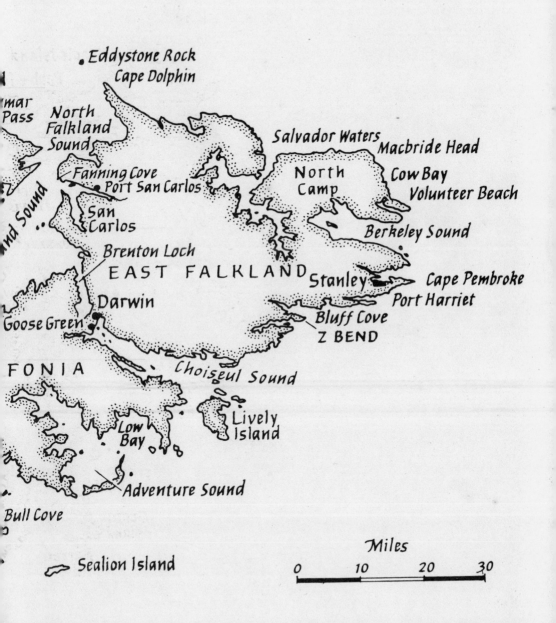

Eddystone Rock
Cape Dolphin

mar
Pass

North
Falkland
Sound

Salvador Waters
Macbride Head

Fanning Cove

North
Camp

Cow Bay
Volunteer Beach

Port San Carlos

nd Sound

San
Carlos

Berkeley Sound

Brenton Loch

EAST FALKLAND
Stanley
Cape Pembroke

Darwin
Port Harriet

Goose Green
Bluff Cove
Z BEND

FONIA
Choiseul Sound

Low
Bay

Lively
Island

Adventure Sound

Bull Cove

Sealion Island

Miles

0   10   20   30

REASONS IN WRITING

REASONS IN WRITING

A Commando's View
of the Falklands War

by
Ewen Southby-Tailyour

BCA

LONDON   NEW YORK   SYDNEY   TORONTO

This edition published 1993
By BCA by arrangement with
LEO COOPER
an imprint of
Pen & Sword Books Ltd.

CN 9941

Typeset by Yorkshire Web, Barnsley, South Yorkshire
in Times 10 point

Printed by
Redwood Press,
Melksham, Wiltshire

CONTENTS

Dedicated to
the Crew of *Foxtrot Four*

Choiseul Sound
8th June 1982

Colour-Sergeant B R Johnston QGM Royal Marines
Sergeant R J Rotherham Royal Marines
LME(M) D Miller Royal Navy
Marine A J Rundle
Marine R D Griffin
MEA(P) A S James Royal Navy

Supplement to the *London Gazette*, 8th October 1982

The Queen has been graciously pleased to approve the Posthumous award of the Queen's Gallantry Medal to the undermentioned in recognition of gallantry during the operations in the South Atlantic.

Colour-Sergeant Brian Johnston, coxswain of LCU F4, was working in the vicinity of HMS *Antelope* when her unexploded bomb detonated, starting an immediate fire which caused her crew, already at emergency stations, to be ordered to abandon ship. Without hesitation Colour-Sergeant Johnston laid his craft alongside the *Antelope* and began to fight the fire and take off survivors. At approximately 2200Z he was ordered to stay clear of the ship because of the severity of the fire and the presence of a second unexploded bomb. Colour-Sergeant Johnston remained alongside until his load was complete. In all LCU F4 rescued over 100 survivors from the *Antelope*.

On 8th June, LCU F4 was attacked by enemy aircraft in Choiseul Sound. During this action Colour Sergeant Johnston and five of his crew were killed.

Colour-Sergeant Johnston's selfless bravery in the face of extreme danger was in the highest traditions of the Corps.

Also in Memory of
Doreen Bonner
Mary Godwin
Susan Whitley

Stanley,
Night of 11/12th June 1982

MAPS AND CHARTS IN TEXT

GLOSSARY

AAF. Argentinian Air Force.

ABU. Amphibious Beach Unit. Small unit, usually part of an LPD's (qv) assault squadron, designed to smooth the passage of men and equipment across the inter-tidal zone. Contains recovery and diving sections as well as a water-farm for re-supply of fresh water from ship to shore.

Action Stations. The state a warship is in when in contact with the enemy. All systems are manned and depending on the threat all hatches and doors are shut and clipped tight to prevent flooding and the spread of fire.

Aldis. Powerful signalling lamp used at sea. Light emission can be reduced to a pinprick and colour changed to red or green.

AMTRAC. American designed tracked amphibious assault craft.

AOA. Amphibious Objective Area.

AOO. Amphibious Operations Officer. Senior Royal Marines officer embarked in the LPD (qv), usually a Major. Responsible to the captain for all amphibious planning and execution. Link between ship and COMAW/Brigade staff during operations.

AOR. Amphibious Operations Room. The command nerve centre of the LPD (qv) from where the CLFTG (Brigade Commander) (qv) and CATF (COMAW) (qv) conduct amphibious operations. Separate from, but alongside, the Ship's own operations room.

539 Assault Squadron Royal Marines. 3 Commando Brigade's own landing craft squadron consisting of a mix of heavy, medium and light assault and raiding craft, plus its own ABU (qv) and engineering support. It is self-contained and equipped for independent tactical or logistic support of land operations where there is a sea, fiord, river, estuary or lake flank.

Assualt Stations. State that an amphibious ship is brought to prior to landing its EMF (qv). Troops are assembled in pre-ordained areas. Guides are earmarked, craft and helicopters are brought to instant readiness and in the LPDs (qv) flooding of the dock may begin. If this occurs while the ship is at action stations (qv) there is often a conflict of requirements as men need to move around the ship which is closed-up for action with hatches and doors shut.

ATG. Amphibious Task Group. See also COMAW.

ATURM. Earlier name for the Royal Marines base at Poole, Dorset. Amphibious Training Unit Royal Marines, home to the SBS (qv) and Landing Craft branch.

AVRE. Armoured Vehicle Royal Engineers. Tank chassis with bulldozer blade and demolition gun operated by Royal Engineers. Used during *Operation Motorman* to knock down the barricades in the Bogside area of Londonderry.

AWD. Action working dress. Usual rig worn in action at sea.

BAS. (3 BAS). 3rd Commando Brigade Air Squadron. In 1982 a mix of Lynx and Gazelle (qv) light helicopters. Employed for anti-armour attack, artillery spotting, communications, casevac (qv), small-scale troop insertions.

BCR. Battle casualty replacement.

The Black Pig. LCU (qv) specially converted for trials in the Arctic.

Blowpipe. Hand-held, optically guided, anti-aircraft missile.

Blue-on-blue. Official description of an engagement between units on the same side. 'Friendly fire' is the unfortunate euphemism for such tragic events.

Bofors. Quick-firing gun fitted to many HM and RFA (qv) ships.

BSA. Beach Support Area. Administrative and logistic area close to the beachhead from where stores and equipment can be distributed forwards.

Camp. The Falklands outside Stanley.

CAP. Combat air patrol. During the campagin this consisted of Harriers loitering overhead likely areas ready for instant action.

Carl Gustav. 84mm, hand-held, anti-tank weapon.

CASEVAC. Casualty evacuation from the front line.

CATF. Commander Amphibious Task Group which, in 1982, was COMAW (qv).

CGRM. Commandant General, Royal Marines. Also Department of:

CinC Fleet. Commander-in-Chief Fleet, based at Fleet Headquarters, Northwood, Middlesex.

Chacon. Very large wooden shipping container.

Chaff. Clouds of tiny strips of tinfoil launched from small rockets to entice enemy radar-guided weapons away from their targets — usually the ship that fires them.

Chinook. RAF twin-rotor helicopter capable of carrying ten tons.

CLFFI. Commander Land Forces Falkland Islands.

CLFTG. Commander LFTG (qv) which in 1982 was the Brigadier commanding 3rd Commando Brigade Royal Marines.

COMAW. Commodore Amphibious Warfare, in command of all amphibious ships in the ATG (cv).

CTG. Commander Task Group.

148 Commando Forward Observation Battery Royal Artillery. Small unit designed to control the fire of NGS (qv). Often put ashore in advance of the main force and accompanying special forces insertions.

Dead Marine. Empty bottle.

Defence Watches. Eight hours on and eight hours off. Watch system with ship at highest state of readiness bar being actually at action stations (qv).

Deltext. Delicate Text. A form of encryption of a signal message hiding a delicate text usually to be de-cyphered and read only by the officer to whom it is personally addressed.

DIS. Defence Intelligence Service.

DNSY. Direction of Naval Security.

DWIS. Defence Weekly Intelligence Summary.

EMF. Embarked military force. Depending on the size of the ship this can be anything from a full Commando Group in an LPH (qv) to a small party of special forces in a submarine.

Exocet. French anti-ship missile capable of being launched from the air, another ship or the back of an improvised lorry. Operated by both British and Argentinian forces.

FCO. Foreign and Commonwealth Office.

FEBA. Forward Edge of Battle Area.

FIC. Falkland Islands Company.

FIDF. Falkland Islands Defence Force.

FIG. Falkland Islands Government.

FIGAS. Falkland Islands Government Air Service operating small Beaver float planes.

FOB. Forward Operating Base. Landing craft base ashore and close to or beyond the FEBA (qv).

Gazelle. Light helicopter used for artillery spotting. See 3 BAS.

Gemini. Inflatable raiding craft. 15′ long with a crew of one and six passengers depending on equipment carried and sea state. Speeds up to 20 knots but considerably reduced as load increases. Powered by single 40hp outboard engine. Can be man-handled, parachuted or launched from a submarine.

GH. Government House.

GPMG. In 1982 the general purpose machine gun. Linked rounds of 7.62mm calibre.

Greasy Spoon. 3 Commando Brigade's travelling, mobile, tactical galley.

Green Goddess. Elderly military fire engine. Many brought out of retirement during the firemen's strike of 1978.

HE. Colloquial use of HEGFI (qv).

HEGFI. His Excellency the Governor of the Falklands.

HMG. Her Majesty's Government.

LADE. Lineas Aereolineas del Estol. AAF (qv) run airlink between the Falklands and the mainland.

LC. Landing Craft, LC Branch or Landing Craftsman.

LCU. Landing Craft Utility. One-hundred-ton landing craft designed to carry two main battle tanks, although this payload has been reduced over the years without an alteration of the vessels' design and construction. The payload was once reduced by the Chief Naval Architect to a mere six tons — an order we ignored, preferring to accept empirical results rather than those of a computer manned by landlubbers. Four carried in the docks of the LPDs (qv) *Fearless* and *Intrepid*. Numerically numbered in each ship from one to four but proceeded by T or Tango for *Intrepid*'s craft and F for Foxtrot for *Fearless*'s. Designed with the LPD (qv) for simple ship-to-shore journeys, they have only a rudimentary navigation fit and no shelter for passengers of which they can (for very short fair-weather journeys) carry about 150 with full kit. They have a crew of seven accommodated in spartan conditions.

LCVP. Landing craft vehicle and personnel. Small plywood-constructed landing craft of about ten tons capable of carrying four tons or 30 fully equipped troops (temperate climate) or a Land Rover and trailer. Hoisted on davits on each side of the LPD (qv).

LFTG. Landing Force Task Group.

Lloyd's Open Form. Initial salvage claim form used at sea.

LOD. Line of Departure. Nautical version of the Start Line (qv) but more usually a notional line drawn on a chart.

LPD. Landing Platform Dock. Otherwise known as assault or command ships. *Fearless* and *Intrepid* employed to the South Atlantic in 1982 with *Fearless* flying the flag of the Commodore Amphibious warfare — COMAW (qv). Designed in the 1950s with *Fearless* being commissioned in 1965 and *Intrepid* in 1967. Displacement of about 12,000 tons but increased by 5,000 tons of water to flood the dock aft in order to float out the four LCUs (qv). They also carry four LCVPs (qv) on davits. Flight deck capable of operating two medium-sized helicopters simultaneously but they can carry up to four. Designed to carry about 400 men, a squadron of main battle tanks plus (for example) 7 four-ton lorries and 20 Land Rovers.

LSL. Landing Ship Logistic manned by the RFA (qv). Six in service in 1982. Named after Knights of the Round Table. 5,500 tons fully laden. Ro-ro configuration. Capable of carrying 16 MBTs (qv) and over 500 troops in austere conditions. Small aft flight deck capable of operating Wessex (qv). Midships flight deck usually cluttered with extra vehicles and wires for mexeflotes (qv). Although designed to land vehicles and heavy equipment directly onto the beach or across a causeway this method was not used during the Falklands conflict. Two mexeflotes are usually carried flat against the LSL's side for offloading from a deep water anchorage.

LVT. Argentinian (American designed and built) Landing Vehicle Tracked. Amphibious, armed and armoured troop carrier that can swim ashore from amphibious shipping and deploy as an armoured personnel carrier.

MB. Moody Brook Camp.

Mexeflote. Low flat rafts manned by the RCT (qv) used after the initial assault to land heavy vehicles, plant machinery and bulk stores. Made up of many individual cells into raft 126' x 24'. In this configuration each can carry 120 tons. Raft may be split into smaller sections carrying approximately one ton per foot of length. Raft weighs approximately one ton per foot in length and is powered by two Harbourmaster 6 cylinder diesel engines. Mexeflotes are transported to the AOA (qv) against the sides of LSLs (qv).

Mirage. French-designed delta-winged supersonic aircraft capable of launching Exocet (qv). 'Dagger' version used for air to ground attack.

MOA. Marine Officers Attendant. 'Batman' in the army, 'steward' in the Royal Navy and 'bearer' in the SAF (qv).

M&AW Cadre. Mountain and Arctic Warfare Cadre Royal Marines. Specialist organization of men trained in mountain and arctic warfare for duties within the Commando Brigade. Capable of operating independently or as leaders for larger formations.

NBCD. Nuclear, Biological and Chemical Defence.

NGS. Naval Gunfire Support.

OCAD. Officer Commanding Amphibious detachment in an LPD. Captain, Royal Marines.

ODM. Overseas Development Ministry.

OP. Observation Post.

PET. Pre-Embarkation Training.

PNG. Passive night goggles. Binocular-style instrument used to enhance night vision. Issued to some helicopter pilots.

PSA. Public Services Agency.

Pucara. Twin turbo-prop, twin-seat Argentinian aircraft designed for counter-insurgency operations. Highly manoeuvrable and heavily armed with rockets, bombs and machine guns.

PWD. Public Works Department.

3rd Raiding Squadron. Initially 3 Commando Brigade's squadron of small raiding craft such as the RRC (qv) and Gemini (qv). Merged into the Task Force Landing Craft Squadron (qv) and later still (in 1984), as Raiding Troop, with 539 Assault Squadron (qv).

RAMC. Royal Army Medical Corps.

RAS. Replenishment at sea. RAS (L) – liquids – such as aviation fuel and diesel. RAS (S) – solids – dry stores; see VERTREP.

RBR. Round Britain and Ireland Race. A two-handed sailing race held every four years.

RCC. Royal Cruising Club.

RCT. Royal Corps of Transport. Among a host of duties they man the mexeflote (qv).

Rebro Station. Sometimes known as a relay station. Radio link used to pass on radio signals either over mountain tops or around headlands. Can be automatic but often manned.

Red Sea Rig. Mess uniform worn by officers in the evening. White short-sleeved shirt with regimental or service badges of rank on epaulettes, regimental or service cummerbund and evening trousers.

RFA. Royal Fleet Auxiliary. The Royal Navy's supply and support ships.

RMSC. Royal Marines Sailing Club.

RRC. Rigid Raiding Craft. 17' long assault craft powered by a 135 HP outboard motor. Crew of one and up to eight passengers or 2,000 lbs of stores. Speeds up to 35 knots depending on load and sea conditions.

RYS. Royal Yacht Squadron.

SAF. Sultan of Muscat's Armed Forces.

SAS. Special Air Service.

SBS. Special Boat Service.

Scare charges. Small explosive charges dropped at irregular intervals over the side of ships in an anchorage to discourage enemy underwater saboteurs.

Scorpion. Light tank of the Blues and Royals.

Sea Harrier. SHAR. Naval version of the Harrier VSTOL fighter aircraft. RAF version in 1982 was the GR3. Equipped with Sidewinder (qv) missiles, 30mm Aden cannon, bombs and rockets. SHAR duties were air-defence and CAP (qv) while the GR3's duties were in direct support of ground forces.

Sea King. Royal Navy medium support helicopter. Anti-submarine version can carry about ten men, the troop-carrying version (Mk IV) about twenty.

Sidewinder. Air-to-Air guided missile carried by Harriers.

SIS. Secret Intelligence Service.

Sky Hawk. Argentinian American designed A-4 attack aircraft. Subsonic and heavily armed with bombs, rockets and machine guns.

SLR. Self-loading rifle. In 1982 the standard 7.62mm infantry rifle.

SNO. Senior Naval Officer usually embarked in a STUFT (qv) to interpret naval orders and command any embarked naval party.

SOA. Sheep Owners' Association.

Spearhead. Spearhead battalion. Rotational duty (usually one month at a time) performed by home-based infantry battalion or Royal Marine Commando. Up-to-strength in men and equipment ready for instant deployment world-wide.

Start Line. A line on the ground marking the start of an attack from where timings and formations can be initiated. If possible a natural physical feature and at right angles to the advance. See LOD.

STUFT. Ships Taken Up From Trade. Civilian ships requisitioned for military operations.

Tab. Parachute Regiment slang for Tactical Approach to Battle. See Yomp.

Three Six Five. '365'. Falklands slang for mutton. Eaten on every day of the year.

Uckers. Naval slang for a fierce version of Ludo. Rules were so contentious that an Admiralty Fleet Order had to be issued laying down the rules to be used in the Fleet. This has not prevented various 'jungle' rules being applied during the hard-fought competitions between messdecks and messes when at sea.

VERTREP. Vertical resupply between ships at sea by helicopter.

Volvo. BV 202. Articulated oversnow vehicle designed for the Arctic but found to be invaluable with its low ground pressure across 'camp' (qv).

Wessex. Royal Navy medium support helicopter for deploying troops.

Yomp. Commando slang for long approach march with full load. See Tab.

Z Bend. Author's name for the twisting passage between East Island and Loafers Cove. Short cut in fine weather between Bluff Cove and Fitzroy settlements.

ACKNOWLEDGEMENTS

Since 1977 numerous people have helped me to write this book, at home and in the South Atlantic, in peace and in war, and have contributed as willingly now as they did at the time.

Some have preferred not to be named, but others I must thank publicly and in particular: Major-General Julian Thompson and Captain Michael Clapp for their endless patience with my queries and for reading, more than once, uncoordinated snippets of the manuscript in its raw state. Without their continual advice, support and counselling now and in 1982 there would be no tale to tell.

Lieutenant-General Robin Ross gave early and invaluable advice on presentation; Lieutenant-Colonel Roger Blundell read the whole manuscript and was polite enough not to comment too harshly; Lawrence Cotterell read the manuscript, commenting at length and with great wisdom; the staff of the Royal Marines Museum, and in particular Ed Bartholomew, checked my version of the history of the Royal Marines in the Falkland Islands; Captain Bill MacLennen of the Royal Marines Public Relations Office helped steer the manuscript through 'the system' — a vital task; Colonel Gerry Wells-Cole confirmed one or two of my opinions; Mrs. Sara Jones read a section of the manuscript and was kind enough to allow me to keep it in; Captain Fred Cook reminded me of NP 8901's communications arrangements in 1979 and Colour Sergeant 'Connie' Francis supplied valuable information about his LCU's duties on 8 June, 1982. Captain Phil Roberts was kind enough to comment on my perceptions of Sir Galahad's routines on that same day from which I was able to clarify some important points. Major Tony Todd's views are as invaluable now as they were at Fitzroy.

I would like to thank Tom Seccombe (lately the Director of Naval Security) for two things, firstly, for moral support in San Carlos on D Day; he will know the second reason!

Lieutenant Steve Nicoll very kindly lent me the original of his Mountain and Arctic Warfare Cadre notebook from his time in Winter Quarrie overlooking the track from Darwin to Fitzroy.

Assistance was given by three former officers in the Welsh Guards who served in the Falklands in 1982: Major Julian Peel Yates commanding Headquarter Company, Captain Robert Mason, Adjutant and Captain Jan

Koops, second-in-command of the Prince of Wales's Company. Without their painstaking scrutiny my story would be incomplete and one-sided, but as the result of this willing co-operation the awful events of 8 June, 1982, have now, I believe, been put into the fullest and most balanced perspective.

They, and everyone else mentioned above, helped with matters of fact but the interpretation of those facts and the conclusions and opinions reached are mine for which only I can bear the responsibility.

Major de Gascoigne's devastatingly sensible comments and observations before and after the 'war' were always appreciated, but, most especially, was the moral support offered during it.

I must thank Leo Cooper, my publisher, for suggesting the whole idea, followed by his, and Tom Hartman's, humorous and patient editorial work in the face of my incompetence as a typist... and, finally Jüri Gabriel, my agent, who kept me going long after I decided that I would rather be sailing than writing.

AUTHOR'S NOTE

This is a love story and during the last fifteen years I have agonized over how to tell it. Despite the mind's ability to erase bad memories, I now realize that my involvement in the South Atlantic was not a bed of roses and there is no point in pretending that it was, even if that truth now hurts. Like all true love affairs, the bad has to be acknowledged as well as the good and my experience is no exception. To recount the tale highlighting only the happiness would be to falsify events – altogether a worse crime than hiding the facts from scrutiny.

By presenting my story in this manner I know I have opened myself to much justified criticism, but I must stand by my descriptions. Many of them are not very palatable, but I believe that they make honest reading. Above all I ask that my critics remember that the whole Falklands saga is an enigma with so many opposing forces pulling in opposition, each passionately believing that their course of action is the correct one – and in this respect I do not even consider the Argentinian view. For many of my early days I was in the middle, and not likely to win under any circumstances and while I do not regret this for one instance it does explain the conundrum in which I so often found myself. One thing I did learn, in large measure, is that while the military mind is trained to select and maintain an aim until the objective is achieved, the political mind (with one remarkable exception) was too often dominated by the twin spurs of personal gain and fear of retribution, making a stated and clear aim a very changeable goal. There is no doubt which principle led to our success.

The object of this love story are islands not people. People are transient, resilient and replaceable; they can look after themselves. Remote islands and their eco-systems are fragile and vulnerable and their inhabitants love them and care for them and their future with a passion not often understood by outsiders.

For my part this love affair influenced the many actions I was to take and, as in all such relationships, rationality in decision making rarely enjoys first priority! This 'affair' was to bring in unequal measures, immense happiness for much of the time, moments of intense sadness, not a little frustration, sometimes distrust and sometimes jealousy. I have, by nature, a happy-go-lucky disposition that relies heavily on the 'it'll-be-alright-on-the-night' approach to life, although this aspect was to be well tested between 1977 and 1979. I am a fatalist and being at ease on my own I prefer to make my own decisions, which, of course, might explain some of what happens between these covers.

As the result of volunteering to serve with Naval Party 8901, the Falklands brought out a side of me that I had not appreciated previously. I became more sensitive to, and more positive about, certain aspects of life and it is no use pretending that, once smitten, I was unhappy to let the place dominate my life for over a decade. But now it is over and I have said my piece I feel very much like Admiral Grey whose final letter from the Falkland Islands in 1836 began thus:

"I will now bid goodbye to the Falklands with a few casual remarks and they shall be very few as I am quite tired of the subject."

I felt strongly, almost possessively, about the Islands and their defence, their seizure, and the manner in which we were to capture them back: so much so that I was bound to be involved in controversial discussions. Some of my comments may, therefore, seem a little personal and harsh, but war, and its prevention, is a harsh and personal experience. It heightens emotions, deepens distrust, intensifies respect and destroys or confirms friendships.

Perceptions, where previously grey or muddled, become polarized and powerful; these are based on individual assessments, with no one person having access to all the facts. A full and accurate view of any situation is never available at the time to help decision making, and only hindsight can show where these judgements have been valid or baseless.

Therefore this is not a history book. It is merely an individual's view of the Falklands in war and peace, before, during and after that Austral Autumn of 1982. Many will hold different views of the incidents I describe − these are mine. For the most part they are contemporary views, some of which have become modified by time and hindsight.

I made numerous mistakes between 1977 and 1982: some things were said (in my log and in public) that, with a wider perspective of events, I would have phrased differently or not at all. Some good decisions were taken that would not have been taken if all the facts had been known. Some actions I now regret, some I shall stand by to the end. All my decisions should be exposed, for without these conflictions a false picture of reactions and judgements would result. No one at any level is immune to these dichotomies where the time available for making a life-affecting decision can be measured in split seconds. We are all prone to making inaccurate decisions which, when executed, can by good fortune lead to success but without that luck can end just as easily in failure, as they often deserve to; hence Kipling's warning 'to treat the impostors [Triumph and Disaster] just the same, and that maxim holds particularly well in these cases. Fear and worry also play their part in personal perceptions, for each man has his own threshold of what is acceptable and what cannot be faced.

A calculated risk plus luck, is not the same as foolhardiness plus luck. 'Getting away' with an action does not necessarily validate the original decision, for that way future strategies and tactics could be based on delusions and the second time they may not necessarily work. Thus it is occasionally acceptable to criticize success.

For any successful military operation there has to be a clear, simple, single aim. The aim of the last two-thirds of this book is to re-distribute some of the credit (which seems to have gone astray) in favour of the amphibious operations, and in doing so, tell the part played by the amphibious ships and craft. It was their duty as components of the Amphibious Task Group to transport, land and then support the 3rd Commando Brigade Royal Marines, itself an integral part of that Amphibious Task Group, and it was upon the shoulders of the Commander of this ATG (known as Commodore Amphibious Warfare or COMAW for short) and his co-commander, the Brigadier Commanding the Landing Force Task Group, that the repossession of the Falkland Islands depended. These joint commanders were supported by the ships and aircraft of the Carrier Battle Group, plus numerous remarkably noble civilian Ships Taken Up From Trade and the Royal Fleet Auxiliary. The operation was essentially amphibious from start to finish (and it began with an Argentinian amphibious operation) and so, through my own version of events, I want to highlight that aspect.

But my story actually starts long before the Argentinian invasion on 2 April, 1982. Between 1977 and 1979 I had the privilege to re-assess the defence of the Falklands, make recommendations to the Foreign Office and the Commander-in-Chief of the Fleet at Northwood, Middlesex, and then implement the newly agreed Concept of Operations. My story ends with the formation of 3 Commando Brigade's Assault Squadron in 1984; a Squadron 'invented' in North Norway in 1972, trialled, *ad hoc*, over the years and then formed in San Carlos Waters.

But now, even after ten years, the subject will not leave me. At the beginning of 1992 *The Spectator* ran a four-week classified advertisement which read:

PERSONAL

Where is Ewen Southby-Tailyour? If
you know contact Meridith. Box No: 066LM

My solicitor suggested we inserted a return 'ad' which would read no more than: "Who cares where Ewen S-T is?" My wife thought it was an ex-girlfriend and forbade me to answer it, while various friends had less attractive and more exotic suggestions. My cousin Robert Tailyour

(Director of Operations Royal Marines and then my 'boss') asked how much it had cost me to insert!

The Director of Naval Security took it more seriously and, on my behalf and after much covert corresponding, found that it was a Mrs Leslie Meridith from San Diego, California, anxious for information on the Falkland Islands before her first visit.

I suspect my involvement − with the Islands! − will not end there.

After any 'incident' it is a military requirement that those involved be invited to 'Render Their Reasons In Writing' to their superior officer: he then decides what action, if any, should be taken to inflict punishment, remand for court-martial, re-apportion blame or exonerate. Praise is seldom an option.

These are my Reasons in Writing covering the part I played in a brief but crucial period of Falkland Islands history. I will leave it to others to decide what action to take.

Ewen Southby-Tailyour
South Devon, 1993.

PROLOGUE

The Norwegian yacht's bowsprit dipped and shuddered as another thundering white-fronted comber slammed into *Capricornus's* port bow. The southerly wind continued to rise through the Beaufort scale forcing the large gaff-rigged ketch to roll and yaw with increasing violence. The Scandinavian, exposed at the tiller in the open cockpit, shouted below for a second mug of whisky-laced coffee before tugging the loose towel tight around his neck. The spume, shaken free from the tossing bowsprit, stung into his face. Here, north of the Birdwood Bank, the seas, though shorter and steeper than their first cousins just one hundred and fifty miles south, had an irregularity nearly as dangerous as the constant charge of those huge 'grey beards of Cape Stiff'.

Twelve miles ahead lay Middle Island and the entrance to Choiseul Sound. *The Vicar of Bray*, the last remaining survivor of the 777 ships that left New York for California in the 1849 gold rush, lay at rest in the mud and shingle off Goose Green's jetty. The American nautical archaeologists, huddled below in the womb-like security and warmth of the saloon, gritted their teeth as the world heaved and lurched. It was not the method of approach to their quarry they had wished, but, in the Falkland Islands, it was the only one available. Being interested in America's nautical heritage was one thing; putting that interest into practice was quite another!

On deck, I pointed out Lively Island ten miles to the south west; low and undulating, distinguishable only by the brilliant white beaches just dipping on the horizon and House Rock, the highest point, jutting proud above the deserted sand dunes. To starboard lay Port Pleasant and the entrance to Fitzroy Settlement. Beyond the peninsula nestled Bluff Cove and a magnificent sheltered waterway that we would visit on the return journey. Shortly, as the Kelp Islands drew abaft the beam, I ordered an alteration in course to bear away into calmer waters: the ship's motion would ease and, with any luck, the sun would break through between the thinning cumulus.

For the archaeologists the journey to Goose Green was a necessity; for the crew it was a job for which they would be paid; for me it was a voyage of exploration and amateur survey.

Alongside, the Black-browed Albatrosses wheeled and soared between the racing crests of the southern ocean. The fold of skin above their eyes gave them a malevolent look that betrayed their peaceful intentions; they were not the only bird life on that huge ocean. Great Skuas, heavy-bodied and purposefully evil, dived and screeched in their endless search, and fight, for food. Tiny, delicate Wilson's Petrels flitted along the dark, marbled valleys, dancing along the surface on their frail legs.

Beneath the albatrosses the 'puffing pig' dolphins (or *Cephalorhynchus Commersonii* to the nautical experts lying miserably below) rolled and played across the bow waves and down the leading edges of the breaking seas.

The skua, follower of death, and the petrel, harbinger of bad weather; dreadful omens of doom to all but the most phlegmatic of seamen.

At 0430 on 2 April, 1982, the sound of helicopters was reported in the vicinity of Mullet Creek, East Falkland Island and at 0515 'three large ships' were seen off Mengeary Point and turning in to Port William.

At 0605 the Royal Marine camp at Moody Brook was attacked without warning. An 'advance force operation' using small arms and grenades was attempting to neutralize the British garrison before they had the chance to deploy to, and defend, Government House, the beaches and the airfield. Due to perceptive Standard Operating Procedures the base was empty — the men having already taken up their positions. While Moody Brook was systematically searched, using phosphorous grenades as pre-emptive fire in the belief that it was occupied, a second party that had landed at Mullet Creek was creeping its way past the lone Royal Marine lookout on Sapper Hill and towards the high ground to the south of Government House. Royal Marines to the east of Stanley were pulled back to meet the enemy now squeezing the seat of government in a classic and unexpected pincer movement.

At 0615 Government House itself, defended by just thirty-one Marines and the Governor's driver armed with a shot gun ("determined to shoot the first Argie that tries to haul down the Union Flag"), came under direct attack for three hours. A second amphibious landing began, this time in great strength and across Yorke Bay beach. Tracked amphibious vehicles forced their way westwards along the 'airport road' until stopped at the outskirts to the town by accurate anti-tank fire. One tracked vehicle was engaged by a 66mm weapon forcing the driver to manouevre his limping vehicle off the road. A Royal Marines' Carl Gustav anti-tank weapon was brought into action, again registering a hit. None of the occupants emerged and the vehicle lay dead in the mud. Fifteen more vehicles took the place of the first casualties and against such odds (now including heavy mortars and machine guns) the remaining defenders were obliged to make a fighting withdrawal towards Government House; only one section made it. In the meantime another Carl Gustav-armed section was attempting to hold up the enemy advance by sinking a landing craft that foolishly assumed it could transit The Narrows with impunity.

The green, tin-roofed colonial building took three hours of machine-gun, rifle and grenade assaults and still held out. Much of this caused a diversion from a small party of Argentinians intent on entering Government House with, it was presumed, the intention of snatching His Excellency. Three of this number were captured after two bursts of automatic fire were aimed through the floor of their hide — a maid's bedroom. During a lull in the fighting an attempt was made to rescue three wounded Argentinian soldiers but this was thwarted by their leader appearing to pull the pin from a grenade. Described by his admiral as 'my best officer' the Lieutenant Commander, shot in the stomach, was to be the first to die that austral autumn.

Lynx helicopters from two British designed and built Type 42 destroyers landed men on the lightly blocked runway and at 0830 the first Argentinian Hercules aircraft arrived with infantry reinforcements. The fight for Government House continued, causing at least three dead and seventeen wounded among the attackers in its immediate vicinity. There were no British casualties and despite disgracefully inaccurate press reports in Britain giving no credit to the Islands' defenders, the Argentinians paid dearly for their 'bloodless' occupation: they were to pay even more.

Shortly after 0915 a cease-fire was negotiated — the term 'surrender' being purposefully avoided by His Excellency the Governor and Commander-in-Chief, Mr Rex Hunt, whose last message to the people for whom he was responsible ended: "I'm sorry it has happened this way.... But I wish you the best of luck and, rest assured, the British will be back". But would they? For had not the defence of the Falklands been treated so casually that it was unlikely that Britain would send the required massive task force to recover them?

Mr Hunt, and the meagre forces at his disposal, had done their best, which is more than can be said for those who allowed this shameful incident to take place in the first place. The questions that will always be asked are:

"Should he, and they, have been put in that position in the first place?

"Why were the forces so 'meagre' when much Ministry of Defence effort had been put into planning their enhancement fewer than three years before, following agreement with Her Majesty's Government?

"Why, with thirteen thousand troops (the eventual total of Argentinians that were to serve in the Falklands) on their way supported by a substantial navy and air force, were there no more than a few hours of warning when that force must have taken weeks of local diplomatic, political and military activity to prepare and launch?"

The Royal Marines and their Commander-in-Chief were repatriated to London while Britain, and the world, watched for the next move — if there was to be one: General Galtieri expected not — and he might have been right but for Britain's Prime Minister and First Sea Lord.

INTRODUCTION

The history of the Royal Marines' involvement with the Falkland Islands is long, almost certainly as long as Britain's formal occupation, although, unlike that occupation, it has not been continuous.

The first Royal Marines to land probably did so under the command of Captain John Byron who left England on a voyage of exploration on 21 June, 1764 with the sloop *Tamar* and the frigate *Dolphin*. After failing to find Pepys Island he entered Port de la Croizade (so named the year before by the Frenchman de Bougainville) to find a suitable anchorage off the eastern coast of Saunders Island. He christened the small creek Settlement Cove and the landlocked harbour Port Egmont, in honour of the First Lord of the Admiralty.

The next year a subordinate of Byron's, Captain John McBride, was despatched to consolidate the Settlement Cove garrison. He arrived on 8 January, 1766 with the frigate *Jason*, the sloop *Carcass* and the storeship *Experiment*. The settlement he established consisted of over 100 men with, among other items they had brought, a prefabricated wooden hut. They added numerous stone buildings, planted vegetable gardens and reared a thriving livestock population. They were well stocked with coal.

After spending the austral winter extending the community, McBride left Saunders Island to carry out the second part of his instructions. After he had "Immediately (completed) the settlement begun last year at Port Egmont," he set about "(finding) any lawless persons ... seated in any part of the said Islands, (and compelling them to) either quit or to take oaths, acknowledge and submit themselves to His Majesty's Government as subjects of the Crown of Great Britain."

One of McBride's ships remained at Port Egmont, while the commander sailed the adjacent coastlines in the *Jason* carrying out his orders. It was well known in London that the French were established among the islands and if 'found seated' they were to be given six months to comply with McBride's instructions or leave, but McBride was essentially interested in surveying the coastline (despite his orders to study the hinterland) and had little time for what happened beyond the beaches. Indeed he held little prospect for the place at all, considering the mountains barren, the climate too windy, the land too boggy, and the penguins and sea lions as vermin.

McBride was, perhaps, an ill-advised choice for the task set him, although he was not alone in being disenchanted with the Islands. Many of his men, and those of his French opponent, had similar thoughts on their situation. A British Marine lieutenant wrote (probably not for the last time): "The most detestable place I was ever at in my life... one wild heath wherever you turn your eye," and a little further east at de Bougainville's Puerto Soledad the garrison's Spanish priest was moved to write: "I tarry in this unhappy desert, suffering everything for love of God." These were to be sentiments echoed down the years by many enforced expatriates.

It was unfortunate that Dr Samuel Johnson, when commissioned to write a paper on the value or otherwise of the West Falklands Islands (in an effort to defuse the crisis of 1770), took many of McBride's views as definitive and, without having visited the Islands himself, described them as being: "...thrown aside from human use, stormy in winter, barren in summer, an island which not even the southern savages have dignified with habitation, where a garrison must be kept in a state that contemplates with envy the exiles of Siberia, of which the expense will be perpetual."

The intervening months saw a number of contacts, mostly friendly in the manner of that age, with the French, unaware that, back in France, de Bougainville had agreed that the Islands should be handed over to Spain.

McBride sailed for England in early 1767 leaving Settlement Cove and the harbour where, according to Byron, "The whole navy of England might ride here in perfect security from all winds", under the command of, firstly, Captain Rayner, and then Captain Hunt of the *Tamar*.

Hunt fell in with a Spanish schooner in September, 1769, and invited him to leave. Shortly afterwards they met again and this time Hunt was presented with papers requesting him to leave instead. This exchange of ultimatums reached a climax on 4 June, 1770, when a force of five Spanish frigates arrived off Settlement Cove. The British could only muster the sloop *Favourite*, commanded by Captain Farmer, backed up by the shore battery of four twelve pounders protected by mud banks.

By 8 June Farmer had strengthened his fortifications (the only stone building being the blockhouse above the tiny inlet) and felt secure enough to send a letter to the Spanish commander inviting him to leave Port Egmont. The commander, Juan Madariaga, suggested that Farmer send an officer to see the extent of the force ranged against him. The news was bad: the Spanish had a force of 1,600 men. Madariaga again suggested that Farmer quit. He refused. The Spanish landed on 10 June and, after a short and spirited defence, the Marines (2 officers and 21 other ranks) bowed to the inevitable. Farmer and his men sailed for Britain on 14 July after a forced delay (among other things the *Favourite's* rudder had been removed) ensured that the news of a Spanish victory reached Buenos Aires and Spain first.

The Royal Marines left behind three of their number buried half-way up the south-facing hill.

In London there was intense indignation, not only at the invasion, but at the Government's failure to foresee and prevent it. The Foreign Secretary (Lord Weymouth) had to resign and, without waiting for a reply to diplomatic protests, a task force was quickly fitted out at Portsmouth.

I am tempted at this point to comment that if we do not learn from history it is bound to be repeated!

British Marines returned to Port Egmont as the result of an order for restitution being signed on 7 February, 1771. Captain Stott, with the frigate *Juno*, the sloop *Hound* and the storeship *Florida*, was despatched and the settlement was handed back to the British on 15 September. Just three years later it was abandoned for, in Lord Rochford's words, "It is neither more nor less than a small part of an economical Naval regulation". In accordance with the custom of the day a small lead plaque was left on the blockhouse door on 20 May, 1774, which read: "Be it known to all nations that Falkland Ysland, with this fort, the storehouse, wharfs, harbours, bays and creeks thereunto belonging, are the sole right and property of His Most Sacred Majesty George III, King of Great Britain, France and Ireland, Defender of the Faith. In witness whereof this plate is set up, and His Britannic Majesty's colours left flying as a mark of possession by S.W. Clayton, Commanding officer at Falkland's Ysland. AD 1774."

The spelling of Ysland in the singular is of interest as Britain did not then lay claim to the Spanish possessions on East Falkland and, indeed, at that stage, acknowledged the Spanish occupation of Puerto Soleded (later named Port Louis) at the head of Berkeley Sound.

The turbulent history of the Islands continued, but Royal Marines (they had become 'Royal' in 1802) were not to appear, formally, until they formed part of the fleet which returned to Berkeley Sound on 2 January, 1833, under the command of Captain James Onslow in HMS *Clio*. This small force had first called in at Settlement Cove and, finding it in ruins, repaired the blockhouse before sailing east.

On 9 January, 1834, Lt Smith (an officer sent to become the first British authority in the Falklands − he called himself the Resident) landed from HMS *Challenger*, installing himself with a twenty-one gun salute the next day. That same day Lt Smith took a party of twenty Royal Marines to seek out a band of murderers from a previous episode. They were not successful and so, on their return, *Challenger's* captain, feeling that this was not in his remit, sailed for Patagonia, only to become wrecked on that inhospitable coast. However, he had left behind six of his Detachment and by March the fugitives had been caught.

From those days parties of Royal Marines continued to play a part in the development of the Islands with detachments helping ashore in all manner of artisan work until the 1960s.

The next formal Royal Marine involvement was in 1849 when a detachment of pensioners (ranging from 26 to 53 years old) and their wives were billeted in Stanley under their Commanding Officer, Captain Reid, and Sergeant-Major Felton. (The capital had moved from Port Louis in 1843.) Although they were treated as civilians they were subject to military discipline for twelve days each year during their 'annual training period'. They came with their prefabricated wooden buildings which still exist in the south west corner of the town, originally named Upper and Lower Row, now known as Drury Street and Pioneer Row.

Thirty-five Royal Marines (commanded by Captain Abbot) and their wives, plus sixty-five children, arrived in Stanley onboard the *Ealing Grove* on 12 January, 1858, to take over the pensioners' duties. Theirs was a hard commission for there was little or no accommodation and even less furniture − turf and peat blocks serving as chairs and tables. They were named, as suited their rather more regular status, The Falkland Islands Garrison Company. They were relieved by another detachment in January, 1863.

However, the Royal Marines' days were numbered when, in 1877, the then Governor, Callaghan, argued that removing the military would save the Colony £1,066 a year: a much cheaper police force could be instituted in its place so, on New Year's Day, 1878, the last Royal Marine left the Falklands.

There were Royal Marines embarked in the battle fleets of 1914 and 1939 but they took no active part in hostilities ashore and it was not until November, 1964, that the Corps was once more involved in the rough and tumble history of this South Atlantic archipelago. HMS *Protector's* Royal Marines detachment was put ashore under the command of Lt Pat Troy as a defence against an Argentinian threat that seemed likely at that moment. Two months before, a Cessna light aircraft had landed on the race course; the pilot planted an Argentinian flag, handed over a letter addressed to the Occupying English Government and took off again. Quite a feat under the circumstances.

Lt Troy's detachment was removed to be replaced by a permanent presence known as Naval Party 8901. NP 8901's duties became of greater military significance when in 1966 a Dakota landed, once again on the race course. The aircraft, belonging to Aerolineas Argentinas, had been hijacked whilst on an internal flight by a group calling themselves the Condor Gang. It sat on the turf for one and a half days before being surrendered to the local Roman Catholic priest. The OC of NP 8901 had, briefly, been taken hostage. Eventually, driven by the cold and the lack of interest from the Islanders whom the Condor Gang had expected to be more welcoming, the 'invaders' were flown home. Later, stripped of everything movable to help it take off from the soggy grass, the Dakota was also flown back. As a result of these intrusions NP 8901 was ensured a continuing position on the Islands.

Despite being charged with the minor offences of carrying firearms and false imprisonment, the Condor Gang were regarded as heroes worthy of a commemorative plaque in their capital. Britain's only physical action had been to despatch HMS *Juno* to take charge of the hijackers, although, in the event, they were kept by the Roman Catholic church and not by the police before being allowed home under Argentinian arrangements. It all added up to acknowledgment by Britain that this was an internal Argentinian Governmental matter, thereby inferring that any incident on the Falklands came within that jurisdiction. It did nothing for the morale of the Islanders and helped to strengthen the view that the Foreign Office was becoming less interested in retaining responsibility for the Islands.

In 1976 a party of Argentinians occupied Southern Thule. Britain's reaction was to do nothing, which included not telling the public – and certainly not the Falkland Islanders. In 1977 there was a genuine and positive 'invasion scare'. The Prime Minister, Mr Callaghan, sent a nuclear-powered submarine, two frigates and two auxiliaries to the South Atlantic, but didn't tell anyone. The Argentinian 'invasion' fleet returned to base. The Southern Thule party remained.

NP 8901, augmented for a few weeks each year when the Ice Patrol ship was in Falkland waters, remained the deterrent to Argentinian threats to the Islands until that deterrence failed in April, 1982. To begin with, their duties in the event of an invasion were to hide in the hills and act as a sabotage or guerrilla warfare cadre, but in 1978 their Concept of Operations was altered to that of a more active defence. They were now required to defend the seat of government and, if at all possible, "buy three weeks' bargaining time in the United Nations". (Presumably the length of time it took for a relieving task force to be prepared and on station.)

The Royal Marines of NP 8901 helped train and support the Falkland Islands Defence Force (the uniformed 'Territorial Army') and the Settlement Volunteers (the civilian militia outside Stanley). From the mid-sixties, when the numbers were few, (roughly the size of a frigate's detachment) the Falkland Island detachment increased to about 40. For a few years from the mid-sixties to the mid-seventies NP 8902 (consisting solely of naval ranks — 2 'pilots' and ten ratings) was also stationed in Stanley with its SRN 6 hovercraft.

1. The author with his son and father (General Sir Norman Tailyour) at the passing for duty parade of NP 8901 on 9 March, 1978.

2. Thirty-six members of NP 8901 on 9 March, 1978. Sitting, second from right, is Keith Pittock. Sitting far right is Fred Cook. Sitting third from right and next to his father (Rear Admiral Horlick) is Chris Horlick. Missing, among six others, is Corporal Steve Newland. Sitting, third from left is the Commanding Officer of ATURM, Lt-Colonel John Hardy.

I

A Wild Call

"I WANT YOU TO GIVE a lecture to the next Naval Party 8901 when they arrive here for their pre-embarkation training in two weeks time." The Commanding Officer of the Amphibious Training Unit, at Poole in Dorset, looked at me across his desk.

The year was 1976. Naval Party 8901 was the official title of the Royal Marines' Detachment (or garrison) in the Falkland Islands, stationed there as a Foreign Office-sponsored show of force acting as a 'trip-wire' against an aggressor. The business of being a 'trip wire' is an unenviable one. The small force is not expected to hold off an enemy assault, but to buy time so that more suitable forces may be deployed with a valid excuse. Trip-wire troops are, by and large, regarded as expendable.

Each year a new 'block' of Royal Marines was despatched to relieve the old for a year's sojourn in the South Atlantic in this outward show of diplomatic determination to 'Keep the Falklands British'.

"But I don't know a thing about them."

"You soon will!"

Neither he nor I could have guessed how prophetic his last remark was to be.

In carrying out the Colonel's wishes I studied earlier post-tour reports, read what literature there was available in the library and travelled to Fleet Headquarters and the Department of the Commandant General, gleaning wherever I could until, finally, so captivated by what I had discovered, I volunteered for service in the Falkland Islands − but was sent to Bickleigh Barracks in South Devon.

22 June, 1977. The Royal Marines Military Secretary was paying his annual visit to the operational units of the Corps and on that Wednesday it was to be our turn in 42 Commando to benefit by − or be horrified at − his prognosis of officers' future appointments and chances of promotion. Although I was happy in the Commando (my duties as Operations Officer were professionally challenging) I had not enjoyed the easiest of relationships with my Commanding Officer. This was exacerbated, on my part, by a long-term illness picked up during the Oman's Dhofar war from where I had returned as a recce platoon and company commander ten years before.

The Colonel was worried that if 'selected for Major' it would be embarrassing if my promotion could not be confirmed after the statutory six months waiting period. He should have been more honest for I knew he felt there were military causes to deny me promotion. I was the officer closest to him in operational matters as the second-in-command was new in his post and keeping 'hull down' due to the dismissal of his predecessor. I was, therefore, whether culpable or not, in the firing line for any errors. In my defence, however, it has to be said that many of the problems affecting the Headquarters, and thus the whole Commando, were to a certain extent of the Commanding Officer's own making and stemmed largely from his eccentric behaviour during a recent three months training deployment in the West Indies.

As was the custom on those occasions the Military Secretary addressed all officers in the Mess and followed this general talk with private discussions with individual officers who had requested them. He added to the list those officers to whom he wished to speak. My name was on that second list.

I sat down. There was no preamble and I remember the words exactly.

"Ewen, it is time you and your Commanding Officer parted company." I was astounded at the directness of the announcement; I thought, too, of the other officers who had so recently been dismissed.

The MS continued: "I'm sorry but I think it better this way and as we are not in the habit of removing COs it must be you." He paused without a glimmer of a smile.

"I'm offering you the post of Officer Commanding Naval Party 8901 as a 'local' major."

The MS paused. Then a genuine smile did cross his face before he continued.

"But never tell your CO that you were a volunteer as he thinks you are going there as a punishment!" Although I had indeed been a volunteer earlier, a posting to the South Atlantic at that stage had not been uppermost in my mind and despite the bravado in front of the Military Secretary I could not pretend, amongst my friends, that it was welcome.

Once I had accepted the inevitable, I was keen that the family would accompany me (despite it being an un-accompanied posting) and it is to her great credit that when the initial shock had passed Patricia fell in with the plans with great enthusiasm and her customary perfection and fastidious organization.

There were very good reasons why wives (unless they were Islanders married to Royal Marines) were not officially welcome. The threat was real and, if an invasion was to occur, the Detachment would be required to leave Stanley and make for the hills with no one being responsible for the fate of any military dependents. Indeed such questions as hostage-taking and blackmail were raised as valid reasons for the servicemen being unaccompanied.

In my case I was determined, and a number of factors helped me in my decision. In our married life, then of ten years, we had only spent two together for any length of time. The life had suited us as far as it went, for Patricia quite often came with me on my travels, but there were other reasons why it was important to me to take my family to the South Atlantic. The Falkland Islands were then, and still are despite everything, a remote and wonderful place for a youngster to see and experience. I felt it would have been selfish to have denied my children (then aged 4½ and 1½) the opportunity of living through their impressionable years without the advantage of witnessing such wildness of nature and such a range of wildlife in natural surroundings. I may well be accused of arrogance in ignoring the rules and my senior officers, and to that I must plead guilty: but I could never have forgiven myself if I had denied my young family this quite unsurpassed start to their lives.

For my part there had been two other reasons for volunteering for a posting not known to enhance promotion prospects. Firstly, it was a 'command' posting, and although the numbers were few − about forty-four marines − it counted as a Company Commander's appointment. As I was unlikely to be promoted Major, let alone beyond that, I wanted to jump at every opportunity to avoid incarceration behind some fun-forsaken desk as a very junior staff officer. I had been lucky enough to have already held a number of command appointments (including three at company level), but as there were no volunteers for the Falklands in those days I did not feel selfish in accepting this latest one. Many officers considered even a desk preferable to the South Atlantic, but how wrong they were and how glad I was to be!

Secondly, I wanted to have the opportunity to explore waters that were largely untouched by the sailing fraternity and to tabulate them for future visitors. From the very earliest days I was helped by a great friend, Peter Odling-Smee. Peter was a recently retired Royal Naval hydrographer who had surveyed Stanley Harbour, Christmas Harbour and the North West Passage off Pebble Island and whose enthusiam for the Islands and their 'nautical' attractions knew few limits. He was instrumental in helping me to appreciate that it would be possible to undertake the private work I had already begun planning. There was, then, no hint of any military requirement to look at the beaches.

I was very conscious, from every previous officer who had served in the Falklands, that alcohol and loneliness were insidious partners. I knew well my own failings and recognized that without my family I would be unlikely to complete my self-imposed task on the one hand and give the total commitment that my Marines required on the other. I knew my faults and the best way to combat them.

The first thing to do was to write to the officer I was to relieve in the Falklands, Nigel Willoughby, an old and valued friend.

At the end of my letter I raised, rather tentatively, the question of my bringing out Patricia and the children. I was braced for the answer as I knew well the restrictions – militarily from the MOD point of view and socially from the Islanders' point of view. But despite Whitehall's views my earlier studies had shown that the more married-accompanied men the Detachment had, the happier and more cohesive it became.

In addition to the possibility of my family's move and apart from all the obvious military questions I wanted to ask, I raised the idea of shipping out my small sloop. The thought of carrying out the surveys from my own yacht in a remote and seldom-visited part of the world was an added spur to my desire to go at all.

I had been brought up under the burgee of the Royal Cruising Club and had learnt of the members' peregrinations through the remote cruising grounds of the world, and yet a glance through the Club's journals indicated that the Falkland Islands had never featured prominently. Here was a chance to put that right as well.

In the end I'm not sure that I did get it right, for as it turned out I could not be seen to be studying the coastline privately when I should have been commanding the detachment, and yet on the other hand I certainly could not be seen to be doing so for military reasons (as part of my duties were to require) for fear of causing undue and understandable suspicion, if not alarm. I was to decide, after much thought, to admit that what I was doing was indeed for private reasons and that I would just have to accept the expected opprobrium. The Governor was to castigate me on a number of occasions for spending too much time at sea, but I was never able to tell him the truth behind my activity.

The problem of the family's move was nearly resolved for me by an unfortunate chance encounter.

On 26 June I was honoured to be invited to a Buckingham Palace Garden Party as a committee member of the Royal Naval Sailing Association.

My heart sank as I noticed the Royal Marines' Chief of Staff making his way towards us. I was in a morning coat and he was dressed in full blue uniform. This particular General was not a favourite among the officers and marines for he exercised a dedicated lack of human interest in his subordinates. He possessed no detectable sense of humour.

"What are you doing here? Why are you not on the Military Secretary's list — and why are you not in uniform?"

I was rather taken aback by this attack, not least because I was there as a yachtsman, and with my Commanding Officer's permission. As far as I was concerned it was none of his business, nor was it his party! However, Patricia was quicker than I and answered for me:

"Oh, didn't you know? There are other ways of being invited to Buckingham Palace than being a Royal Marine General."

He turned to her:

"Well I hope you like your husband's next appointment?"

"Yes. I'm thrilled. We shall be together for the first time for years, and I have a number of friends in Argentina with whom I can stay on the way there and back."

He turned back to me: "I thought you understood that it was an unaccompanied posting!" and without waiting for an answer the General strode away. We had been left in no doubt that Patricia's move to the south would be blocked at every turn.

When Nigel's return letter was received it helped us to make up our mind and increased our determination to carry out our original plan. We had never expected help from the service and we certainly never asked for it but what we hadn't bargained on was active prevention of our plans.

Nigel was honest in his answers.

He reminded me that in his earlier reports he stated that he was, in general terms, against wives accompanying the Detachment. He had one accompanied Corporal, but this did not affect the Detachment at all. With his current experience he felt that he had now changed his mind and as far as his own wife was concerned he:

"... would enormously appreciate her company, help and support in what is certainly an unusual community. Her presence would greatly reduce the strain on me and would be to the benefit of the Detachment. In principle therefore I would encourage you to bring Patricia out if you can possibly manage it. It would turn what is basically an unaccompanied tour with lots of disadvantages into an unforgettable experience for you both."

His initial comments were not overshadowed by his subsequent, and sometimes gloomy, synopsis of the practicalities of life for expatriate families. Firstly, expense. Nigel outlined the basic cost of travel, despite the possibility of a RAF indulgence flight across to Washington. It all looked horrific but feasible. Next, food:

"It's probably fair to say that rents compare favourably with UK married quarters and that the cost of living in terms of staples is markedly lower (eg beef ten pence a pound). Cheap (though not totally duty free) booze is available and one would not be running a car or spending much on luxuries or going out to dinner as these facilities are not available!"

He had a particular message for Patricia:

"Life is hard work for wives out here," he wrote. "Many houses are peat-heated. Peat has a certain charm, but it is a laborious charm – lots of fetching and carrying, and it is a somewhat dirty fuel ('clean' dirt though!). There are no convenience foods so food preparation is long-winded by comparison with home. Many wives actually regard this as an advantage. Deep freezes are plentiful.

"Medical is OK. Dentist is intermittent.

"There is a nursery class (private) but I'm not sure of details. Education in general is poor, but at 5 – 6 the consensus seems to be that it is OK. It is at the later stages that the isolation starts to pull the standard down."

He was generous about the social scene which, bearing in mind his bachelor status and position in the community, was interesting.

"There are enough nice people about for life to be bearable and the social scene can be quite hectic. Very much a question of making your own entertainment, though. No TV. Local broadcasting plus BBC overseas for 4 hours a day, films though the RMs. Some of us reckon that there are advantages to the above."

The answers on sailing were as positive:

"Next," he wrote, *Black Velvet."*

"Provided that you can fix it I think it would be a marvellous idea to bring *Black Velvet* out. A glance at the 50:000 map of the Falklands will show you that every settlement is accessible by sea. What it will not show you is that there are lots and lots of hazards, most of them completely uncharted. However, Jack Sollis, the master of MV *Forrest* (your ship) has a lifetime's experience of Islands waters, so expert local knowledge for any planned inter-island voyage is immediately accessible."

This was the most encouraging news and went far beyond the amount of advice I was expecting. I pricked up my ears at so much – the loneliness, the uncharted waters, the chance to sail back: the excitement of it all.

Planning then started in detail. Patricia visited Thomas Cook to ask for any itinerary they might have for private travel to the Falklands (they didn't), and I contacted the Falkland Islands Company on the possibility of *Black Velvet* being shipped out.

I also wrote to the Assistant Military Secretary to see if I could sail her back during an extended end-of-tour leave.

"The Commandant General would be disposed to look favourably on a 'little extra leave' should you be unable to complete your passage home within your foreign service leave entitlement.... I have therefore consulted with the Captain of the Fleet, who considers that it would be no bad thing for your Detachment to have a focus of interest, and that the return voyage would gain much in the way of publicity for the Corps."

I was grateful for this decision of the Corps, which only served to remind me just how good the Royal Marines are at indulging some of its members' way-out projects. Many are turned down but usually for very practical and overriding military reasons. I have never been afraid to ask to carry out some private expedition, and have been turned down more than once, although I also believe that it is often more time-consuming and painful to seek permission than it is to receive retribution! It is a question of knowing when to apply this theory.

Thomas Cook returned a most helpful letter detailing the services by British Caledonian Airways or Aerolineas Argentinas from Heathrow to Buenos Aires but from there to Stanley via the southern Argentinian oil town of Comodoro Rivadavia was, they thought, by courtesy of the Air Force. They were not too sure and they certainly had no timetables. One suggestion was the Air France Concorde service from Paris to Rio. It was very tempting.

The most helpful of letters was written to Patricia by the wife of one of the two Royal Air Force technicians (on a two-year accompanied posting through the Overseas Development Ministry) whose duty it was to service the Beaver float 'planes used for civilian inter-island travel and the regular airmail service of letters and small packages. Jean Hall, at Nigel's request, wrote eleven pages of comprehensive advice answering all the mundane but necessary questions. Jean had anticipated, from her own earlier experiences on arrival, everything that we would need for moving out a young family and setting up house from scratch in Stanley. Invaluable though Nigel's advice was, the views of a service wife were even more so. Through Jean's eyes we first became aware of the daily advantages and disadvantages of domestic life for an outsider in Stanley.

The whole business of taking the family came to a head on 30 November when I was summoned, without warning, to call on the Chief of Staff to the Commander-in-Chief. I had called on the Admiral before but on this second occasion I became suspicious when ordered to arrive in full Lovat uniform — the usual sign that, as some joker put it, it would be an interview without coffee! At least I was spared full 'Blues' with sword and medals.

There then took place a conversation nearly as ludicrous and as one-sided as that that had occurred on the lawns of Buckingham Palace. I stood at ease in front of the Admiral while the Fleet Royal Marines Officer, Major Taylor, stood to one side. This did not help as I was referred to by the Admiral throughout, in the third person, as Major Tailyour. Clearly the Royal Marines' Chief of Staff had reported our

Garden Party conversation to his opposite number in Fleet Headquarters.

Major Taylor was asked if Major Tailyour realized whether or not his future appointment was an unaccompanied posting. I was then asked the question and my answer repeated back to the Admiral via the Major. After this farce had run its course I was told, via Major Taylor and repeated to me, that I was not to take my wife without express and written permission.

The meeting was over. Outside, the FRMO apologized for the rather childish manner in which it had been conducted. I shrugged the episode off as being of little consequence and one that was certainly not going to affect my plans; although I did not say so at the time. Militarily, I understood the reasoning behind the view that wives should not accompany their husbands to the Falkland Islands, but as it was a risk I was prepared to accept, and as the arrangements were being conducted without help from the MOD, I felt that my private problems were of little interest to the naval staff. The wrath of 'the system' was worth risking for the sake of the superb experience awaiting my young children.

My conscience was slightly relieved when I received a letter from Nigel saying that the Governor had heard that the MOD were taking a rather "left wing view" of my plans to bring the family south, but as far as he, the Governor, was concerned, he was my Commander-in-Chief 'in situ'. I was to continue planning. This was great news, although I continued to keep my plans private at the United Kingdom end. In accordance with tradition and good manners I had written to His Excellency the Governor and Commander-in-Chief, Falkland Islands (known by all as HEGFI) acknowledging my appointment as "Officer Commanding Naval Party 8901 under your command". Towards the end of January I received a letter from Mr J.R.W. Parker, HEGFI himself. It was most welcome, not least of all because of the second paragraph:

"We are particularly looking forward to meeting your wife who will make a very welcome addition to our small community, as well as being a great help to you in the somewhat isolated circumstances of your posting."

We were all on our way!

II

A Clear Call

I LEFT 42 COMMANDO on 18 November with a glad heart. Although life as the Operations and Training Officer had been testing, headquarters duties were not to my liking as it had been all training and no operations, apart from joining the Commando in its last days in Belfast to understudy my predecessor. I had found working for the Commanding Officer a rather trying experience which neither I nor my fellow officers put down to being all my own fault.

The stories of the Commando's West Indies tour in the spring of 1977 on the island of Vieques are well-known by those involved and who will remember, with confused feelings, very many bizarre incidents such as the loss of, and commando-wide search for, a 44DD 'bra' belonging to the Commanding Officer. It was last seen with each 'cup' over the head of the Motor Transport Officer and the Quartermaster as they danced an impromptu *pas de deux*, their arms round each other's shoulders at a late night officers' mess party in a coconut grove!

It was time to look forward. I drove to Poole on 21 November, met many old friends that evening and woke on the Tuesday to dress, rather self-consciously, in a Major's uniform for the first time.

Two of those who joined me at Poole that first day were the Detachment Second-in-Command, Second-Lieutenant Christopher Horlick and the Sergeant Major, Colour-Sergeant Keith Pittock.

Shortly after my appointment to command the Falklands Detachment had been announced, the Assistant Military Secretary had offered me an outstanding junior officer as Second-in-Command. "He has never put a foot wrong and you will be a fool to refuse him."

I wanted an officer able to act independently, within the guidelines of 'the book' but not dominated by it. I wanted an officer with some individual spark and excitement; I asked for Chris Horlick. Chris had been serving in 42 Commando as a rifle troop commander under training and I liked his style. He was superbly fit (a candidate for the SBS selection course) with a great sense of humour; he didn't take life too seriously and was responsible and intelligent. Above all, he was not frightened to take calculated risks, nor was he frightened to argue his case. He was not a 'yes' man and yet knew when to accede to a senior officer's wishes. The

Assistant Military Secretary readily agreed to him joining me. I could not have wished for a better companion.

There was, though, a small problem. Chris was still a Young Officer Under Training and as such would be wearing the rank of a Second Lieutenant for a few more weeks. In a commando a Second Lieutenant is seen for what he is — exactly that: under training. In NP 8901 he would take on many complicated tasks and responsibilities and I wanted to give the Detachment (and especially the Senior NCOs under his direct command and control) no excuse for believing him to be so inexperienced. It could have been argued, quite understandably, that the character of the man would see him through, but I could not take that chance. Early that first morning — before Chris had had time to appear in public — I presented him with Lieutenant's badges of rank. He was sworn to secrecy. Nobody noticed, but I believe it made a fundamental difference to his standing within the Detachment.

There were more serious matters to be tackled. The senior NCOs were due to join the following week, with the bulk of the men the week after. In the meantime the advance party had a large shopping list to contemplate. We had to draw up a comprehensive training programme; organize the transport of our heavy baggage in large wooden chacons; order the dry foods we would need for the year; book training and field-firing ranges; attend numerous briefings; conduct practice ceremonial parades; inspect and alter uniforms; undergo continuation training in the use of the fifteen-foot Gemini inflatable assault craft; send the armourer on courses for Second World War equipment so that he could maintain the Falkland Islands Defence Force weapons; order our year's supply of NAAFI stores (how much Coca Cola, beer and whisky would forty-four men drink in twelve months — how much port would I?); fix security courses for those needing them; book courses in stores accounting and petty cash funds; attend briefings from the Falkland Island Company office in Whitechapel (the Admiralty Agents for the upkeep and repair of Moody Brook camp — our future home); fix butchery courses for the corporal chef; arrange intelligence, naval and military briefings; apply for extra security clearance for myself and the signals NCO; send a suitable corporal on a cinema projector's course and the whole Detachment on escape, evasion and survival courses and exercises. This comprehensive list increased as we read through previous reports of pre-embarkation training and the lists of what they had lacked.

Required reading was the *Shackleton Report* and the previous year's Intelligence Summaries. We needed to open up a Registry with the appropriate filing systems and establish each man's next of kin and documentation.

The most important desk to be activated was that of the Detachment Sergeant Major. All Detachment Sergeants Major, whether they are embarked in ships or Naval Parties or for special one-off operations, and regardless of rank, are known as "the Sergeant-Major". Such was Colour-Sergeant Keith Pittock. On a minor scale he had to manage the full range of a Commando RSM's duties but in miniature. Although this made the responsibility slightly less daunting the pain of failure would be as severe; none the less so because we had an 'active service' role to perform.

Keith Pittock had begun life as a Landing Craftsman but, in his words, had 'seen the light' and volunteered to change his specialization to that of Drill Instructor! In my view he had gone the wrong way, but we need drill instructors, and his sharp wit, well-tuned sense of humour and methodical approach to life were to be invaluable. He also possessed a high degree of sensitivity to the feelings of others; an attribute not often associated with the parade ground. Keith Pittock was to become a lifelong friend; we had some differing views on the occasional matter, but, as with all successful OC/DSM relationships, these cemented rather than destroyed mutual respect.

Two events helped us to get organized quickly in such a short time. The first was the firemens' strike of that winter and the second was the generous offer by my brother-in-law of the use of his grouse moor for our military training and survival. The firemens' strike caused vacant spaces on some courses, while whole field-firing ranges became available as courses were sent *en bloc* to man the *Green Goddess* fire engines.

David Williams-Wynn's offer of Llanbrynmair in North Wales was a generous and magnificent gesture that removed from us the tedium of military training areas with their necessary but intrusive restrictions.

We needed to practice teamwork in a number of military techniques that form part of an individual's Royal Marine training: long range patrolling covering great distances with heavy loads, reporting on enemy or relevant activities, escape and invasion coupled with living off the land were all skills we needed to exercise together and in the smaller teams we would be split into once in Stanley.

The wildness of Llanbrynmair was perfect and we would not need to use (even if they had been available) any training staff; although I did manage to obtain the services of a corporal from the Mountain and Arctic Warfare Cadre who was delighted to get into the snow-covered mountains of North Wales and away from his fire-fighting duties.

For my part, and in addition to taking part in all of the above, I attended numerous Ministry of Defence and Foreign and Commonwealth Office briefings. By far the most important I attended was the first, addressed to the future employment of the Naval Party in the Falklands in peace, and its actions in case of invasion. It was held in the Directorate of Naval Plans on 1 December, 1977, and the day after the rather one-sided interview held with the Chief of Staff in Northwood at which I had been ordered not to take my family south.

The meeting was attended by at least one other Royal Marines officer; of my rank, but a year or two younger, this major was known for his staff rather than his regimental acumen and could think of nothing worse for his career than a year in the Falkland Islands!

The current task of the Detachment was outlined for my benefit although I was, of course, *au fait* with the general pattern of what was then required in case of hostilities. This introduction was followed by the exciting news that starting with the handover to our own successors a new defence strategy would be in place and operational. Naval Party 8901 would, in the future, take on an active defensive posture around Stanley instead of running into the hills to observe and disrupt. We would be what I was to call the 'Buffer Detachment' between the old and the new; we would still be a trip-wire.

Not only was this an exciting challenge but it had its chilling aspects.

Firstly, it seemed even to my limited knowledge (of the terrain) that forty-four men were wholly inadequate. Secondly, it was to be me, a 'local' Major, who would re-write the comprehensive plans for approval at Cabinet level. I wasn't too sure that I was the right man to make such fundamental decisions, although I was happy that as a Royal Marine who had served mostly in Commandos or at sea (and almost always in a 'command' capacity) I probably had as much experience as any of my age and seniority, but to be asked to link in my military assessment of what might happen and how we should be prepared to react to the altogether unknown quantities of the political and social aspects was a tall order. We were not being invited to defend a typical piece of north west Europe so loved by the military tacticians of the era, but a thriving, albeit tiny, capital city about as remote from help as it was possible to be. I just hoped that the support I would need when alone would be total.

"What is the new requirement exactly?" I needed at least a little guidance.

"Up to you, militarily, but when you meet the FCO they will give you the political necessities and priorities. We expect you to buy them some bargaining time in the UN − that sort of thing."

"How long? How? What if we fail?"

"Discuss this with the FCO, then when you get out there make your own assessments. You will need to look at improving your communications externally and internally, increasing the scale of defensive weapons, setting a 'notice to move' time and assess any useful beaches for any re-invasion or re-supply if your deterrence and the UN fail. You may need to decide how far out from Stanley and Government House you will want to halt any advance and in that context we shall need to look at the position of a new barracks." I pricked up my ears at the mention of beaches for military use and instantly thought that here was the ideal cover for my private work, but, as I have explained, I was to reverse that decision for local reasons

Before my main FCO briefing I was brought up to date with the military aspects of United Kingdom/Argentinian relationships. Mixed in with these preliminary briefings was the added and interesting dimension of perceived Russian aspirations in the South Atlantic, the littoral countries of South America, the Cape Horn route, the Antarctic continent and the associated fishing and mineral rights. Partially as a result of this possible third party, it was also made absolutely plain that the British Government (then Labour) wished to be seen to be acting positively to a number of threats (bi-lateral and tri-lateral) to the relationship between the powers that laid claim to the Islands in the middle; one a spurious claim and one *de facto*.

In March, 1976, Argentina had succumbed to a military government whose openly declared aim was the 'recovery' of 'Las Islas Malvinas'. Later in that year, and not made public among the Islanders until over a year later, was the Argentinian occupation of Southern Thule. Shortly after this Argentina withdrew her ambassador as a direct result of Lord Shackleton's visit to the Falklands and Britain was forced to follow suit. In 1977 there were intelligence reports of troop movements in southern Argentina and the possibility of an expeditionary landing on South Georgia, to counter which Mr Callaghan ordered the despatch of the nuclear-powered submarine HMS *Dreadnought* and the frigates *Phoebe* and *Alacrity*, plus two auxiliaries. They were, as I was being briefed, patrolling as a deterrent: a deterrent unknown to those whom we wished to deter. Also in 1977 the Argentinians captured by force six Soviet trawlers and a factory ship 'on the high seas' and then without warning in November the Argentinian Navy cut the fuel supply to the Falklands and announced that no longer would its ships fly the British courtesy ensign while in Falkland Islands waters. Early military action against the Falkland Islands seemed inevitable to everyone except those who were paid to know.

The main FCO briefing was held in a basement conference room during the week of 12 December. I sat on one side of a large table, flanked by and opposite a number of civil servants and diplomats. The background to the present, undeclared crisis was explained; the impact of the recently released Shackleton Report discussed; the Argentinian military capabilities presented (although I was surprised that no one was able to answer the one question I had at the end − their army's parachuting capabilities), as were the British Government's ideas for the future. I was privy to the developments then underway and which were not to be made public until Mr Callaghan, who was then, of course, no longer Prime Minister, admitted them in the House of Commons in March, 1982, just as the South Georgia 'scrap metal invasion' was at its height.

All this should have alerted the Government to the need for a proper defence policy and contingency plans. Instead of which they continued with an unrealistic trip-wire defence based on forty men eight thousand miles from reinforcements enforcing a three-week bargaining period. None of this, nor the eventual signs of Britain's reduced commitments and capabilities (the proposed demise of her amphibious capability for instance) would have gone unnoticed by the Argentinians living in Stanley, and certainly not by the Junta. The surprise was that the invasion took place when it did − and yet like the wrong type of winter snow on a Home County's railway line it was greeted with almost total disbelief in London − but not in Stanley.

The July 1976 *Economic Survey of the Falkland Islands* was a fascinating document commissioned by the Labour Government from Lord Shackleton. As it was not required to (and nor did it) discuss the sovereignty issue it was largely ignored by the Argentinians. Apart from ninety points mostly concerned with the economy which were studiously and mischievously misinterpreted to Parliamant by the then Foreign Secretary (Anthony Crosland) it highlighted two aspects of importance to the military. Lord Shackleton had written his optimistic report with a view to arguing that with an economically viable Falklands Islands there was a greater chance of persuading the FCO that they were worth the political fight in resisting any Argentinina claim of sovereignty − which is where Crosland came in by arguing that "this economic strength would require considerable Argentinian cooperation...and we cannot have that unless certain political issues are raised," which was FCO-speak reversing Shackleton's proposals for economic independence.

But there was an added if unspoken twist to this paradox, for although there were very clear problems with the internal economies of the colony (mostly the direct effect of too small a labour force, an undiversified economy, a near monopoly by the Falkland Island Company and an extraordinary degree of absentee landlordism) most of the islanders were there because they liked the slow, rather personal pace of life and did not want their home to become an area of economic expansion if that expansion meant a degradation of their way of life. It was not for any outsider (even one as eminent as Lord Shackleton, I was to be told) to impose unwanted industry, with all its attendant horrors, on such a community. Yet it was this lack of self-confidence and self-esteem due to the poor economy that was at the root of so much. Crosland again: "The Survey further recommended certain major capital projects, [in addition to lengthening the runway, which I discuss in a moment] notably a pilot fishing project, which would bring the total recommended expenditure by the UK up to some pounds sterling 13-14 million.... But for the rest we cannot at this time accept the more costly recommendations. The overseas aid budget, recently cut in the December public expenditure exercise, would not stand it. There are more urgent claims from much poorer communities."

Considering that between the years 1951 and 1974 the United Kingdom gained, at the Islands' expense, to the tune of over eleven and a half million pounds there was a disingenuous ring to the FCO assessment which was not lost on the Islanders, who knew, as did Shackleton but twisted by Crosland, that an estimated 98% of their gross national product was re-invested in Great Britain or its offlying islands (Channel and Man). In a paper presented to the Royal Geographical Society on 15 November, 1976, Lord Shackleton highlighted this important but little-known (outside the Islands) and well-concealed (inside the British Treasury and FCO) fact: "Far from living off the British, the British have been doing very nicely out of the Falkland Islanders....Far more has come back to Britain in the way of profits than has gone out in the way of investment. More importantly, we concluded that the Chancellor of the Exchequer has, over the years, taken twice as much out in tax as has gone in in the form of aid to develop the Falkland Islands." This would not have been music to Crosland's ears.

Nor did many of Crosland's 'poorer communities' have such a threat hanging over them that could be countered, partially, by an increase in self-confidence. That self-confidence could have been restored in the Islands by a more positive attitude over the main concern − a firm declaration that there was nothing to discuss on the sovereignty issue. Instead the Kelpers were offered grandiose schemes that relied heavily on Argentinian participation and British money. Considering that up to the 1980s Britain made a profit from the Islands this last was hardly beyond the Kelpers' expectations. When coupled with their almost total reliance on the Falkland Island Company and the whim of absentee landlords, it is not surprising that there was a distinct lack of self-confidence among the Islanders which was highlighted in the Report. The Islanders had the answer, but it was only partially explored by Shackleton: nationalize the FIC, bring the profits back in to the Colony and diversify the land ownership, if necessary, under Government control.

Militarily, the airfield was the most significant part of Shackleton's report. "The permanent airfield [which had been started in 1974 to replace the 'temporary' one built with American equipment by an Argentinian workforce — and who were seen off from BA by our Ambassador] should be strengthened and extended to a length necessary to receive short- and medium-haul jets and part-loaded long-haul jets."

It was accepted, in private, that the airfield extension (for which the ground survey had been conducted) would assist in the defence of the Colony and so would not be in Argentina's interests, although nobody seems to have noticed that an extended runway, in addition to allowing larger civilian aircraft to land, would be available for Argentinian fast jets. It is important to note that this aspect of the Report was vetoed by the Falkland Islands Government itself (with civilian aircraft only in mind), resulting in a Falkland Islands broadcast stating that there were other deliberations to be taken into account, "the wider political and financial considerations, including the framework for co-operation with Argentina". The 'beneficial' effect of this apparent appeasement by the Falkland Islands Government was to be felt in 1982 when the enemy's fast jets were unable to operate from Stanley and so were forced to fly from the mainland. What had started out as a 'sop' to Argentine wishes — and against many British and Island wishes precisely because it was just that — was to prove a bonus to our own war effort. A paradox indeed.

Shackleton's intention had been to show that the Islanders could be financially independent and that nothing should therefore have depended on closer ties with Argentina — hence the longer airfield. But this was not how Crosland presented his reading of the report, during which he felt able to announce that more talks would take place with Argentina to "raise fundamental questions in the relationship between the Islands, Britain and Argentina".

No wonder all this kept the Islanders suspicious.

So that was the situation. NP 8901 were to defend the Islands by force and in doing so prevent any form of attack against Government House for at least three weeks. We would be just forty-two men with no defensive arms or stores. Our only offensive weapon would be the standard self-loading rifle and three two-inch mortars with the enemy's objective (Government House) only three miles from the beaches and airfield, and our base, from which we would have to deploy with the minimum of warning, another three miles further away. Even if the enemy were not to invade, a peaceful sojourn in an idyllic and forgotten corner of the globe while we re-aligned the Island's defences was looking less likely.

Further meetings with CinC Fleet's staff, CGRM's staff and the officers in the Directorate of Naval Plans came and went. Not one officer by whom

I was briefed had been to the Islands, nor had any civil servant or diplomat. Indeed in my Pre Embarkation Training (PET) report before leaving for the South Atlantic I commented, as had my predecessors, that, apart from the immediate problems and discussions on what was happening at that moment 'down south', I learnt nothing new from the FCO and, as Nigel had, I regarded the large scale of the meetings a waste of everybody's time. In addition to which it had been quite clear from the main FCO briefing that, had they not been under government pressure, the officials concerned, being apparently heartily sick of the subject, would have let the Argentinians have the Islands. One diplomat said to me privately, as we left the 12 December meeting, that he wasn't sure that any long-lasting effects would be felt if we abandoned the Islands to the Argentinians. Disgracefully, he wasn't thinking about the inhabitants or their wishes!

It struck me that the Commander-in-Chief Fleet and the Department of the Commandant General Royal Marines had concurred with the Secretary of State for Defence that a new Concept of Operations needed to be introduced in the light of recent Argentinian actions, but that the Secretary of State for Foreign Affairs and his FCO were out of step with the Ministry of Defence's concurrence. Mr Callaghan himself could have taken any action he chose to face up to the Argentinian Junta (with Parliamentary and United Nations approval) but decided not to − apart from the unknown despatch of the submarine.

The practical aspects of preparing ourselves continued, with the weather around the middle of February, 1978, perfect for our needs. A deep covering of snow lay across the Welsh hills and the lakes were well frozen.

By coincidence the terrain was as bleak and unforgiving as that over which we would be operating and, as luck would have it, the temperatures on the moor that winter were lower than any we would experience in the southern hemisphere.

We conducted field-firing back on Dartmoor, lengthy approach marches across the bogs and tors and then back to Poole for the final weeks and our Passing for Duty parade. A thoroughly satisfying, hard and worthwhile training period was over, the success being due in a large part to the patience and resilience of the staff at Royal Marines, Poole. The final ceremony was held on 9 March with the occasion greatly enhanced by my father taking the salute. Leave followed which in our case was spent in a near orgy of farewell dinner parties and the final laying up of *Black Velvet*. She was not to come, for her one-way fare was almost exactly the same as the return for Patricia and the two children. Something had had to give and the yacht lost. It was a sad decision but the right one and, as it turned out, a fortuitous one for I was able to see more of the country from the deck of 'our' patrol vessel the MV *Forrest* and visiting ocean-going yachts than I would have done from that of a twenty-four-foot sloop.

At the last moment one of my marines came to see me. He had served twice in previous NPs 8901 and for one commission in HMS *Endurance*. His girl friend in Stanley was pregnant and as he hadn't seen her for eighteen months wasn't too sure what to do about it. I explained that there were three 'spare men' training with the Detachment for just such eventualities; he could take one of those places and stay behind. He chose to come with us. I thought at the time that it was a noble decision, but it was not until we arrived that I was to discover that the girl in question was allegedly carrying her sixth child: each one supposedly had a different father, and she was not yet, we were told, twenty-five. She (in white) and my marine (in blue uniform) were to marry in the Cathedral attended by His Excellency the Governor.

I had a lot to learn about the Falklands way of life!

III

The Gull's Way

AT EIGHT O'CLOCK ON 29 MARCH, 1978, I said goodbye to Patricia, Hamish and Hermione at the cottage and drove to Poole. The next place we would meet would be at Stanley Airport on, we hoped, 8 May.

The Detachment arrived in Montevideo, by courtesy of Air France (after flying via Paris, Dakar, Rio de Janeiro and Buenos Aires – where we were not allowed off the aircraft) to be met by an officer from HMS *Endurance*. So far so good! Once we had settled in to the ship, a local anglophile named Sam arranged for the marines to be taken on a run ashore, whilst myself, Chris and the ship's officers would be given dinner in one of the many restaurants he seemed to own. It must have been jet lag and lack of sleep but the next thing I remember was waking up sitting with my head on my arm in a totally strange and empty room. I looked round – nothing but empty dining tables; in front of me on a plate was a bill for twenty-four people totalling what appeared to be the GNP for the whole of South America. The others had 'done a runner'. I hardly knew what continent I was in, let alone which city. Panic...but my misery was short-lived. Suddenly through the door burst my new-found friends, led by our Uruguayan host. Much raucous laughter and more tequila. I was safe, though it had been an anxious moment!

We sailed the next morning, 1 April, 1978, and at eight o'clock on the morning of 5 April I was summoned to the bridge. HMS *Endurance*, her white and crimson hull caked in drying salt after a boisterous passage south, began the turn to starboard for the entrance to Port William. To port lay the Tussac Islands with the unseen but best known 'wrecker' of them all, the Billy Rock, off their seaward end. Ahead and slightly to port was the wonderful sweep of Yorke Bay and Gypsy Cove with the Stanley roof tops showing intermittently above and beyond the majestic sand dunes; a pleasant surprise to the first-time visitor by sea. I muttered something about it looking beautiful only to be stopped by the Captain: "Judge no ice until crossed." I could have added another couplet from the old Norse proverb: "Nor maid till bedded" – but bit on my tongue!

The ship could not have been kinder during the intervening days. Captain Derek Wallis and his officers and ship's company were more than generous in their desire to make our transition from the Rest-of-the-World to the

Falklands as painless as possible. Indeed some of the ship's company had moved out of their own mess decks to make room for my marines. Everywhere there was kindness, and not a little sympathy for our future.

Around the ship the sturdy and evil Arctic Skuas fought and screeched; alongside, Commersons Dolphins rose and dipped in graceful arcs; among them, and with much more commotion, tiny gentoo penguins porpoised and darted. The sky was overcast but clear, the air thin, cool and bracing. The wind from ahead was strong and beginning to rise, bringing with it a hint of moisture that, although slight, would soon be driven through the thickest of clothing.

Endurance turned hard to port and shot through The Narrows; then quite suddenly the whole of Stanley was laid before us along the sloping southern edge of the harbour. Peat smoke blew north-eastwards, the sweet, cloying smell invading the bridge through the open wing doors. At nine o'clock the ship came to her anchor a few cables off the Public Jetty from where a small vessel was slipping. Also red hulled with white superstructure, I recognized her instantly from photographs and descriptions: MV *Forrest* was bringing out the departing OC NP 8901, his Sergeant Major and their welcoming party.

With *Forrest* loaded and our farewells said, we embarked for the short journey to the Public Jetty. The 'old' detachment were waiting, there were many renewed acquaintances before we were off under the stares of a small handful of Kelpers anxious to see what the 'new boys' looked like.

Moody Brook, two and a quarter miles west of the jetty, did not come as a surprise. I had read too much and studied too many photographs for that. Outside, cold and uninviting, inside warm and snug with the smell of peat-smoke well-embedded into all the soft furnishings and thin prefabricated walls. The interior was clean and neat, the outside was not.

That evening Nigel and I changed for drinks with the Governor. Mr Jim Parker, large and avuncular, and Deirdre, petite and charming, greeted us in the colonial style (but tin-roofed) Government House at the start of a relaxed evening in comfortable arm chairs by a smouldering and very warm fire.

On the second day we began discussions in earnest after a walk around the Moody Brook real estate. Nigel briefed me on the work he had completed so far on the new Concept of Operations and on the progress he had tried to make with repairing and renovating Moody Brook in the short term. For the longer term, the progress he had made on choosing a site for the new barracks (to match the proposed new Concept) was aired at length.

I was to hear confirmation very quickly that my private assessment in London was correct: up to then only lip service had been paid by the FCO towards the likelihood of an invasion and that that alone had, perhaps subconsciously, influenced many of the Islanders' views of how seriously their defence was being taken. They were of course not to know that a very real threat had been averted by Mr Callaghan sending a small task group a few months earlier. Their perceptions were being understandably clouded by what they saw in the Islands, the continued occupation of Southern Thule (which they now knew about, the delay and lack of action doing nothing for their confidence in the sincerity of the FCO) and the state of NP 8901. With my recent 'London' experience it became instantly clear that the realities of life in the Falklands with its daily worry of an invasion were not appreciated in Whitehall where the rest of the world dominated the thoughts and minds of politicians, diplomats and members of the Ministry of Defence. On the spot, invasion was a continuous subject of conversation − not just once a month or once a week but every single day.

Nigel had studied the new role of the Detachment and had come to the easy conclusion that, as constituted, it would be incapable of resisting an invasion under the proposed new Concept of Operations, especially as this would be a role for which it would not be re-complemented. When the idea of re-tasking had been first mooted (but with no increase in size) he began from the very first of the principles − defence of the seat of power. No longer would we rush into the mountains to play at guerrilla warfare while the United Kingdom prepared a task force (a notion that itself had hardly been credible) but from now onwards the Detachment was required to prevent or delay a landing of an unspecified strength for three weeks and, if that failed, to fall back towards Government House and the protection of the life, and status, of the Governor.

In London I was told to keep the enemy at bay while either the United Nations forced a political solution or the Royal Navy and Royal Marines arrived to 'sort it all out'. If the enemy backed off from the 'trip-wire' we would have won, but if he was not put off we would lose badly and bloodily. To be a credible trip-wire the enemy would have to believe that the United Kingdom would retaliate with force, but, for our part we were not too sure that this would happen, and we had no reason to think that the Argentinians saw it any differently. Certainly all the diplomatic signs were not in our favour in this respect.

What could be in our favour, I argued, was a faint hope that the Argentinians would back off for long enough to think about it if we were to force them to fight among the civilian population. To do so the enemy would have to make the conscious decision to incur casualties in the pursuit of his aim and in that brief time vigorous diplomatic pressures would be placed upon him. All this presupposed enough warning to block the airfield, mine the beaches and set up a defensive line through Stanley. The trip-wire, in my view, had to be at the landing sites, not at the gates to Government House.

The fall-back positions in case the enemy did not trip, or he ignored the inevitable political ultimatums, were to be decided by me and along with these assessment the Concept of Operations would be approved (or disapproved) by CINC Fleet and CGRM before being presented to the Government.

To be in the slightest part a credible military deterrent we would now need heavy machine guns to cover the landing beaches; we would need mines to block the beach exits and we would need explosives to crater the runway, although this would be pretty final if the invasion turned out to be a false alarm! We could always block it with vehicles but this would only be a temporary measure easily removed by a determined enemy. We would need passive defence stores like barbed wire; we would need mortars to cover the approaches to Stanley; we would need anti-tank weapons; we would need enough vehicles to mobilize ourselves quickly; we would need modern communications for internal command and control; and we would need a twenty-four-hour-a-day signals link with Whitehall. We would need (although this was not in the original instructions but arose from the requirement to have a more viable workforce) a detachment that was trickle drafted and not block drafted, and to make this workable and more at ease with the local society we would need the key members to spend at least eighteen months in the Islands – 'married accompanied'. The men would need to be paid properly in addition to their basic pay to allow for the privations suffered by their families at home and to make up for the not inconsiderable loss of freedom and necessities (let alone luxuries) incurred by living in the Islands. None of these things we possessed on my arrival.

Such was the state of the defence of the Falkland Islands in 1978, and, verging on the farcical as it did, it was hardly surprising that the message perceived in Buenos Aires was that it was unlikely that Britain would come to the military aid of a colony it so clearly was not interested in defending politically or militarily in the first place. Given all these facts, it is odd, perhaps, that Argentina did not invade earlier, and yet if she had waited for just a year success would almost have been guaranteed politically and certainly militarily.

This was therefore my 'shopping list': assess the current situation, write the Concept of Operations and seek approval before writing the Standard Operating Procedures, demanding the stores, weapons and equipment needed to practice those SOPs and then, finally, choose a site for a new custom-built barracks.

Out of the projected Concept would fall the refinements I have just mentioned, the new barracks requiring the longest lead time – a proper barracks in the right place and capable of being defended. In the meantime the structured and systematic refurbishment of 'The Brook' to make life more pleasant under such extreme conditions was to be put in hand as a temporary measure.

The 'old' NP 8901 left on 8 April and as they steamed out through the Narrows in HMS *Endurance* to the traditional firework salute from the ship, watched by less than half a dozen Kelpers, we felt isolated and alone. We knew it would not be easy, we knew we had to fight on a number of fronts but nothing prepared us for the intransigence we were to meet. With the unhelpful benefit of hindsight over ten years later, I wonder if that fight was worthwhile, for we achieved little in practical terms and when the invasion did occur the trip-wire was swept aside as swiftly as the political condemnation. Much of the defence equipment that we were to request as the result of our new orders was not to be sent until the Spring of 1982 (four years hence) and by a fearful irony was on the charter ship I was to board at Ascension Island. I can only guess at how different things might have been if quicker action had been taken and the Detachment had been able to defend more effectively itself, the beaches, the landing sites and, finally, Government House. The principles and facts of our defence strategy might have been better understood by the Argentinians if we had been equipped as agreed and on time and had been allowed to practice our procedures. They would have seen a more resolute desire and, maybe, have stood back just that little bit longer. The Islanders, too, might have had more faith in Great Britain if they had seen our (and their) desires met with alacrity by the FCO (who had agreed this new strategy in the first place) instead of the very clear delaying tactics which were to take place. But this is in the future.

Once the old Detachment had left we were able to take stock of our inheritance. There had been valiant attempts by every succeeding Detachment to improve their physical lot in some way but each one seemed to have met with opposition on two fronts: the Civil Service at home in the form of the PSA at Croydon and the Falkland Island Company in Stanley. It was the duty of the FIC to maintain the Royal Marines Barracks at Moody Brook by repair and rebuild as necessary, for which they were paid handsomely by the MOD (Navy), yet it was this aspect of our life that caused more trouble than any other. To this day I do not understand the reasons for such reluctance on the part of the FIC to honour official obligations. Their lack of attention to our needs was to produce various knock-on effects, one of which was that the local people saw us, their defence, living in such squalid conditions that they were forced to the conclusion that, if so little attention was being paid to the fundamentals of our existence, then it boded ill for the more expensive and vital components of our presence. They seemed not to know that much of it was the fault of their own Company, preferring instead to blame the MOD and FCO who, in this respect, were blameless.

Of course not everything was the result of a lack of care and interest from 'outside' agencies. A bullet hole existed in my office ceiling as the result of a marine's failed suicide attempt a few years previously. Nigel apologized for its presence, saying he had always meant to get it filled in. Horrified that such a symbol of the depression that could occur should have been allowed to remain, I promised myself to have it at the very top of my list of things to do. It was still there when I handed over to my successor.

The most urgent concern in those early days, and one which had a direct bearing on our future operational status, was communications. Internal communications were based on civilian-style sets and, although insecure, they were adequate for our needs: they were also compatible with the Island-wide network, allowing us to keep in touch with settlements without any military formalities. Indeed, on Sundays the duty Royal Marines signaller at Moody Brook ran the complete Falklands communications network.

The initial and main worry to me, and previous Detachment Commanders, was the link with the United Kingdom and in particular with the Whitehall Communications Centre known as Whitehall Comcen.

The teleprinter link capable of receiving and sending encrypted messages was run by Cable and Wireless and only operated from 0800 to early evening. As I noted in a letter to CINC Fleet's staff, "The comms problem should be looked at now. For instance, during the night it is not possible to contact England by any means whatsoever; except when HMS *Endurance* is here which is only four out of every twelve months. I hope 'they' do not know this." But I'm sure they did.

The routine which my Signals SNCO (Sergeant Fred Cook, later to be commissioned) inherited from his predecessor was to open up the teleprinter link at 0800 with some brief informal chatter to the London operator indicating, covertly but 'in clear' that all was well and he was not talking with an Argentinian pistol at his head. On one alarming occasion, due to some little local difficulty, the whole of the Islands remained incommunicado with the rest of the world for three days and when Sergeant Cook did get through it was obvious that nobody had missed us at all!

For the first week we sat back and took stock. We drew up lists of priorities, established areas of responsibilities, took advice locally and from Northwood and then, on 1 May, 1978, and with HE's consent (which was not necessary but tactful, as he was the Commander-in-Chief) I wrote a firm signal of intent to the Fleet Royal Marines Officer on the staff at Northwood.

The first thing I wanted was a visit by a team of reasonably senior officers from the operational, logistics and personnel branches of Royal Marines' Headquarters. I also asked for a representative from the Department of the Environment, for it was they, and the PSA at Croydon, who held overall responsibility for the state of Moody Brook through their agents on the Islands, the FIC.

Before we arrived the PSA had conducted a survey of Moody Brook and concluded that recent minor improvements had been acceptable, but we considered that they only 'decelerated the rate of deterioration' and in this respect my signal also called for the immediate removal of the imaginatively named Belsen Block (the scene of an even earlier suicide). It was (and is to this day) a huge, reinforced concrete structure built during the 1914–1918 war to house the diesels and generators that powered the naval signal station – for which Moody Brook was the accommodation. Designed to withstand naval gunfire, this attribute was mercifully never put to the test in either World War, but it was easy to see that it would have been a success in this respect. Moody Brook accommodation was evacuated at the end of the First World War and condemned for human habitation. It was reinstated during the Second World War and again evacuated and condemned at the end of those hostilities. To some minds it was the ideal place to house a detachment of Royal Marines: three desolate miles from Stanley – and no bus stop.

Our deterrence, even before 'the change', relied in large part on our ability to deploy at little notice and with great speed from Moody Brook. To do this all traffic had to cross the Moody Brook Bridge between us and Stanley. The weight-bearing ability was suspect as the structure only remained horizontal, and above the Brook itself, by courtesy of what was described in my signal as 'retired hovercraft jacks'. Only light-weight vehicles were allowed to pass, and while this was no real problem (one four-ton Bedford was permanently off the road and the other had been written-off), it meant that the other legacies of the hovercraft and wireless station days had to remain, for there was no method by which we could remove their rusting and unsightly detritus. We had to accept it, but it, too, did little for our morale. Nor was it possible to backload the forty-nine large, wooden shipping containers (chacons) that also littered the camp, although uses were found for some. Indeed without about ten of these we would have had no food stores, stationery, ready use lockers or ammunition stores. One chacon had acted as the terminal for a particularly enthusiastic radio ham and one, by some inexplicable piece of manoeuvring (social and physical), had ended up on the Public Jetty in Stanley where it did sterling service for the crews of visiting ships in conjunction with an enterprising young island girl known only as 'The Yellow Submarine'! (Financial independence was there for some.)

The tragedy of all this was that Moody Brook's geographical position, forgetting for a moment the military position, was ideal. It was, or should have been, a very beautiful and desirable place to live, by Islands standards. The view down the length of Port Stanley was stunning; it was far enough away from the capital to be isolated from many of the petty day-to-day problems and yet near enough for most social or domestic needs. But it was a pigsty of a place: the buildings were not weather-proof; an open and cracked sewer ran through a fresh-food store; the vehicle tracks were deep canals of mud and the camp was surrounded on every side by scenes of desolation, rust and decay. It was easy for an outsider to tell us to ignore the local sights and not to be so sensitive, but to those of us for whom it was home for thirteen months the view was not the same.

Even without sewage the chacons were not the ideal storage for food and within two days of arrival we destroyed 150 pounds of decomposing meat.

My first signal began: "Unless a full and progressively planned modernization programme is approved we are unable to do more than carry out a periodic repainting and minor home-improvement scheme. Currently and for the foreseeable future our priority is self-maintenance to the detriment of our military duties, but I consider this is vital to overall welfare of Detachment."

I ended this magnum opus with the following statements:

"Only first hand knowledge can impress the seriousness of these and other problems affecting our viability as a military force. Our living conditions and inability to appear properly equipped cause regular and embarrassing comments from locals who do look to us to maintain high standards of alertness and administration for their defence."

I followed this opening signal with a four-page letter to the new Fleet Royal Marines Officer, Tim Downs, about to become a staunch ally.

"Starting at the top there seems to be a great deal of muddled thinking over what our real task is. Certainly we do not seem to be equipped nor manned for any of our likely roles. There is little we can do except physically guard the life of HE. Any question of defending Key Points (KPs) or Vital Points (VPs) is unrealistic due to our numbers. The Falkland Islands Defence Force (FIDF) is only a little more than a morale booster. Given warning, we could delay an amphibious landing, but not if it was preceded by a sudden arrival of two or three transport aircraft on the runway (which is only a few hundred yards from the only likely beach) with an advance party to secure the beachhead – or vice versa. That is the worst case but even at the best, and most likely, we are largely impotent and can only be used in an observation or minor defensive role. The aim of this letter is not to discuss our Concept of Operations but to point out that due to the conditions under which we exist any discussion on our role will be highly influenced by present admin and associated difficulties....

"The Islanders see this and wonder, with every justification, what our military tasks must be, for they have never been told. I am already sick of the number of remarks to the effect that we should be replaced either by the Royal Engineers or, worse, 'a proper fighting regiment like the Scots Guards....

"The communications side of things is a muddle....

"A formal shake-up has got to be made now and firm proposals drawn up and acted upon. The geographical position of the Camp is also a contributory factor in making people wonder why we are here....

"As it happens HE wants us to keep a low military profile at the moment.... However, I have carried out a number of TEWTS (tactical exercises without troops) and start exercises next week to cover the most likely military problem areas....

"The locals are very friendly and seem sympathetic to our problems... but at the moment they see our treatment as being indicative of the lack of real interest shown in their defence by Whitehall."

My final and handwritten words were:

"I would, seriously, like to spend two years here putting the new show on the road. The country and people are fabulous – well worth fighting for."

I was to remember these words time and time again, but I never retracted them. The letter was dated 4 May 1978.

The reference to the Royal Engineers was to become a much-exercised point by the Governor and some senior islanders who reasoned, with understandable logic, that if our presence alone was the deterrent and (as our duties in the event of an invasion were to hide in the hills and not fight) it would have made more sense for the military unit to be one that could in peacetime offer some skills to the community. The Royal Engineers were seen by many as representing the best of both worlds. As it was, the Detachment was often called upon to carry out mundane tasks and the balancing of these with our normal duties was one requiring great diplomatic skill, which I am not sure I possessed in the right quantity.

Patricia, Hamish and Hermione were due to arrive by courtesy of Lineas Aerolineas del Estol at 0930 on the 8 May. I watched from the control tower as the 'plane flew downwind along a sunlit Port William only to disappear into a thick bank of fog that suddenly rolled across Cape Pembroke peninsula. For the next two hours we listened to the droning of engines before they faded away to the westward. Forty-eight hours later the aircraft tried again, successfully, allowing a very relieved but thoroughly exhausted family to step onto Falklands soil. Their long journey was over but not without cost. The two very young children were suffering badly from some form of stomach poisoning picked up in the squalor of Comodoro Rivadavia. The return to the mainland for a further two nights without any sustenance had done nothing for the children's already poor health and Patricia's usually robust constitution. No attempt was made by the airline or hotel to help with food or drink (or even to understand the quite obvious problem) forcing Patricia to storm the inadequate kitchens in search of food. At 26 Ross Road West good food, much sleep and a welcome cocktail party helped our flagging senses of humour in time for us to fit quickly into Stanley's leisurely pace as a complete family. I was glad of their presence and their superb moral support to my efforts.

The CINC Fleet staff were quick to respond to my signal, although not all their news was good. We were to receive a visit later in the year, though I would have preferred it sooner; I was to establish ownership of the Belsen Block with a view to its destruction; there was the slimmest of chances of funding being available for the building of a new barracks; the case for an extra Land Rover was accepted but not for a second (operational) four-tonner as it was assessed in Fleet HQ that the 'fighting element of the Detachment could all fit into the three Land Rovers you have' (which showed that even in the military headquarters in England there was a lack of understanding of our predicament, since even under the existing 'rules' the whole Detachment was required to leave Moody Brook for 'guerrilla warfare activities'(!), including the cooks and clerks). But mine not to reason; we had made an initial point and as soon as we could study the ground and draft the first proposals for the new Concept of Operations the better.

There were other matters that needed our attention and patrolling, *Per Mare Per Terram*, was one of the very positive ways by which we could show our presence, not only to the Islanders in their settlements but to any third party interested in the less populated areas. Another way to show and explain our presence was for me to meet and talk with locals at every level in Stanley. Right from the very beginning my full involvement in these two vital aspects were to be curtailed or prevented.

The FIG owned the small coaster MV *Forrest*, named after an earlier Roman Catholic Minister, the Reverend W. Forrest McWhan, who had been particularly popular and who travelled the Islands extensively in his pastoral duties. When *Forrest* was bought and sailed out it was appropriate, and rather touching, that she should be named after the minister. Her duties, too, would be as popular and widespread throughout the Colony.

Although *Forrest* was owned by the FIG she was chartered by the Royal Navy for NP 8901 duties at £45,000 per year. This was a pretty constant source of revenue for the Government and the act of taking *Forrest* 'off charter' for whatever reason, was one that required careful consideration by the Officer Commanding. I had to weigh up the loss of revenue to a comparatively poor community with the Navy's need to get value for money. The Islanders, particularly those in 'Camp' (the country beyond Stanley), gained twofold by this arrangement for while she was on charter she would invariably take mail and consumable and perishable goods around the settlements. Officially we were required to charge commercial rates to avoid unfair competition with the FIC's own coaster MV *Monsunen*. While this was right and proper, it was not always easy keeping the accounts up-to-date. Luckily even the FIC realized that our itinerary so often changed that any packages would only reach their destination on an 'as available' basis and so sensible and blind eyes would be turned towards those settlements whose 'sea mail' we did take for a nominal price. Bulky items such as sacks of flour or sugar were usually dealt with more formally, as was the occasional passenger.

Forrest was skippered by the redoubtable Jack Sollis, who had earned his BEM during the Second World War and who had subsequently been awarded the MBE for his nautical service to the Colony in a succession of previous vessels over the intervening years.

Jack was much respected as a seaman, but his personal reputation among a number of settlement managers seemed to depend on how much private work he was prepared to accept for their individual convenience at the expense of the military. Some unscrupulous managers did try to play us off against the FIC's more expensive but more reliable (as far as the itinerary's timings were concerned) MV *Monsunen*. I managed never to take *Forrest* 'off charter' during the year, whilst giving the settlements as good a service as I could, which was fine for Jack's reputation and good for the community.

There was room for manoeuvre on all sides, providing settlement managers did not presume too much. One in particular did. Within a few days of my arrival in the Colony the manager of Hill Cove 'tried it on with the new Major'. Although it lost me credit with the Governor and the settlement I won a moral victory which, had I lost, would have been fully exploited throughout our year. The incident involved a brace of

English-born sheep-dog puppies he wanted brought to his settlement before their quarantine period was complete. I refused his imperial request with a firm but polite telegram, to receive in reply:

"Refusing to carry puppies for ten to twelve hours when there is no other transport available seems poor thanks for the hospitality yours and previous Detachments have received on this station. Reconsider your decision and inform me soonest."

HEGFI had been sent a copy and ordered me to comply. I told the Governor that we could not run, or alter at the last moment, a military patrol on which numerous other people were already depending, at the whim of an arrogant manager intent on breaking the quarantine laws. This was an error: the Governor and he were great friends and indeed the Governor was about to announce that he had successfully recommended the award of the OBE to the man in question. I arranged for the dogs to be sent by air but the damage had been done.

This rather stupid incident followed shortly after a meeting with HE in which he asked me to persuade Patricia to be his eyes and ears in and around Stanley. His aim was to have a 'spy' who would report back to him on the morale and opinions of the city at 'Spinning Guild' and 'Womens Institute' level. I explained as tactfully as I could that that was not why my wife was joining me. It was only afterwards that I surmised that perhaps that had been the unspoken reason why he had made it so easy for Patricia to come south. Either way these two incidents formed a barrier between myself and HE that was never bridged — and, indeed, was to be compounded, for shortly after the second interview I was ordered formally to restrict my contacts to those not on the following list:

The Parliamentary Councillors

The Medical Profession

The Education Department

The Falkland Island Company Executives

A subsidiary list of named personalities

This was not going to be easy in a community of eight hundred all told, with my children at the local schools, the FIC responsible for the upkeep of Moody Brook, our dealings with the hospital at professional level and my involvement as the Garrison Commander with the Councillors who were all employed in daily tasks within the community and with whom I had to work at varying levels.

I was also refused permission to patrol the most important area of all — the Jason Islands.

Back at Moody Brook I continued planning for the OC, the DSM, the QM and the signaller to be married accompanied for a tour of between eighteen months and two years. To this end we would need housing which could perhaps have been incorporated into the new barracks. The daily upkeep of the camp, for so long neglected by the FIC, would have to be sharpened up to tide us over the interregnum before the new accommodation was approved and built. Support for this was easily obtained.

Thankfully a calming influence was being exercised by Tim Downs on our behalf at Northwood. He received my suggestions with restraint and patience. He wasn't the only one.

One of my briefing officers in London had been a venerable and retired naval officer who had spent much of his life in Naval Intelligence. 'Percy' worked for DI4 and became a regular correspondent. On 5 July I expressed concern over the lack of intelligence from Government House and the restrictions on our training and asked if there was anything ulterior in this. His answer was that there was nothing known in DI4 to prevent us being kept informed or carrying out vital practices and that DI4 assumed that these restrictions were 'whims of HE's': they were not MOD policy. The British Naval Attaché in Buenos Aires sent regular intelligence reports to HEGFI, but as these were not trusted in Government House I was not privy to them. Additionally, and according to HE, any form of military manouevres would arouse suspicion among the islanders, and yet I was constantly being asked by the islanders themselves what contingency plans we had exercised recently. It was impossible to win and was a matter which I believed, against the Governor's wishes, should have been discussed openly with the Falkland society. That chance was to come but was itself to be the cause of further distrust between myself and His Excellency.

One point that, whilst not directly affecting our role, had a marked effect on morale was the case for some form of Local Overseas Allowance. This was one of my hardest fought battles and was to influence my opinion of those responsible in London for naval pay, allowances and service conditions. The eventual refusal of any sort of allowance (which, for want of a better description, I nicknamed Embuggerance Allowance) was quite unjustified and certainly immoral. My initial euphoria over this was caused by the Chief of Staff's letter to the Director General of Naval Personnel Services, Rear Admiral Baird. In it he outlined our case in the clearest terms and, whilst accepting that LOA was a non-starter, he, too, argued for a special allowance. Admiral Baird agreed all that was said.

LOA is given to servicemen living abroad and is designed, in simple terms, to make up the difference in the cost of living compared with that in UK. It goes without detailed comment that no LOA is paid if the cost of living stands below that at home. On the face of it this might, conceivably, have been the case in Stanley, but there were other considerations in the equation. The Detachment spent over a year away from their families, the longest formal separation throughout the armed forces. There was no leave home other than compassionate, and little opportunity for local leave other than within the working environment. Our families even had the free railway concessions removed from them, which meant that wives left in service quarters far from 'mum' were not assisted throughout the year.

We had no concession postage rates and telephoning home was hugely expensive and not reliable. What made it worse was that HMS *Endurance's* ship's company, including the RM Detachment, were in permanent receipt of sea-going LOA even when ashore and living in Moody Brook, for periodic training exercises. By no stretch of the imagination could life at sea be judged more expensive than life in Stanley! Coupled to that, they had regular runs ashore in well known flesh-pots on the way to and from the Antarctic (and I do not include Stanley in that reckoning, despite valiant efforts by the Yellow Submarine). The ship was only away from the UK for six to eight months. We did not grudge them one penny but it was difficult to explain to NP 8901 why this anomaly existed. I gave up trying.

The issue had been confused by the answers given by an earlier Detachment Commander on a periodical LOA review form. He had been too honest! When asked, for instance, what the cost of a taxi was or how much did it cost to get a suit cleaned or to buy a banana or to eat out, he replied NIL, for these 'luxuries' were not available. Of course these answers helped to give the impression that life in Stanley was ridiculously cheap. What he should have said, with a clear conscience, was that you could hire a Land Rover at an exorbitant daily rate, suits could be dry-cleaned by arranging to send them to BA on the weekly flight at a vast price, and oranges cost over one pound each if you ordered them from the mainland. He argued that alcohol was duty free; it may have been, but FIC freight charges took care of that 'perk'. These are just a selection of small but significant examples to show how the earlier case had been denied and why we had to pursue a different form of allowance to make up for all the manifold little difficulties and expenses that face a marine living abroad. My (and the Chief of Staff's) arguments were to fall on the increasingly deaf ears of Admiral Baird as I was to discover much later via Tim Downs. "Baird has walked right back on his previous enthusiastic support and now says he is not convinced.... I don't know who has got at him (HE?)."

I became desperately sorry for my marines. How does one face the Detachment with the news that 'they' in London with their well-kept ivory towers and weighting allowance had refused to acknowledge the privations

3. "We were very happy at 26 Ross Road West." This picture was taken from the beach.

4. Hermione being hoisted on board the wreck of the *Lady Elizabeth* in a mail bag.

5. "Sunday afternoons were spent exploring the local wrecks and sand dunes". Waiting for the tide to recede before visiting the wreck of the *Lady Elizabeth* with Hamish, Hermione and Patricia.

6. "The redoubtable Jack Sollis" - Master of the MV *Forrest*.

under which we were forced to live? The answer is with shame and embarrassment.

One of the aims of the patrols was to visit the settlements in order to train the settlement volunteers. The local defence force was divided into two distinct parts. The uniformed 'reserve' was supplied by the Falkland Islands Defence Force (FIDF). Based in Stanley it was a properly constituted and organized military formation. The less formal Settlement Volunteers were, in effect, the eyes and ears of the Colony, on whom we relied heavily. These gentlemen were trained in the use of issued small arms and in observing. They were of course not required to sit all day long on the headlands watching the western ocean for invaders, but simply to give notice of any signs of landings. If a landing did take place they were trained to report its size and composition and the type and range of weapons and equipment (radios for instance) that were being used.

To my mind the most important use of *Forrest* was as a presence around the less inhabited corners of the archipelago. I wanted everyone to know, including the Argentinian Airforce Lieutenant-Colonel who ran the Stanley end of the LADE airline, that there would be no part of the Colony un-visited or un-watched for more than a few weeks at a time. I did not want some isolated group of 'enemy' to think that they could land unseen on a remote islet and then announce after some time that they claimed squatters' rights as they had not been discovered for eighteen months. That way lay embarrassment – and yet that is what, in effect, was happening in Southern Thule.

With a coastline of over 15,000 miles there is a vast length only occasionally watched and many more miles which are never watched.

I did not see the patrols as being a deterrent to a large-scale landing but as a passable deterrent to opportunists who might want to try and establish a foothold. The message I wanted relayed back to BA was, 'Wherever you might land you will be discovered very soon'. That alone would be an achievement.

In all this I needed Jack's full co-operation and understanding and it of course fitted in with the orders I had received in London of being seen to be a more aggressive form of deterrence than simply rushing into the hills.

As a start the first patrols were around East Falkland, dropping off small parties of marines at various settlements so they could get to know the inhabitants before making their way back overland. The aims were threefold: the settlements would get to meet the new Detachment, the marines would get to know areas over which, Heaven forbid, they might have to fight, and they would maintain a good standard of physical fitness relevant to the terrain.

We were required to keep 75% of the Detachment in the Stanley area 'just in case' but by the time Chris Horlick, who co-ordinated the sea and foot patrols, had subtracted the men required for vital maintenance, those involved in the daily round of buying and cooking food (six swedes here, half a pound of carrots there and all from retired kelpers who protected the individual seedlings from the wind by growing them inside open-ended beer tins — of which there was a huge supply), the drivers, the airport guards, the lonely lookout in his hut on Canopus Hill, it meant that the numbers available for patrolling were less then 25% of the Detachment. However, by some clever juggling (and probably a certain sleight of hand, for getting the marines away from Stanley was crucial to the maintenance of morale) he managed to establish a workable routine.

As the sea patrols were purely observation patrols, designed to send a message to any potential aggressor, these required the minimum of service personnel. Life on board *Forrest* was not to the liking of many and certainly not for the faint-hearted or weak-stomached, nor for those who found long hours sailing past uninhabited coastlines boring. I was often the only military passenger!

The first sea-patrol left Stanley on 19 April for a daytime round trip via Bluff Cove to drop off the first land patrol.

I wasn't yet sure how to set about my task of studying the coastline and on that first day took a simple blank-paged logbook, my forty-five-year-old Leica camera and a pair of binoculars. Rather self-consciously I reported to Jack on his bridge.

From this very first patrol onwards Jack Sollis and his long-suffering crew entered into the spirit of my study. Whatever reason they thought was the one for which the work was destined, they asked no questions. They were also glad of the seatime, for it was the only way to supplement with overtime a less than generous wage.

The journey to Bluff Cove was uneventful with "*a light wind from the south west, moderate swell and slight sea, cloudy with sunny intervals*". Throughout the subsequent months I spent at sea round the coastline this was probably the most frequent entry in my log. The Islands are certainly windy — four times as windy as, say, Plymouth, on the south coast of England — but they have been given a reputation they do not deserve, mostly by the more lurid journalists who do not know, do not understand or are not prepared to learn, the truth.

Billy Rock ("*dries 7 feet*") was left to port. Jack turned to me:

"The most dangerous rock in the Islands — probably over fifteen wrecks. Some say that if you dive you can see three on top of each other." I opened my virgin logbook and began the first of one hundred and twenty-six pages of sketches, charts and notes.

Cape Pembroke — "*overfalls, particularly with a southerly wind*" — and the only aid to navigation throughout the archipelago: at least that was so in 1978 when the lights marking the 'Narrows' at the entrance to Stanley Harbour were haphazard in reliability and the light on Mengeary Point was non-existent. There should have been a light above the beach at Blanco Bay as a leading mark down Port William, but even the charts described it as 'occasional'. It was considerably less frequent than that! The light on Porpoise Point had not been seen in living memory and was reported in the Admiralty Pilot as being 'unreliable'. Like Cape Pembroke, it too has had a chequered career, although unlike Pembroke it has not been continuous in operation.

We sailed past landmarks that were to become familiar but were then unknown to me. Our destination suddenly opened up as a slash in the strata-ed cliffs:

"Bluff Cove entrance very difficult to see...anchored off the entrance bearing 0100 true in four fathoms over mud. Ashore by Gemini through gorge...small boat landing at hut on west side − anchorage over mud opposite in one and a half fathoms. Suggest a moor if ship is longer than fifty feet. Difficulty could be experienced in turning."

This entry was to take on a greater significance a few years later, as was the next where I described the passage through the channel separating East Island from Islet, or Loafers, Cove on the mainland to the west, the Z bend.

We returned that evening with my enthusiasm for the Islands now total.

A number of Argentinian Airforce families lived in the Stanley community with whom they were on friendly if somewhat distant terms. They were employed by the Argentinians to run the Stanley offices of LADE which at that time ran a haphazard (usually once a fortnight) flight between the Islands and the rather seedy oil town of Comodoro Rivadavia. The 'commanding officer' was Vice Commodoro Eduardo Carnossa; tall, urbane, goodlooking (so I was told by the girls) and gentlemanly, he was accompanied by his wife, a stunningly attractive South American woman. I found that we had many interests in common, but was expressly forbidden to 'fraternize' with him, although he and his wife were to be found at many Government House parties. I wondered if, like me, he had been sent to the Islands as a 'punishment'!

On 26 June the Officers' Mess was to entertain the Governor and Mrs Parker (plus one or two others) to dinner at Moody Brook. I had decided that mussels steamed in white wine and oats would be the first course, so, in a wind chill well below zero centigrade, I had collected them before dawn from the shallow waters of the Canache to the east of the town. Arriving back with a full bucket at 0830 I was in time to watch the receipt of the first batch of signals kept overnight in the Whitehall Comcen for our daily re-contact with the outside world.

The first signal was personal for me and announced that 'Their Lordships had approved the promotion of Captain SES-T to Major on the 31st December 1978.' This came as a shock for there had been no doubt in my mind that it would be an impossibility. It also instantly, and erroneously, assured me that my handling of the NP 8901 situation was being met with approval.

I telephoned Patricia while Chris Horlick opened the champagne. In the middle of this celebration a knock on the door by the duty signaller (who doubled as the sentry) heralded the arrival of Vice Commodoro Carnossa. My instant reaction was that he had come to congratulate me, thereby confirming the private view that they knew more about NP 8901 than we did!

This visit was most irregular, for although I had no reason to refuse him permission to enter the camp — we had no secrets other than the appalling conditions under which the Falklands deterrent existed — he had been forbidden to visit by HEGFI. On this occasion there was clearly something amiss and he was invited in without hesitation. His view of our deterrent value was probably strengthened by the sight of me in mussel-collecting clothes and Chris Horlick in a uniform of sorts drinking champagne at 0845. I offered Eduardo a glass and after a tiny sip he suddenly walked to the window-sill to put his head in his hands while tears streamed down his cheeks and across his fingers. I was acutely embarrassed.

He turned: "Why does no one like us? Nobody here likes or trusts us. We've even won the World Cup and still nobody likes us!"

There really was nothing I could say and, anyway, he gave me no chance, for, as suddenly as he had arrived, he put down his drink and walked back to his vehicle.

I liked the civilized and aristocratic Vice Commodoro who had once been the military governor of a southern Argentine state. He was to be immensely helpful when the time came for my family to leave and I hope that some day our paths will cross again so that we can thank him.

At last the news I was really waiting for came in a hand-written letter from Tim Downs.

The inspection was to be brought forward and Tim would be part of it. It was now timed for the end of July, giving me nine months to get action taken after the problems had been witnessed at first hand. Before they left England it was vital that the first draft of the Concept of Operations be sent back so that questions could be prepared in advance of the on-the-spot-look.

There was some 'practical' good news. Spares would be sent for the non-serviceable four-tonner and, surprisingly, for the written-off one which had never been mentioned by me, although that did not alter the official view that we needed neither! When the spares did arrive they were all for left-hand drive vehicles: the stores system, using its initiative, assumed that as we were abroad we must be driving on the right!

Kelp Gull.
Larus dominicanus

IV

Backing and Filling

NOT ALL OF OUR THOUGHTS were directed towards the future.

Personal and domestic affairs kept me alert and the Detachment's welfare problems and solutions kept Patricia and the Sergeant-Major on their toes.

From the family's point of view we were lucky to have been offered 26 Ross Road West, a government-owned prefab-style bungalow separated from Stanley harbour by a narrow, rough road and the beach. It was the third most westerly house, towards the seaplane hangar and a mile and half east of Moody Brook itself. On taking possession I asked for the keys but there were none and, as there was no crime, we never missed them. The house was surrounded by a wooden paling fence enclosing small gardens at front and back and the ubiquitous peat-shed. The kitchen cooker had only recently been converted from peat to oil and we burnt peat in the drawing room fire. The roofs and walls creaked like an old sailing ship in the gales but unlike them the interior remained warm and dry even in the harshest of weather. We had brought out a very few of our own pictures and a tiny selection of silver bits and pieces for decoration and reminders of home but they were hardly needed. The views from all the windows were stunning and compensated for any lack of paintings or photographs. We were very happy at 26 Ross Road West!

I bought a light blue, 'series one' Land Rover, petrol-driven with a home-made, plywood, removable hard top. It cost £800 and in England would have long since been broken up for spares, but it never once stopped and we sold it on for what we had paid for it. For the first six months we were also lent the newest Land Rover in the Colony, taking delivery of it straight from the charter vessel. It had been bought by Alan and Carol Miller of Port San Carlos who, by coincidence, were off to England the week the vehicle arrived. This was a most generous gesture and allowed us to boast that we owned the oldest and the newest Land Rovers in the Colony.

The children were settled into the local schools — Hamish into the junior school and Hermione into the play school. Patricia joined neither the Spinning Guild nor the Women's Institute and did not gather scandal. I bought a make-it-yourself spinning wheel from New Zealand and she was taught to spin privately, and very well. The restriction on our social habits by the Governor we ignored. We had to ignore them or sit in total isolation in number 26, and that is not our style. However, as a result we were often 'off' the guest list at Government House, although on one memorable occasion when we were 'on' Patricia was treated so rudely that we felt it was not worth the hurt. It was all rather sad.

A number of expatriates were prepared to ignore the Governor's rather strange orders and we did enjoy many happy evenings around peat fires with copious quantities of Argentinian wine for which I quickly acquired a strong liking, making a change from the Chilean whisky Jack would serve on board *Forrest*.

Weekends and summer evenings were spent among the sand dunes of Yorke Bay, Pilot Bay and Gypsy Cove and to liven these regular and frequent excursions I built a number of sledges that we would tow behind the Land Rover along the water's edge. The children revelled in this mix of aquaplaning and tobogganing; so did Chris and I, although it was to become rather dangerous as our experience and boldness increased. The toboggans, and flat tin trays, were excellent fun down the fronts of the high and steep sand dunes.

All around was the wildlife — penguins, albatrosses, skuas, dolphins, petrels. We would sit on the headlands and watch the Puffing Pigs and Peals Dolphins surf in on the breakers to leap clear and backwards as they reached shallower water. They would swim out to sea to start all over again, obviously enjoying it for the sheer pleasure it gave. I studied and painted them for hours when at sea and wrote a detailed report for the Cambridge Dolphin Survey Project which they very kindly described as being "the most interesting and comprehensive notes that (we) have seen since the survey began".

In the winter the walks at the sea's edge took on a different meaning. There was also peat to be collected from friends who would allow us to buy from their own sheds. We would walk up the slopes of Tumbledown and Two Sisters, Goat Ridge and Mt Harriet; we visited Mounts Longdon and William, Sappers Hill and Wireless Ridge and the coast at Mullet Creek. The only missing ingredients in those halcyon days were the dogs and foresight!

The Bosun dinghies and Geminis were used for recreation although not without raised eyebrows in the winter months; fishing trips were made by Land Rover to the Murrel River and Chris and I would often tow a seine net on foot (but in immersion suits) through the shallows of Yorke Bay. Huge and delicious mullet were the quarry which the Detachment cook, Corporal Lamerton, would batter, deep fry and serve in newspaper. The Islanders are not generally fish eaters and so any frozen fish landed from the foreign trawlers or factory ships to thank the community for taking a sick seaman or for supplying fresh water were sent to Moody Brook galley. In the evenings we would occasionally set up a projector at home and watch some very out of date 16mm film after a gourmet meal of goose (those shot as part of the scare programme at the new airport), trout, mullet, mussels or lamb more tender than any in England. Fillet of beef was available at 11 pence a pound and all this allowed Patricia to put her more exotic *Cordon Bleu* course ideas into practice. Although hard work, for there were no butchers, bakers or fishmongers, we delighted in this way of life.

To an outsider all might have appeared serene, and in many respects it was, but there were, inevitably, strong undercurrents at every level of our military and private lives.

The Detachment experienced two attempted suicides. The first was a genuine attempt, the second less so and conducted during the annual inspection with an overdose of drugs by the Leading Medical Attendant — as good a time and as good a person as any to emphasize the despair that could be wrought by the place.

The first 'suicide' was altogether a more unpleasant affair involving a naked Senior NCO, a naked mistress, hot bath, sharpened knife and a darkened house during a Sunday evening thunderstorm. With 'I love you Heather' written in blood on the wall (the blood had dribbled down beneath each letter) I doubt that Hitchcock could have bettered the script. I had been 'forced' to find the victim lying bloodstained and naked in the bath as the Sergeant Major (whose job I felt it was!) pretended not to know where it was.

Other problems came and went. I resisted the call from Government House to have a marine sent home and was proved right when the Chief of Police eventually announced that the plaintiff, a publican, had been more drunk than anybody during the alleged incident.

One late morning on my way into Stanley I recognized a well-known Land Rover outside 26 Ross Road West and slammed to a halt. Inside was a familiar, and most personable kelper helping Patricia to relight the cooker. I took her through into the drawing room:

"Get rid of him!"

"Why?"

"I'll tell you later."

When he had finished his work I was taken to task before explaining that that particular man had (so we were told up at the Brook) been in prison for four major sexual crimes: buggery, incest, bestiality and rape, some more than once. He was, though, the only oil-fired cooker expert and a delightful Islander. Prison was not a serious punishment as the

40

inmates were often given the key to their cells so that they could let themselves out for meals. The harshest punishment was the 'Black List' whereby anybody could apply for anyone else, providing there was good reason, to be denied alcohol, not only in public places but also at home. The only serious anti-social crime that I was aware of during our year was a young man who was caught with three hundred pairs of knickers in his bedroom that he had 'nicked' off washing lines. It was a delightfully safe place to live.

When the infrequent cruise ship visited, the population of Stanley could be doubled by tourists. It was then that as many members of the Detachment as could be made available would play football on the pitch alongside Government House. Hidden in the Land Rovers would be all our weapons, radios and spare ammunition ready for instant action.

On aircraft days we would send a Land Rover with plain-clothed, apparently unarmed marines to the terminal where they would mingle with the alighting passengers (whose names would have been announced the night before over the evening broadcast) and keep an eye on the AAF crew. This was a covert operation, although well known by all, including the flight crews. If the aircraft was waiting any length of time the FIC would offer a vehicle and the uniformed Argentinians would be taken to the Company's West Store to stock up with duty-free drink and small consumer goods at a fraction of the mainland price. This facility was also available on Sundays when the store would open especially for the Argentinian Air Force — an opportunity denied kelpers in from Camp for, sometimes, their one day of the season or even year.

It almost always struck me that the aircrew were too many for such a small airplane and such a short flight from Comodoro Rivadavia, but I was usually warned, locally, not to 'rock the boat'. My reports to DI4 were not so easily suppressed.

To keep our friends in the United Kingdom in touch with our lives we would compile tape recordings usually full of nothing more complicated than the children reading personal messages and the sounds of the wildlife as heard from our front door. One tape, though, was rather more serious and with a deliberate attempt at foreseeing the future Chris and I sent a spoof and heavily clichéd report 'From Our War Correspondent' which began with the words: *A pall of smoke hangs over this beleaguered city as from my hotel bedroom I can see Argentinian tanks and soldiers taking up fire positions, while from the direction of the airport and beaches comes the unmistakable chatter of machine-gun fire....* It was not meant as a joke.

One piece of news was the award of the Wilkinson Sword of Peace to NP 8901 in general for their community work over the years, but to Nigel Willoughby's Detachment in particular. Nigel, a helicopter pilot, had flown the Beaver seaplane (after some intensive self-instruction) during a prolonged absence of civilian pilots, thus keeping the islands and settlements in touch. The news of the award was announced to the Colony through the *Falkland Islands Times*, a grand-sounding publication 'roneo'd' off fortnightly and, apparently, distributed worldwide.

The paper, not known for the class of its reporting nor its accuracy, described the military facts with unusual precision, but in the next edition the readers took over. To an outsider it was a disturbing episode in the light of so much good that had been achieved by NP 8901 over the years.

Anonymous letters had always been a feature of the *Falkland Islands Times* but this was one that I read with more interest than most, for it affected us directly:

"It was with profound shock and anger that I learned of the award to our local Royal Marine Detachment of the award of the Wilkinson Sword Peace Prize. It seems ironic that a band of men who have inflicted more damage on our community than any other should be honoured with this prestigious award.

"The utter stupidity and lack of thought behind the Wilkinson Sword award can only be equalled by the bestowal some time ago (21st July 1976) of the Freedom of Stanley on that same (sic) Royal Marine detachment. This gesture, was actually proposed by one of our own elected councillors.... However, this impressive and expensive 'gesture of gratitude' could have been justified had the Royal Marines actually done anything to deserve it...they have inflicted terrible and, I fear, irreparable damage to our community and they are still destroying our population.

"For too long now the exodus of women with marines has been treated as something of a joke.... There are some people who would defend the marines by quoting the small things they have done which may benefit the community in the short term. But these are, I repeat, small things that do not benefit us in the long term. No matter how much they contribute to charity, or how many of them entertain us on the radio or fly 'planes during pilot shortages, they will never be able to make up for the harm they have done and are continuing to do.

"As a military force also they are useless.... If our giant neighbour decided to invade these islands he would swamp our meagre defences. We should do away with this small but troublesome force.... If Britain will not give us a real defence then we would be better off without any."

The following issue of *The Times* contained three letters supporting the Royal Marines but the deed had been done and numbers of people were openly in support of a few of the remarks made in the first letter. The authorship remained in doubt and still is, although I had my very strong suspicions, and still do. The parents of a Falkland Island girl had presented themselves in my office one lunchtime and, after inviting them into the mess for a gin and tonic, they suddenly produced a collection of polaroid photographs taken of their daughter with one of my marines. They were, to say the very least, intimate, and, quite understandably, very upsetting to the parents who then demanded that the pervert (there was nothing perverted that I could actually deduce) be sent home immediately.

Much as I supported their distress I had to point out that the incident had been obviously carried out with the full participation (and as far as I could make out, the full enjoyment) of their daughter and that any marine to be dismissed from the Colony for such an 'offence' would become public knowledge within minutes, adding, certainly, public shame to their private embarrassment.

The matter was dropped, but I long harboured the view that the subsequent anonymous letter was the result.

Other letters appeared: "We are grateful for what the Marines have done for us.... Has this islander done anything to benefit the Islands large or small...would he/she waste his valuable time running to Port San Carlos and back for the sake of £110 which would be donated to the museum and not a penny to his own pocket?... Would he go to all the trouble of organizing sponsored walks, charity balls, etc for the benefit of the Senior Citizens of Stanley? ...No doubt the answer would be 'No, I couldn't be bothered .... No, I haven't got the time.'... A lot of other people are leaving the colony. Why? For the simple reason that the Falkland Islands have very little to offer them."

Another letter, written by a woman, contained the following: "They contribute a lot towards the Islanders who aren't more interested in sex and boozing − whether illegal or in married bliss − and Boy, if you opened your eyes a bit you'd see how corrupt the Islands are becoming − you should give them a Wilkinson Sword for simply coming here. As for the local dames flitting to the UK with the Royals − I DON'T BLAME THEM − look at the ill-mannered drunks a lot of women have to face when they decide to take the plunge and try their luck with a local. My God, at least the UK men treat their wives as something they love, not as a punchbag when he's had a few too many while he's been out to the pub and left his spouse to cook his supper and in some cases feed his kids."

In addition to some (but not all) staunch letters of support for the Royal Marines, Islander was now set against Islander, with us rather bemused, but not wholly surprised, in the middle. We had to remember that everyone knew everyone....

Despite partial agreement with the original sentiments, another anonymous author wrote: "Why not bring out married Marines with their families....Would it not be possible for our Government to offer incentives to marines married to local girls to remain and work in the Islands."

Perhaps it should be pointed out here that under two per cent of Royal Marine/Falkland Island girl marriages lasted beyond five years. The Detachment before us married eleven out of an estimated fifteen eligible girls, and my Detachment was to have four, of which to my present knowledge two have lasted, one in the Islands and one in the United Kingdom, fifty per cent being a remarkable achievement.

Other letters contained snippets of common sense aired for the first time by the Islanders and it was heartening to see that a number of our proposals (unpublished at that stage) were being put forward independently.

All this, and much more, in a paper described within its own pages by a senior member of Stanley society as "purveying infantile smut...more usually confined to lavatory walls". At Moody Brook we agreed with the author of these lines and if we read *The Times* at all it was often to marvel at the public bickering and invective contained within its few, badly typed pages.

Our perceived value to the Colony had earlier been put into the same perspective when, in 1972, Ian Strange managed to write a 328 page 'standard work' on the Islands (reprinted in '81, '83 and '85) without once mentioning NP 8901; and the Royal Marines only in the context of the 1982 conflict; but then he was not an Islander (by their definition) and had served in the Parachute Regiment! He was, though, a good friend whom I managed to help out on a number of occasions.

To an outsider it always seemed strange that projects − the new school hostel in Stanley and the Darwin Road were examples − were set in train without much thought of manpower. In Stanley itself there was chronic over-employment with many men and women undertaking two or three jobs, making the sacking of inefficient employees almost an impossibility for there was no one to replace them. A prime example was the only 'digger' driver whose alcohol intake (as admitted to me by the Director of the Public Works Department) was well in excess of fourteen pints of beer every day. The empty beer cans strewing the countryside wherever he was working became known as Bobby's eggs. For three particular days running he successfully cut the power line between Moody Brook and the town generator as he drove his machine to work to dig clay for the road, thus severing our vital link with Whitehall just as we were due to open up each morning.

It was little wonder that friends within the ODM and FCO would tell us in private that their patience was in short supply when dealing with the

Falklands and their internal problems, let alone their external ones. But the Islanders had strong arguments on their side, for they put into the British economy (private and public) considerably more than they received in return. It was also wrong for outsiders to criticize the way of life of the colony, especially as in such matters as honesty, diligence and hard work under difficult conditions they had much to teach us. They had been the staunch occupiers of a piece of British real estate for a very long time and had been the tangible proof to any would-be invader that they were a stable community to be taken over only against strong opposition. It was a pity that these attributes of steadfastness over their future were not matched by the FCO. The kelpers had 'kept them British' when others had wanted them to be otherwise and, in doing so, had staved off the aspirations of a number of potential occupiers, Russia included. Although it was easy to blame them for allowing the FCO to take such a loose attitude towards their own future they still deserved better and more positive treatment. The Islanders' greatest mistake was to accept a decline in self-respect, but this, in turn, was often based on the lack of investment due to a poor return on their GNP – and for that most blamed the FIC.

At last I had time (and, by then, a modicum of experience of the ground and military problems) to look in detail at the Concept of Operations. Firstly it was necessary to put myself into the Argentinian mind and decide what the aim would be and how they would set about achieving it. With the Governor, we came to the conclusion that the Argentinians would assume that the people were oppressed by the British Crown and would wish to be relieved of that first. Therefore they would aim at the seat of power with as little disruption as possible to the civilians, who, we assumed they would assume, would be waiting to break out their long-hidden blue and white Argentinian flags. Thus the defence of Government House had to take priority.

Allied to that would be delaying tactics. Depending on how much notice we would receive we could try and stop them at that most crucial (and most easily upset) phase of amphibious or airborne landings – the transition from air or sea to consolidation on land. Our first lines of defence were therefore the airport and the co-located beaches which, by natural coincidence, were also the most ideal for amphibious landings. My remit to buy three weeks bargaining time in the United Nations was one thing, but we reckoned that in the face of the expected onslaught even three minutes would be optimistic – but ours not to reason with the political decision, no matter how unrealistic. HE suggested that all we would achieve would be forty dead marines and in this and associated matters we were totally in accord.

I planned, therefore, to block the old and new airfields with any spare vehicles and these were earmarked, but the beaches were not so easy, for there were, in total, about two and a half miles of sand in Yorke Bay, Pilot Bay and (if they could find a way through the kelp) Surf Bay. We considered special forces landings in the dozens of small coves and bays surrounding the Stanley peninsula but as small groups of men could land anywhere, whether sandy, rocky or 'cliffy' we had to take steps against only those landing areas close to the objectives.

Ideally, and if the defence was to be taken seriously, we would need to mine the beaches, place barbed-wire entanglements, cover the exits with heavy mortars and machine guns and have permanent lookouts. I expected the initial thrust to be seaborne with the aim of moving the half a mile or so inland to capture the two airfields. Short of blowing craters in the new airport there was not much we could do, and, as that could happen during a false alarm it was not a move I considered further. We had no explosives anyway, apart from a limited amount of plastic.

Although I always hoped we would have some diplomatic warning of a day or so, it was clear that to defend the beaches and landing ground with rifles (and a handful of two-inch mortars − a favourite of mine as a personal weapon since the Dhofar War) was not really on, so we planned to block the runway and simply observe the sea approaches from well prepared and camouflaged OPs. I could only afford two four-man sections for these tasks anyway − hardly an opposed landing for the Argentinians by any standard. It was best that, having observed the landings (and delayed them long enough for the rest of the Detachment to reach their main defensive positions), these two small sections would then conduct a fighting retreat to their main defensive positions in the Stanley area bringing with them up-to-date intelligence.

This trip-wire philosophy might, just might if it took place actually among the houses of Stanley, make an aggressor who thought he had come to relieve an oppressed and Argentine-friendly society, stand off while negotiations took place. It was, let's face it, a forlorn hope, but was in line with my instructions. So I planned the first line of defence to run north-south along the eastern outskirts of the town, the second, to which we could deploy if given less notice was right through the town and the third and most likely was simply around Government House and the person of the Governor himself.

In addition to all this I had two other considerations. The most important was to get out of Moody Brook the instant there was any hint of an invasion. I believed that our base would be the target for the first pre-emptive strike and this would take place, with no warning whatsoever, from the air, naval gunfire or special forces. I gauged that we would have less than five minutes, if that. We therefore were to live for the remainder of the year at five minutes' notice to quit The Brook and head straight for GH, from where, if there was still time, we would deploy as far forward as luck and the enemy would permit.

The second consideration was intelligence for those back in England who would need to know what had happened, how, in what strength and, if possible, with what plans for the future. The civilian reaction in the face of such a *fait accompli* would also be useful to the FCO and MOD.

With two section commanders I sited the bunkers covering the beaches to which they would deploy on first call-out. Each was well dug in, strongly fortified and contained the rudiments for a lengthy stay, except for ammunition which would be carried in at the time. I did not expect them to fight 'to the death', rather to show that we meant business while, if necessary, falling back through the pre-planned 'trip-wire' positions. At each position the enemy would have another opportunity to gauge his position vis-a-via civilian casualties and political opprobrium. At the end − and assuming that the enemy showed no signs of hesitating − I wanted live Royal Marines close to Government House. One position was placed in the rocks of Yorke Point and overlooked Gypsy Cove, Yorke Bay and Pilot Bay and the coastline out to Cape Pembroke lighthouse: the second in the rocks at the peak of Hookers Point faced northwards across Surf Bay and westwards down the road to Stanley. Both these positions also covered the airport. The Yorke Point position was exposed and easily cut off, so, as an alternative, depending on the exact nature of the landings, we also prepared a position on Ordnance Point with a Gemini assault boat hidden in the kelp of Hadassa Bay for escape to Government House.

We prepared a line of defence, but without the civilians knowing of it, north-south outside Stanley and another cutting Stanley in two. These were not mini-Maginot Lines but simple, recce'd areas with the Marines becoming familiar with each possible site for personal protection. Through a certain amount of social subterfuge every peat shed, hedge, garden wall and outhouse became a well-known defensive position.

Sites for slit trenches around Government House were recce'd and we moved a chacon into the grounds as a ready-use ammunition store. Detachment Headquarters and the third section would move to GH, regardless of how much warning we had, from where they would monitor and control the battle.

One problem never solved was the location of the huge ammunition store in two concrete, water-logged magazines two and a half miles east of Government House and close to the entrance to the Canache; an undefendable area almost certain to be taken by the enemy within minutes of his landing by air or sea. By any standard an extraordinary place to keep our bullets and bombs.

As the communications (or lack of them for half the day) had been a serious worry not only to us but to the FCO, early in our year we set up a covert radio station under the tin roof of Government House. In the attic and close to the billiards room was a disused compartment. In this space Fred Cook placed a radio set with the aerials stretched between the chimneys. This last manoeuvre was conducted at night as it was important that nobody knew of our covert link with the outside world. The 'cover' was nearly blown when Fred managed to drop a reel of aerial wire down a chimney, but happily it was retrieved from a ground floor fireplace without being compromised! Over the weeks we practised communicating with Diplomatic Wireless Stations in Kinshasha and Walrus Bay, for which I had supplied the initial great-circle bearings. This space and the arrangements were unknown to the inhabitants of Government House who would allow my senior NCOs to play billiards in the upstairs billiards room, during which time Fred spoke to the FCO via Africa. They played a great deal.

To solve the intelligence-gathering problem I chose the fourth Corporal and his section of four Royal Marines to be the 'covert' team. Whilst the others would change positions during and between exercises so that they became familiar with all the land likely to be fought over, the covert OP team remained the same. It was vital that nobody knew of their existence nor their operational duties and certainly nobody (including the Governor and the remainder of the Detachment) was to know of the position from where they would observe, unseen by enemy and civilians alike. Everyone thought they were 'the reserve' (for which they practised occasionally to keep up appearances) and no questions were ever asked.

Beneath the rocks that run along the south-facing summit of Cortely Hill (and immediately opposite Government House) we built a heavily defended sanger. Much of the structure was natural, and the stronger and more camouflaged for that; with a few man-made refinements it was almost impregnable. The idea was not to fight from it, but to remain hidden. On leaving Moody Brook when the alarm was sounded this team would make its way along the back of Wireless Ridge and, via a well-rehearsed but concealed route, into this OP. Their duty was to observe everything that took place in the town opposite, judge the strength and determination of the enemy, his weapons, his command post positions and gain as much military information as they could before deciding on a suitable time to make their escape. On occasional Sundays I would walk Patricia and the children over and around the OP (without them knowing it was there) just to see if they could discover it. They never did.

The escape route was also well-recce'd and practised. From Cortely Hill they would make their way, with as much or as little haste as was compatible with remaining undetected, to a similar hide dug into the shallow cliffs overlooking Campa Menta Bay on the north coast six miles to the east of the entrance to Port Salvador. It was an overland journey of about thirty-two miles. Travelling only at night it would take them roughly four days, although this would depend on the time of year (length of the nights), enemy activity and weather. At Campa Menta Bay, and from their secure hide, this small team would contact the outside world using pre-dumped equipment, food and clothing. They would, if required, lead in the first wave of any re-invasion across the beach which could, then, accept two LCUs. A more likely task was to meet and brief any initial special forces or 'advance force operations' team. I chose the men for this task very carefully indeed.

Initially, I wanted to discuss my views with someone away from the Islands to see if I was on the right track and so on 29 June I wrote another lengthy letter to Tim Downs clearing my mind and the way ahead as I saw it:

"Our main aim must be to defend HE and Government House.... and our (present) SOPs cover that adequately....From there the Concept becomes more difficult to define...the range and type of enemy and options open to him....The threat here is not so easy as, say, in the Radfan, Borneo or Dhofar mountains. Originally it was agreed that the Concept of Operations should be no more than a statement to the effect that we should be prepared to react flexibly to any emergency that might occur!

"It must be assumed that the Argentinians would not want the Islands without the co-operation of the Islanders. Without the Islanders the Islands would be of little value as no Argentinian is likely to live here...and yet, uninhabited, they would be easy prey for a third interested party — Russians? Thus the invading force would see itself as a liberating army and would do all in its power not to alienate the locals. But as a show of force it would be much to their initial advantage to take out Moody Brook with a pre-emptive air strike or naval bombardment. Likewise we do not see ourselves 'fighting on the beaches nor on the landing grounds' for, although we might hold up their advance, it would not take them long to destroy us, leaving the way open to march on Stanley and the seat of Government. But if we were to force them into a position of having to fight us around GH they would probably back off to a bargaining position. To attack us under those circumstances would almost certainly mean forcing them to inflict civilian casualties and this they could not risk doing.

"I accept that given enough warning that an invasion was likely to occur we would seriously hamper their efforts but forty dead heroes for the sake of a delay of a day or two is not good military practice. (HE's words which I thoroughly endorse!)"

In the same letter I continued my moaning about the accommodation for the Marines and again argued with the DOE inspection report that had stated that the "Marines are happy with their conditions"! I was even quite conciliatory towards the Falkland Island Company for once, but the reason for this unusual attitude has long been forgotten!

I ended with a plea: "Please, if you have space, can you bring 1 lb of Twinings Earl Grey tea (preferably in quarter pound packets)."

My worries over the amount of warning we could expect (or not expect, as seemed the more likely case due to our cut-off position) were exercised in one of my periodical ramblings to DI4. An underlying concern that never seemed to be appreciated was the amount of practice that the Argentinian Airforce was getting and in this lay the seeds of many suppositions for my fertile imagination.

I asked to be on the distribution list of the Defence Weekly Intelligence Summaries and I asked for support from the Defence Intelligence team in the MOD to overturn the Governor's decision not to allow me to Buenos Aires:

"The feeling in GH is that for us to be seen to be doing anything military is to arouse suspicion among the islanders (and the Argentinians!) so we are very drastically curtailed, although the locals do expect us to be ready to meet any contingency....They are always asking what we can do in an emergency and state that we would be useless because of our numbers, but when I ask HE to allow me to practise I am told 'No' for fear of giving rise to speculation.

"The overt Argentinian presence has begun to give me cause for worry. In addition to the weekly Saturday flight of a piston-engined Fokker F27 from Comodoro Rivadavia the AAF began an additional jet F28 service direct from Buenos Aires on Wednesday 17th May. It is difficult to see the commercial reason or viability for this; in addition it means extra expense to the Colony's coffers and manpower.

"There were hardly enough passengers to warrant one aircraft and certainly not two. As it is the F28 often arrives with one or two people and occasionally none. The thing I do not like is the number of pilots getting practice at landing at the airport. On the second proving flight they flew down with about twenty pilots for fifteen circuits. This was the same day as an Argentinian naval aircraft overflew some Polish fishing vessels at anchor in Berkeley Sound. The AAF pilots of the F28, when asked by me about the second aircraft, which was plain to see, denied all knowledge.

"The Argentinian Airforce has asked for permission to build an underground fuel installation at the new airport but, up to now, the FIG has not agreed. It is difficult to know why they need this facility as the aircraft flies in with so few passengers and from only three hundred miles away that it can hardly need refuelling. Forty Argentinian labourers are planned to come down in the austral spring (September) to build a jetty at the Argentinian YPF oil terminal just to the east of the town."

Still on the subject of military manoeuvres and intelligence I ended this letter with an arrogant but necessary statement:

"I tried to sail MV *Forrest* around the Jason and Beauchene Islands the other day but was firmly put off by HE as it was felt that this might give cause for speculation again. This followed much comment (the Islanders remember the Southern Thule cover up) about how did we know that they were not sitting on those islands already. My point is (and has always been) that we should be seen to be patrolling at regular intervals so that they would know that no unauthorized landing will go unnoticed for any time....in fact I shall sail around the Jason Islands at the end of August or beginning of September without telling anyone until it is over and think of some lame excuse for having done so!"

A letter was also received from the Naval Attaché on the matter of my intelligence briefings in which he said he could not brief me unofficially and suggested I keep pestering the Governor. He also told me that he had sent the head of the Argentinian Marines to the British Army exhibition in England and then on to "spend a few days with the Royal Marines...it all helps cement friendships and will undoubtedly strengthen the Argentinian Marines' healthy respect for our Corps. No bad thing". Certainly no bad thing!

DI4's beach intelligence officer was his usual supportive self:

"I really can not throw any light on the problem HEGFI has with the Naval Attaché in Buenos Aires and why he will not let you receive any intelligence − most odd," and went on to explain that he did not believe that the British Government had the slightest intention of "grasping such a prickly nettle so near to a possible election and, although the 'Argies' are pressing for more talks, they probably see it that way as well".

He was interesting in his assessment of the wider picture vis-a-vis Argentina and the Chileans and suggested that while they were at each other's throats the last thing they wanted to do was "to involve themselves in warlike activity against you. This will not necessarily stop them encroaching further into the unoccupied FI Dependencies next season."

A little later I was to write to the Assistant Fleet Royal Marines Officer that "We are waiting to see if Argentina and Chile go to war on Thursday. It might affect us quite considerably". An aspect of this possible war, unappreciated outside the Islands but assessed in the South Atlantic by those who knew the area and mentalities well, was that Argentina might seize the Falklands as an airbase from which to attack Chile, an added dimension to our concerns. However, in the meantime DI4 continued:

"I appreciate your frustration with the difficulty of doing any realistic exercises. We are putting our devious minds together on this problem. We might hatch something out of the egg."

I was glad to have established this steady flow of two-way information and found that it made working for two masters with differing views on how the defence of Stanley should be conducted rather easier than it might have been.

One 'battle' I lost concerned the security procedures at the airport. HEGFI ordered that we should strengthen our presence on 'plane days' and, whilst I was keen, it was on the condition that the arrangements remained covert in dress and arms. Indeed he asked for little more than was actually happening, although neither he nor the airport manager knew that. In addition to the 'normal' team, I had long established a second and even more covert Land Rover with a fully armed section to be nearby. Now, even the normal team had to be openly armed and in uniform. Somehow this did not accord with the other order about us not carrying out military drills for fear of speculation. I did not understand this double-dealing. Without wishing to divulge that we already had more armed people on the spot than he realized I explained that this openly armed presence was against my advice. I was told to do as ordered and have two uniformed men with loaded weapons in the passenger reception area and one in the control tower. I had already arranged that the first man on to any aircraft was Les Halliday, the Harbourmaster and Chief Customs Officer. Having checked the passenger and cargo manifests before anyone disembarked, he would give me (or the duty SNCO or Corporal present) some innocent sign that all was well and that he was not a hostage as he stepped first off the aircraft in advance of any aircrew or passenger.

These new airport security arrangements were put into practice immediately with no complaints from the locals, the airport staff (including the Argentinian air traffic controller) or the AAF pilots. It was only I who then viewed them with some misgivings.

At last the visit for which I had fought so strongly was upon us. I had waited with some trepidation, for although I knew I was not popular with the Governor nor with certain sections of the MOD at home, I had been trying, against some surprising opposition, to carry out the instructions so clearly given in the FCO and MOD. I remained puzzled by apparent intransigence but often put it down to the lack of understanding by those in England of the practicalities of life on the spot and the nervousness of those on the spot to do anything that would either make the locals suspicious or the Argentinians angry!

The flight containing Colonel Dick Sidwell and Major Tim Downs arrived on time on 26 July. I (and an armed Royal Marine) had joined the air traffic controller and airport manager (Gerald Cheek, then a Corporal in the FIDF) in the control tower. The other person present, as always, was an Argentinian, for although English is the international language of air traffic control, the LADE pilots refused to speak anything but Spanish when 'on finals'. It was pure cussedness on their part and nothing else. Once the plane had taxied below us I walked across the tarmac and followed Les Halliday on board. He turned left for the cockpit while I met Dick and Tim in the cabin.

It was the greatest pleasure to meet old friends and allies and to know that they would now be able to help process all that needed to be done, using first hand knowledge of the problems. However, as Dick Sidwell left the aircraft with Les, Tim took me aside for a few seconds.

"Ewen," he whispered loudly in my ear, "you're in the pooh. Just let everything ride for the first day while the Colonel gets the feel for the place. People are not happy with you back in UK and the chances are that you may be the first officer in recent years who will not have his promotion confirmed after the statutory six months."

I tried to ask a quick question but Tim pushed me through the aircraft door. My elation at their arrival had been dashed. However, a saving grace was that the numerous responses from Tim and DI4 had always been positive. I was pretty confident that once the Colonel had seen the problem he might be a little more convinced of my arguments, if not wholly converted.

That day was spent in settling the two visitors into Government House, briefing them at 26 Ross Road West and introducing them to the sights and sounds of the Falkland Islands. I purposely did not want them to arrive at Moody Brook 'naked' as it were of the atmosphere of the Colony — and I wanted them fresh after a good night's rest. The general mood of the Colonel seemed to indicate that he had come down to tell me to shut up and put up with the embuggerances of the job and get on with carrying out my instructions with as little fuss as possible. I did not argue that that was precisely what I was trying to do whilst meeting resistance from all sides.

The following morning, after a quiet family supper at home followed by a whisky or two around the peat fire, Colonel Sidwell inspected a Quarter Guard in the mud and frozen slime outside the entrance to the Galley, the only space suitable. The wind was strong from the west and it was midwinter.

After the formal start to the day we began a tour of inspection of the camp which should have been conducted in the manner of a captain's Sunday rounds at sea — almost to the point of issuing the inspecting officers with white gloves! The Marines had done their best and, where they could make it so, everything was immaculate, but the rotting food stores, the noisome and open drains through the back of the galley, the wet and dry rot in all the walls of the men's accommodation, the bizarre magazine arrangements, the extraordinary accounting system whereby the Quartermaster every day bought an egg here, a cabbage there, and somewhere else a handful of leeks from local families to feed his 42 mouths, did nothing to impress in the way that an inspection of Bickleigh Barracks would have done. Equally unimpressive were the stripped down four-tonners without spares, the appalling condition of all three Land Rovers, the piles of rusting junk dating back to 1914, the Belsen Block's crumbling cement walls, the ambiguity of our defence instructions, the isolation from Whitehall Comcen for twelve hours in every twenty-four, the lack of any form of allowance, and the absence of any form of relaxation facilities except an overcrowded and expensive bar selling warm tinned beer.

It sounded like a long list of complaints and perhaps it was, but it was the first time that any visiting officer had seen the problem at first hand and not have it tucked away for the sake of getting a good report. I had campaigned for this visit for the benefit of my Marines and (if it does not sound too grandiose) for the benefit of the Colony. I was not going to miss a trick now that I had achieved the first of my aims.

Two-thirds of the way through the morning, during which time I had hardly opened my mouth, Colonel Dick suddenly announced that he had seen enough for the moment and ordered me to meet him alone in my office. I put the remainder of the inspection on stand-by and led him past the one partially-serviceable typewriter with struggling clerk, and into the inner office.

He sat in my chair and called for a signal pad before looking up at me as I stood in front of him. I suddenly thought that what he had seen had convinced him that here was an OC unable to put up with a few privations and unable to look beyond the minor irritations of his position, and, of almost more importance, incompetent to assess the military situation and decide the future requirements. I had blown it. I was instantly confirmed in this view as he looked closely at me without a hint of a smile and said:

"Ewen, you've been a bloody fool." He stopped and let that bald and true statement sink in. A fool I probably had been, but it had been with the best and most worthy of intentions. I wasn't quite sure how to react. I wanted to defend myself, my actions and behaviour, but I did not want to exacerbate the situation.

Then, quite suddenly, came the turning-point of my pre-war involvement with the Falkland Islands and its defence.

Colonel Dick smiled and spoke clearly and plainly: "It is far worse than you have explained in all your signals. I am absolutely astonished that things have been allowed to go this far — not only in material and social degradation but as far as your duties are concerned. Please leave me for half an hour or so and I shall meet you for a drink in the mess. We shall carry on with the inspection after lunch. Your real mistake is that you have not argued the case properly."

I saluted and left my office leaving the Colonel writing beneath the bullet hole. Tim was warming himself by the peat fire, a gin in his hand. He smiled at me and told me of Colonel Dick's first reactions. I breathed one of the deeper sighs of relief.

Dick Sidwell's signal was a masterpiece and, although lengthy, it was not a word too long or unnecessary. It addressed everything — pay and allowances, new barracks, Concept of Operations (he agreed my assessments and suggestions), transport scales, complement, communications — every single aspect that had been my concern. It went further and deeper than I would have dared and was directed at exactly the correct level. It took the form of an intravenous injection right into the heart of the Commander-in-Chief's and Commandant General's organizations.

The visitors stayed a week — they could not have stayed less — and left on the Wednesday F27 flight for Comodoro Rivadavia. In the meantime we walked the likely sites for a new barracks if permission was to be given for one; we cajoled and encouraged the Falkland Island Company and the local DOE to take a more positive interest in maintaining The Brook; we sited the defensive positions and, although told of its position, we did not, for security reasons, visit the covert OP; we assessed the sense of married-accompanied appointments and trickle drafting; we discussed communications and equipment, defence stores and weapons; we gave a cocktail party for all the Stanley establishment, including members of the society with whom I had been forbidden to mix. We went for long walks across the beaches that, we believed, would see the initial stages of any invasion.

For the first time I felt not only that I was on the right track but that all that I had been charged to achieve was now well under way and, although local difficulties would continue to exist, I would receive the backing necessary from the FCO and MOD in England. I was warned, though, that this backing would not always be obvious, for there were fears, expressed in later letters, that to upset the Governor in public by apparently disagreeing with his dicta might not be the best way forward; but forward we would go nevertheless.

That, then, was the mood with which I was left as the F27 took off into a westerly gale for Argentina on 2 August, 1978. As it happened things did not get better in the Islands. Indeed they noticeably deteriorated in most respects, as we shall see.

Wandering Albatross

V

The Whale's Way

HIS EXCELLENCY LEFT FOR ENGLAND and 'consultations' a fortnight after my visitors and, although it should not have been the case, a certain relief was felt in a number of quarters, not least by Mr John Massingham, the Colonial Secretary, who then became Acting Governor. He had never hidden his dislike of Mr Parker from me (which I thought was odd), and nor had the Governor hidden his dislike of John Massingham (which I thought was even odder).

HE's departure heralded a number of events. The chief of FIGAS, an elderly, prickly gentleman, but an outstanding Beaver pilot, called to demand that the security at the airport, so sternly required by HE, be removed immediately. While I agreed that a less overt presence (as had been the case) was better all round, the new system had been at HE's insistence. I stood my ground in support of the executive decision.

John Massingham agreed to my visiting Buenos Aires to receive a full military intelligence brief (the first I would have received during our stay) and a blind eye would be turned towards any proposed patrol around the outer islands and in particular the Jasons. I was also due to address the highly influential Sheep Owners Association (SOA), to be followed by a less formal question and answer period. This talk and discussion had been given the blessing of the Governor before he left.

The Falkland Island Company accepted the need for a formal 'work book' of outstanding tasks to be completed at Moody Brook, while I continued to assess the best place for a new barracks. In addition, I was to put the final touches to my Concept of Operations and continue to press the case for a different method of manning the Detachment allied with the appropriate pay and allowances reflecting our quite unique position within the British armed forces.

I looked forward to the following months with renewed excitement and, although socially we were still not totally welcome in many houses, because I had segregated the Officers' and Sergeants' messes at Moody Brook, the visiting officers had managed to impress upon many expatriates and kelpers that this was not some form of stand-offishness on my part but a vital aspect of good military discipline and command.

I reported back to DI4:

"I am addressing the SOA this Thursday and will explain very carefully the situation as I see it regarding the practising of military drills in the Stanley area as I believe that it is HE and not the locals who are preventing this. The SOA have in the past been our most ardent critics, but in fact are only so as they have never had the reasons for our presence properly explained. There is no mystique.... Of course I will not divulge the detail of our new Concept but simply impress that there is positive action being taken and that full co-operation would be much to our collective advantage.

"This also includes the patrolling of the *Forrest* around the outlying islands at regular intervals, say every two months. I now have reason to believe that since my last letter the feeling is that it was not the wish of the islanders to stop me patrolling...but HE putting a fictitious point of view which they do not hold. He is embarrassed about the Southern Thule affair and thinks that even if we said there was nothing on Beauchêne or the Jasons nobody would believe him as (the government) has lost credibility. Therefore the feeling is that it is better not to put us into the position of having to answer the question in the first place. *Forrest* is probably the most important deterrent we have...as she can monitor the waters and islands regularly ensuring that the presence of anyone would not go unnoticed long enough for them to claim squatters' rights as seems to have happened elsewhere.

"On the same subject it has been reported to me by the manager of Sedge Island that many thousands of Fur Seals have been disturbed off the Jasons and have come ashore on his island. The feeling is quite clear that something has forced them off the Jasons at an unusual time of the year. Although this information has gone no further than me as people are always edgy here, there has to be a cause.... I will be looking in the third week of September."

One of the first positive actions to take was to block off the 'old' Hookers Point airstrip that had been laid by the Argentinians some years earlier. The Acting Governor sent me a formal request to 'make this so'. The runway consisted of aluminium planks and was designed by the USA for use in the Antarctic. Before the new Airport became operational Hookers Point had been in regular use by the F27, but was now only used by Rob Pitaluga of Gibraltar Station and Bill Luxton of Chartres who both flew private Cessnas. With their concurrence we could block half the airstrip and still leave them plenty of room to land and take off.

The last thing we wanted to do was to turn the Falklands into a fortress. We were not at war with anyone and the Islands were too peaceful to bring the many military aspects into prominence, but we did need to know that with the minimum of notice we could activate all kinds of measures which, until needed, would remain out of sight but not out of mind. Invasion may have seemed a far-off possibility to Whitehall, but, as I have explained earlier, it was a daily and continuous concern to those on the spot.

Pretty quickly I received a reply from DI4. Whilst being positive, it did not help me in my balancing act between public loyalty to my Commander-in-Chief on the spot and the duties I was required to undertake. In the end, while trying to placate the Governor and meet his wishes, I was often forced into subterfuge.

"I wonder what caused the seals to leave the Jasons? No doubt you will find out next month when you have a look. Certainly there is a need for you to be able to survey your parish. I find the Governor's attitude a bit odd.

"You will be aware that the Argentinians are much concerned with their dispute with the Chileans over the Beagle Channel award and its implications. On the internal front you will know that Videla is now President, having retired as Army CINC, and General Viola has taken his seat in the Junta. The old war horse Admiral Massera [whom I always assumed would be the spearhead of any decision to invade the Falklands] is due to retire on the 15th September and hand over to Admiral Lambrushini. We might see Massera trying to enter politics through his contacts in the Peronist camp, but he may well find that when he has lost his position as CINC Navy and Junta member he has no effective power base left.

"The Argentinian military are finding increasing problems arising from their break with the US. I would expect Videla to try to improve his image if he can, but the Human Rights mud has splashed a lot of people and whitewashing the present regime will be a difficult task − and the odd person still gets 'disappeared'.

"PS. I personally believe that while the Chileans and the Argies remain eyeball to eyeball in Patagonia you are far less threatened. However, if the quarrel is settled your problems will re-assert themselves rapidly."

If unofficial, I was beginning to receive sensible and clear background intelligence. Certainly without this regular link I would have been unaware of the Junta's changes and those within the senior ranks of the armed forces. It was an odd position for the garrison commander to be in when the only news of his possible adversaries came in informal correspondence.

In the midst of all this life did continue, and in time for HMS *Endurance's* departure from England I was able to write to Fortnum and Mason to order a personally made-up hamper. I wrote to the ship's First Lieutenant, Lt-Cdr Tom Allen, with whom I had spent long evenings in lighthearted banter on the way south, enclosing a number of requests. Most were concerned with staff inspections and audits, but I ended up:

"Is there any chance that you can bring a pig (dead) for which I will pay and a Stilton or two and a brace of pheasants (also dead — for which I will also pay) in your deep freeze for the New Year. I will have plenty of draught beer waiting by then."

I had taken to the Islands in *Endurance's* wardroom 'fridge' a small bottle of our own well-established yeast culture plus a year's supply of hops and malt; mixed with the Falkland Islands water it was producing quite excellent beer and probably the only draught beer in Stanley made from the real ingredients.

But by October things had begun to get out of hand to a worse extent than had existed before 'the visit'. I had heard nothing from 'home' except the odd rumour from the officer earmarked to relieve me. In a fit of exasperation I poured out a new sob story to the patient Tim Downs back in Northwood.

"I thought it was time I let you know how things have been going since your visit as I am worried that we could be losing the momentum as far as the marines are concerned.... The problem is, in part, worsened by the fact that the Falkland Island Company have not lived up to their promises. I have chased and chased but with little effect. I had hoped that your visit might have put a bomb under Harry Milne [the corpulent Stanley Manager of the FIC] but sadly this was not the case. He is simply not interested in our problems other than as a money-making concern. I became rather rude to him the other day and ruffled his feathers — something I suspect nobody has done before as he is regarded as the benevolent uncle.

"We have trouble with John Massingham over the airport security. The head of civil aviation — a known opponent of the Royal Marines — [which was always odd since Nigel Willoughby had pulled his Air Service out of a hole when the pilots were unfit to fly for much of the time due, allegedly, to drink] said that the only people responsible for security at the airport were the airport authorities and that the Marines were an embarrassment to him. I requested a meeting of all interested parties to thrash out this problem — to which I was becoming an innocent pig in the middle between HE — absent in the UK — and the Head of Aviation. Not one statement of mine was accepted and I was even told by the Acting Governor that I was inexperienced in military matters compared with his years in Africa. He ordered me to withdraw from the airfield....My loyalty to HE remained intact, despite his orders being against my advice in the first place.

"This feeling of not being appreciated is felt over a number of the good works we are carrying out for the locals....The number of requests we receive is incredible....We took the whole of the West Falkland sea mail around the settlements (due to *Monsunen's* sudden unserviceability) having to alter considerably long-standing patrol arrangements. Not one word of thanks but two formal complaints that we were late....On the previous trip one settlement refused to ask any of the Detachment ashore for a cup of coffee after they had worked some hours offloading cargo thereby saving the settlement much time and money. Jack Sollis even asked if they could come ashore for a walk but he was told by the manager that Royal Marines were not welcome at San Carlos. [With a new manager, and very different circumstances, attitudes were to change! ...and it has to be said that this last incident was an isolated case.]

"On a different subject you will be interested to know that, to my face anyway, HE considered your visit to be a waste of time. He pays only lip service to our presence and continues to demand that we keep a very low profile for fear that any move we make will panic the public — hence talk of a new barracks or a major rebuild at the Brook would appear, to his eyes, to indicate an escalation of the threat. Before he left, HE ordered me to stop the planning for a new barracks saying that he will take it on. There is no doubt that he did this to stop any more talk or work on the subject.

"I have fought and fought to be given regular briefings but am simply told that it is his job to decide when I should receive information. What a way to run a deterrent. The politicians and FCO are the biggest threats to the defence of these Islands — but On! On! I suppose."

Some of this (and very much more) was pretty small, pretty petty stuff but (and it was an important but) the community treated the MOD/HMG with contempt on one hand for being unable to prevent an invasion (I agreed with them on this point but the criticism rubbed off on us) and yet looked to us for that very deterrence. Under those circumstances the most petty example took on huge proportions and is why I mention them now. The significant aspect of the criticism that we received was that it was continuous and not just the occasional isolated barb; and for that I felt sorry for the Marines whose efforts were treated so contemptuously. They were far away from family and friends, trying their best to help a society they had not volunteered to live among. There were, as always, more wonderful cases of understanding, consideration and help than otherwise, but these, as with many cases of quiet support and approval, were not made in public.

But there was progress, if only marginal and patchy. The news, good and bad, came as always in letters from Tim Downs. New communications equipment would be sent as soon as possible so that we could continue the long-distance 'panic' circuits with which we had been experimenting from the roof of GH.

(The communications equipment did arrive but it was badly damaged in transit.)

The trickle drafting of the Detachment was turned down, which was hardly surprising, but the sadness was that the key players would not be appointed for any more than a year and so there was no question of married-accompanied tours. I always believed that to have the main pillars of the Detachment on longer married tours would have helped as a buffer between the Marines and the Stanley society.

Although I had nearly been prevented from bringing Patricia with me, her presence was of inestimable value to the Detachment — a point that was not lost on the new, and much enlightened, Chief of Staff in Northwood, as I explain later. Hers was the only shoulder for the younger Marines to cry on when they had problems at home. A typical example was when two of the detachment wives had miscarriages followed by a flat 'no' from London to my request for compassionate leave. This, and other such domestic crises, needed a woman's touch at our end and from a woman who was part of 'the team' for it was essential that the Islanders did not know of such personal dramas and tragedies. It was quite within our experience that the less pleasant of the Stanley female and male population would single out men with problems and work on them in the bars and pubs to try and divide the Detachment.

Tim Downs wrote: "The new build project is looking quite good; a rebuild on the present site is likely to be as expensive as a new build on a new site. Fleet are just getting up steam and have got the Quartering people and PSA on the move.

"'G' Branch seem quite happy with the revised Concept of Operations and even accept (your) SD!!" This was a quite valid comment on my lack of staff training, spelling, grammar and punctuation as well as my adherence — or lack of it — to the accepted method of writing staff papers.

The 'terms of service' were still in the hands of the Royal Marines' Chief of Staff, the officer that had accosted Patricia and me at the Buckingham Palace garden party, and who was, clearly, continuing to exercise his lack of understanding of the men and their problems. I knew we would get no help as long as he had any influence. Tim Downs again: "I have failed to get any financial help and COS to CGRM is adamant that your post (and any others) should remain unaccompanied even if it was extended to eighteen months. However, it has been agreed, in order to give you better continuity, that the Second in Command will change three months before the rest of NP 8901 and the Sigs SNCO, one general duties corporal and the Quartermaster will change at least one month early. This will not happen until the next detachment hands over in 1980."

Life became dispiriting enough for me to express it home:

"Patricia finds the life depressing (although like me she has immersed herself in numerous hobbies and interests) as it is unpleasant to be in a society where one is automatically disliked for being what one is rather than for oneself. The Marines find this attitude particularly wearing. We continue to do good works but more often than not at the expense of our morale as we are regarded as a useful source of ready labour for all the projects that the Government and PWD are unable to tackle: particularly now the Darwin Road project is under way. This has removed all the labour force in the Colony as FIG are now paying excellent wages and overtime. We have no crew for *Forrest* and a number of settlements have been denuded of hands."

Not long afterwards, the FIG persuaded the Overseas Development Ministry to supply an Islander 'land' 'plane but only after the FIG agreed to build, at their own expense, a hangar. Consequently the Darwin Road was to be halted after one year and a mile of progress so that this new project could be completed. The Colony was going round in little circles and, as so often, with us in the middle.

A particular case in point was raised when, out of the blue, I received a copy of a letter written by a senior officer on CINC Fleet's staff to the MOD department responsible for the procuring of equipment asking what possible reason could I have for needing my own 'naval' aircraft. It was stated that during a recent visit to Northwood by HE he had said that I had put a case to him that, 'for the increased effectiveness of NP 8901' the provision of a third Beaver aircraft, flown and owned by the Royal Navy, 'would be of value to NP 8901's routine duties round the colony'.

I had asked for no such aircraft and, even if I had thought it would be useful, I knew that the chances of getting it would have been slim indeed and I would have been held to ridicule. My name was very definitely being taken in vain and I did not like it.

But, at that time, life still had to go on. On 1 November, 1978, the old Hookers Point airstrip was removed by a gust of wind. My intelligence report at the time described it thus:

"At about 0300 a sixty to seventy knot gust of wind from the south lifted the whole of the temporary airstrip like an enormous wing (it was cambered along both edges) and flipped it over to the north for almost its whole length, except the westernmost 200 yards. It must have weighed about 1,300 tons. The planks were then torn apart and scattered over a wide area. The net result is that we are now left with the packed subsurface of sand which is still usable by a Cessna. The speculation is whether or not the Argentinians will sell the remains to the FIG or remove them as was the original plan. The pieces would be most useful to the locals. The Argentine press accuse the Chileans of sabotage! Any news on the likelihood of war?"

HEGFI returned to his Colony on 15 November in what was described at the time by the Acting Governor as a 'terrible' mood. Certainly it took ten days before he summoned me for a debriefing of the previous weeks – an unheard of slight but one that was apparently offered to all Heads of Department. When it was my turn it manifested itself in treatment that would not have been out of place between a martinet of a Commanding Officer and a very young recruit.

"To start things off," I wrote to Tim, "I was accused of writing the original letter to the *Falkland Times* – a preposterous suggestion – before he began to say that 'Colonel Dick Sidwell was a thoroughly bad man'...then he stopped himself. I was 'the worst OC he had come across and certainly ran the worst Detachment'. That's fine by me but a number of other Heads of Department have been told the same thing about me. This may be true but I don't expect the Governor to make those personal feelings public.

"The airport security arrangements have been cancelled with a public castigation of me which is galling as they were HE's wishes and being carried out against my advice at the time and, anyway, were in operation for nine aircraft days before he left with no complaints from anyone. I was then accused in various minutes circulated through the Secretariat of disobeying his instructions...to save his face as he was being accused of being too military by others in the Government. He felt it easier to blame me. I gave up the argument when he invited me to become Governor if I felt that I knew the wishes of the people better than him. As it had been against my advice in the first place I felt rather annoyed.

"Why doesn't he come clean and tell the FCO, the MOD and the Islanders he doesn't want the military here except as cheap labour or the source of new aircraft or harbour launches? Certainly our military position at the moment is verging on the farcical."

As so often I sought solace and peace from this turmoil by driving to the local wild places with the family. One of the great escapes within easy reach of Stanley were the numerous wrecks, of which the *Lady Elizabeth* at the eastern end of Port Stanley was the most impressive, if not the most historic or important. Only a very few times in the year was it possible to reach the ship across the sand and we took this latest occasion to get on board. Hamish and I could climb up a chain hanging down her starboard side but Hermione had to be hoisted up inside two mail bags. Our combined efforts failed to lift Patricia! These periods of private, family enjoyment were very good for our souls.

It was at the end of one of these Sunday afternoon excursions that we returned to the Officers' Mess for tea in front of the peat fire when I became aware of Sergeant Cook, the signaller, working away in the cypher

7. "Driving can be a slow and tortuous business averaging only 4 mph across 'camp'."

8. Leopard Beach, Carcass Island. A prime example of the Islands' beauty.

9. Black-browed albatross nesting on Westpoint Island.

10. Fortnightly Argentinian Air Force F27 flight from Comodoro Rivadavia.

room in the roof. He eventually emerged trailing a long length of teleprinter tape behind him.

"Bad news, Sir!"

"What is?"

"We've just received an 'officers deltext' signal which is for your eyes only but we don't have the correct key cards. I've asked them to re-send it in common old crypto and promised the operator that I won't look."

I was puzzled. I knew that deltext signals were almost always only sent when an officer was in serious trouble. I also knew that, as it was from CINC Fleet's Chief of Staff himself, it was indeed serious, but what on earth had sparked this off on a Sunday?

The message had been written − this much we discovered − on the Friday, but it had taken two days to be passed through the Whitehall Comcen. I was pretty certain that, although unpopular with HEGFI (for, I believed, honourable reasons), I had done nothing to warrant such attention from home.

I waited an anxious few hours before it came through in a different code and was deciphered by Fred and brought to the wardroom.

"I think you're in the pooh, Sir. I'll wait in the Sergeants' Mess while you read it."

I read it:

"For Major Southby-Tailyour from Chief of Staff.

1. In his telex 304 of 5th December to the Foreign and Commonwealth Office about the Minister of States' meeting with Councillors in early January, HEGFI refers to an indiscretion on your part in referring in a semi-public address:

a. To your campaign for new barracks for an enlarged accompanied draft

b. Adversely on present and past capability of NP 8901 and

c. Other unhappy things.

2. HEGFI also refers your assiduous cultivation, against advice, of Councillor Miller.

3. Request your side of the story to these allegations plus any background.

4. You should know that Sidwell/Downs recommendation for accompanied tours has not been accepted but that new barracks proposal is being actively considered. There is no intention of enlarging detachment but staggering some reliefs being considered.

5. Am also signalling HEGFI in hope of closing matter.

6. He will not be aware my para ...."

The rest was garbled but believed to refer to the last paragraph.

My first impression was that I really was 'in the pooh' as Fred Cook had suggested. I sat, poured a port and puzzled over the message and the causes behind it. The main clue to the seriousness of the signal lay in the expression 'and other unhappy things'. No CINC Fleet Chief of Staff would surely, I thought hopefully, use that casual expression if there was not, somehow, just a chink of humour to leaven an otherwise strong rebuke or at least an understanding that there must be a second side to the story worth listening to.

The most important aspect of the signal was that here was a chance, finally, and at the most senior level possible, to explain the dichotomy in which I found myself vis-a-vis the FCO in the UK and MOD's desires for the new-look defence of the Colony and those of the 'on-site' FCO representative.

I would not have another chance to put my case, and so, stalling for time in order to prepare what was up to then the most important 'reasons in writing' letter I had ever been asked to 'render' I sent off a signal in clear saying that I would be replying 'by the next available Argentinian aircraft'. This not only gave me time but alerted him, I hoped, to the difficulties we experienced with communicating satisfactorily.

For the moment I would put my cards on the table to the Admiral and let him and his staff — and that of the CGRM — come to their verdict on my behaviour.

In full, my reply read as follows — and I would not have changed one word of it with any amount of hindsight:

"Sir,

"I have the honour to reply to your signal of the 8th December 1978.

"The meeting to which His Excellency refers was a private, informal talk with members of the Sheep Owners Association; the Chairman of which is the Stanley Manager of the Falkland Island Company. The meeting was held four months ago on the 17th August shortly after the visit of Colonel Sidwell and Major Downs. I addressed the meeting with the full knowledge and concurrence of His Excellency.

"At that time, and partially as a result of the inspecting officers' visit, speculation over the future of the Royal Marines Detachment was rife at all levels of society.

"I informed the Sheep Owners Association that the inspecting officers, whom many members had met, had looked at all the factors affecting NP 8901 and had returned to England to present their report. Nothing classified was discussed nor anything which was not already public knowledge and which had not been openly talked about by His Excellency. During the meeting I endeavoured to be as circumspect as possible bearing in mind the fact that members already knew a great deal about our circumstances. This information has been gleaned over the years from a multitude of sources. It is a very small society. I felt that it would have been contrary to good, honest relations to have denied facts that were well known from long before our arrival. This is the only talk I have given; it has effectively put a stop to all serious rumour and speculation. I felt that this should have been my aim at the meeting.

"I have never openly advocated a larger Detachment (although I have discussed this subject in official circles) nor have I ever commented on the capability of NP 8901 other to state that, given warning, we would give a very good account of ourselves. I am not in a position to comment on the terrible gossip that can abound in the clubs and pubs of Stanley and which is sometimes attributed to myself, second-in-command or senior non-commissioned officers. I, myself, have never visited a Stanley pub.

"My desire to put a case for having certain members of the Detachment accompanied is well known and the practicalities of this were discussed by the inspecting officers with civilians during their visit. My wife and children are with me in the Falkland Islands which I believe has been a great help to me in this difficult society and, consequently, I believe, of great benefit to the Marines.

'Other unhappy things' could refer to my determination to practise our skills, procedures, security drills and patrols. I am most restricted in this respect, the reasons for which are difficult to understand. This restriction in itself gives rise to questions from locals concerning our presence here when we do not appear to exercise in preparation for eventualities.

"I am extremely puzzled by my 'assiduous cultivation' of Councillor Miller. There is ex-councillor Sid Miller and his youngest son councillor Tim Miller. I have met Sid Miller three times; once at a Government House cocktail party, once at a cocktail party I gave in the Officers' Mess for the inspecting officers and, finally, at the Sheep Owners Association meeting. I have never been to his house nor has he visited mine.

"I have met Councillor Tim Miller twice. Once at a private cocktail party and once at a cocktail party given by me in the Officers' Mess for members of the Sheep Owners Association. He is the manager of the Walker Creek settlement which I have never visited. I hardly know him or his views.

"On my arrival His Excellency instructed me not to mix socially with Councillors, the Medical profession, the Education Department, the Falkland Island Company executives and a few named individuals. In a society of under one thousand people, and apart from the strangeness of the request, this has proved to be impossible. Since their departure the inspecting officers have kept me fully informed of the progress being made as a result of their report. I have never felt it necessary to resurrect my original 'campaign'. We are extremely grateful for all the help, support and guidance we are receiving.

"In conclusion I wish to state that the Detachment continues to help the community with a wide range of projects. I believe that this is proving to be a very happy and successful tour for the Marines.

"I have the honour to be,
Sir,
Your obedient Servant
SE Southby-Tailyour
Major, Royal Marines
Officer Commanding Naval Party 8901"

There was nothing more to be said. I was not surprised that my efforts − or perhaps the manner in which I was going about them − had given some offence to His Excellency, but I had thought that I was aiming in the right direction and certainly in the direction ordered in London. I was aware, as I have shown, that HE seemed to be pursuing different policies not only behind my back but behind that of the MOD and possibly his own FCO. That, at least, was my perception at the time. I believed that it was also the perception of the Fleet Royal Marines Officer.

Apart from His Excellency, my speech to the SOA (which seems to have been a major source of complaint) was remarkably well received by the members. A transcript of the question period was sent to me, at my request during my 'reasons in writing' research, which included the following:

"Mr Hardcastle: Major, if I may say so, that is the best thing I have heard for quite some time. I have been renowned for my criticism of previous Detachments for the simple reason that until this morning I had no idea of just what their role is. Nobody has had the courage to define a policy.

"Mr Goss: Could you clarify the ways in which you would like to improve or extend your training of the force if the population were to allow it?

"Major S-T: If an offensive enemy landed we would deploy immediately from Moody Brook. We would like to practise this at odd moments. Also we would like to practise street fighting in Stanley.

"Mr Blake: If I read the situation correctly, the Royal Marines are to now act as a delaying force until a major force arrives. Have you any assurance from HMG that if the occasion arose will there be a back up or will there be just a note of protest?

"Major S-T: Something will happen militarily but I cannot be more specific than that. For us our first stop on deployment will be

Government House from where we will deploy forward as a delaying force as required.

"Mr Cockwell: I would like to express my appreciation for Major S-T's frankness and can only comment that if we had a similar co-operation from Government Departments things would improve no end.

"Mr S Miller: It would seem to me that the Marines are at a considerable disadvantage with the present defence system at the airfield.

"Major S-T: I'm glad somebody mentioned that. Arrangements are well in hand for considerable improvement in security arrangements.

"Mr Pitaluga: These restrictions on street manoeuvres. Can the SOA help?

"Major S-T: Yes. Spread the word and support us."

It can, of course, be seen that whilst keeping the detail confidential, some of these points were at odds with local FCO thinking and policy and quite clearly it was extremely galling to HE to find them being aired in public. I accept that criticism entirely, but, as is also shown, the most influential members of Falkland society shared the MOD's views on their defence.

At about the same time my DI4 contact warned me that both Chile and Argentina were 'hard at it in the world arms market' and that Argentina in particular had purchased some 25 Israeli Mirage V aircraft. Just to add a spark of amusement he sent a newspaper cutting from the *Eastbourne Herald* informing its readers that their local Member of Parliament, Mr Ian Gow, was 'heading south' to the Falkland Islands which were apparently ruled by a 'military junta'. "What," Percy wanted to know, "was I doing and why didn't I keep DI4 better informed?" He ended up with the request to send him details of my cabinet in due course. There was a PS:

"Should I have called you 'Excellency'?"

There was a PPS:

"No war before Christmas — writing separately."

Then, at last, came the first real sign that I had the backing I needed to vindicate my actions. Although the visiting officers had given me their full support there were some doubts in my mind concerning views at high level. The Chief of Staff's reply and a second letter from him were the spur I needed to continue the line I had started so long before. In the first letter I was told, quite informally, that no further action was intended and that I was to 'feel free' to write to him with any problem that might crop up.

The second letter was even more positive; although it should have made my relationship with HE easier, in some respects it made it worse, for, despite a 'green light' to forge ahead with plans I still had to work directly with the Governor.

The opening paragraph began:

"I have been aware for some time that HE the Governor has been pursuing a line on Moody Brook Camp that is different from the line that this Headquarters is following. I am also aware that this situation is causing you some embarrassment."

After a few more paragraphs of a sensitive nature the Chief of Staff ended with:

"I look forward to seeing you when you return and would also hope to have the opportunity to meet Mrs Southby-Tailyour."

This was excellent and positive news. The new Chief of Staff was Rear-Admiral William Staveley, an ex-Commanding Officer of HMS *Albion* from northern Norway days when I borrowed his landing craft, and Lt Roger Dillon (his OCRM), to set up the first Landing Craft forward operating base. These two letters gave me the confidence I needed to face the immediate future with renewed vigour.

My renewed vigour was being matched less and less by Keith Pittock, the Detachment Sergeant Major. For some time the DSM had been bowed down by the lack of progress we were making with the maintenance of the camp and with our truncated military training. Coupled with a slight but continuous, and rather touching bout of homesickness, he was, on a number of occasions, failing to sustain the Detachment's morale. I had tried discussing things with him and counselling him, as had Patricia, but with little effect. I therefore decided that if he was to play the part of DSM to the full he needed to be jolted. Militarily I thought that this would be unfair and unwarranted, so Fred Cook (whose support was vital if the plan I had was to succeed) and I hatched a plot that, although aimed at Keith Pittock, could be taken as an attempt to sort out all the other despondent members of NP 8901.

The whole Detachment had been supportive in the overall efforts to better our terms of service; all had supported my call for longer and accompanied tours for key members and of course all had supported the call for a more realistic financial recompense other than the simple separation allowance which, anyway, only affected the married man.

Whenever a classified signal came tapping across the teleprinter the duty signaller had to call for the Signals NCO. Only he and I were security cleared, and to a higher than normal category due to our involvement in the signals trials which went through Diplomatic Wireless Stations in countries with which I had long assumed we had no formal connections. Sergeant Cook would then take over in the attic's cypher room. The DSM, who had a right to know most things that were going on — even if sometimes Fred or I had to weed out some of the more exotic bits to reduce the security — would obviously be brought in after the censoring process had taken place. On the morning in question a signal was 'received' by the duty signaller who, recognizing the sensitive nature of the contents, called for Fred making quite sure that the DSM heard. The normal procedure was followed, with Fred, acting with a certain amount of theatrical exuberance, bringing the tape in to me past the DSM and clerk in the outer office.

Behind my shut door Fred and I waited until a suitable period had elapsed, when, in a loud voice, I asked Sergeant Cook to fetch the Sergeant Major. He stumbled into the office as the door was opened.

"Ah, Sergeant Major. We've just received some quite excellent news from London."

"Oh yes sir?" Keith Pittock's idea of good news did not always match mine.

"Yes. You know we've been fighting to have various members of the Detachment married accompanied and on an eighteen month tour — plus all sorts of other things to enhance the value of NP 8901. Well, at last CINC Fleet have agreed to some of our suggestions and are asking us to implement them before we leave. I think you had better read the signal; then we can decide how and what we tell the men."

I handed the Sergeant Major the flimsy signal with lengths of tape stuck across the pages in the manner of an old-fashioned telegram. So far everything had gone as normally as the Sergeant Major would have expected. He read:

"Confidential/Staff in Confidence

"From: Chief of Staff to Commander in Chief Fleet

"Personal for OC NP 8901

"Reference (Here followed a whole series of very real looking references.)

"After long and detailed study by this Headquarters and the Department of the Commandant General Royal Marines and in conjunction with the Foreign and Commonwealth Office it has been decided that the case for having certain members of NP 8901 married and accompanied makes sound sense.

"It is therefore planned that the posts of OC, DSM, DQMS, Sigs NCO, Chef and Carpenter and Vehicle Mechanic, be married accompanied forthwith.

"However, as it is impractical for the present incumbents to alter their personal arrangements this will take effect with their successors.

"In order to allow your reliefs to make the necessary arrangements for such a move and to allow the next NP 8901 to join as a formed team the whole of the present Detachment will be required to remain in post, unaccompanied, for an extra six months.

"We know that you will take this aspect of this most satisfactory arrangement with your normal fortitude. You may take satisfaction in a well argued and presented case resulting in positive action.

"Letters containing details of new travel arrangements and handover will be sent shortly. PARMS and DORMS will be amended accordingly. NNN."

The Sergeant Major read this bombshell slowly; he then read it again before allowing it to drop to the floor. He faced the window with his head resting in his hands, his elbows on the sill.

"I don't bloody well believe, it Sir. I don't bloody well believe it." He turned and looked at me.

"The bloody Admiral can tell the wife. I'm not going to!" and he stormed out of the office slamming the door.

Fred and I looked at each other. While I should not have employed the signals sergeant to take part in a serious joke against the DSM, it was in all our interests that Keith Pittock came back into line, and this was the best way I could think of shocking him into that.

I opened the door and confronted him. "Look, you've supported all the arguments. Don't you see we've won a major battle?"

"No I bloody well don't." I had the first inkling that I might have gone too far.

The aim was to make him see that life could be worse. He pushed past me and went to his cabin.

Somehow the 'buzz' got out. Various Corporals and Marines who would normally have no reason to be across in the headquarters wing of Moody Brook found an excuse to visit the orderly room.

"I hear we've got an extension − excellent news."

"Christ, Shep," − the Detachment Clerk, Marine Sheppard − "how the hell do I ask for a discharge?"

I listened from the hidden sanctity of my inner office as marine after marine gave his unsolicited opinion of an extra six months in the Falklands. The surprising thing was that about ninety percent were happy to stay. It was a heartening verdict.

Although the 'bite' (in Royal Marine parlance) had been aimed at the Detachment Sergeant Major I felt it should run its course as an indication of other things but by noon it was time that the truth was out. All the Corporals and Senior NCOs were invited in to the Officers' Mess where Chris and I poured drinks. With my back to the peat fire and without looking at the prime recipient of the joke I apologized for my little dig at their expense. All took it in excellent part with much laughter. All, that is, except Keith Pittock. He drank his drink, put the glass on the mantelpiece and to a deathly hush announced that he would:

"...get even with you Sir. Some day, somehow, I'll get even with you." He left the room.

Cruel perhaps, but from that moment on he was as good as he had ever been, and probably even better. He was, in truth, quite one of the best, but things had been getting him down in recent weeks and the sudden glimpse of just how bad things could be brought him up with a round turn. All should have been well that ended well but he was to be as good as his word and he did get even with me — with considerable interest. To this day he has the original signal as one of his prize mementos of the Falkland Islands!

Despite a number of disagreements, HE and I were able to discuss the long-term problems of the Falklands and their neighbours. An added complication that we considered was the possible intervention by the Soviet Bloc if Great Britain was to acquiesce to the Argentinian claim or failed to take remedial action after military occupation. We believed that it could have been as short as three weeks before Russia moved in — almost exactly the bargaining time I was to 'buy'. The Falklands under British rule was one thing, under Argentinian it was quite another matter and whether or not America would intervene against Russia in support of Argentina's membership of the Organization of American States was an uncertain factor in the equation — especially if the transition had been by force in the first place. This was an interesting theory I expanded later at the Royal Naval Staff College.

Of one thing every one was certain, the Islands without the Islanders would be useless to the Argentinians. It had been estimated that two-thirds of the population of Patagonia is of northern European stock, the true Argentinians preferring to live in a climate more in sympathy with their Latin/Spanish backgrounds.

One of my duties was to investigate all Soviet Bloc ships that put into Stanley's outer harbour and it was here that one of many amusing incidents occurred, this time on board a Polish fish-factory ship. I had visited her before and on this latest occasion was welcomed by her Captain in the middle of a Sunday afternoon. He was dressed in a dinner jacket and myself and the harbour master, Les Halliday, were ushered into his stateroom.

"Ah, good morning, Major," he had greeted me, and then, in a mock expression of embarrassment, had put his hand across his mouth to mumble, "Oh, sorry! I'm not allowed to know that, am I?"

I always dressed in the hope that I would be taken as a crewman from the Harbour Master's launch. Shortly after that I had looked, casually, up at the foremast aerials to be told in a quiet voice that nothing had been added since his last visit! We repaired to his cabin for too much vodka in exchange for a bottle or two of Famous Grouse. The stewards were immaculate in black bow ties, spotless white shirts and well-pressed black dinner-jacket trousers and served cakes and drinks in a manner that would not have been out of place in Claridge's. This particular Captain was a capitalist in everything but name, even to the point of owning a sizeable apple farm in his native Poland.

The increased number of seals on Sedge Islands, which I had mentioned to DI4, continued to puzzle me and in an effort to discover the ecological reasons I approached the Falklands fauna expert, Ian Strange. Ian, in his quite inimitably enthusiastic manner, wanted an instant patrol of the Jasons to discover the cause. Apart from taking a military look, using the ecology as an excuse, there was a third reason why I was keen to sail around those distant islands.

There was just a chance that we might find traces of the converted steel tug *En Avant* in which Simon Richardson had sailed from Rio de Janeiro on 1 November, 1977, bound for Smith Island in the South Shetlands via Stanley. Among his crew was H.W. Tilman, an acquaintance from my childhood days when I lived in a sister ship (a Bristol Channel Pilot Cutter) to those he made famous with his 140,000 miles of high-latitude cruising and exploring under the Royal Cruising Club burgee. It was a forlorn hope that we would find her or any trace of her crew, but, as is well known, survival on these islands for lengthy periods is not uncommon. It was certainly worth the effort of looking and I felt that I owed it to such a fine man.

There was, too, the wreck, in Falkland folklore believed to be 'of sixteenth century vintage, stranded high and dry in the middle of an island with three skeletons inside'. Some even believed that this could have been one of the ships separated from the *Golden Hind* in 1578 in the latitude of Tierra del Fuego. The island was supposed to be anywhere between the Falklands and Cape Horn, but a popular assumption was that it could be Jason West Cay, the westernmost islet of the whole archipelago. It had never been visited, let alone landed upon.

Ian's desire was coupled with mine, and so, armed with these good excuses, we approached Jack Sollis. Although under my direct and total command for any task I deemed necessary, we felt that under such circumstances, and having been specifically ordered not to visit the Jasons for military reasons, we should discuss the matter with *Forrest's* skipper.

Jack, whose suspicion of any form of dictatorial government matched mine (although mine had to be more covert than his or Ian's), felt that it was very much our duty to establish why the breeding patterns of the Fur Seal had changed. It was certainly not beyond the imagination that either illegal hunting of these animals was taking place among the Jasons or that something even more sinister was chasing them eastwards – human occupation for instance.

Without wishing to ignore totally HEGFI's wishes, we sought and got approval to visit South Jason only. This was the closest of the Jasons to habitation and, therefore, presumably to HE's way of thinking, as it was within sight of Carcass and West Point Island, not likely to be inhabited by Argentinians anyway. By visiting just this island we would not be compromising his stand on such patrolling. South Jason was good enough for me and represented the edge of a very thin and lengthy wedge as far as the future was concerned.

We left on 26 September for a long patrol that, as a model of a combination between my military duties, my private surveys and an ecological detective tour, was as comprehensive as any.

Sailing south-about from Stanley we anchored in Bull Cove on the very tip of Lafonia by Porpoise Point, quite one of my most favourite and desolate anchorages. There was no moon, but the kelp banks, very close by, showed brilliantly in the crystal starlight. The next morning I wrote in my log:

> "0545. Barometer 29.74. Clear, beautiful morning. Fresh breeze from the west. Beautiful colours of the early sun on the tussac – pure golden syrup. Rich dark-blue water. Anchored on edge of kelp. Gentoo colony ashore on SE edge of Bull Cove....Dozens of Stinkers following us. Only one Black-browed albatross. The coastline is featureless and not well charted to the west of Bull Roads. Advisable to stand out into south end of Eagle Passage before turning NNW. See previous notes but if heading for Port Stephens keep well south of Barren Island. The stern of the wreck of the Craigie Lee can be seen in the kelp."

Our second night was spent alongside the jetty in Port Howard where we were entertained to dinner by Sid and June Lee after a very English lunch of roast beef with Richard and Grizelda Cockwell at Fox Bay East.

> "28th Sep. Up at 0600. Beautiful still morning with no clouds and outstanding colours. Took the Gemini to the upper reaches of the northern end of Port Howard to survey both arms for a winter mooring for yachts."

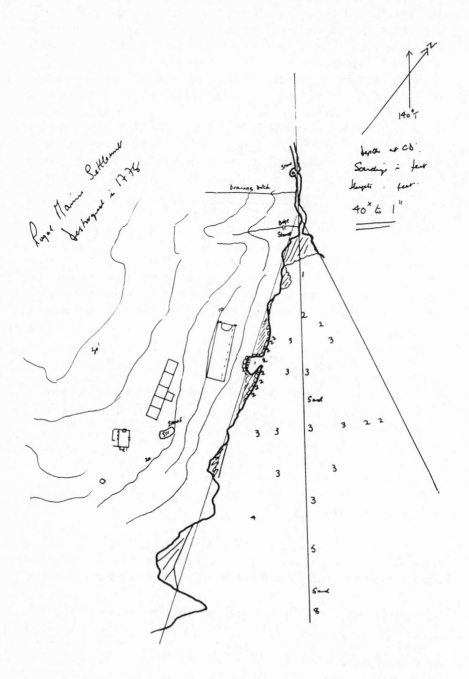

Royal Marine Settlement
Destroyed in 1776

Drainage Ditch

depth at C.D.
Soundings in feet
Heights . feet.
40ˣ to 1″

140°T

All the while I was sketching and note-taking while listening to Jack's running commentary on the islands and shoals we passed — some charted, some not — or that barred or marked our passage. It was a wonderful routine. My 1934 vintage camera and watercolour brushes were working overtime: no matter what the time of day or night I was on deck observing. For the more familiar passages I would often navigate to test my notes, so that I could confirm earlier recorded comments or look for any factors I might have missed. It was non-stop. Even when anchored (especially when anchored) there would be more to study: often from the Gemini when I would be away with my sextant, a hand-bearing compass and lead line. On these occasions I was more at peace with the world and myself than at almost any other time in my life. It was certainly the most perfect antidote to the troubles, real and imagined, that lay in permanent ambush back at Moody Brook.

Settlement managers would ask what was the purpose behind my jottings. "Pure pleasure," would be the answer: "One day I want to return in my own yacht and know where I am going." Nothing more than that.

The evening of the 28th was spent off Saunders Settlement having dropped mail and supplies at Pebble and Kepple Islands. On anchoring I took the Gemini away to visit the original Royal Marines settlement in Settlement Cove. On the western edge of Port Egmont, Commodore John Byron wrote on 15 January, 1765, that "The whole navy of England might ride in perfect security from the winds". I had walked alone across the hill once before but this was my first visit by sea and I found it very much as Admiral The Hon George Grey had described his first visit in HMS *Cleopatra* on 23 November, 1836:

"Of the old Settlement we could discover foundations of what appeared to be a row of barracks and houses built with some regularity of plan, but the Spanish Authorities had endeavoured to destroy all trace of habitations and had not left even the remnant of a wall standing."

Neither did I have any difficulty in finding the settlement and mooring alongside the tiny stone wharf designed for ships' whalers, longboats — and Geminis.

The low and crumbled cookhouse and accommodation walls were plainly visible on the skyline and the slightly more substantial storehouse just above the landing site was still in excellent condition, considering its age and turbulent history. The scene could not have changed one jot during the previous one hundred and forty-one years and probably not for the earlier sixty years. Helped by Sergeant Cook and a Marine we drew a reasonably accurate map of the settlement and took soundings of the small creek. Up the hill towards the north-west and hidden in the diddle-dee were the graves of three Marines who had died in an earlier confrontation.

22ʳ Feb: 1979

Barometer 29.25. Wind N. f2. Overcast at 0550, (Bar 29.72).
Northerly swell. slight. Slight SW sea running. Impossible
to land at Sedge Island so making course for the north
of the Jasons.

Sextant angles indicate that the gap between North
Fur Js: and Seal Rocks is wider by 2½ cables and
that Flat Jason is shorter by 2½ cables.

Tens of thousands of BB Albatrosses — a truly fantastic sight.
Also two huge Wandering Albatrosses making the B-B
look tiny! Many shearwaters and shags. Many Peales dolphins.

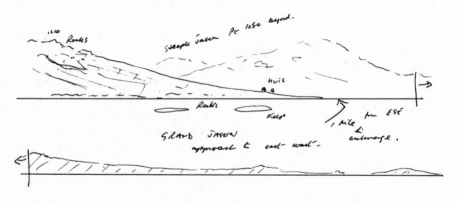

GRAND JASON
approach to east-ward.

1415ʰ Entered the shallow bay beneath the huts of
Grand Jason. Anchored in 10 fathoms ½ a cable
out over a rocky bottom. However there is
a very sheltered (except from the NĒ) cove about
10 yards across beneath the shearing shed which is
80 yards from the shore. (The kelp is easily
negotiated by a yacht or dinghy. The accommodation
hut is 150 yards from the shore. Fresh water
and a Jackass Colony. Slight rain. Sailed
for Stanley.

I hoped then, and resurrected my hopes in 1982, that someone sometime would care for these resting places with the same diligence that the graves of later defenders of the Colony were given. Sadly, as I write, I have yet to hear that this has happened.

Time pressed and at 0930 *Forrest* sailed from Saunders for Sedge Island, and the irrepressible Wally and Phyllis McBride, to anchor off their seal-crowded beach and opposite the point where, some years back, the honeymoon couple had floated a large wooden cargo container ashore. They 'rolled' it up the beach to just above the highwater mark and lived in it for six months whilst building a small bungalow further inland. Today we were progressing their 'civilization' a step forward by helping them to mark out the proposed airstrip. It was usual on these occasions to deliver the bulk goods, mail and beer that could not be carried in the periodical float-plane flight. The unusual thing about this particular visit was that Wally insisted that we then drank his three months' supply of beer with him and Phyllis in celebration of the imminent opening of his airport. We promised to re-stock him on our return journey!

On, then, to Port Pattison, the stunningly beautiful anchorage off the Carcass Island settlement. Before rowing ashore for dinner with Rob and Loraine McGill I again took the Gemini off to the eastern extremities of the anchorage to sound and record. The night ashore was spent in superb comfort and amidst outstanding hospitality. It was around these more remote settlements that we met the true Falkland Islander, for while there were obviously many in Stanley, there were, too, less attractive elements. Here, around the outer settlements (and apart from just two, who were expatriates anyway) I met the genuine Islander working every hour that God gave him, and her, to export goods for the benefit of the Colony's GNP, and working against sometimes crippling charges from the FIC and a less than three per cent return for their labours.

At 0630 on 30 September we left Carcass to starboard and sailed parallel with Gibraltar Reef for the southern corner of South Jason. As far as the eye could see the sky was 'bulked out' with Black-browed Albatrosses and Giant Petrels, amongst whose hordes were the less graceful but, in some respects, more attractive Silver-grey Fulmers, Cape Pigeons and Whale Birds. Below the ship's forefoot and along the bow wave the Commerson's and Peal's Dolphins rolled and accelerated, dived and surfed.

There were no seals, but, of greater importance at that moment, there was no sign of anything else either. While we stuck reasonably closely to the route we had agreed we did stretch a point and circumnavigated Elephant Jason anti-clockwise just to make sure. Ian with his binoculars and I with my sextant pursued our different roles. The fur seals must have had a more natural, but no less worrying reason, to have moved eastwards.

Human presence would have been an easily remedied problem. Nature was probably posing something altogether too difficult to solve.

By 1200 we were back in Westpoint Island anchorage and ashore with gin and tonics in the Napiers' very English-style house and garden from where we were able to report back, with no question of us hiding any secrets, that there were no Argentinians on the closer Jasons. To satisfy myself, and DI4 in Whitehall, we had to patrol the farthest islands; but at least we had managed the first blows to the wedge.

The Napiers' hospitality is difficult to escape but reluctantly we were on our way after lunch, bound initially for Grave Cove so that I could sketch and tabulate the anchorage, before we ran southerly and fast through the Woolly Gut and on towards Stevelly Bay.

I was very keen to visit Stevelly Bay, not only for covert landing-craft reasons (although I explained in public that it always sounded like the most ideal yacht's anchorage) but because I had been told that a short distance inland and to the east at the head of Port North was a long low valley with a hard and level floor capable, without much preparation, of taking a C130 Hercules aircraft. That type of information, although of no real use in 1978, was exactly the sort of thing that needed to be stored away for future reference. The Argentinians had craft capable of landing earth-moving equipment and they had an abundance of Hercules.

Some strange tidal eddy washes ashore a whole range of nautical bric-a-brac from the South Atlantic. A frogman's flipper and a submarine's smoke float caused some quite fantastic and alarming rumours in the Stanley pubs; an unnamed ship's lifeboat (empty) has arrived here, as have whole tree trunks from Chile and in 1976 seven sperm whales were either washed ashore or deliberately stranded themselves, their bones still visible in the sand.

We anchored before dusk in the desolate but safe and kelp-free spot between the Bense Islands. Jack and I sat on the upper deck drinking Chilean gin (an acquired taste) watching the Puffing Pigs playing around the cable, their brilliant white flanks lit by the dying sun. They carried these dappled crimsons and yellows down through the clear water, darkening all the time until they merged into black before suddenly rocketing up into the sunset again. It was an impressively peaceful moment and as far removed from the bickering and traumas of Stanley as I could have wished.

Dinner, with Argentinian red wine, was the usual mutton, known, for obvious reasons, as '365'. Not many enjoyed *Forrest's* cooking, but I did. Breakfast was always curried, minced mutton plus, with luck, a chicken's egg, and without luck a penguin's. My children found these eggs delicious, but as the white remained opaque or translucent, no matter how it was cooked, much of my distaste was influenced by the visual senses rather than the palate's. Lunch was always cold mutton with copious dashes of Lee and Perrins' Worcester sauce (an excellent combination), mashed potatoes and swedes and, if lucky, this would be followed by 'pussers' tinned pears and sweetened condensed milk. Dinner, always, was roast mutton with mashed potatoes and swedes and, alas, 'pussers' tinned pears, but, if fortune was really with us, tinned peaches! My only regret was the absence of tinned sardines, for when alone at sea I have often existed on nothing else except a tot of whisky — eleven days being my 'record' so far. The sardines, incidentally, are better and less monotonous if first flambéd in gin!

Sailing at 0600 the next morning, we passed close to Crouching Lion Rocks, well named as anyone who has been to Trafalgar Square will testify; Landseer would have been proud of the likeness. Turning north-east for Roy Cove and after dropping mail, wheat and sugar, we headed for the most westerly inhabited island — New Island — past the prominent wreck of the *Glengowan* lying, as though anxious to be off, with her stern in the kelp and her jibboom pointing to the open sea. To follow the peaceful weather of the previous few days we dropped the anchor in a full gale with rain and sleet showers from the west, and a rising glass. Unknown to us, the plan had been to barbecue mutton ashore with the one family 'in residence' but instead we were invited for a traditional meal of roast mutton round the peat fire.

Beaver Island, Weddell Island and Fegan Inlet came next.

Fegan Inlet enticed me to write encouraging notes about safe anchorages for yachts, with the roofs of the settlement just visible over the saddle of land that separated it from Port Stephens harbour. Peter Robinson met me on the foreshore, from where we took a box of plastic explosive, a cartouche of detonators and a roll of detonation cord to his embryo airstrip. In the middle was the tip of a rock formation, the removal of which was impossible by any other means. After an hour or so of cutting it away in small pieces — since to have blown an enormous hole would have left a very soft patch, no matter how it was filled and rolled — we sailed for the north and home via a night stop at Westpoint Island. It was on this memorable occasion that the dinner developed so successfully that even Jack Sollis was enticed into taking part in an impromptu eightsome reel afterwards.

The next morning we slipped from Westpoint early for a meandering route to Stanley while I checked many of the northern islets and reefs before we closed with the coast east of the entrance to Port Salvador and the series of small coves and useful looking-beaches between there and Macbride Head.

Although lengthy, this was a very typical patrol. Much cargo had been delivered. I had filled in many pages of the notebook and taken dozens of photographs and sketches; we had checked on an environmental mystery, confirmed the absence of Argentinians on the inner Jasons and recce'd one airstrip and prepared another. We had 'been a presence' around the Falklands, all without mishap and accompanied by much laughter. Personally, I could ask for no more than that.

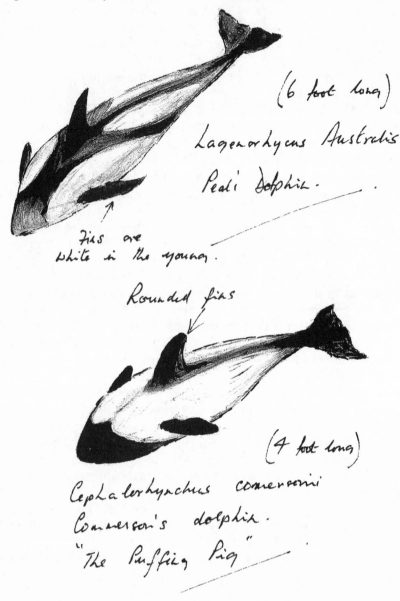

(6 foot long)

Lagenorhycus Australis

Peali Dolphin.

Fins are
white in the young.

Rounded fins

(4 foot long)

Cephalorhynchus commersoni

Commerson's dolphin.

"The Puffing Pig"

VI

Homeward Bound

THE DAY AFTER MY RETURN from the Jason Island patrol my cousin William Tailyour and his stunning American wife came to stay for a week. To William (an ex-gunner and Major in the Royal Marines Reserve) to travel to such a remote place from their house in Connecticut was not out of the ordinary, but the look on Amanda's face at the airport when the F28 took off again without them was altogether something different.

Facing me with a much alarmed expression she said, having noticed the complete lack of any other aircraft in the area, "Where is it going and how do we get home?" I explained that it was going back to Buenos Aires, a mere twelve hundred miles away and that it would be back in a week's time. I omitted to tell her that the schedule and its reliability were entirely in the hands of the Argentinian Air Force. Despite her initial reaction to being marooned, the week was a highlight in our tour, for they were kindred spirits and great fun.

Work, though, dominated, and in particular the long-running and tedious sagas of the state of Moody Brook camp (let alone any improvement or re-siting), the local security and state of readiness of the Detachment and the practice of our new routines dogged our life.

We were also in the middle of the tourist season with no check on who landed from the cruise ships and, even more surprising, no check on the number of pilots it apparently took to fly in the twice-weekly flights. These officers continued to be wooed by the FIC store, despite much local misgivings. The more forgiving – or the more naive – assumed that the reason for so many 'pilots' was a not unnatural desire to purchase whisky at a tenth of the price in Buenos Aires. The more astute saw this regular influx as a means of the AAF getting as much practice at landing at Cape Pembroke as possible, by as many as possible. I was not taken in by the 'whisky' theory and nor were DI4. For a Colony with a near-paranoia over their future, the lack of any form of check on tourists or restriction on pilots was difficult to fathom.

Some visitors were more than welcome and Cindy Buxton was one. In the Islands to carry out a recce for her proposed filming of the penguins and wildlife on Steeple Jason, she was worried about the lack of a suitable partner to share the work on that isolated island. There was someone, but

Cindy was convinced that 'she' would not accept. In describing her proposed companion it became clear that I also knew who she had in mind.

"Are you by any chance thinking of Annie Price?"

Yes she was – and did I know her? I had been best man at the wedding of great friends of mine when Annie, whom I knew well anyway, had been chief bridesmaid. She was a resourceful and gifted 'stills' photographer in her own right. Cindy asked me to write and sow the seeds of the idea; so I did, and between them they produced quite one of the most beautiful wildlife films.

Len Hill of Bird Land at Bourton-on-the-Water in Gloucester arrived with his cross-country, amphibious, eight-wheeled Argo Cat. Len, one of life's real people, had earlier bought Steeple and Grand Jason as wildlife reserves. Unwittingly he gave me the best possible excuse to patrol those islands, and this we did, with him and his 'machine' being lowered over the side off the only landing-point of Steeple Jason and just below the huts that Cindy and Annie would eventually live in.

During our passage for Len's islands from Carcass Island on 26 February, 1979, (with HE's full permission) I described some of the most amazing sights of my time in the Falklands and ones that will never be forgotten. Among pages of navigational notes and data I wrote:

> *"We are here (off the north end of Flat Jason) at just about slack water (high water springs – which is not the recommended tide but the right time) the chart shows dangerous overfalls at any other time. Now there are thousands of sea birds feeding in the upwelling eddies that bring jelly fish to the surface along with other goodies that they find so delicious......South of the Fridays I can safely say that I have never seen so many birds at once. As far as the horizon the air is thick with Black-browed Albatrosses, Sooty Shearwaters, Rock Shags – tens of thousands – all massed like Starlings over an English field at migration time. Quite fantastic. Many albatrosses too gorged to fly. Many penguins – Rockhopper and Jackass. Sorry! There must be over a million birds in sight. Arctic Terns, Tussac Birds and never forgetting the dolphins – the Peals and as always my favourite, the Puffing Pig.*

Sadly Len was to die whilst flying back from a later visit to his adored islands shortly before the Argentinian invasion. He was spared the horror of watching the rape of the island's sanctity, but he is irreplaceable as a penguin enthusiast.

A particularly fascinating visit was that of the Norwegian sailing ship

Capricornus. Her arrival coincided with a team from the National Maritime Historical Society of America (NMHS) led by Dr Eric Berryman of the University of New Mexico, Albuquerque. Their aim was to visit the wrecked *Vicar of Bray* whose hulk lies at Goose Green. There was no suitable craft available except *Capricornus* and so I put the two in touch, with myself as interlocutor and navigator. The arrangement worked well and, as a result, the NMHS completed their survey of the *Vicar of Bray*, the Norwegians gained some useful employment, I experienced some unbelievable sailing and we all became excellent friends.

Before this, HMS *Endurance* had arrived out from the United Kingdom and passed through on her way south. It was an exciting moment of the tour, for we were no longer isolated. She brought with her well-needed moral support, although it was not long before the Captain (now James Lord) suffered at the hands of HE – to the point that in a later letter he had to explain his reluctance to bring his ship in to anchor to drop a sick marine: "I am actually quite keen not to come in to anchor because not only will it waste valuable time but I might get trapped by those ashore whom I am happy to leave alone at the moment." At least he had a choice! The direct result of this was a signal sent to me on board *Capricornus* from HE demanding my presence back in Stanley to take charge of the arrangements to accept *Endurance's* helicopter with the casualty and to despatch the mail for her and the British Antarctic Survey team in South Georgia from whence she had dashed. The Beaver float-plane was scrambled and flew direct to Goose Green where it moored alongside the yacht. The photograph of the two together sums up, for me, so much that I enjoyed about my way of life.

With the end of my tour in sight HE began to try to tidy up his relationships with the Naval Party and with the MOD, with the idea, we suspected, of having one or two of his ideas in being before my successor arrived. The running of *Forrest* was a point in case. Government House insisted that, for the benefit of the Colony, she should now be run as a Government vessel; they owned her but could not afford to run her so this idea was a puzzle. Actually, it was not much of a puzzle for the reason soon became apparent. The Royal Marines would no longer be responsible for the patrol programme or itinerary. As the result of a lengthy brief from me, the Directorate of Naval Plans saw a parallel with the third Beaver float-plane and nipped the plan in the bud. In amplification I had to remind the Secretariat that the Colony gained £45,000 per year through the chartering arrangements as they stood, which included FI Government work as well as much inter-island ferrying – all for free.

In this vein of trying to secure a number of *faits accomplis* a less than welcome visit took place that strengthened my suspicion of the Governor's true intentions towards the Royal Marines' presence in the colony. A Royal Engineers major arrived without warning to 'inspect' NP 8901! The first I heard of his presence was the day after a reception at Government House when someone quite innocently asked me what had kept me away, since I was the only 'head of a department' absent from the welcoming party for a Major Leivers. Although no one had any right to expect to be invited at any time to GH I was a little surprised that, as the senior officer (of only two) in the colony, I had not been aware of this officer's arrival. On enquiring, I was informed that HE had specifically removed my name from the 'standard' guest list and that the Major was in the Falklands to visit the RE warrant officer and REME Staff Sergeant who were on loan to the PWD. That was fine, and nothing to do with me but....

The next day Major Leivers arrived unannounced at Moody Brook with the statement that he was there to inspect the camp formally at the express instruction of HEGFI. I was not amused, although it tied in with the Governor's long-stated aim to have the Royal Marine Detachment replaced by soldiers who could work at civilian trades. I was well aware of HE's insistence, in opposition to CINC Fleet's wishes, that Moody Brook's problems, present and future, were to come under his direct and personal control.

The Major told me that 'someone in London' had told him he would be discussing with the Governor the viability of sappers replacing marines in order to build the new camp and then stay on as the military deterrent. I was angry but I was also astounded that this had been fixed not only behind my back but behind those of CINC Fleet and the Commandant General. Apparently, through weeks of signal exchanges, this visit and its reasons had been prepared between HE and an RE Brigadier in the MOD.

It was now necessary to wing off yet another warning shot to MOD. The return letter from Colonel Dick Sidwell firmly closed the case. "We are grateful to you for alerting us to the Leivers affair; it has allowed us to forestall the Governor and take quick remedial action." As I suspected, neither the Engineer-in-Chief nor the 'someone in London' (a Brigadier Wheatley) had the slightest intention of suggesting, let alone approving, the replacing of the Royal Marines with an 'Army' Party 8901.

Then, almost suddenly, it was all over and despite all the work at home and in the islands I had nothing practical to show for our efforts apart from some new vehicles. The Concept of Operations and Standard Operating Procedures had been approved, but without weapons and defence stores, they were impotent policies.

A last flurry of signals. A last report to DI4. "There is a twin-engined Argentinian plane based here for a week 'checking' the radio beacons." A last series of visits. Ian Gow, MP for Eastbourne, who managed to horrify HE by reciting at a GH reception the whole of that poem about a visit to a zoo and a 'orses 'ead 'andle, was accompanied by his 'pair' MP, David Lambie (Ayrshire Central) who spent much of his time with the marines in their bar telling them they should demand single cabins. They were not actually impressed, for not only are they conservative by nature but most of them preferred the communal atmosphere of the small dormitories. Both, though, were delightful and formed a most amusing double act at the various dinner and lunch parties Patricia and I gave. We were to miss their erudite and witty repartee.

The first sign for me that not everything was falling on the stony ground of Government House came in the following entry in *Hansard* under 'Written Answers' for 23 February, 1979:

"Falkland Islands.

"Mr Gow asked the Secretary of State for Defence what proposals he has for improving Moody Brook camp in the Falkland Islands: whether he has any plans to re-build the Royal Marines camp at a site closer to the airfield: whether he will list the special allowances paid to Her Majesty's Forces in the Falkland Islands: what criteria he applied when deciding on the rate of those allowances.

"Mr Wellbeloved: The Property Services Agency is to undertake a feasibility study in the near future into ways of improving accommodation at Moody Brook camp. At the same time an assessment will be made of the possibilities of rebuilding alternative sites. Members of Her Majesty's Forces in the Falkland Islands receive the normal allowances to which they are entitled: there are no special allowances for Her Majesty's Forces in the Falkland Islands."

Not surprisingly, I recognized the wording of Ian Gow's questions, but, equally, we all recognized the ambiguous nature of the reply and in particular the fact that there was not even a hint of a study into any special allowance. I knew that Admiral Staveley and his staff were as upset as we were and I knew, too, that he would not let the matter rest there.

Towards the end I was desperate to be able to pass on to my relief some fruits from our labours, for, right from the very beginning, I had been determined that we would take the brunt of the 'new look' in all its aspects and pass on a going concern to the next NP 8901. To a large extent I failed, but there were some small victories – personal and military. For instance I had been the first person known to have landed on the Eddystone Rock, although I had failed to make a similar landing on the rear offside hoof of Horse Block Rock. The new Concept of Operations was approved at Cabinet level (perhaps my greatest achievement); a revised scale of defensive and offensive weapons had been agreed and arrangements for their procurement set in motion; the new communications links were well tried, and if not fully established, much of the ground work had been completed; the transport situation had been vastly improved with a regular turnover of new Land Rovers (plus an increase in scale), and the two four-tonners back on the road, but the Brook was still dominated by the Belsen Block; the bridge was still impassable, officially, by anything more than a long-wheel-based Land Rover and the hundreds of tons of rusting junk still lay in heaps all around; a concrete parade ground had been built, though this was more to keep the mud and filth out of the buildings than as a plaything for the Sergeant Major.

I had alienated the FIC but we had seen substantial improvements to the accommodation, largely through our own efforts and at the cost to our military duties. I had, very sadly indeed, alienated the Governor, but many of our arguments and disagreements were undeniably due to the fact that we were working for separate 'departments' of government who were perhaps themselves not always pulling in the same direction. I am sure, too, that there would have been much harmony if we had not been the 'Buffer Detachment' charged with such a radical change in the defence policies. Patricia had avoided spying for the FCO and in the last three months the locals (expatriate and Kelper) had begun to realize what we were trying to achieve. Suddenly we were invited out almost continuously. We had just one court case and that involved a woman, and 'my' NP 8901 only married four girls − almost an all-time low! We had two attempted suicides and I had sent one corporal home for using the Belsen Block for expressly forbidden trysts with various undesirable and untrustworthy women.

Patricia, Hamish and Hermione left the Falkland Islands on 16 March, 1979, about two weeks before we were due to sail in *Endurance* (and after her own series of farewell parties), helped in considerable part by Vice Commodoro Carnossa. I shall always remain grateful to him for his kindness in this and other matters − a civilized man of the utmost courtesy and charm whom, I always suspected, was involved in something of which he did not approve.

It had been sad saying goodbye to the family, for towards the end Patricia had begun to relax into the lifestyle. Hamish and Hermione were more than upset, for, to them, the Islands had always been a paradise compounded, not thwarted, by the absence of life's trivia such as television and discos, although they were a little young for the latter. It gave me immense pleasure to watch their understanding of wildlife and its own imperatives develop so early in life.

Just before the family flew out Tim Downs arrived with a small team from the PSA to establish, on the ground, the site of the new barracks.

This was much to HE's public annoyance, but at the insistence of CINC Fleet. They arrived just in time for an emotional end-of-tour party in the men's canteen at which the Marines and Junior NCOs presented me with the most generous gift of a silver goblet which I still use to this day.

At yet another party the Sergeants' Mess presented me with a piece of polished mahogany (no doubt illicitly 'salvaged' from some wreck) with a large lump of Falkland's rock balanced on top. On a brass strip along the side were engraved the words *Never Leave A Stone Unturned* — a reference to all that each one of us had tried to achieve. Hidden beneath the stone in a small compartment was a miniature bottle of stout. It was all very symbolic, and continues to dominate my studio.

The final party I attended was given by the Stanley doctor and his wife, Keith and Mo Dunnett, who had been loyal supporters from the very beginning, along with a very few others on my 'forbidden' list. The whole of the Sergeants' Mess had also been invited to this happy and carefree occasion among some very trusted and valued friends.

I was slightly below par at the Dunnett's party (but only as far as dancing was concerned) for the day after Patricia left I was 'given' a vasectomy by the second Stanley doctor. He had been helped in this task by Sister Diane Ryding, but as I was keen to assist at the operation she had been told to leave the operating theatre yet remain hidden behind a screen in case of emergency! Di had become used to the Tailyour family's medical problems for she had been on duty when Hermione chopped off the end of her left index finger trying to stop the invasion alarm which Hamish had wound up one Sunday lunch at The Brook. On another occasion we had to rush Hermione to the hospital with a sharp piece of kelp sticking through her lower lip. Di was to go on to greater things with the International Red Cross in, among other places, Beirut, Afghanistan and Ethiopia, where she was awarded the Florence Nightingale Medal — an amazing woman.

The last three days before our relief's arrival were spent cleaning the Camp, while we were billeted around Stanley. The new NP 8901 arrived at the Public Jetty on Sunday 25 March and after full briefings and tours of our various defensive positions I reluctantly sent my final signal to the Commander-in-Chief of the Fleet (copy to the Department of the Commandant General Royal Marines) stating that the command of the Falkland Island's garrison now rested with Major Sandy Lade....But there was no doubt in my, or Sandy's mind that if there had been an invasion in the subsequent five days I would assume command of both Detachments.

On the final day Keith Pittock came to me clutching a formal invitation from the First Secretary for him to attend a farewell party in Government House. Later that evening I bumped into the Sergeant Major, clearly the better for what had obviously been a very good occasion attended by every head of department with champage and a full buffet lunch.

That same evening I introduced Sandy formally to His Excellency at GH but my own official farewell took place a few hours before *Endurance's* planned departure with me standing in front of HE's desk while he told me in three minutes that I had been a 'thoroughly bad OCRM, although my Detachment had saved the day for me by behaving impeccably'. His last words were to the effect (and this surprised me more than anything else connected with my relationship with HE) that I had strong moral convictions and that that was about my only plus. It was a sad note on which to leave a society I had tried, at some personal expense in emotion and effort, to serve not only in accordance with my own conscience but the wishes of my masters at home. That may sound a bit pompous now but I believed I deserved better of the Governor no matter what his private views of my endeavours might have been.

After I had left Sandy in GH, I spent my last night in the Falklands quietly and at peace, in marked contrast to the rest of the Detachment!

As HMS *Endurance* sailed out through The Narrows on the last day of March, 1979, I stood alone on the upper deck. The Detachment were already below, tasting their first 'real' draught beer for over a year. They did not look back; but despite all the worries, the fights, the soul-searching and the hurt, I did look back. I looked back with the greatest possible affection. It had been in many respects an alien experience far removed from anything to which most middle-ranking Royal Marines officers are accustomed. In this I had been given immense moral and practical support from an amazingly patient team of friends and advisers at home, not forgetting the members of my own NP 8901. I was sad in particular because I knew that if I had managed things differently at the beginning there might have been a chance that faster progress would have been made, but I had been working against some unexpected odds. I pondered, too, on whether full acquiescence to the Governor's continual stream of contradictory wishes would have made life any more tolerable. It might have done in the short term, but in the end I was bound to follow the requirements from home rather than those on the spot.

But there had been so much personal pleasure that far outweighed the military and professional setbacks and as Stanley's coloured rooftops dipped below the sand dunes of Yorke Bay my thoughts were out in the far islands and settlements as viewed from *Forrest's* decks. They were also with some very close friends in Stanley who, too, had made the tribulations worth the effort.

I turned below for what I, if no one else, considered to be a well-earned pink gin. Away from the wind and the screech of the Arctic Skuas, I promised myself I would return — but the next time it would be under sail and under my own conditions.

KING
PENGUIN

VII

North by East

THERE WAS A SECOND FINAL STING: at the last moment we were ordered to fly by RAF to Brize Norton after four days waiting in Rio. It was usual for the outgoing Detachment to embark in *Endurance* and be dropped off in Montevideo for a civilian flight via Rio, Dakar and Paris. This was ideal for it meant an arrival at Heathrow at a civilized time of the day with our families able to meet us by public transport. It also allowed those members of the Detachment who wished, to be given the equivalent of the civilian air fare so they could make their own way home as best suited them.

A number of Marines had opted to motorcycle through Brazil, Central America and the USA using this cash; one had made arrangements to hitch round the world west-about. This last bombshell, when it came in the last few days, required the Marines to return the fare money advanced to them and which, in most cases, they had already spent on their own arrangements. I wrote a vigorous signal explaining that at the end of just over twelve months the last thing we wanted to do was to spend four days in a cheap hotel in Rio before flying by 'crab-air' back to Oxfordshire to arrive, inevitably, at 0630 on Sunday 8 April.

Four nights in Rio would have been excellent value on the way south but at the end of a year and a bit in Stanley it was bad news. I warned London of the dangers of my Marines being mugged or spending their hard-saved cash, as well as the possibility that they would return home with various diseases. The official answer was that 'if the members of the Detachment could not look after themselves against the former problem and be strong enough to avoid the latter they were not worthy of their service'. I thought this answer to my signal was a poor joke until it was reinforced by some unidentified Whitehall warrior. We arrived in Rio after a most comfortable journey in *Endurance*, whose ship's company appeared to have a similar sympathy for our new predicament as they had for us on the way south!

Four men were robbed of every cruzeiro with which they had been issued by an exceptionally unsympathetic British Consul. The Consulate knew nothing of our arrival and took the first three of our four days to find enough local money, during which time we existed on the few notes we had managed to bring from the Islands and which, because they were Falkland Islands currency, were not acceptable anyway. It was a most unhappy and unpleasant interlude, compounded when I learnt later that two men arrived home with some form of sexually transmitted disease.

The only light moment of the journey occurred when the two-hundred-gallon water tank above the Sergeant Major's head burst as the Boeing 707 landed heavily at Buenos Aires airport *en route* from Monte to Rio. As we were not allowed off the aircraft he sat in the sun at the top of the steps drying himself for an hour or so, much to the amusement of the lads.

It was raining at Brize Norton and only a few of the wives had been able to make the hastily changed rendezvous because of schools, travel, the time of day and the day of the week. The 'system' had the last laugh.

There were many de-briefings to be undertaken immediately on return. The various staffs were anxious to have the benefit of my first-hand knowledge of the problems; the FCO was anxious to discover why there were apparent discrepancies between what they had asked me to undertake and the manner in which I tried to execute those wishes. The Royal Marines Chief of Staff (who had not changed in my absence and who was remarkably conciliatory considering his earlier attitude) seemed to be full of praise for the progress which we had made (on paper) although he agreed with me that not only were the conditions under which I was forced to carry out my duties difficult but that there should have been no barriers anyway. I explained that, contrary to FCO belief, the Islanders were anxious to have a viable defence and that that defence should be openly seen to be in place and efficient. I had to explain, too, that quite often what was said in public did not always accord with what was said in private in the Islands and that included conversations with visiting parliamentarians and press. I explained that even after a year of pretty intensive study I was still not certain what anybody really wanted and that that enigma was confused by conflicting instructions and views from Government House and the FCO. The airport guards were a prime example of the Islanders wanting one thing when talking to me and quite another when discussing it with HE. It was almost too much to comprehend!

My most satisfying de-brief was that held with the Chief of Staff to CINC Fleet, Admiral Staveley, while Patricia was summoned to call on the Admiral's wife for a debriefing of the social and welfare problems. I assumed that this was with a view to the 'Fleet' having a better and more balanced and factual idea of the living conditions in order that a renewed case could be made for realistic allowances.

Other things took over my life again and the Falklands began to recede

93

into an already crowded past. I navigated the expedition in the North Sea first mooted by the American team in Goose Green and I re-commissioned my yacht *Black Velvet* with the intention of selling her at the end of the season. I also ran the emergency office during the 1979 Fastnet Race — a most sobering week.

I had been appointed to the Naval Staff College at Greenwich which was, against all expectation, immense fun. My selection came as a surprise but no less welcome for that and I benefited hugely from the experience. It was also just before the 'moratorium on defence spending' and we were well served with foreign and interesting 'home base' visits.

Amphibious operations loomed large in our deliberations — the Falklands did not!

At Greenwich I had time to reflect and consider the present and future of the Islands in an orderly and logical fashion and with all the help available at such a place of learning. All the muddle over the wider issues of what I had been tasked to achieve and what I had tried to achieve were more easily analysed in the calm atmosphere of South East 10.

I argued strongly with visiting lecturers over the importance of the Islands if, for instance, the Panama Canal was blocked in time of tension and Russia had completed her encirclement of the South Atlantic and was ready to move further westwards. I argued the case of the economic importance of the Islands vis-a-vis their proximity to that part of Graham Land most likely to have recoverable minerals should World opinion ever allow their mining. I argued their strategic importance to the United States and put them into the same category as the American 'occupation' of Deigo Garcia in the Indian Ocean. I became, in short, not only boring on the subject but obsessed with their future, short- and long-term. My fellow students would groan quite audibly in formal lectures if the South Atlantic was ever mentioned for they knew full well that there would be a supplementary question from me at the end.

Nobody thought for one moment that the Islands would be invaded; the earlier rebuffed attempt was still 'secret' and the Southern Thule expedition was not seen, in Great Britain anyway, as anything too serious, otherwise Callaghan would have done something about it, wouldn't he? Back in the less confrontational atmosphere of London I was able to re-hash all the very real fears that actually faced those on the spot and put them across with increasing confidence to my fellow students and members of the Directing Staff. I would not suggest that any of my forecasts fell on deaf ears but the East-West nuclear and conventional stalemate with the possibility of war on the central front was more topical. The battles on the flanks of NATO and a North Atlantic anti-submarine campaign in support of convoys were subjects closer to the aims of the Staff Course.

I took the teasing in good heart but – and this is not hindsight – I was saddened by a general lack of interest that seemed to mirror the attitude presumably being adopted by the FCO. As soon as I, at Greenwich, stopped worrying about the Falklands the happier everyone would be.

My course thesis was, naturally, titled *The Falkland Islands – A Personal View* and rightly or wrongly a number of well rehearsed themes ran through it. As I was to write just two years before Argentina's invasion:

"Territories no longer need to be conquered by force of arms; force of threat is often enough. During the last six years Soviet expansion of this kind has taken place in the Indian Ocean and those parts of Africa (notably the west coast in this context) where this policy was deemed to be, and was proved to be, the most effective. This policy has already begun, and is becoming more evident in the South Atlantic. This brings, once more, the Falkland Islands into focus but with a much more sinister backdrop. Argentina is in danger of joining Russia in this method of modern expansionism – albeit for different reasons."

Later in the same paper I was to conclude:

"In addition to all these problems let us look at an even more sinister side of Falkland Island affairs – that of their strategic importance. Russia is keen to support revolutionary movements in the Atlantic littoral states of South America; she already has sea ports on the Eastern side of the South Atlantic and it is only to be expected that she will start looking on the western side to complete the encirclement. The (possible) loss of control of the Panama Canal by the United States must be of significant importance, for who knows to whom the Panamanians will deny access in the future. In time of war, too, it only takes a very small amount of explosive placed by a subversive party to render the canal unserviceable and without this route the Cape Horn passage would increase in military importance. In 1991 the Antarctic Treaty is due for revision, a significant landmark for the future as neither Russia nor Argentina, amongst others, recognize Britain's claim to Graham Land and the vast deposits of mineral resources. By coincidence that part of Antarctica is the most valuable and is the closest to the ice-free ports of the Falkland Islands. There can be little doubt that any change in Falkland Islands sovereignty would affect the integrity of Great Britain's claim to Graham Land and could possibly be seen as a wider will to abdicate."

I had discussed earlier in the paper the local resources that could be recoverable: "such as the estimated £40 million a year from the sodium and calcium alginates obtainable from the Kelp; the estimated 20,000 million barrels of oil beneath the continental shelf to the north of the Islands (US Geological Survey); the sustainable white fish catch of 140,000 tons per year from the local waters (twice the then estimated world total catch) and two thirds of the world's protein requirement from the krill (particularly important to Russia since the American grain embargo on cattle feed to the USSR). As a 'wider will to abdicate' I also mentioned the impending removal of the ice patrol ship HMS *Endurance* first announced (but not generally known − unfortunately, to Sir John Nott's disadvantage − to be as far back as this) in 1975. It was interesting to note that the British Government dismissed the importance of krill, believing it to be an unpalatable food. Tell that to the Japanese! I had come to like krill as a delicacy on hot buttered toast.

The last paragraph read:

"Taking into account the historic and economic contribution of the Falklands to Great Britain I believe that there is a strong case for British aid to the future of the Islands, but this aid will not succeed in its long-term purpose unless it is accompanied locally by actions to reverse past policies; (I had referred in the text to the status of the FIC and the long held desire by many for its nationalization) policies which have contributed to the present state of economic and social decline. In particular there must be a change in the pattern of investment by the companies operating in the Falklands and by the Islanders themselves. A greater willingness on the part of these groups to plough back increasing proportions of locally generated funds into local investment and so reduce the flow of funds to Great Britain is of paramount importance. This would not only be the best demonstration of their commitment to their own future but would show Argentina and any others that at last the Islands were prepared to take the future into their own hands. A new-style Falkland Island Government better suited to the Islands' needs would provide the necessary encouragement and guidance for this change of direction in the Falkland Islands economic future − thus ensuring the least chance of serious outside intervention."

At the bottom of this last page after it was returned from being marked I wrote: "but it isn't happening and the invasion will!"

This was a private document presented to show an ability to argue a case on paper, but it did encapsulate my public thinking throughout the Staff Course. As such I felt as strongly then as I did before and indeed, as I still do, but it is not for outsiders to tell the Islanders how to manage their own piece of real estate: we should be thankful that some have had the strength of mind and body to colonize the place for over one hundred years, thereby ensuring that the mother country has a foothold in that most exciting, promising and valuable part of the world. Many saw them as merely a collection of barren islands, but their status as gateway to the nearest and most accessible piece of Antarctic (and to the Pacific) has

11. "As always the widlife diverted our attentions from the problems in Stanley." Female elephant seal on Carcass Island.

12. "I had no difficulty in finding the old settlement and mooring alongside the tiny stone wharf designed for ships' whalers, longboats - and Geminis." Original Royal Marines settlement on Saunders Island.

13. *The Black Pig* in a Norwegian fiord north of the Arctic Circle shortly before the Argentinian invasion of the Falklands.

14. Training in the 'floating-off' technique for launching Geminis from a submarine. First Lieutenant with stopwatch.

never been forgotten by the Islanders, though all too often overlooked by transient politicians.

The halls of academe were fine for six months but I was restless to get back to my Marines and the boats. That is not to say I did not enjoy my time at Greenwich. I did, but at the end I was ready to return to the practical side of things. The Military Secretary wrote to tell me that if I was to consider a future in the higher ranks of the Royal Marines I should accept a Ministry of Defence staff job but would I consider taking over command of the Landing Craft Branch. There was no contest, and so, fully realizing the restrictions that would be placed on any promotion, I accepted with alacrity.

A few days before the end of the course, the First Lieutenant of the College took me aside and in a very conspiratorial manner told me that two members of the Naval Security Service were waiting to interview me over lunch. "It doesn't look too good, sir!"

I paid not a jot of attention to the lecture but sat for an hour and a half racking my memory to see what on earth could have caused Naval Security to take such a public interest in my past − or even present. Nothing specific came to mind, although numerous little snippets kept returning to haunt and taunt me as I sat uncomfortably through the lecture on, I think, Naval Control of Shipping in time of war. There could have been plenty from a distant past; indeed I had once been interviewed by the Director of Naval Security himself, the notorious, but much loved, Colonel 'Black Jack' Macafee, about one or two things from well before my marriage. The interview had then been conducted across a personal file which had certainly measured not less than a terrifying two and a half inches thick, but which turned out, thankfully, to be full of old newspaper cuttings, bogus signal messages and letters that referred to no one in particular, known in Naval Security circles as 'The Fat File Treatment'!

The First Lieutenant in full uniform with silver-knobbed walking stick escorted me, much to the smirking of my fellow students, across the quadrangle towards one of the many small anterooms that lead off the main wardroom. I was, to put it mildly, very worried indeed and I've no doubt that it showed. With a great sweep the huge tall doors were opened to reveal Colour Sergeant Keith Pittock and his Warrant Officer already well outside a number of beers and a delicious cold buffet.

Keith Pittock watched my initial look of fear turn to relief and, with a smile as broad as mine was non-existent, said:

"I told you I would get even with you, Sir. Now I think we're quits."

We certainly were and he was the winner by a long way. The four of us enjoyed a long and hilarious lunch which was worth every pound on my mess bill.

The course was marred for me in December by the sudden and unexpected death of my father from a heart attack just a few days after his sixty-fifth birthday. He had viewed with amusement, and jealousy, my antics in the Falklands and had been a great supporter of the surveys, for whatever reason I was pretending to carry them out. He had, too, fought quite unashamedly for better conditions for NP 8901 through his friendship with Keith Speed (his local MP and sometime Minister of State for the Royal Navy) and Ian Gow.

I was to miss father's humour and outrageous sense of the ridiculous. To me he had been the living proof that the highest ranks could be achieved unconventionally. He was hardly staff-trained (a matter of much amusement to him) but had risen without this being an impediment to end as the Commandant General Royal Marines in 1964 and during the intense period of what at the time were known as the Healey Cuts − the first of the more recent exercises putting the future of amphibious forces under serious review. He had, too, been instrumental in obtaining for the Corps its latest role − the northern flank − without which we may well have suffered irreparable emasculation or even annihilation. He had been a friend of Lord Mountbatten's to the extent that when the Governorship of Bermuda had come up for re-appointment in 1971 Mountbatten had been father's sponsor. (Gibraltar and the Falklands had also been mentioned!) He taught me that ambition should not necessarily be allied to promotion and that to gain anything in life risks had to be taken. He would often quote the Duke of Montrose if he found me dithering on a decision. "He either fears his fate too much or his deserts are small..."

My mother had died eight years before, just as the final decisions were being made for the Governorship. Against all family advice, father decided he could not face the task without her and withdrew his nomination. It was an understandable decision but a sad one.

But life had to continue and once funerals and Thanksgiving Services were behind us I took on my new role as the 'boss' of the Royal Marines Landing Craft Branch.

New defence cuts had forced upon us the prospect of the total demise of the Landing Craft Branch when we were warned that certainly one and possibly both the Assault Ships would be put on the disposal list, and *Hermes*, the only Commando ship still in commission (and she had, anyway, reverted to the anti-submarine role) would also be sold or scrapped.

Part of my job at Poole was to continue the practice, each winter, of the inshore Arctic warfare tactics in independent support of the Commando Brigade that we had first attempted in 1972. To do this I would fit out by fair means or foul (money being unavailable for even conventional trials) one of my one-hundred-ton LCUs (Landing Craft Utility designed to carry two main battle tanks) to operate in temperatures down to -30°C. She would be transported to north Norway in the 'duty' assault ship (*Fearless* or *Intrepid*), replacing one of those they carried in their internal dock.

It was during just such an exercise in the winter of 1981/1982 that we loaded into *Fearless* a landing craft named, eventually, *The Black Pig*. Her cox'n was Colour-Sergeant Brian Johnston who had left his own *Foxtrot Four* behind at Poole for the duration of the winter deployment. Other cox'ns had helped me and many landing craft officers over the previous winters, but none were as willing to take the calculated risks required to reach beyond the limits of 'the book' as Colour Sergeant Johnston. His crew were Sergeant R.J. Rotherham, Marine A.J. Rundle, Marine P.A. Cruden, MEA A.S. James and LMEM D. Miller.

VIII

Invasion

BETWEEN JANUARY AND MARCH, 1982, and well north of the Arctic Circle *The Black Pig* had helped us push to even further limits our knowledge of camouflage (static and on the move), movement through ice, nautical ambushes in the narrows and a host of other military/nautical skills — skills previously untried since the 1940 Norwegian Campaign when such luminaries as 'Blondie' Hasler (later of Cockleshell Hero and single-handed sailing fame) had operated minor landing craft in support of the French against the Germans in the same waters.

Before 1972 landing craft had been tied very much to their parent ships, which meant that if the shipping left the amphibious operating area landing craft support was lost to the Commando Brigade. In the Mediterranean, Persian Gulf and Far East this loss of mobility had been acceptable as the troops moved inland but in North Norway the problem was more acute. Fiords bisect many lines of advance and offer the only guaranteed methods of movement in winter when enemy action or avalanches can close valleys and roads and blizzards prevent flying. Without the sea lanes this loss of flexibility can seriously hamper the Commando Brigade.

In 1972 the Commanding Officer of 45 Commando (Lieutenant Colonel Sir Steuart Pringle — as he then was) approached and asked if *Fearless's* craft, which I was then commanding, could be detached for a night raid while the ship went to sea. Surprisingly, my Captain, Simon Cassells (later Second Sea Lord), took no persuading to let me detach two of the LCUs, allowing me to establish a Forward Operating Base (or FOB) on the edge of the fiord, with my Headquarters in one of the holds of the lead craft. As the whole of the Commando could not fit in my two craft I asked HMS *Albion* if she would lend me her four LCAs (as they were still known). Her OCRM, Lieutenant Roger Dillon, of whom more later, had crewed for me in the 1970 Two-Handed Round Britain Race and would be a superb ally in this experiment. That night we loaded 45 Commando into the boats, secured the LCAs alongside the larger LCUs to produce only two radar echoes and showed (when necessary) the lights of fishing craft.

The Commando was landed fifty miles away just short of the head of Reisenfjorden, across unrecce'd beaches (another radical departure), from where they attacked the defending Italian San Marco battalion in the rear, while we returned, again undetected by Norwegian Coastal Forces. The Italians were not amused, nor were the rather stuffy NATO umpires whom Colonel Pringle had 'forgotten' to brief. Two nights later we carried out a similar raid with two companies against a Norwegian Coastal Artillery Fort on the island of Grytoy.

As far as I was concerned that set the scene for the forming of an independent landing craft squadron, and it was to practise the skills necessary for tactical and logistic support in an effort to convince the senior officers that *The Black Pig* had been converted. This 'new' art included the embarkation of the tactical headquarters of the Commando Brigade; establishing a small mobile hospital or dressing station alongside the area of operations; setting up a mobile rebroadcast station giving a horizontal relay which was much more difficult for an enemy to locate compared with the static sites on the mountain tops; transporting and then launching and supporting small-scale raids from a mobile and hidden base and, the most exciting skill of all, covert navigation, which included experimenting with paint schemes and camouflage on the move in shallow water among similar-sized icefloes we had cut off from the ice along the fiord edges or against the cliffs.

We had used a number of conventional craft in the intervening years but 1982 was the first time that we had a dedicated trials craft and not a pristine one from either Poole's training cadre or from an assault ship. We were then able to paint the LCU in whatever colour we chose without embarrassing anyone but ourselves. I wasn't sure what colours to use for this last experiment but anything was preferable to light grey. People who have not experienced the Arctic have often expressed surprise that anything other than white would be effective. I didn't then know what the most realistic answer was and went in search of *Fearless's* bo'sun. The only colours he could let me have in any quantity were black and dark brown. Much to the surprise of all involved, including the crew, we painted *The Pig* in fetching disruptive patterns of these two very dark shades. Against the fiord edges she disappeared and we never looked back. When people ask I tell them that the colours were the brainwave of my artistic mind, but the truth is far more prosaic!

At the winter's end I managed to avoid the journey home in a RAF C 130 aircraft, for not for nothing are passengers known to the loadmasters as SLF − self-loading freight − and given the appropriate treatment.

While everyone shared a common view of travel by RAF 'air trooping' not everyone agreed with me that the best alternative way home was by sea.

HMS *Fearless*, and her Captain, Jeremy Larken, had given us superb support throughout the winter deployment and I wanted to repay him and many of his officers, chiefs, POs and ratings who had helped us.

To thank them all I threw a Black Velvet party in the tank deck as the ship rolled and pitched her way south from the Arctic. *The Black Pig's* crew mixed a vast amount of champagne and Guinness in the same dixies that, a generation before, would have contained the daily mix of rum and water.

We arrived in good order at Plymouth on 19 March, 1982, and I returned to Poole to write my trials report, pack for leave and prepare for the handover of the Branch to Roger Dillon after Easter.

I had arranged to attend a course in London on 'Oil, Islam and the Middle East' for the last two days before leave and persuaded Poole's Chief Training Officer, Major Mervyn Wheatley (a well-known *bon vivant* and great friend), to come with me. The Thursday night, the first and only night of the two-day course, coincided with the monthly dinner of the Royal Cruising Club of which Mervyn was not then a member; but it was a good opportunity for him to meet many who were. We went to bed very late.

I was woken on 2 April by the ringing of a telephone and a voice that I instantly recognized as my Adjutant's asking for Mervyn Wheatley. Believing that our illicit absence from the university, for which the MOD were paying our fees and London subsistence, had been discovered, I feigned ignorance of anyone of that name at that address – wrong number. No, the Adjutant insisted, it was the right number and he hoped that Wheatley would be able to tell him where Ewen Southby-Tailyour was. I came clean.

"You bastard! Where the hell have you been?"

I explained that we were off to the University that moment. A little late, I agreed.

"Forget about the bloody University. The Argentinians have invaded the Falkland Islands and you are wanted back here immediately with all your charts."

"You're joking!"

"No I am not."

He had every reason not to be amused.

On the journey to Poole we managed to obtain snippets of news. There was no official word that the Islands had been invaded but all the signs were there. They just weren't being confirmed by the FCO.

We mused over the likely route any Royal Marine involvement would take and were certain, even at that stage, that it had to involve the Commando Brigade. Our limited knowledge of recent politics and fleet dispositions showed that this was possible but that it would take some time to activate, and might not then have been large enough or in time. We had failed to deter adequately. Would we now be able to attack adequately? – a much more costly exercise.

The Royal Marines, surprisingly, were unaware that as early as 29 March plans were being hurriedly prepared for a naval task force to be despatched south. These plans were being drawn up on blank pieces of paper for there had been no contingencies for such an event despite so many warning signs. As the embodiment of the Royal Navy's ability to project power ashore it remains a mystery why the Commando Brigade had to wait until 2 April to be stood-to, for by that time a sizeable fleet (by post-Suez standards) was already being mobilized, redeployed and sailed: thanks to the one military leader who held an unshakeable believe in the ability of his service. Admiral Sir Henry Leach was the First Sea Lord (also standing in as Chief of Defence Staff in his absence abroad) and alone among the service chiefs was prepared to offer, with justified optimism, a military solution. The army in particular wished to have little to do with what they thought would be humiliation and the area of operations was too far away for any sensible RAF involvement.

A car met us at Poole railway station and rushed me straight to the Colonel's office where his instructions were as clear as his Adjutant's had been some hours earlier.

"Pack your kit, take my car and report to the Brigade Commander in Hamoaze House as soon as possible."

As before, no time was to be lost. I tried to lose no time but there were one or two tasks that had to be completed before leaving Poole, possibly not to return.

The Landing Craft Branch had been mobilized, an action made considerably easier by the order being received just before everyone had left on leave.

The two Landing Platform Docks, HMSs *Fearless* and *Intrepid,* had been earmarked for disposal but contrary to a popular misunderstanding had been reprieved as the direct result of a visit by Mr John Nott (as he then was) to HMS *Fearless* and Royal Marines, Poole, on 23 November, 1981. (I had been a member of the presentation team formed to convince the Secretary of State for Defence of the importance of amphibious warfare in general and specialist ships in particular. It is popular to condemn Mr Nott for his decisions but he had the courage to listen to informed argument 'at the coal face' and reverse his earlier orders. This is an aspect too readily overlooked on purpose by those not prepared to give credit where it is due.)

The LPDs are 13,000-ton ships with a small flight deck and a dock. They can operate support helicopters from two spots, while beneath, the dock floods to float out four one-hundred-ton landing craft (Landing Craft Utility or LCU) each designed to carry two main battle tanks. The ships also carry four smaller landing craft (Landing Craft Vehicle and Personnel) on davits, each of which can carry thirty troops equipped for temperate climate operations. Internally the ships can embark a squadron of tanks with their own supporting wheeled vehicles or a total of about 85 mixed Land Rovers and four-tonne vehicles. Their 'passenger' load is about 300 men in normal conditions but this can be almost doubled for short periods. The ship's complement is about 550. I say 'about' for over the years various additions and subtractions had been made to each ship.

Instead of 'disposal' it had been decided that one of the ships should be on duty with the second in what was euphemistically called 'preservation by operation', another name for deep refit with the crews dispersed throughout the fleet. In 1982 *Fearless* was 'in commission' with *Intrepid*, just into her 'P by O' as it was known.

The wartime role of my men at the Landing Craft base was to man the off-duty LPD with the Officer Commanding Landing Craft Branch designated as the Amphibious Operations Officer. The AOO (invariably a Royal Marines major, although not necessarily a landing craft specialist) is the Captain's amphibious expert, a link between him and the embarked force, and, when the ship is flying the flag, the staff of the Commodore Amphibious Warfare. A fully trained landing craft captain always commands the Detachment of about one hundred. I had been the Officer Commanding *Fearless's* Amphibious Detachment (OCAD for short or, in the Sergeants' Mess, known more colloquially as Oh Christ Another Disaster) for three glorious years in the early 70s.

That was the 'war' plan. This time, the only time it had been enacted, the men who had come ashore from *Intrepid* when she paid off had joined Poole to release those on training jobs to go to sea in *Fearless*. So, the men then at the landing craft base were already a trained team and it was reasonably simple for them to rejoin their old ship. The ex-AOO was still available and so Major Malcolm Macleod returned in that capacity, which was just as well for I was to be required elsewhere although as I mobilized my 'new' command I did not then know that.

That morning, in the train, I had started a log, not knowing quite what prompted me to jot down events so soon into what was yet an unlikely involvement from my point of view.

"*There has been no problem with the recall due to the efficiency of the 2IC (Tim Barratt). Thank God for excellent people on whom one can rely at all times but particularly in times of crisis, so now − 1700 − off to HQ Commando Forces in Plymouth.*"

The Brigade is actually stationed about a mile or so from Commando Forces but on this occasion and for those early hours much of the planning was being conducted together in Hamoaze House and not Stonehouse. As soon as I entered the familiar building it was obvious, at least to my untrained eye, that at this stage such close co-ordination with the HQ staff was vital and made absolute sense. All the orders coming from London were received and processed by the General's staff; it saved time and effort to have the Brigade staff on hand to discuss and interpolate reactions to each piece of new information.

A swarm of staff officers, commanding officers, clerks and signallers mingled in hasty activity. Arms and papers waved in the air; groups of anxious-faced men ebbed and flowed like amoeba. I was reminded of the floor of the Stock Exchange on a busy day and wondered 'where on earth would I fit in to that well-trained team'. If I had given it any thought at all (and apart from the brief discussions in the train I hadn't) I would have expected to be milked of the notes and photographs that I possessed, thanked, and then sent back to Poole to supervise the employment of my men into an operational ship already with its own AOO. I would not have expected to play any further part in the saga.

I reckoned without Brigadier Julian Thompson, an old friend. In Aden he had been the senior subaltern when I commanded a half-troop at Dhala on the Aden/Yemen border. Later on he had been the Brigade Major, serving at times in HMS *Fearless* when I had acted as the amphibious adviser to the then Brigade Commander on the practicalities of the art. Julian was also the only other person to whom I had lent my yacht, the first *Black Velvet*. He was to become the Commodore of the Royal Marines Sailing Club when I was the Rear Commodore.

The Brigadier was standing in the middle of the room surrounded by questioning staff, issuing instructions calmly and absolutely clearly, as though born for the moment. He has a highly intelligent and quick mind and had learnt, through his close study of military history, not to repeat others' mistakes. He knew exactly what he wanted and was refusing or accepting all types of advice from his service advisers with their specialist knowledge. He wanted more of some commodities, less of others. Each suggestion was considered, weighed up and decided upon. He was in his element and I remember thinking what a superb stroke of luck that this latest crisis was occurring during his command of the Brigade.

We did not know at that moment if all that would be required of the Brigade would be merely to sail and poise — a well-established and vital factor in Amphibious Warfare useful for bringing pressure to bear without commitment. All we did know was that deploy we must and there was no point in doing that without a balanced force ready for absolutely anything: traditional Amphibious Warfare routines, traditional Royal Marines work.

As it was the Brigadier who had called for me I felt that it was to him that I should report. Feeling as though my part was too minor at that stage to warrant an intrusion, I hovered in the background waiting for a sensible moment to interrupt.

Julian saw me 'poising' and turned:

"Have you brought your maps and charts?" He knew about my earlier work through the Royal Marines Sailing Club.

"Yes, Brigadier."

"Right. Come and tell me all you know."

To tell him all I knew would have taken rather more time than he had and would have consisted, apart from describing a year of practical experience, showing him over a thousand photographs and numerous pencil and watercolour sketches. I had under my arm at that precise moment a role of annotated Admiralty charts and a box of slides and prints − a small selection of what was on offer.

"Brigadier," I said, "I have about a hundred and fifty drawings, over a thousand photographs, two hundred pages of notes and a dozen or so annotated Admiralty charts. It might take some time." Seeing an opportunity slipping away unless I struck, I added, "and I'm not going to tell you a thing unless you agree to one condition."

I thought as I said it that I might have overstepped the mark.

"What is that?"

"You take me with you."

"Done!" he said. I was on my way and there was no further discussion.

"Now, come and tell me where we start."

We sat down in a corner with the Brigade Major. They both listened for a few minutes and then stopped me. My enthusiasm had taken over.

"The best thing is for you to prepare a brief for everyone who needs it and I will slot it in to my first Orders Group. At the moment we need to know all about the Islands − where they are, what they are like − nothing specific. Just get us all thinking along the same lines."

The two officers left and I sat down again. A catch-all brief was required and one that could, for the time being, be all things to all men. The first person to hear it was the Brigadier himself an hour or so later, taking rough notes as I spoke.

I decided that it was as well, before anything else, to get across the topography and climate. Under these two general headings I spoke of the painfully slow 'going' across country, the beaches and coastline, the settlements, the absence of roads, the sparse population, the lack of food, water and repair facilities outside the tiny communities and even there these would be very limited indeed. This was an important point to emphasize at the very beginning. It was, in my mind, vital that everyone understood the physical problems we would face if called upon to land — for that would affect the equipment, stores, clothing and food that we would be packing in the hours left to us. We had to get this right at the very beginning.

Various staff officers sitting in at this first informal brief followed the Brigadier with individual questions.

The quartermasters wanted to know about the availability of fresh food and water. There was none, at least not in the quantities that they were interested in. I had to repeat this unpalatable fact many times.

The transport officers wanted to know about the availability of petrol and the 'trafficability' of the ground. There was no fuel in the quantities that they were hoping for and 80% of the 4,700 square miles was covered by peat bogs. In my humble view, I suggested, the Volvo oversnow vehicle with which the Brigade was equipped would be a Godsend.

Boots! Everyone wanted to know what to wear and what to advise their men to pack. I made it clear that although 'wellingtons' were ideal for daily work something more military was required for long-distance cross-country movement carrying heavy loads. I thought the ideal boot would be the heavy leather 'ski march' boot with which so many of the Brigade were issued for North Norway. The weather would be turning foul as we spoke — if it had not already started to do so — and snow would lie on the ground for about seven days in each month. And so the questions went on.

I needed to make a cool clear-headed assessment of the help and information I could offer and then tabulate that into military form filtered of all unnecessary 'civilian' detail. (I was to change my mind on this point.) It needed to be assimilated easily and quickly by those to whom the area was as unknown as the far side of the moon.

I drove home to write formal lecture notes slightly surprised to find that the long day had only ended at midnight. It felt like 0400.

The 3rd of April, and it already seemed as though the saga had lasted considerably longer than one day. That morning I set up my 'shop' in the old ballroom of Hamoaze House with a blackboard and easel alongside a trestle table on which I placed just about everything 'Falklands' I possessed. To leaven the military bread a little I reversed my earlier decision and displayed examples of Falkland Islands wool, spun and raw, and various articles of local culture and art. It was as well that people immersed themselves as fully as possible in their subject and be given an all-embracing view of the place that was to dominate their lives for the foreseeable future. The Islands had to be brought to life in as wide a dimension as practicable.

On a small three-foot by two-foot map I scribbled rather quickly in blunt, felt-tipped pen the briefest of résumés against the most likely places in East Falkland where we could land or anchor. Alongside San Carlos for instance I wrote:

"Sheltered. Dominated. Good forming up positions. 65 miles by land from Stanley. 92 miles by sea."

Bay of Harbours (and Low Bay) was described as:

"Sheltered. Few landings. No dominating features."

Cow Bay:

"Poor tracks to Stanley. Bogs. Good beaches but open to the weather and the enemy."

I drew arrows along various land routes from the possible beaches or helicopter landing zones. One set of arrows approached Stanley from the north-west via Douglas and Teal Inlet, another marked a southern route from Darwin via Bluff Cove and yet another suggested a route from the upper end of Port Salvador via Mount Kent.

It was a much pored-over map.

During the morning I pieced together the slides for the initial briefing due the following day and discussed many aspects of the Islands with the Brigadier. The thought uppermost in an amphibious commander's mind must be the where and how of the first foot ashore. Until recent years the 'how' had not been a problem — we had had the ships and helicopters: the 'where' was not usually a problem either for we had intelligence and contingency plans for our NATO, and most likely 'out-of-area' objectives. The 'where' in 1982 was about to be discussed in great detail. The 'how' was to become a real worry.

The two commando helicopter squadrons (845 and 846 Naval Air Squadrons) were earmarked for the Brigade, which was hardly surprising as their *raison d'être* was to support it, and there were already rumours that the troop-transport problem would be solved by the Peninsula and Orient Steam Navigation Company. The ships we should have had simply did not exist any more. *Bulwark* and *Albion* (Commando Ships converted from 24,000-ton aircraft carriers) had been scrapped, whilst HMS *Hermes*, although once converted to a similar role, had reverted to anti-submarine duties. Just occasionally she exercised in her secondary, commando carrying, role.

Many things drove home to the practitioners of the amphibious art the emasculation we had already suffered and with which we were further threatened, but nothing did so more convincingly than the lack of troop lift ships with helicopter spots. With the loss of these specialist ships from which an initial assault can be launched in strength the country had lost a major defence option and in April, 1982, life was going to be difficult enough anyway against superior numerical forces without the added restraint of being unable to use our primary form of swift assault — the medium lift helicopter — when we were to need it most.

But the only multi-spotted ship available in April was the one LPD with just two spots. Transporting a Brigade (and one that was nearly the numerical strength of two) to the Amphibious Objective Area (the AOA — or, put very simply, the anchorage and hinterland where the first foothold would be placed) would be one thing — at that moment unresolved — but getting it ashore in an assault posture was going to be quite a different problem no matter what ship, short of a 'flat top' was offered up. The two aircraft carriers were already earmarked to operate Harriers; there would be no room for marines until the last minute (if at all) and that would mean a helicopter cross-decking operation from whatever troop transports we were to be given. There were none with even one helicopter flight deck.

The rumour that the cruise liner SS *Canberra* was about to be requisitioned was, if true, excellent, even if she was unable to land her passengers in assault, but it was a start.

The logistic support of the Commando Brigade (not usually involved in the initial landings) was to be carried, as always, in their specialist ships, the Landing Ships Logistic. LSLs were, and still are, 'maids of all work' (named, though, after six Knights of the Round Table) with two helicopter spots, although the forward one is usually cluttered with vehicles or the restraining wires for the side-carried mexeflotes. These 'mexes', low, flat, self-propelled barges of up to 126 feet in length, are capable of carrying one ton per foot in round figures. Although slow and ponderous, they are invaluable for landing heavy equipment in the absence of suitable beaches for their mother ships.

At 5,500 tons the LSL can carry 500 military passengers, but of greater importance is their ability, in time of war, to land heavy equipment such as tanks, repair and supply vehicles or bulk fuel, directly onto the beach. This is obviously an evolution not conducted until the beachhead is well established and secure. Despite their obvious advantages, they were not assault ships.

Unknown to us other than via the rumour network, the previous afternoon, 2 April, the General Manager of the Peninsula and Orient Steam Navigation Company had been summoned, with his Fleet Operations Manager and his own Assistant, to attend a meeting in Whitehall "within the hour."

Among many questions concerning fuel and resupply was: "Can

Canberra land heavy helicopters on board and if not is there anywhere that can be converted to accept them?"

While in the Mediterranean *Canberra's* log for that day read the same as it probably did for most days:

"Course and speed as necessary for the comfort of passengers and to achieve planned ETA in Southampton, England."

Late that night the Captain, Dennis Scott-Masson, received a telex:

"...advise urgent, repeat urgent by return, estimated time passing Gibraltar — signed Peninsula."

The immediate reply read:

"ETA Europa Pt 042200."

A military planning party were on their way the next day, joining the ship during her brief and unscheduled stop in Gibraltar. Few knew the meaning of their presence on board, or indeed, perhaps, that they were on board at all.

On 5 April P & O received a letter from the Department of Trade which, considering the import, was remarkable in its brevity:

"The Secretary of State for Trade in exercising the powers conferred upon him by the Requisitioning of Ships Order 1982 hereby requisitions the SS *Canberra* and requires you to place the said vessel at his disposal forthwith.

"The vessel should proceed immediately to Southampton Berth 105.... A further letter will be sent to you regarding the charter party arrangements which it is proposed to apply to the SS *Canberra*."

I particularly liked the reference to the Charter Party!

At 0730 on 7 April *Canberra* secured alongside her usual berth in Southampton, as instructed, and immediately began the transition from cruise liner to amphibious transport or, in military parlance, LSLL — Landing Ship Luxury Liner!

Whatever facilities for transporting men to the Amphibious Operating Area *Canberra* may have possessed, she could not boast a flight deck capable of accepting even a Scout helicopter. If helicopters were to lead the assault the men would have to be transferred to a 'flat top' well in advance of H Hour, for even the two proposed helicopter spots would not have allowed a simultaneous landing in force. If landing craft were to spearhead the assault then they would still have to transfer well in advance to a ship with suitable docking or mooring arrangements (rather than the tiny side ports). None of this could take place within the AOA for fear of compromise and the lack of surprise. As she was already earmarked to carry three of the four commandos or battalions that made up the 'bayonets' of the Task Force she had to be involved in the initial assault. But how? Either way men would have to be cross-decked. A landing craft transfer pre-supposed good weather (in the south Atlantic in autumn?), a lee under the land (which land?), air superiority (the air threat was formidable) and plenty of time (always a commodity in short supply). Although in the future, the method of landing is uppermost in a staff planner's mind when conducting the loading of the shipping and the move out from the home base.

Although we knew that *Hermes* was to accompany us south we knew that she could not sail with a commando embarked, for her primary role had been altered to that of anti-submarine warfare and to that would be added the role of 'Harrier-Carrier'. At least just for the landings, she could, we hoped, embark a commando for that vital and near-instantaneous first foot ashore; and if that was in the dark she could be back on station supplying combat air patrol (CAP) shortly after dawn. Or so we thought. All this pre-supposed much, but held the seeds of many thoughts in the early days.

It was, as Julian Thompson pointed out:

"Flight decks or the operation is off!" We were given flight decks but only enough for limited cross-decking, administration and logistic re-supply, not for an assault. (Incidentally, as I write this in 1992, we still have no flight decks and thus no assault capability.)

The day wore on. Snippets of news filtered down to Hamoaze House. One battalion of the Parachute Regiment would come under command. This was indeed excellent news. The CO of 22 SAS, Lieutenant-Colonel Mike Rose, telephoned offering his Regiment's services. Ships of all sizes and shapes began to appear on the itinerary; all the LSLs were earmarked; *Canberra* would have two helicopter spots, not enough for assault purposes but useful for cross-decking and communications. The carrier group of *Invincible* and *Hermes* was due to sail on 5 April.

I started the second day of the crisis with an early drive into Hamoaze House. Julian Thompson presented a full briefing of the problem as he saw it. This briefing began at 1000 with, traditionally, the 'ground' paragraph. It was the second of sixty-nine presentations that I was to give on the Falklands during the campaign.

I had been told to make my introduction as informative as possible and to impress upon the audience that the Falklands were no ordinary place in which to be going to war. I had to emphasize that we were not discussing a 'typical piece of north-west European countryside' as so many had assumed, partly, I suspect, because they are a British colony at the same latitude south as London is north.

I began my part of the 'O' group with a true story. Before flying to the Islands in 1978 I had met an imperial woman at a farewell cocktail party. She announced to me, and the other guests, in a loud voice that her husband had been appointed Governor of the Falklands.

"But he had to turn it down as I can't stand the heat, y'know!"

At that moment I switched on the slide projector to show a shot of the wreck of the *Lady Elizabeth* snowbound in a summer blizzard.

I spoke for about twenty minutes with a continuous display of slides to illustrate every point. The sunshine; 1,600 hours a year compared with Plymouth's measly 1400. The rainfall: only 25 inches a year. The temperature range: between an equable 21°C to a mere -6°C (warmer than Norway). The wind; an average of 17 knots in the austral winter increasing to 18 knots in the summer (the single most dramatic difference — Plymouth's average is 4 knots!). The sea temperature range: between 9-11°C in the summer and 3-6°C in the winter. I reminded the audience that the Islands lay south of the northern limits for icebergs and that the extreme northern limit for pack ice was only 200 miles south.

I explained the settlements with no outlying population; the lengthy coastline of about 15,000 miles surrounding 4,700 square miles of land 85% of which was covered with peat bog. I explained the lack of transport or roads and the slow speed of advance across country (four mph for Land Rovers and only one mph or less for fit men on foot); the dearth of communication systems other than private wireless transmitters; the absence of newspapers and television. In many respects I conveyed the feeling of a small Utopia, providing one liked isolation and was self-reliant. I meant it that way. There may be many faults, to British eyes, in the Falklands way of life, but I did not want to dwell on those or even suggest them. I wanted, on purpose, to instil a feeling of revulsion that such an idyll could have been threatened by an outsider.

I sat down to a surprised silence. Although most COs had discussed the place with me individually, having it brought to life with slides and a strong script amid the formality of a military briefing was quite another matter.

Various Brigade staff officers then followed with more prosaic matters until the briefing was summed up by the Brigadier. We were now all part of a team, with one aim and that team was part of an even greater band. I felt that we had crossed the first of many start lines.

As we broke up after two hours of intensive exchanges and questions, Mike Rose, with his second-in-command from 22 SAS, tapped me on the shoulder. I had not met Mike before but his 2IC and I were acquaintances from the Oman where I had commanded a company of the Northern Frontier Regiment in the Dhofar war. Mike needed a private brief covering possible landing sites and detailed information on problems such as the building of hides outside settlements and survival in general. He was keen to understand more about the possibilities of infiltrating the civilian population of Stanley. I was able to help on all counts.

I was summoned from this private briefing by Julian Thompson. He and Mike Clapp, now the Commodore Amphibious Task Group (COMAW, to his colleagues and staff) were off to brief the Commander-in-Chief Fleet, Admiral Sir John Fieldhouse, at Northwood, who had now taken on the mantle of Task Force Commander.

Mike Clapp and I had met a few times over the previous months. An officer with a devastatingly calm manner under all conditions, he was the first Fleet Air Arm Observer to have commanded a Buccaneer squadron, and in action during the Borneo campaign. Some, more senior to him, saw his very quietness as a sign of weakness and exploited this shamelessly; but not those who served with him and saw the challenges put upon him and the manner in which he met those pressures. Although we did not know it then Julian Thompson and Mike Clapp would be the architects of the initial first foothold, without which everything that was to happen subsequently would be still-born. The Commodore's duty was to land the Brigade in the right place, at the right time, in the right order and without significant loss, after which Clapp's ships would revert to supporting the land forces, while, throughout these operations, and the lengthy sea approach to the AOA the Carrier Battle Group would defend the amphibious forces in the air, on and under the surface and with naval gunfire and fighter ground-attack aircraft. Nobody in amphibious forces believed, even then, that there could be any other successful method.

From the beginning COMAW should have answered directly to his commander, the Flag Officer Third Flotilla (or Flag Officer Carriers and Amphibious Ships in the old parlance) and we expected this highly experienced officer to be given overall command at sea. Rear Admiral Derek Reffell was an expert in Amphibious Operations and knew many of the personalities (he had commanded the assault ship HMS *Albion* and had himself been COMAW), but we were to wait in vain for this appointment to be made and instead an officer with no previous experience of amphibious or air warfare was to assume command of the Carrier Battle Group with the responsibility for protecting the amphibious shipping. It cannot be denied that this caused a number of unnecessary problems, for although COMAW was to be told that they were three separate commanders (the third was Thompson as the Landing Force Task Group Commander) with equal access to Northwood, the Carrier Battle Group Commander was to "meddle a great deal and muddy the waters." A more attentive *'primus inter pares'* (for that is what Rear Admiral John Woodward's appointment was to be) would have made for smoother and more equable decision-making, although better still would have been Admiral Reffell as the on-the-spot commander with the appropriate rank of Vice Admiral.

I grabbed my briefing pack and drove to The Longroom football pitch to join a Lynx helicopter. Major General Jeremy Moore was also attending the briefing, although at that stage he was not in any executive command; but it was his major formation that was on its way and he was responsible for all commando forces and their supporting arms.

At Northwood we were escorted by armed Royal Marines down 'The Hole'. This underground, nuclear-proof headquarters of the Fleet was dug alongside a rather more spacious and airy modern office block on the surface. I knew 'The Hole' from various previous incarnations, not least when I had been the Assistant Fleet Royal Marines Officer on the Commander-in-Chief's staff, responsible for all Royal Marines afloat in destroyers and frigates.

We entered the air locks and descended towards the bowels. To any sailor or marine it was similar to entering the 'citadel' of a warship: vast, heavy, airtight doors; long, straight passages; artificial lighting; artificial air; the hum of distant generators. All that was missing was a gentle pitch and role of the deck to make us feel really at home.

From the start, though, I felt out-of-place. There were seven of us in all, central to the briefing, while senior staff came and went bearing intelligence up-dates, questions and answers.

Vice Admiral David Halifax, the Chief of Staff, sat with CINC Fleet and an admiral I had not met before, but whom I recognized as FOF3, the officer we hoped would be despatched to join us.

My log describes the briefing:

"*I started the briefing by explaining the country and the weather in the FIs. COMAW expressed a desire to sail with his task force complete (the Battle Group having sailed in advance). It was agreed that there was no question of an assault taking place on the Islands until the sub-surface, surface and air battles had been won. In the middle of this meeting a Flash signal was received from HMS* Endurance *saying that he had been ordered to leave the area as he was within waters claimed by the Argentine. At the end of his signal he said 'Should I act belligerently?' Not bad for a ship miles from help with only two Bofors against an enemy frigate.*

"*There was much discussion on the way the land battle should be fought when it came clear to me that everybody in the room assumed the islands were some extremity of the Northern European continent. It is taking time for people to realize that this situation differs so much from NW Europe.*"

I made a note to emphasize this point even more strongly as it was clear that I was not getting the message across. I'm not sure that the problems, particularly of the speed of men and vehicles across country, were ever really understood by those back in the United Kingdom.

"We all agreed (quite extraordinarily, I was involved in the discussions) in the end that a naval battle followed by an unopposed landing and then a blockade with demoralizing raids on the enemy might be the best solution to bring him to heel. Major Roger Blundell, [a particularly great friend of mine who was my daughter's godfather, and with whom I had spent many happy hours sailing,] *was in attendance throughout and kept very busy indeed finding the answers to numerous questions.*

"It was agreed that an ultimatum should be issued and a cordon sanitaire declared on the 11th April with any transgressor sunk by the nuclear submarines now on their way.

"The problems over Canberra's *flight decks were aired and I again emphasized the importance of air cross-decking in the likely event that it could not be carried out by boat.*

"In the corridor outside and on our way to his private office the CINC took the Bde Cdr and me aside and said, 'It is going to be a sad and bloody business and I only wish I could offer you more ships'."

The visit achieved two firm commitments: amphibious operations were now clearly in the Commander-in-Chief's mind, as up to then our only mission had been to sail as quickly as possible to show political intent, and that being so it was agreed that no 'opposed' landings would take place and any that did would not do so until air superiority had been achieved.

"The 'on the spot' command aspects were not discussed, at least not within my hearing, but we all presume that Admiral Reffell's presence will mean his appointment as overall commander.

"On arriving back at Plymouth we debriefed the Bde HQ and COMAW staff and then home very late where I found Patricia in a bit of a state as the press, TV and news all day long seemed to have been extolling the virtues of the Argentinian armed forces while ignoring our own capabilities. Let us hope their patriotism prevails in the end."

The scenes of the huge build-up of Argentinian forces shown on the television seemed to be repeated *ad nauseam*. I caught a glimpse before turning in and was disturbed to find the coverage one-sided, with emphasis placed on the appalling weather and ground conditions that any British force would face against an overwhelming number of well dug-in and, by then, acclimatized enemy troops. There were, too, appropriate comments on the foreign and defence policies that had allowed this avoidable action to take place. It was a little late for the media to vent their corporate spleens; they should have done so with each successive defence cut and each Anglo/Argentine débâcle.

Early the next morning the Brigadier and I climbed back into the Lynx to head east again, this time to meet and debrief the ousted NP 8901 and the Governor, Mr Rex Hunt, due to arrive that morning from Montevideo via Ascension Island. For a landing craft officer I was already getting too much flying time.

As we boarded, the Brigadier asked me to prepare a list of questions to put to the incoming Marines that would help us in the final moments of our preliminary planning. I scribbled in my note thirty-five points including:

What has been the recent weather pattern?
Situation over the stay-behind OP.
How far has the road to Darwin been built?
State of Fitzroy road bridge.
State of Moody Brook bridge.
State of the private airfields.
Position of FIC.
Position over Admiralty fuel depot.
Position/state of old airfield.
Cable and Wireless aerials.
Were the troops equipped for living in the FIs?
State of the wrecks.
Position of Polish/Russian factory ships.
State of airfield facilities.

The Lynx stood back for the RAF VC 10 to land, parking two minutes later close to RAF Brize Norton's VIP lounge as Mr and Mrs Hunt and the Royal Marines were escorted in. Time was very short. To meet the 'team' in the lounge was a gathering of people; there were no formalities apart from the usual 'good mornings'. Perhaps it was hardly the home-coming the ex-prisoners of war were expecting; that would have to come later. The Governor, the officers and a few NCOs sat around low coffee tables where we joined them. Behind us officials hovered; one kept up a running commentary on the telephone to, apparently, 10 Downing Street. I was told that it was Mr Jerry Wiggin, the Minister of State for Defence, who seemed: "*rather bemused by the whole event.*"

Others in the background were members of the FCO, a major from the Army School of Intelligence at Ashford in Kent and members of the DIS, SIS, SAS and SBS.

I began the session by rattling off my questions first; almost every one giving rise to supplementaries. Most were answered by the 'new' Detachment OC, Major Mike Norman, rather than by the man with the greater experience of the Islands, Gary Noott. Later I was to write:

"Gary was in a slight state of shock and dazed whilst Mike knew little about the islands but only about the defence of GH."

I had hoped that Gary Noott might have been able to answer some of the questions that Mike, with his limited time in the Islands, simply could not have done, but he was not very forthcoming and, in many respects I learnt little of real value or that I could not have eventually worked out for myself once the facts of the invasion became known.

One of the problems I was anxious to explore was the whereabouts of the 'covert' section that had so carefully been written into the SOPs three years before. A report from the section which should have hidden opposite Government House before making their escape to Campa Menta Bay would have been invaluable, but everyone had been committed to the battle, which we had felt in our day would have been a poor use of resources against the expected odds. The loss of one section from the 'order of battle' would have made little difference to the outcome, but would have been a useful intelligence gatherer and, as originally intended, a briefing party for any advance force operations.

The questions were self-explanatory although I did not feel able to elaborate at the time why we needed to know, for example, the state of specific wrecks, nor the reason why we wanted to know which expatriates had stayed behind, nor why we needed to know the position of the Polish and Russian fish factory ships. In the background some surprised expressions were noticeable, but I kept my reasons to myself.

A pattern emerged of a colony taken by surprise by an army equally surprised by what it found. For their part the Islanders did not rush onto the streets waving long-hidden Argentinian flags which must have been rather disenchanting to the invader.

The enemy had come expecting to live off the land as far as food and water were concerned and be able to move across country by a fast and extensive road system. The answers to my questions showed that numbers alone would not make up for the lack of pre-planning that had accompanied the invasion. Too many men needing food and water could be a problem and would require a massive and continuous airlift which, given the promise of the day before, should be easily prevented. Their intelligence had been poor and they would suffer. The answers also showed that a naval blockade would be the best start to hostilities but no more, before a physical re-possession took place against an army reduced by poor morale, hygiene and nutrition. The army was largely conscript without the training and will-power to exist on survival rations alone. The more hardened regular soldiers would be better off and have a professional understanding of how to combat low morale brought about by meagre supplies and limited or non-existent shelter, but they were, apparently, in the minority. As we were to discover, the airlift I warned would be so vital to their war effort, once started, was to continue with little interruption by the British right up to the night before the Argentinian surrender.

The Brigadier and the General followed my lengthy question period with discussions on men, equipment and communications.

During the previous days we had gathered snippets of what had occurred militarily on the day the Islands were invaded. Now we were able to hear first-hand of the battle that took place and the immediate events that led up to it. There was talk at the time that the Royal Marines Detachment did not put up much of a fight and that the Argentinians had been ordered not to shoot to kill. I originally recorded this as fact, but I was wrong, as the ferocity of the attack against Moody Brook testified. My original SOPs had assumed that any attack would start with a pre-emptive strike against the Royal Marines barracks and in this I had been correct. Putting the Detachment at five minutes' notice to quit their accommodation − not necessarily five minutes' notice for action but to be away from the Brook − had been justified. Although the Noott/Norman detachment had had time, more than five minutes, to get out it was still gratifying to hear that, despite the loss of the camp, all men had been able to deploy to their pre-arranged positions.

The intensity of the attack against Government House, when it came, also dispelled any view that the Argentinians had meant no physical harm. Certainly no such orders were issued to the Detachment, allowing them to impose severe casualties amongst the Argentinian forces who led the assault. In the end I believe that better field craft, better camouflage, better fire and movement and better training were the dividends that paid most and ensured that all the casualties were taken by the enemy.

"Heard, too, that the 20 marines under A/Lt Mills from HMS Endurance had been landed at Leith Harbour in South Georgia and had shot down a Puma helo with small arms and damaged an Argentinian corvette with a Carl Gustav − good show.

"They were then captured and along with the British Antarctic Survey teams taken to Argentina. I can't understand why the Argies

118

have decided to repatriate the POWs as they would have been good for bargaining but maybe they don't expect us to fight back. They may be wrong about that.

"It became clear that the Argie SBS landed before dawn — possibly by helicopter in the Mullet Creek area then split into two parties attacking MB and GH. It would appear that they walked past the Sappers Hill OP without taking any interest in it. They have destroyed MB which was empty. Rather a pity really as, despite my efforts over the years, (and that of many other OCs) to have it replaced, suddenly I have become rather fond of it! Also they will have destroyed Patricia's curtains and cushions and my pictures. Once the dawn assaults had gone in, LVTs were landed at Yorke Bay and the airfield secured.

"Then they advanced on GH and a fire fight of about 1½ hours took place.

"One of the LVTs was engaged by a Carl Gustav from Surf Bay OP and nobody got out from it after it had stopped.

"Another LVT had a burst of GPMG fire through its open rear door. The door was shut and it moved on. Other LVTs were hit by 66 and 84mm but they just 'wobbled their bottoms and moved on'.

"Their prisoner handling at the beginning was fair and correct although there were no formal interrogations. The officers were split from the men. As they were moved back through the successive formations and units the treatment became worse and more contemptible."

I had not met Rex Hunt and was keen to do so for I had heard over the years what an effective Governor he was and the perfect choice for such a community. Before he left the VIP lounge, and with no wish to delay his departure for home, I thought hard for an excuse to introduce myself.

"Excuse me Sir. I have a Governor's flag taken after the Queen's Birthday parade in 1978. It never found its way back to GH. You might like to keep it." I didn't mention that a Wood Cottage mouse had eaten away a large section of the Falkland Islands crest in the middle. It was a lame reason for butting in but the only one available at the time.

"I would indeed — but my suggestion is that you get down there and put it back where it belongs!"

"I will."

On our arrival at Hamoaze House at lunchtime, Julian Thompson allowed himself a brief moment of irritation. The Royal Navy had announced that it was appointing a captain to be the senior embarked officer in SS *Canberra* and therefore, by inference, in command of the military units that would be sailing in her. It was the ideal catalyst for the Brigade Commander to appoint a deputy and have him sail in the liner. Colonel Tom Seccombe, a much respected and experienced commando officer who had served in almost every theatre of operations since he began his career, was exactly the man to be the buffer between the senior naval officer and the three strong-minded, strong-willed commando and Parachute Regiment commanding officers. It is difficult to say what problems this appointment prevented but it was a move much appreciated by the embarked forces. I mean no disrespect to the Senior Naval Officer, whom we meet later, but who was unknown to most of us then, but Colonel Seccombe's appointment was a shrewd move.

I was released early that afternoon, having completed my final round of general questions, briefings and de-briefings. The details would follow once we sailed. Everything that we needed had been earmarked and was either already at sea or on its way to a loading port. Like other members of the staff, I had 'personal admin' to sort out, not having had a quiet moment at home since well before April Fool's Day, so I drove home in my old, green Morris Traveller, sombre at the thought of the morrow, but also elated beyond belief that I was involved in something in which I could give positive and unique help.

Once again I was disturbed to find the television showing seemingly non-stop shots of Argentinians pouring into the islands while deriding the likely size and potency of Britain's answer. The children were upset to see 'tanks' rumbling past our old house. Suddenly they too realized the awfulness of what was happening to the place they knew and loved so well. The abiding image I held of my family throughout the conflict was to be of Hamish and Hermione watching those televised scenes.

I bought extra watercolour paints, films, started my packing and then slept well.

IX

Outward Bound

AN EARLY TELEPHONE CALL on the 6th had me scurrying out of bed only to be told that I was to remain at home until called forward for a 2330 flight that night from the Stonehouse Barracks Longroom football pitch. I was to join HMS *Fearless* by Sea King.

It was a relief! For the first time since the crisis began I could concentrate on the family and my personal affairs before setting off for an indefinite period of time − unlike the certainty of an exercise when one can plan ahead more constructively. Although this uncertainty existed, I was sure that we would be away for at least three months. Already we knew that we would have to stop somewhere to re-stow equipment and vehicles, carry out rehearsals and, possibly, diversionary landings. That much was guided by geography and our own philosophy of amphibious warfare and took no account of United Nations' prevarication − a real enemy to our timings prediction − and the resolve or otherwise of our Government. Deploying from the country quickly was the present priority as a show of determination. After that who knew what would occur?

The Government's resolve was already apparent − strong and unequivocal. From the military there was another aspect of amphibious warfare on offer to the Government, in addition to the speed with which we had reacted: the art of poising that I have mentioned earlier. Amphibious forces are a deterrent, over the horizon, that can advance without taking territory, can withdraw without giving up ground or losing face, can keep the vital element of tactical surprise intact right up until the last moment and which can then be wholly committed or act in small parts, can probe and re-probe at will and unexpectedly and can be added to or reduced with ease and with secrecy.

That last night before sailing I spent hours on the telephone answering questions from anxious relatives and friends, tying up odds and ends, cancelling plans for sailing races, holidays and lectures. One person I did manage to contact was an Islander on leave in England. Leif Barton was a member of one of the oldest Falkland families and married to 'Hamish' Maitland who had worked for the Grasslands Trials Unit during my time in the Islands. I needed her help with four questions:

1. Which Kelpers were in the UK whom we could contact for specific information on various areas?

2. A list of all radio 'hams' in the Islands with their call-signs and frequencies, and, if possible, their main contacts outside the Islands.

3. A list of all the occupied settlements in the Islands together with their owner's and manager's names.

4. Any Argentinian sympathizers among the Islanders both in the UK and at home.

I knew this last list would be short, if it could be compiled at all.

Just as I was about to put the receiver down Leif made a remark I was never to forget and one on which I based a number of ideas and suppositions concerning the long-term future.

In the Islands, three years before, I had often discussed the Kelpers' predicament in the likeness of Damocles and the sword above his head. As long as the threat of invasion existed there was concern and worry, probably of the unknown rather that the actuality. It was, for instance, accepted that some facets of Argentinian involvement in everyday life were more convenient, and would come more cheaply from that country than from the United Kingdom — domestic oil, tertiary education, medical support and air mail for example.

"Ewen," Leif said, "the sword has fallen. There is no threat any longer. It's happened." As a piece of Falkland Island logic it was unbeatable; nor did it mean, in any way, that she approved — indeed quite the opposite — but I understood very clearly what she meant. The fact that it could be replaced by a greater threat in due course did not occur to either of us.

"The TV news is now a little less dramatic about how bloody and difficult our job is going to be. I hope they go on giving us support because the wives and families will need their morale boosting more than we will for we will be very occupied and will, anyway, know the truth and not have to read between the lines of the media reports."

The call to embark at the football pitch came at 1700 for a flight at 1800. There was little time to make the RV as the inward journey against the rush hour could take three-quarters of an hour. It was fortuitous that there was no time for lingering over farewells at home.

I needn't have been in such a panic for only the fire crew in their white fearnought asbestos suits huddled out of the drizzle in the lee of the spectator stand. A trailer with our suitcases soaked up the West Country showers. Behind us lay Plymouth Sound, flat and grey and lifeless: occasional squalls off the northern shore of Drake's Island, intensified by heavy rain, clawed at the surface. Tiny white wavelets bomb-bursted outwards, providing the only colour in that drab scene. The Island, a hundred feet below and a third of a mile away, was only just visible. It would have been a depressing evening at any time. We took photographs of each other: Hermione in tears, aware only that whatever was happening was not good news, Hamish anxious to see a helicopter at close-quarters and Patricia in a sombre but calm mood. It was one of only two moments during the saga that I wished I was somewhere else, preferably at home in front of the great open fireplace or peacefully at anchor off a tree-clad river bank.

Slowly the other staff appeared. Through the mist and with little audible warning two Sea Kings rounded the eastern coast of Drake's Island to settle gently but suddenly noisily onto the grass.

Julian Thompson came across to Patricia and shouted above the din: "Don't worry about Ewen. He's too valuable for me to let him out of my sight and I will be nowhere near any action!" It was good for Patricia to hear but I hoped it wasn't going to be true.

We had said our last goodbyes before the others arrived, which was just as well for Hamish only had eyes for the nearest aircraft as we struggled into its belly with our small cases. The heavy luggage was loaded into the second machine. I have never travelled in a Sea King with every seat full and assumed because of this that HMS *Fearless* was close. I was wrong and through the port window behind my head I watched the familiar cliffs of first Bolt Tail, then Bolt Head, Prawle Point and finally Start Point flash past above us. We were flying low and fast to the south east for a rendezvous somewhere towards the Portland end of Lyme Bay. I didn't mind so long as we could land when we got there and didn't have to return because of weather to go through the whole 'farewell' process over again. Talk was impossible. Lines of silent faces nodded and shook with the aircraft's natural movement accentuated by buffeting from the southerly near-gale, some, eyes half closed, others wide-eyed; all forced into deep individual thoughts. Despite the lack of verbal contact there was an air of personal tension.

After an hour the familiar flaring of the aircraft as it lost speed before turning sharply over a brilliant white and translucent green wake were all the signs we needed before *Fearless's* stern moved slowly aft below the open door. From now on we could only look forward to victory or defeat, political or military, before thoughts of return would be allowed to dominate our minds. We had crossed the second startline with Soggie Oggieland, as the sailors call Devon, already far away.

Fearless was steaming westwards into a damp evening and through a slight swell and moderate sea. I didn't linger on the flight deck longer than it took to gather my few belongings, although I did stop at the top of the ladder by the flight deck control caboose, (known as Flyco) long enough to see all my heavy kit offloaded from the second helicopter. I had once watched my trunk and two suitcases being ditched into the English Channel from a net underslung below a Wessex as the aircraft came in to land on the old Assault Ship HMS *Bulwark* at the start of a three-month Mediterranean deployment.

The Brigadier and Commodore seemed pleased with the speed and efficiency of the loading and sailing and with the general arrangements for the special kit and equipment that had been assembled. All acknowledged, though, that without an aim other than to sail as hastily as possible it was difficult to know for what we were planning. Now that we had actually cut our ties with the mainland we could assess what had been achieved. Were the stores and ammunition scales likely to be correct? Was the equipment and balance of supplies adequate for the unknown duration, the fickle climate, the unfamiliar ground? Nobody knew.

My first impressions are best described in the words of the moment:

"Arrived onboard Fearless *somewhere in Lyme Bay I imagine, after an hour's flight. Conditions are pretty difficult. The two officers' accommodation 'flats' are covered one layer thick with Compo boxes as a false deck — luckily I am a short officer. There are stores and supplies everywhere. 4L1 mess deck is used as officers' accommodation.*

"I have been put into 02-22, a four-berth hole of Calcutta. Late night into bed as dreaded coming to the squalor and discomfort. In normal times four in the cabin would have been junior officers with little kit and still overcrowded. We have four Majors/Lt Cols with every possible piece of equipment and nowhere to stow it or to work. The gap between my bunk and the one above is so narrow that I cannot lie on my side or turn over without disturbing the guy above: and if I have one of 'those' dreams it could seriously embarrass him. Decide that I will have to seek alternative accommodation tomorrow. Too cramped to write anymore."

It was indeed cramped. Helped by a superbly cheerful wardroom staff, we had slowly disentangled ourselves and our kit from the aircraft and the piles of luggage at the forward end of the flight deck. The already long-suffering but equally cheerful Mark Gosling (the ship's Amphibious Operations Officer, responsible for, among other seemingly more important aspects, the accommodation of the entire embarked force) allocated us sleeping spaces. I'm not sure that he knew I was coming as I was not on the Brigadier's or Commodore's manifest. The junior officers had been allocated a ratings' mess deck (and were better off than almost any of the other staff — although it did take a day or two for them to realize this), while the more senior officers were in the two- and four-berth cabins. The most senior officers had their own permanently allocated cabins of one or two berths, although in some of these cabins extra camp beds were lashed to the deck.

At the last minute Mark, with glee, announced that as I was a friend he had found me a bunk in a four-berth cabin along the port passageway. It seemed like a good idea until I came to make use of it. By doing so he did me a great favour, unwittingly, for if I had spent that first night on the gunroom deck (as some did) I may not have been so moved to take subsequent action.

Early the following morning I padded along to the senior officers' bathrooms. Baths are *verboten* at sea for they waste precious water, even more so with the ship at 'overload plus'. I hoped that this tiny room leading off the showers had not already been allocated as some spare store or office space. It hadn't; but just to pre-empt any similarly inclined freedom-seeker I moved in my charts, slides and note books to make it look official. After a decent interval to allow Mark to recover from his patient and overwhelmingly tactful exertions of the night before, I asked if I might take over the bathroom as the Falkland Islands chart store, intelligence office and cabin. He was delighted for he had an officer who did not approve of being on a mess deck in the bowels of the ship and so was anxious to move him to a cabin. Personally I thought that any wide-open and pleasantly chaotic officers' mess deck (whether in the bowels or not) would be preferable to cabin 02-22! My decision to move out seemed to please everyone.

A friendly word with the ship's chippy and I had a chart table across the bath; a camp bed from the Wardroom Chief Petty Officer fitted alongside; my charts and kit filled the bath. It was nearly perfect; perfection itself being achieved when I realized that I could hear none of the incessant (but necessary) ship's broadcasts that broke into our lives every few moments during those difficult settling down days. Later on I would not be able to hear the regular and heart-chilling "Air Raid Warning Red, Air Raid Warning Red, the ship is under air attack." Peace and quiet. Luxury of a sort.

The first full day at sea (7 April) was spent by most people coming to terms with their new environment. There were some who had not served at sea before, most notably the two troops of the Blues and Royals with their light tanks, and, while the overcrowding was strange to us, the whole thing must have been a nightmare to them, but they fitted in quickly with humour and forbearance.

"News from Argentina is worse. Call up. 5,000 troops in the Islands and so on. Talks of mining the beaches — lengthening the airfield but this surprises me as it falls away to marsh at the beach and is rocky to the east. Perfectly possible but it will take time. Indeed it was originally planned to be much longer but cut short on FI Government insistence so that only Argentinian a/c could operate — such was the desire to appease their neighbours although at least fighters may now be unable to use it.

"Someone has put a notice on the door to my bathroom/office/cabin which reads 'Dependency of the Falkland Islands — Sovereign Territory — do not invade'. Some other joker has written underneath — 'Water conservation officer. Port only'."

These first few days were noticeable for the subdued atmosphere among many of the embarked force. The weather was not good and, perhaps, the frenetic activity of the previous days had not helped. People seemed to spend longer than usual finding their sea-legs. Thank goodness I have never suffered from sea-sickness, or ever taken a pill, and so was able to use this breathing space setting up my information centre with all notes, photographs and charts tabulated into orderly piles. I was pleasantly surprised to find that I could think of nothing that I had left behind.

During our second evening on board the wardroom was packed for an introductory talk on the Islands in general. There were no military undertones to the discussion. It was aimed at getting everyone thinking along the same lines from the outset. What we were going to do about the problem would come later. I covered everything I could think of with slides illustrating each facet of life: the style and system of government; history; education; currency; commerce; sheep; stamps; beaches; hinterland; weather; survival; wrecks; settlements; travel; krill in ships' intakes; birds as a flying hazard; peat bogs, stone runs, seal wallows as hazards for troops. Everything. I played a tape of wild-life noises and even managed a passable imitation, myself, of a gentoo penguin!

The most common question asked was: "What are they like?" The press had not helped with over-dramatic descriptions of the weather, although such vague expressions as 'Dartmoor surrounded by the sea' (quite accurate) or 'The Hebrides but sunnier and windier' (not bad) were among the more acceptable phrases. The point made was that they are quite simply unlike anywhere else.

After the talk and before changing for dinner, which I am glad to report was still held in Red Sea rig, I wandered, deep in thought, up to the starboard bridge wing. The weather was now poor with low flying cloud and a moderate to rough sea. I leant over the wooden-capped bridge-coaming and faced the wind and drizzle, for I needed a few minutes to think long and hard about what was facing us and my part in it. There was already a danger of my becoming too involved with the intimate planning, and that was not a good thing. Once or twice already I had had to stop and think before answering a question about some of the islands — Kidney Island off the entrance to Berkeley Sound and Carcass Island off the north coast of West Falkland. If this was to continue, I was going to have to balance my judgements very finely indeed if the information I gave was to be of any positive value. My love of the Islands was in danger of smothering my desire — indeed my duty — to give balanced objective assessments of places and plans. I went in search of the Brigade Commander.

Whether or not he and his staff, and Mike Clapp and his staff, had also come to the same conclusion I did not know but we agreed there and then that I would not be part of any planning team. I would answer questions, and comment only on plans once they had been drawn up, and even then only as far as the practicalities of such a plan were concerned. This would save me the embarrassment of having to decide, even subconsciously, on the angle to pitch my advice. Carcass Island (for instance) would have made an ideal 'stone aircraft carrier' for Harriers under certain circumstances but I would never have been able to face Rob and Lorraine McGill again if their beautiful and much loved paradise was to become the focus of our own attentions; worse still, any Argentinian retaliation resulting from our use. It was best, we decided, that I would describe, and leave the decision making up to those whose knowledge and understanding of the Islands was based only on military assessments and imperatives.

Slowly a routine grew out of the apparent chaos of those first days. Individual briefings at any time in every twenty four hour period became a regular feature to add to the routine evening staff briefings. In the tiny closed-circuit television studio I made a video of my lecture for distribution throughout the Amphibious Task Group, although I never knew if it was used, for I still spoke, face to face, to every man in the Commando Brigade. Perhaps it did get as far as the Carrier Battle Group and 5 (Army) Brigade (it certainly should have done), but I never found out.

The staff were all friends with whom I had served at some time or other earlier in my career. The Brigade Major, John Chester, had a no nonsense approach, a short temper kept under control and a sense of humour that would manifest itself quite unexpectedly. He was very easy to work with from my point of view, but, of more importance, he was well trusted by the Brigade's Commanding Officers.

David Baldwin, a staff officer without portfolio, had been the DAQ (or staff officer responsible for logistics and the personnel side of things) before handing over to Gerry Wells-Cole shortly before the invasion. He was one of very few men in the Task Force that I met who never lost his sense of humour or proportion of what we were about. This belied, though, a positive and determined desire to achieve perfection with amazing patience in all things he did. The decision to keep him on 'for the duration' was an inspired one.

Gerry Wells-Cole, a large officer, navy cricketer and family man with six children, had taken over the unenviable task of DAQ from David Baldwin; another positive character with a devastatingly calm way of making his point forcibly and with compassion. This last attribute was to be tested often, especially when dealing with the casualty lists, and was never found missing. Much of the campaign's success was 'logistic' and for that, too, the Brigade would be grateful for his presence in this thankless but indispensable task. (Surprisingly, his name was not to appear in the honours list.)

Ideas developed. To begin with the Brigadier's and Commodore's staff moved systematically around the islands producing plans for landing in all possible areas with mix-and-match forces depending on the natural and man-made circumstances. I was on call throughout the day and night to answer specific questions, each small presentation being preceded by a juggling of the slides so that not only were they different, which kept me fresh, but were absolutely relevant only to that specific area under discussion.

Many times a day the Brigadier's personal staff officer or the Commodore's secretary would seek me out with the request to call on the appropriate commander clutching maps, charts and photographs of 'such and such' a place. I would then lay out the relevant documents on the deck in front of the armchair. Most of these sessions were held late at night with the Brigadier in his dressing gown. He would point with his big toe: "What's that place like?" The foot would circle above a coastline and drop, quite suddenly, onto a desolate piece of Falklands territory. I would follow the descending toe and answer immediately or at least in enough detail to satisfy him that it was no good or that I should go away and get the full notes of that particular target. Although neither he nor Mike Clapp drank a drop during those days they were kind enough to allow me to appear with the occasional bottle of port while I tried to keep up with their very fertile minds and almost butterfly-like perambulations around the coasts — all fifteen thousand miles of them.

"Good beach, but narrow and shallow, good exits for troops and light tracked vehicles. Difficult approach but safe from enemy observation. The LCVPs will have no difficulty in the dark but the LCUs may ground five or so yards off shore. Will accept two LCUs at any one time or four

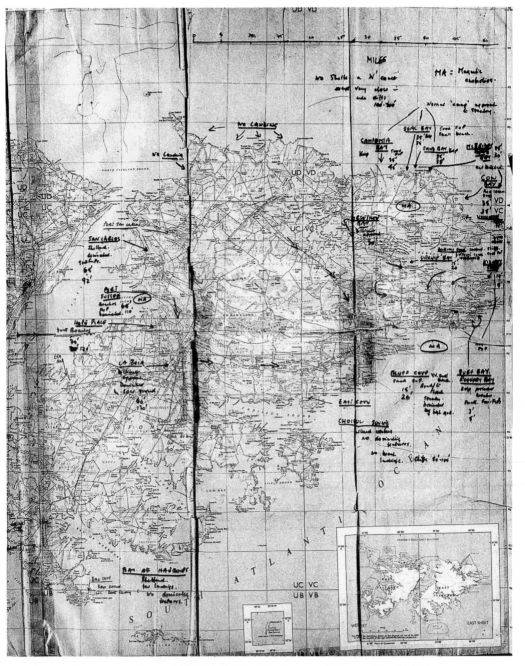

15. 2 April, 1982. "On a small three-foot by two-foot map I scribbled rather quickly in blunt, felt-tipped pen the briefest of resumés against the most likely places in East Falkland where we could land…and drew arrows along various land routes from the possible beaches and helicopter landing zones towards Stanley." Not a bad guess!

16. HMS *Fearless*.

17. The Great White Whale.

LCVPs. No mutually supporting beaches but not overlooked by high ground either. Open to the easterly swell which only occurs on one day in ten — and to exocet-armed aircraft. Submarines will have a clear and deep approach."

"Right. We need a full illustrated brief in two hours' time, now what about...here?" Feet or hands would descend upon another stretch of coastline.

I was constantly at full stretch trying to double-guess the commanders' minds and. then, when they pointed to somewhere unexpected, remembering as fast as I could if I had ever visited that particular place and if so what I had found. Was it tabulated in my note book? Did I have photographs or pencilled sketches? Was it covered in the *Admiralty Pilot*?

I had been joined in this exercise by a most valuable officer who, too, had personal reasons for going back. Unlike my love affair, John Thurman's was a double romance for he was engaged to the Governor's daughter whom he had met whilst serving with Gary Noott's Detachment. When the Islands were invaded he was with Diana Hunt in Greece on his end-of-tour leave, having been relieved early, in accordance with the decison made during my time in command.

John had walked nearly as many miles across the featureless plains as I had sailed past them, and arrived equipped with an astonishing collection of colour slides. To save time we indexed all our information together and divided the 'lecture aids' into easily referenced boxes so that we could quickly put together any presentation on any part of the Islands and from any aspect at the drop of a hat, or a big toe. The same slides were often needed for very different lectures one after the other and sometimes simultaneously. As we had no facilities for copying colour slides once we had sailed it was vital we kept very close tabs on them.

John, the most patient of men, took his task very seriously indeed. He was invaluable to me and eventually was to be much in practical demand by various units, for he knew the way across country better than most.

Our knowledge was constantly updated by photographs and snippets of information from Islanders on leave in the United Kingdom, but a paradox was that John and I probably had a better overall knowledge, for although many Kelpers knew everything there was to know about their own settlement few knew much about anywhere else in the detail we needed. John and I were able to piece together and dovetail into complete packages the information on, say, neighbouring settlements. Often we would be presented with photographs with vague descriptions on the back such as "View of islands near Salvador" and then spent many hours deciphering exactly what piece of coastline or what angle of a settlement we were looking at, and, having established that beyond doubt, then add the information, sometimes from very old pictures indeed, to our jigsaw.

During these early days we scoured the fleet, by signal, for any slides we could borrow for our mobile library. We did not worry about the subject. Almost any view, even if it was in the background to a family picnic, was of value if it showed landmarks or the 'going' under foot or a distant headland for identification of a beach. Information from those in England formed part of the regular mail, free-dropped into the sea alongside the fleet from a few hundred feet. Performing miracles for morale, the RAF Nimrods delivered papers (private and service), videos and newspapers direct to individual ships. Any reservations we might have harboured earlier about the embuggerances of travel by RAF Support Command were dismissed as we were kept informed, and in touch with home.

Our dossier on the Islands grew. The planners started off knowing nothing, but John and I like to think that by the time the Brigade landed they knew as much about their destination as they did about their operational areas in north Norway.

So it developed, with us returning to emphasize the same place many times, and sometimes not at all, as each option was filed away for possible future use, or never to be seen again. As far as I was aware at the time we had no directive that allowed us to harden our ideas to any specific area or task. Were we, for instance, to capture an outlying island as a show of our capability or were we to wait until the Argentinians capitulated politically or militarily through lack of will or lack of resources? I remained content not to know of any specific aim, for that way an unwelcome degree of subjectivity would have crept into my answers.

The fact that we had sailed ready for war (or, at least, equipped for it) in so short a time was proof enough of our intentions and was in itself as clear a message of the Government's determination as could be given. Galtieri's belief was that we would do just that. Sail. Nothing else. He believed that, after a suitable admonition in the United Nations against his initial invasion, the world would tire of Britain not accepting the new status quo. Any sympathy we might have accrued would evaporate with time, leaving us with no option but to accept defeat and go home. Initial American analysis had us being defeated − to the point that, unknown to us, they were prepared to send an aircraft carrier if we were prepared to man it. But as it happened international pressure did not build up against us to begin with and we could feel honourable about our military objectives. I'm not sure what happened to the aircraft carrier.

Individual briefings continued non-stop.

"Comment on the possibility that the enemy may have extended the runway in either direction."

"Can the SAS land by parachute in the valley to the north of Wickham Heights?"

"Which side of Tide Rock should a frigate pass?"

Colin Howard, the SBS Operations Officer (a friend from Pangbourne, who epitomized the dedicated professional, able with wonderful equanimity considering his job and responsibilities, to maintain a steady view on life and its humorous side), needed answers to all manner of questions to do with submarine operations and the insertion of his men into otherwise inaccessible coves and bays.

So the questions came and were answered, sometimes satisfactorily, sometimes less so, for we were not the experts others kindly had us to be and there were gaps in our knowledge.

After about ten days or so it was time I stopped being general in my approach and began my own own, non-military, brainstorming exercises on specific geographical locations. I therefore drew up lists of all the possible beach landing sites throughout East Falklands and, with John, prepared a list of possible helicopter landing sites that would either be in support of any beach operations or that could stand alone in advance of any seaborne assault. We divided the slide boxes up into easily processed areas so that the time from a question being asked to us being able to produce a comprehensive and structured presentation would be counted in minutes rather than hours. We took no account of any operational considerations. That was 'their' job, using our notes as a basis for discussion out of our earshot.

Having tabulated the beaches, including those that could not remotely have offered anything sensible except perhaps for the smallest of special forces landings, it was time to concentrate on survival.

I reminded the staff of the immense and continuous daily problem I had had of feeding my small Detachment of forty. This lack of food would help the attrition of the enemy's morale and fitness to fight unless he was supported regularly from the mainland. Fresh meat was available, but surprisingly few sheep are seen across the hills. Apart from the obvious examples of shipwreck or air crash, survival, by which I also included the ability to live off the land, could be the order of the day for many of the ground troops and it was as well that they learnt the problems peculiar to the Islands early on.

I started the Survival Paper on 10 April. It ran to seven pages and contained such gems as the usefulness of the Leopard seal when dead: its claws and teeth used as flensing knives or fish hooks; its skin for clothes or shelter; its intestines (when dried) as string for making the shelter or as fishing lines; its blubber for lamps and cooking and its meat for food, each eye containing enough vitamins for a man for twenty-four hours. I noted the value of diddle-dee roots for making a fire regardless of how wet the weather; how to catch the Upland Goose (this suggestion nearly backfired); where to, and how to, catch fish and collect water; what to eat and, of more importance, what not to eat. This last list was very short for there is only one poisonous berry (the Pig Vine Berry) and only one dangerous animal, the Leopard seal. I did not recommend eating any animal that fed off offal (particularly sheep offal), for the danger of liver fluke and hydatidosis was high.

After I had presented the survival notes as a lecture, the Brigadier decided to have a copy issued to every man in his formation, including the aircrew. I whittled the notes down as best I could and distributed hundreds of copies.

Also on the 10th we heard, officially, the news that Britain was declaring, with effect from 0400Z on 12 April, a 200-mile exclusion zone around the islands. I noted in my log that this was only a day later than planned by CINC Fleet on 3 April and showed what an excellent prognosis had been made so early on. It was heartily welcome.

This 'blockade' would then be followed by a naval surface, subsurface and air battle to enforce the declaration. A landing on South Georgia would follow (which was the first that many knew of such a plan) with a landing on an undefended part of the Falklands as a prelude to further action. It has to be said, though, that this last was not in accordance with the views of the Carrier Battle Group, who, we were told in *Fearless*, believed that the solution lay solely with the blockade.

On this day, too, there began to creep into my log strong references to the suspected power of the Argentinian Air Force. From my own limited experience I knew this to be a worry, but then all enemy air power is a worry to amphibious operations during their early and delicate stages. This worry was to dominate much of my thinking as we approached the Islands, for I knew that if 'they' got it right the prime targets would be the slow and ponderous landing ships and craft as they built up the logistic supplies ashore. It was the obvious weak link in any operation of this nature and a link that was not only weak in its ability to duck and weave and defend itself but a link which the troops ashore would need to defend vigorously before they could begin any advance. Some believed the carriers would remain the prime targets after a successful landing. I did not. In retrospect I probably became over-obsessed by the problem, but then I was not alone.

The original promise made at Northwood would have to be honoured if we were to land with any hope of victory. Attacking troops need an advantage, it is militarily accepted, of at least three to one in their favour *on the ground* and with superiority, if not supremacy, in the air. With this numerical factor in our case reversed and increased, the air factor was not only vital but without that superiority it would be suicidal. This was amphibious warfare not the central front. It was the promise that no land offensive would take place until we had that superiority that made us hopeful of a satisfactory outcome. That we would never achieve even air parity over the AOA and the enemy's air bridge was never to be broken was something we did not then know, thank goodness. Those who claim that this was not the case should be reminded that many of us did not once see a British fixed-wing aircraft throughout the campaign. In the first week alone in San Carlos we saw well over two hundred enemy aircraft and even on the last night of the war something like fourteen AAF Hercules flights landed at Stanley!

My log over the next five days or so tells of long briefing sessions in the Brigadier's cabin, General Haig's continuing shuttle diplomacy, intelligence on their mining activities, that 8,000 troops were now in place and the length to which the airfield had been extended. I believed this last to be:

> "...bluff on their part. I certainly do not believe the airfield extension. They have had a long time to dump food but water for 8,000 may give them a headache...
>
> "11th April. Easter Day. Matins and Holy Communion in the morning − a time to think of Patricia, Hamish and Hermione. We must fight the Argies but it does seem all slightly unreal. Which isn't a very Christian thought but then they weren't very Christian in the first place...
>
> "briefed the Naval Gunfire Support Officers on suitable fire stations for the frigates...
>
> "2300. Fearless has been ordered to Ascension Island 'with all despatch'. Good − let's get going!...
>
> "12th April...spent 7½ hours today in the Brigadier's cabin with slides of beaches and possible landing sites. A plan could be to hold the McBride Head peninsula then advance slowly south − stake out the Green Patch settlement area and secure that. Discussed Uranie Bay, Diamond Cove, and in particular, Kidney Cove. Pointed out good covert landing areas south of Stanley for SBS ops...
>
> "called to the Commodore's cabin at 2230 to discuss insertion of SBS with Brigadier and COMAW. SBS will go in on 18th to observe. If they are caught they will say they were part of the original NP 8901...

"Others, outside the Amphibious Task Group, are also studying the options. They were talking of Low Bay in a signal from CINC Fleet. Never heard of it — think they must mean Cow Bay — unless they mean the Low Bay in Lafonia which is laughable as a landing area — operationally and physically. Cow Bay — not a bad beach but terrible hinterland....

"Now producing info for Brigadier on likely enemy strengths the settlements could support. Food and water and so on. I have calculated how long they could last if they kill all the sheep and cattle...

"Brigade and COMAW staff gave a cocktail party in the evening (13 April) for the ship's officers — a most relaxed affair and a good tonic...spent 3 hours after dinner briefing Brigadier and service advisers on positions of assets if I was Gen Menendez guarding Stanley. Brain working overtime. Bed at 0330. Long day...

"14th April...another non-stop day preparing brief for CINC Fleet when we arrive at Ascension Island — must emphasize our problems in moving across country: about 1 mph on foot and 4 by vehicle...worked all afternoon and evening on FI beaches...for Top Secret signal to London...explained that kelp (which they seem terrified of) is no problem to a local and can be more of a help than a hindrance...love of certain areas does not help objectivity...briefed the Staff Medical Adviser on medical problems in the Islands...wanted to write to Patricia but simply no time and too tired...

"15th April...briefed the Bde Cdr — just the two of us — in the afternoon. Now discussing setting up FOB/FAB on an island in the west from where we can operate. Westpoint — Steveley Bay — Carcass — etc. Discussed all the beaches but I have the very distinct impression that his heart is not in this series of options and that he is being pressured from outside. Certainly it will take time to build an airstrip (particularly if we do not have full-time air cover) and it still will not solve the problem of getting the Brigade across Falkland Sound. Briefed COMAW's staff on all the beaches...crossed the Equator — I think — at about 2030. No jubilation!"

The reason for our dash from England was well established and understood, but we needed now to sort ourselves out into a more military posture. We needed to carry out a rehearsal landing somewhere which, itself, could form part of a deception plan. Rehearsing is an integral part of Amphibious Warfare for it exercises everyone from the Brigadier and Commodore down to the junior section commanders or cox'ns in the exact nature of the landing so that 'on the day' it is a familiar process with as many as possible of the avoidable wrinkles ironed out. It also ensures that, despite inevitable confusion caused by weather, the enemy, breakdowns in communication or equipment, everybody still understands the aim and has a good idea how to unscramble the problem at his particular level.

Amphibious Warfare needs careful, detailed, considered and precise planning, practice and execution. All phases of warfare demand a similar input, but with surface, air, subsurface and land warfare in the scales and balanced against cross-decking requirements, helicopter and flight deck availability, landing-craft launching and loading difficulties in the sea state plus weather factors, beach gradients, trafficability, exits and surf height at the end of a long undefended water gap and including a logistics tail at sea in different incompatible ships, every aspect takes on a massive significance.

It is not an haphazard assault onto a beach − any old beach; it is highly complex and demands an immense amount from junior leaders. Lance Corporals in command of landing craft, for instance, are, for a number of vital minutes, entirely responsible for the timely landing of men and equipment. A landing may be approved at five-star or even Prime Ministerial level, but, in the most crucial phase twixt ship and shore, it is often up to the Corporals and Senior NCOs to 'make it so'.

Crossing the watergap is that time when any amphibious force is at its most vulnerable to its two greatest enemies, weather and defensive fire. It is in that area where things, if they can go wrong, will go wrong − spectacularly!

To help reduce the risks I was offering beaches of every type; beaches that would, by themselves, be large enough to contain the whole Beach Support Area (BSA); beaches that were co-located with others to produce alternatives on the day in case enemy action or bad weather intervened, and mutually supporting beaches in case we landed wholly by sea. This last situation would call for a whole series of beaches in the same area so that the troops, once landed, would be mutually supporting in defence. They should also be able to defend the Beach Support Area from all directions.

Any beach had to be easily secured from enemy counter-attack, it had to be free of enemy in large numbers and each beach or set of beaches had to be defendable against air, sea and land attack. Each beach area had to have protection from the elements and be able to accept 'traffic' in all but the most terrible of weathers. Over the days it became clear which beaches, and therefore which options, the staff were putting onto a 'short list'. Just occasionally I was asked to re-describe some landing place away from the main thrust of their thoughts, but often this was in order to dismiss it finally.

We all wanted a peaceful solution, or one that could be achieved with minimal loss of life, and into that category fell the air and sea blockades, but we were also mindful that such actions, even if they work, do not always produce a lasting solution.

GENTOO
PENGUIN

X

Ascension For Orders

ASCENSION ISLAND WAS THE half way stop; the watershed after which there really could be no turning back of the Brigade; the natural break to re-load and re-plan, to train and rehearse. *"Ascension Island for Orders"* I had written in my log after the manner of the old sailing ships who would be sailed from London to clear the docks. Their captains would receive simple sailing instructions: *'Falmouth for Orders'*. This became as emotive a catchphrase as it was an order, for it invariably heralded the next outward-bound leg of a round journey to destinations often unknown and almost certainly the other side of the globe. The analogy to our own situation was perfect.

Ascension Island is the tip of a seamount at the northern end of the Mid-Atlantic Ridge, rising from the sea bed to 2818 feet above sea level. Barren and rocky, with little vegetation, it lies close to the divide between the doldrums and the south-east trades. The highest peak, Green Mountain, is aptly named for it is on its higher slopes that the only plants are found in any profusion. This elongated cone is the extinct remains of a comparatively young volcano and there are traces of another thirty-nine smaller eruptions. The whole island covers no more than thirty-four square miles with about 1100 inhabitants centred around Georgetown, off which we were anchored. The Island is richer in fauna than flora, at least at the lower levels, although a number of animals had been introduced artificially for obvious reasons. Rabbits, wild goats and partridges formed a staple diet in earlier days. The Green Turtle lands between December and May to lay its eggs and there are large sooty-tern breeding colonies. This much I knew from books and geography lessons, but I looked forward to seeing for myself. I was to be disappointed, not with the trade description but the lack of time ashore I could manage.

Our anchorage was to lie in the lee of the south-east trades and the south equatorial current and beneath the long streamer of cloud that drifts smoke-like downwind from the peak of Green Mountain. Either side of the anchorage, but out over the long and untenable Atlantic swell, the sun shone. We were to remain in shadow for three weeks: I'm tempted to say metaphorically as well as geographically!

The meetings scheduled for this half way stop were vital, we knew that,

137

and would begin with a meeting of minds between our two Task Group commanders and the Carrier Battle Group Commander, Admiral Woodward, the Flag Officer First Flotilla (FOF 1), who had sailed with his ships from the Mediterranean on the completion of Exercise Springtrain. The day before we arrived at the anchorage (16 April) we came within range of a Sea King, making it possible for Admiral Woodward to fly north to meet us.

"Gentlemen − Admiral Woodward!" We all stood, awkwardly, for the ship was rolling gently and our chairs were crowded into the suddenly-not-so-spacious Commodores dining cabin usually used for his and the Brigadier's own small briefings and brainstorming sessions. Just about every staff officer, naval and marine, was in attendance. It was warm and humid with the glaring fluorescent lights adding nothing good to the atmosphere. The normally cool bulkheads were long since covered with cork boards to which were pinned and stapled every conceivable map, chart and list. Fuel states of ships, machinery states of ships, medical states of crews, positions of escorts, Argentinian ships and submarines (a bit blank that one) including any shadowing Russian tattle-tale intelligence-gathering trawlers, maps of the Falklands, nautical charts and military going maps, aircraft serviceability updates, weather charts for our present position and, as far as the meteorological officer was able, for the islands, a chart of Ascension Island. There was not a square foot left. It helped to keep the temperature high.

We sat as bidden. The Admiral strode in, tall and unsmiling. He was to give us his views on how things might develop at sea and to discuss with our own commanders how the three of them would approach the morrow's briefing with the Commander-in-Chief. This day was to be a joint session to ensure that we all spoke with the same voice, for it was essential that the three complementary aspects of the Task Force presented a united view and one that could with ease be dove-tailed into the Commander-in-Chief's perceptions and orders. During the journey south there had been dialogue between the two naval Task Group commanders and the Task Force Commander (CINC Fleet), so there should be few surprises on that front. There had been less dialogue between the Landing Force Task Group Commander (Julian Thompson) and the Carrier Battle Group Commander, for there was no requirement. Woodward would react, it was presumed, to the amphibious needs if and when the necessity arose, and for that link Colonel Richard Preston, Royal Marines and an ex-Commanding Officer of Poole, had been seconded to his staff and with whom Julian Thompson had almost daily conversations.

We had been warned of FOF 1's abrasive manner but naively assumed, up to the very start of the meeting, that his irascibility was reserved for his own formation and that with us he would be more attentive to our aspirations, problems and plans. We were to be disappointed.

Rear Admiral Woodward, a submariner, was already treated with suspicion by the Amphibious Flag Ship's embarked staff officers (Naval and Marine) who had hoped that an officer with an understanding of air and amphibious warfare would have been given overall command at sea. Some, including the press, saw Woodward as a dynamic and brilliant staff officer and in his command of the Carrier Battle Group (if I may be so presumptious) these attributes were well in evidence, much to the whole Task Force's advantage. Examples such as his safeguarding of our meagre air assets, the decision to sink the *Belgrano* and his control of the vital naval gunfire support were all war winners, but as a first-time operational commander he did not, very sadly, gain the confidence of his amphibious subordinates (to paraphrase a Nelsonian principle). Not that the Amphibious Task Group nor the Landing Force Task Group were subordinates: they were all equal beneath Admiral Fieldhouse in Northwood. If we had hoped for an officer who would listen with a careful and open mind to the experts in their own specialist fields, then not only were we misled but we were astonished to find little understanding of our affairs or (of greater significance) an apparent willingness to learn.

The absence of FOF 3 was, and still is, difficult to fathom.

Eight years after the campaign Julian Thompson was to write to me:

"It became clear to me, and I believe to Mike Clapp, when we were down in the Falklands two months ago, that he, Woodward, would still try to claim all the credit for the success of the operation himself. At the same time he was saying that until he read my book (*No Picnic*), he did not understand what our problem was!"

Heaven knows, we tried to tell him on 16 April!

My log says everything about the meeting except to emphasize that at no time were we given any confidence in Woodward's ability to estimate correctly the potency of the Argentinian Airforce as it would affect amphibious landings. We came away with the very real fear that it was being swept aside as being of a lesser degree of concern than the surface and subsurface threat − his own specialization. After the war it was explained to me that Woodward was a declared opponent of the Royal Navy continuing to operate fast jets at sea in defence of the fleet. Those of us who had seen the Argentinian Air Force and who had discussed flying with their officers knew that amongst all their servicemen they were the most likely to take the war to an enemy. Flying jet fighter aircraft accords perfectly with the image of the fast-living, fast-playing, hot-blooded temperament of Latin America. To tell the land forces that the air threat was not their problem, as happened, was to indicate a naive assessment of ground warfare, and particularly amphibious warfare. Men and stores crossing the water gap in slow landing craft and vulnerable helicopters operating from ships restricted in their movement is precisely the point where enemy aircraft (or even a few men with machine guns or anti-tank weapons) can seriously alter the day. It is the most delicate of occasions and needs the utmost protection of any phase of war bar none.

Admiral Woodward dismissed the Brigade Intelligence Officer's offer to give his own most carefully constructed assessment of the Argentinian Air Force as it was likely to affect the amphibious forces, with the words:

"Don't bother me with that. I know all about their airforce." It was hardly tactful − even if he did know as much as he said he did.

The treatment of my offering was even more peremptory. Immediately afterwards I covered the meeting in as calm a manner as I could muster. In quoting from this extract I do so deliberately and with embarrassment, but to change or delete words now would falsify feelings at the time and that cannot happen if a true account of contemporary views is to be presented.

"A remarkably tiring day so far. Spent mostly briefing Admiral Woodward whom I thought desperately arrogant, argumentative and bullying − all hiding a great insecurity. Not an amiable meeting either with the staff or, according to the Brig and Cmdre, with just the three of them afterwards. He tried to dictate but as he will only transmit and never listen we did not get very far with having a sensible discussion. He sent me out of the briefing after I had had the nerve to produce my charts with all my corrections on them and not a pristine one; (What do you know about the Falklands, boy? is not the way to endear himself). The silly bugger didn't realize that they are the only charts in existence with all the up-to-date beach and shallow water information. A new chart is useless for this sort of briefing. So, as far as I'm concerned, he went away knowing nothing at all about the Falklands.

"He seems concerned only with landing on the outer islands to build an airfield capable of taking Phantoms and C130s before landing on Lafonia, but as he wouldn't listen to me with my charts he did not hear just how unsuitable that place is from the RM and RN points of view. Anyway we would have a fearful bottleneck to pass if we approached the objective (which must be Stanley) overland from that direction. We should not plan for anything that gives the enemy time to re-group and counter-attack or prepare his defences accordingly. Nothing must delay any attack on Stanley which, surely, must be the *aim. I also get the impression that he really believes that the only way to success is through his air and sea blockade and that the Commando Brigade is rather an embuggerance."*

This meeting and its lack of success was to dominate our thoughts. It certainly hardened opinions. In the days to come whenever signals (known irreverently by the Naval Staff as Windygrams) were received from the Battle Group they were read against the background knowledge that it was likely to be a dictum and would not be seeking advice or confirmation. The meeting did nothing for morale nor our faith in the Admiral's ability to support any amphibious phase with the degree of concern we felt it was due. This may not have been the case in practice but it was our perception, and a most genuine cause for concern in *Fearless* at the time − an unnecessary and added worry. We realized that sympathy for, and understanding of, our problems was to be in very short supply.

"All afternoon and evening − till 0130 − spent discussing yet more beaches. Beaches with the possibility of operating Harriers and Helos. If we can get the Harriers ashore to a base soon after the landings then the worry of losing a carrier will be lessened and we can look forward to close air support over the AOA and advancing troops.

"Tried to go to bed 5 times! Kept being stopped for yet more info. Finally gave up and wrote a simple guide (in matrix format) to every beach on West and East Falkland. It covers approaches, gradients, trafficability, security, likely observation points − theirs and ours − exits, hinterland, going under foot and possibility of helo/Harrier pads, navigational dangers, distances to Stanley by land and sea, size vis-a-vis numbers and type of craft that can use it at any one stage, reliability of info and so on. Massive document, much of it from memory, much from my original note book and sketches, much of it from the marked charts so recently dismissed.

"One of the columns contains The Kelp Factor (out of ten) although as I have written in various signals kelp quite often guards the better beaches and certainly marks any isolated danger on the approach. Most useful stuff, kelp, to those who know how to identify the different types and who have the experience to use this knowledge with care. Kelp, offshore from a landing, can take the sting out of breaking seas and reduce the scend. It is unlikely that mines will be laid in the stuff. All the larger landing craft should be able to pass through slowly, and even the RRC and IRC can do so with care. It also makes it easier to navigate isolated dangers in the dark. Invaluable stuff! Turned in at 0600."

I felt that the Beachcomber's Guide, as it was finally christened, exhausted my itinerary of beaches. It was not, of course, the definitive article on detail but merely a quick guide for personal use by staff officers and commanders – especially the SBS. Detail would be offered as required. I just prayed that I had the information correct, for I knew then that so much was about to depend on the value of my knowledge.

At 0800 on the 17th I woke to put the finishing touches to the Idiot's Guide to Falklands Beaches and then photocopied copies for individual officers before scrounging a long-needed cup of sweet tea from the Commodore's pantry where his steward and the Brigadier's MOA were preparing their respective senior officers for the day.

Royal Marines officers have Marine Officers Attendants, not batmen. They are a special breed and invaluable in the field or on board a ship. Years before, in HMS *Fearless*, Marine Underwood was my MOA. An immaculate man, he would not let shipboard tasks interfere with his daily work. One morning, with an Admiral embarked, we were at action stations with everybody (including the Admiral) dressed appropriately. Every cabin, mess-deck and space had been cleared for action. We set off on formal rounds to stop immediately at my cabin which I could see was not ready for war. The Admiral looked in. Underwood turned from making the bunk: in starched shirt, pressed trousers and a broad smile he announced that he was sorry for any inconvenience, but surely, everybody appreciated that Royal Marines always have clean sheets on Mondays! No more was said.

Ahead of us lay an interesting day and one to which we had been looking forward for some time. The anticipation of better things to come had been heightened by the hoped-for contrast with the meeting of the day before. Many of us were anxious to have our faith in the command system renewed.

"*We shall see, but I think this may be where things start in earnest with a proper briefing, and re-stow for war rather than leaving the country in a political haste.*"

We knew that we could rely on the forthright and vastly experienced Brigadier and the equally experienced, and sensibly calm Commodore to fight the Amphibious corner with the utmost clarity.

As we waited on the flight deck I gazed across the open anchorage. For those of us with vivid imaginations it was possible to see the British Fleet, one hundred and sixty odd years ago, at anchor in the same swell beneath the same cloud waiting for news that the Emperor Napolean (in captivity on St Helena seven hundred miles to the south-east) was about to be sprung by an approaching French Fleet.

Ascension as a deterrent (with its Royal Marine garrison) may have been of value then, for Bonaparte was never rescued. Now it was acting again in a parody of history. Another fleet waited to spring hostages from the successors to the original French settlers of the Falklands. It reminded me too that the Spanish claimed the Falklands from the French and the Argentinians claimed them from the Spanish. The original French settlers had come from St Malo and had even given them the name by which the Argentinians still called them. St Malo had once been a British possession. I wondered if that fact had ever entered the equation!

The staff (with me as a hanger-on) flew in a Sea King to *Hermes* where we were ushered straight into the Commander-in-Chief's briefing. Admiral Fieldhouse sat, flanked by his Air and Land Deputies − Air Marshal Curtiss and Major General Moore − along the outboard side of the packed wardroom.

The Commander-in-Chief gave his assessment of the likelihood of success in the United Nations. He reminded us that the British Government was determined in its purpose to re-take the Falklands by whatever means. He was not hopeful of an agreed settlement either directly with the Argentinians or through any international forum. Then, almost as a finale, he gave his aims. These left us in no doubt about the immediate future and paved the way for what many of us knew and hoped would be inevitable.

Firstly, we were to establish a maritime exclusion zone; secondly we were to establish an air exclusion zone.

So much we already knew.

Thirdly, and of the utmost interest and importance to the amphibious members of the audience (but probably not to those whose faith in the efficacy of the blockades was absolute) we were to: "*Plan to land on the Falkland Islands with a view to re-establishing British administration.*"

I have quoted exactly what I wrote in my log as the Admiral spoke. There was no talk of moving out of any beachhead. Indeed at that stage we were only to plan a landing. It was, though, precisely what we had been doing day and night since 2 April but it was good to hear it from the C-in-C himself. We were not to be a deterrent in waiting, we were not going to poise and posture, we would land when the time was right. Although the executive instruction had been to plan, few of us were in any doubt what that meant. No matter how effective blockades might be, only men on the ground could finally and effectively establish domination over an enemy in such situations. That was our task. If by landing we could achieve just that, so much the better, but if not we would be in an excellent position to exploit the enemy's weaknesses at times and places of our own choosing from a secure and well-established ground base. Poising in the South Atlantic autumn was not really practical. I suppose we could have hidden in the lee of South Georgia but any quick dash from there would be challenged by the Gods of the southern oceans. I felt, as did a number of others, that if we were to land we would do so straight from Ascension Island. The Start Line was here. The bulk of the cross-decking would take place here. If we left here we would land without stopping elsewhere.

At the meeting with Admiral Fieldhouse it was announced that the Brigade would be enhanced further by the 2nd Battalion the Parachute Regiment which, coupled with the already-present 3rd Battalion, was particularly good news. There was yet more good news.

The Brigadier now had five commandos or battalions under command which he considered to be the maximum before complications of logistics and command took charge of operations, not least of which would be the capability of the Commando Logistics Regiment itself which would be stretched beyond any previously accepted limit. This enlarged Commando Brigade, consisting of what the component members considered to be Britain's finest infantry (and why shouldn't they have indulged in a little pride, justified or otherwise?) was to face an enemy force believed to be in excess of 10,000. It was clear that more battalions would be needed, and as no more could sensibly be taken under command, a Divisional Headquarters would be despatched. The land forces were now to be doubled almost at a stroke. Paradoxically all would call on the resources of the one Commando Logistics Regiment.

I noted in my log that there was no doubt that the First Fifteen had been chosen (as opposed to the First Eleven, for it was more likely to be a bloody slogging match more in keeping with rugby than cricket).

On our return from *Hermes* I found further good news waiting for me in my bathroom: a fascinating letter from Roger Blundell. Roger, the Fleet Royal Marines Officer on the Commander-in-Chief's staff, (who, I was sorry to see, had not been included in the visiting team) answered many of my more private fears. It was a pity he had not come to Ascension for we could have indulged in the most scurrilous chat between these four walls and ironed out one or two concerns. As it was, his letter was perfect and put the seal on any morale problems that might have risen from our perceptions of how our aspirations were being viewed back at home. Another superb morale booster was a letter from Colonel Robin Ross whose personal letters of support and encouragement were eagerly awaited – especially important to me as he was a particularly great friend who I knew was missing being with us. His time was to come when, as a Major General, he commanded with outstanding success Operation *Safe Haven* in Kurdistan a few years later.

That evening we went through all the most likely options now that we knew that the landings would be seaborne.

"Brainstormed landings at San Carlos with Brigade Commander."

It was the first time that San Carlos had been purposefully brought to the top of any list. Some have been kind enough to suggest in various books and publications that the choice of San Carlos was largely based on my views. This is not so. At this stage I made no comment about the best or the worst attributes of the place. I merely laid before the planners the physical aspects of the area (among many others) as an option. The decisions, and the credit for the choice, belong to Julian Thompson and Michael Clapp. If I had been wrong in my assessments of the beaches then I could fairly be blamed for feeding false information, but to give me any credit for choosing San Carlos would be an error, although all along I had liked the choice for both helicopter and landing craft operations.

No matter what I said, good or bad, about a beach, it had to be checked out by the SBS. Some of the beaches I had suggested as being worth a look proved to be unsuitable for amphibious operations and some that looked, on the chart, as being unsuitable I could recommend. Campa Menta Bay on the north-east coast of East Falkland fell into the first category. Four years earlier I had chosen this as the site for our arms and communications cache from where we (or, rather, the stay-behind-section) would call in any special forces. During the intervening years, and quite out of keeping with most beaches in the Falklands, there had been a marked build-up of sand or silt totally altering the beach gradients since my initial survey in 1978. The SBS were about to find this out for me.

San Carlos represented an area that had the least defects and the best balance between the military and naval requirements. It was not perfect, but it was less imperfect than anywhere else under the circumstances. The fact that it was to be unguarded by the enemy was an added and vital component in the final decision-making.

San Carlos waters had many attributes. There were beaches around its edges beneath dominating hills; the hills and high ground could be mutually supportive against any enemy counter-attack; it was outside the range of any known enemy gun positions; the waters themselves were landlocked for the most part and would not suffer from heavy surf (a vital consideration once we lost the helicopter assault option); the entrance was easily blocked against submarines; air-launched Exocets would not be able to engage ships in the anchorage itself; aircraft flying over the hills or round the headlands would have very few seconds to identify and engage a target; and, a political and human restraint, the danger to civilians would be absolutely minimal. These were all factors in San Carlos' favour.

There were certainly factors against. It was as far from Stanley as it was possible to be, apart from southern Lafonia; the entrance to Falkland Sound and the entrance to San Carlos waters would be easy to mine; it meant a longer transit through the Total Exclusion Zone, much of which would have to be conducted in daylight if we were to arrive with plenty of time to cross-deck and load landing craft so that they could all sail together in a simultaneous assault. Ships in the anchorage would have very little time to select and engage enemy aircraft, and if, as we already suspected, the carriers would be way to the east it would give our own fighters a very limited time overhead in our direct defence.

For some time the Brigadier had been very taken with the idea of a landing on North Camp but I suspect this was before he knew of the removal of *Hermes* from our plan. Cow and Volunteer Bay had been given much thought: excellent beaches; hard ground useful for Harrier pads but otherwise a boggy approach to Stanley, which was too close. There was a bottleneck at Green Patch. The beaches were too exposed to the east, with all the subsequent military and weather implications.

There was always Berkeley Sound. This would have made a good AOA and, with a near-perfect beach at its head, it caught the imagination; more so, perhaps if helicopters with which to take the high ground to the south had been available from a multi-spot ship. There was no military bottleneck, troops would have been deployed very close (but outside the range of all but the largest of the enemy guns) to the final objective; the going to Stanley was as fair as one could expect across camp. The swell in the Sound only reaches difficult proportions during the rare easterly gales, although preceding these a nasty short sea gets up quite quickly. There was the very real danger that of all the options we might choose, this was the one most likely to be mined.

Around Macbride Head there were a number of beaches close to each other, not shown as such on any chart (including, we hoped, Argentinian ones) over which individual commandos and regiments could land. The seizing and holding of an area so close to Stanley certainly had its attractions as a bargaining and intimidation factor but the physical disadvantages outweighed the good. It was perfectly feasible and was never far from our minds as a useful fall-back position.

Port Salvador presented itself for some time as an ideal place, militarily, from where to break out of a beachhead. Once inside the narrow entrance there is a network of beaches with almost more manoeuvering room than can be found in the upper reaches of San Carlos. The troops would be deployed straight into the hills overlooking the final approaches to Stanley. The real naval problems were the possibility of mines in the entrance, though we were to ignore this threat in the entrance to Port San Carlos, and the possibility that the approach could be blocked by other means – sinking a ship for instance, ours or theirs. Its many attractions were dissected to the full. For a main assault though, it would be difficult to defend against determined air strikes as the surrounding ground is low enough to allow aircraft to pick a target some way off but high enough to thwart early warning. Teal Inlet, at the head of the south western arm of the waterway, was always considered by Julian as a staging post, if not as an initial assault area, if we landed to the westward.

Further west there was nothing until San Carlos and from there nothing until the south coast of Lafonia (although I studied Brenton Loch for other purposes).

Many times I was called to the Brigadier's or Commodore's cabin to discuss the merits or otherwise of Lafonia on the south coast of East Falkland. Port North also featured in these perfunctory discussions.

Lafonia had absolutely nothing to recommend it at all. If Adventure Sound had had any useful beaches the Sound itself would have made a passable AOA for the shipping, although a little restricted due to numerous shoal patches. Added to these uninspiring facts (including low ground with easy approaches for enemy aircraft), the land approaches across appalling ground for infantry and tracked or wheeled vehicles towards another bottleneck, Goose Green, made it militarily a nightmare. Up until the last moment we were directed to look again at this place, much to the rising frustration of a number of planners in *Fearless* who did not wish to be constantly bombarded with what they considered, partly on my recommendation, to be a non-starter.

The Carrier Battle Group seemed to favour this area, but those suggestions were quite rightly and understandably made in isolation of the military requirements.

Eastwards from Lafonia there were a number of beaches, some with impeccable references – as beaches – but few with much else to commend them to Amphibious Forces. There were many poorly charted reefs, most landing areas faced directly to seaward and all were within very quick reinforcement distance from Stanley or the Goose Green garrison.

On West Falkland, Port North possessed one excellent beach, Stevelly Bay, but that was all. It was too far west of West Falkland with the problems that this would entail. There was only the one beach and not much room behind it for a BSA. The question would then be how to supply forward if the helicopters were busy: certainly not by boat nor vehicle. The dominant factor that seemed to be influencing those in the

Carrier Battle Group was the thought of finding an area which could take Hercules and Phantoms. Extending east from the upper end of Port North was an ideal valley that could, with some considerable work, and more time and equipment than we would have, be turned into such a runway, but this would need to be protected offshore and from the air and would tie up much shipping. Nobody denied the fact that the use of an airfield of such magnitude would be invaluable, but penalties would be paid.

I had included some of the more obvious beaches on West Falkland, just in case, but I knew that if the Brigadier and the Commodore had their way there would be no such landing, for it would mean, at the very best, a secondary assault across the Sound against a well-prepared and expectant enemy. The Sound would also prove to be a huge obstacle for the re-supply of any advancing troops, unless we then double-moved all the logistics. We could have kept them at sea, but the feeling was strong that one bomb into a logistics ship could ruin thousands of tons, whilst one bomb into a dispersed Beach Support Area would have less of an adverse effect.

There were, too, other problems that needed to be addressed. The main troop carrier *Canberra* was not an assault ship. Whether the men disembarked by helicopter or by boat, to launch three battalions/ commandos would take an inordinate amount of time on D Day. Two helicopters at a time would be slow enough from the forward and midships flight decks, but men in their ones and twos through the loading ports into an LCU heaving alongside would be altogether a different game. We needed, too, to restow all our kit so hastily packed in England. We needed to carry out a full-scale rehearsal.

Ascension was fine for the re-stow, but it was too far from the AOA for the cross-decking of men. Any cross-decking to ships with helicopter spots or with integral landing craft would need to take place just before the last moment when overcrowding would be acceptable for a few hours, and yet not so close to the last moment that this pause would jeopardize the time and place and flexibility of H Hour − the very attributes vital to successful amphibious operations.

Nor was Ascension suitable for the rehearsal. We were too far in time from the landings and so had no idea what needed rehearsing and in what order. There were no beaches and no suitable areas for manoeuvres.

Some tried to argue that South Georgia, once re-taken, would provide the perfect place for such exercises, but it is separated from the Falkland Islands by nearly a thousand miles of inhospitable waters down-wind. Unless the most extraordinary reversal of the weather system was to occur men would arrive for the assault in poor order after their transports (some of them very weather-sensitive indeed − the LSLs in particular) had bashed into the seas and winds at a slow eight knots or less. The weather in those latitudes can be extreme.

I am not sure when the bad news was made public but I noted something to the effect around that time in letters home. We would not, after all, have HMS *Hermes* for any helicopter assault. She would be too busy flying Harriers. Privately, and taking no other aspects into consideration, I was appalled by this news. The assault could have taken place in the dark with the pilots using night vision goggles. (I had no idea then that only four sets were available and only four crews trained in their use.) We did not expect the Argentinian Airforce to fly by night and so the Harriers would not be using the flight deck. I assumed, too, that the second aircraft carrier, HMS *Invincible,* would be standing guard off the AOA and that after the initial assault had taken place they would both resume Harrier operations.

I had also assumed that any final cross-decking would take place from *Canberra* to *Hermes* the day before so that two Commandos would be ready, in tight but by no means unusual conditions, for a dawn assault, with frigates and *Invincible's* aircraft providing the air defence and Combat Air Patrols before *Hermes* launched her own Harriers at, say, H+2. Perhaps many of us at my level did not know the details of the air warfare picture, but the situation had many parallels with our practices in the northern hemisphere. Admiral Woodward quite rightly had pointed out that he would hardly have enough aircraft to defend himself, let alone the AOA, and to stop *Hermes* flying Harriers until well after dawn was, presumably, a very large factor in the decision, which was, anyway, made in Northwood. On D Day, both aircraft carriers provided CAP and yet we were still attacked with considerable impunity.

Many of the plans had been made on the assumption that at least one, if not two, Commandos would take the surrounding high ground or perimeter defences before any movement across the beaches. Now everything would have to cross the beaches from landing craft, including those units with long approaches to the perimeter defences on high ground. Cross-decking or no cross-decking, it would take a very long time. A string of beaches co-located but separate and mutually supporting would need to be used, each one, preferably, beneath individual units' high-ground objectives. It was all rather unsatisfactory but it did help narrow the choice of destinations.

This was then to be an amphibious operations in the '80s and a very backward step from the 1950s and the first time helicopters were used in an amphibious assault – at Suez. On 6 November, 1956, 450 men of 45 Commando and 23 tons of stores were landed from 7 miles offshore in 83 minutes and yet the Whirlwind helicopters from 845 Squadron could only lift sticks of 5 men, the Sycamores just 3. My father was 45 Commando's Commanding Officer.

It was all a consequence of the demise of the Amphibious Fleet presided over by successive Governments. We did not have the right ships for the job, but we would have to make it work. We would damn well make sure it worked. A positive attitude of the British serviceman that has not always been beneficial to his future: "If you can win by improvisation then why did you need all the expensive equipment?" would more than often be the Whitehall retort, oblivious of the sacrifices at the sharp end of such a philosophy.

Before turning in, John Thurman and I were ordered to brief the SBS onboard the RFA *Resource* the next morning. This came as no surprise, for we knew that shortly the SBS and SAS would be deployed ahead of the main force, as is common practice in most amphibious operations. Beaches, no matter how well they may have been pre-recorded or even recced, must be checked and checked again. *Resource* was due to sail south with the Battle Group at any moment. It was essential that the SBS had the benefit of our joint lecture.

Cape Pigeon

"Whale Bird"

Daption capensis

XI

Doldrums

THE SBS AND THE SAS were on their way south and, although they would remain under the command and control of the Commodore Amphibious Task Group, the Carrier Battle Group would be responsible for inserting them by frigate, helicopter and submarine. Their tasking would be directed on behalf of the Brigadier and Commodore (after full consultation with the two special forces commanding officers) by the Royal Marines Liaison officer on the Admiral's staff, Colonel Richard Preston. It was with him that the Brigade Commander would have daily discussions on the secure radio link, but otherwise there would be no communication between the Brigadier and the Admiral, and in many respects there was no further need. Woodward's responsibility in this regard was co-ordinator not commander. After the war it was assessed that the landing of special forces was his most important function in the period 1-12 May.

The link between the Commodore and the Admiral was of more importance, for it was the Carrier Battle Group that would protect the lightly armed ships of the Amphibious Warfare 'squadron' for their approach to, and operations in, the AOA. During the initial stages at least (and probably for much longer, depending on the way the ground battle developed) the Carrier Battle Group would be in direct support of the troops ashore, with highly accurate naval gunfire producing a greater rate of fire and a heavier round than the 105mm guns of the supporting Royal Artillery Regiment. This support would extend to shore bombardment of the enemy's offensive support capability such as Stanley Airfield and ammunition dumps, as well as his artillery emplacements. The naval guns could far out-range those of the enemy.

Resource was ordered to sail by, and in company with, HMS *Hermes*. This was rather earlier than expected and happened without much conferring with the military. Left behind on the island were a number of valuable items of kit belonging to the special forces, who were not amused.

The sudden departure of the Battle Group preceded a signal stating in effect: "I'm going on down to fight the war — you follow on as best you can". It was hardly inspiring stuff. The hard-pushed staff who had masterminded the quite unparalleled and speedy sailing from the UK (and the now equally amazing but unsung re-loading and re-stowing at anchor off Georgetown) considered it an unnecessary and tactless comment. It followed a signal (sent before our arrival in Ascension by the Flag captain, Middleton, in *Hermes*) which had appeared to have an earlier ring of exasperation about it: "There are 4,700 square miles of Falkland Islands and only 10,000 Argentinians, ergo only one enemy to every two square miles. What's the problem?"

If Woodward had ever listened he and his team would have known what the problem was, militarily and topographically. As it was, these signals and comments did not help either Julian Thompson (who was to describe Woodward's "staccato procession of pedagogic questions [as bearing] little resemblance to the facts as we saw them") or Michael Clapp (or anyone else in the Amphibious Task Group) have much confidence in the grasp on reality held by many in the Carrier Battle Group, and were considered, at that stage, to be more of a hindrance than a help to our planning.

There were real and valid reasons why the Amphibious Task Group could not yet sail. The re-stow had now to reflect the priorities of a landing totally by landing craft, rather than the earlier political aim of being seen to deploy with haste from the United Kingdom. This juggling of vehicles, men, equipment and ammunition could only be finished satisfactorily once all the LSLs and troop ships were together. In addition, everybody from Brigade Commander to rifle section commander and from Commodore Amphibious Warfare to junior radar operator had to train in the convoluted landing techniques forced upon us by the non-amphibious shipping. We also needed to wait until the first aspects of the Commander-in-Chief's plans had taken effect. There was no need for the troops to sit-out the South Atlantic storms at sea whilst the blockades slowly whittled away at the enemy's ability to fight efficiently. If South Georgia was not to be used (and we hadn't yet captured it back) then Ascension Island was the place to be. It was also within commuting distance of Northwood for senior staff officers to come and go if necessary.

Early in the morning of 19 April I was summoned to the Brigadier's cabin to spend some hours following his feet as they roamed across the maps and charts sprawled across the deck. The choice of beaches had suddenly taken on a greater importance and significance, since we now knew that we would have to conduct the main landings by sea. As I left, Julian Thompson called me back. I sat down for another private meeting that was aimed, I guessed, at clearing his mind over the area that we had been discussing. I knew that he wanted to feel that he had been to every place that we covered. He needed that personal feel for every inch of coastline on which we were focusing. In Norway, Denmark and north

Germany the commanders knew in advance exactly where their men would be deployed in the face of a Soviet threat. They knew the ground intimately and were able to plan for every possible contingency: always an advantage over likely adversaries.

Here, in the South Atlantic, very few of us indeed had visited the area now at the hub of every thought and even fewer had visited with a view to fighting across it. Every day we delayed gave our adversaries that advantage that we enjoyed in NATO. Now it was John's and my task to saturate the Brigadier with briefings on every aspect so that he could feel that any decision that he would eventually have to make – or advise the Commander-in-Chief to make – was, as it were, from personal experience. So intense was the need for knowledge that he pointed to a large-scale chart showing the kelp fringes to a bay and asked if the minutely-drawn squiggly symbols represented individual strands of seaweed. I had to confess that, though detailed, no charts and sketches (not even mine!) could be as precise as that.

The weather, the kelp (in patches, if not individual branches), the scenery, the beach, the hinterland, the local people and personalities, names, numbers of dogs, way of life from settlement to settlement, vehicles, everything that a local would have known by a more natural process, was required. It was the first of many such fascinating discussions which forced John Thurman and I to cast our minds back for the smallest possible detail of any visit. As I got up to brief the OC SBS I was stopped again by an 'over the spectacles' stare.

"*Canberra* arrives tomorrow. I want you to get across when she is ready and arrange to lecture to the two Commandos and the Parachute Battalion on board. I want everyone in the Brigade to know as much as they possibly can about the Falklands. Don't home-in on to any place in particular, but you can show pictures of everywhere we have discussed. When decisions are made you will need to brief in greater detail on specific places. One last thing, what do you think of San Carlos?"

I knew exactly what I thought of San Carlos, although I knew what I thought of the other possible options as well. I liked them less than San Carlos, but it had not been my position up to then to say so. Our thoughts had been galvanizing slowly, but now, without troop-lift helicopters, with an increase in speed. Any simultaneous lift by landing craft would be slow and ponderous and would have to take place at night with all the attendant timing and navigational problems that I had long envisaged.

As a landing craft officer I was professionally delighted, but as a Royal Marine I was appalled at this turn of events. I took no pleasure in knowing that the landing craft branch, of which I was then the professional head, was to spearhead any re-taking of the islands. Helicopters were our main *modus operandi* with landing craft more suitable for following up and for small-scale raiding and reconnaissance. We had been practising the offensive use of specially adapted large landing craft to insert and support men behind enemy lines in North Norway, and the Raiding Squadron were anyway well versed in those techniques, using helicopters and submarines to lift their RRCs and Geminis. We were not, though, ready for the simultaneous landing of the equivalent of three commandos to spearhead any main brigade assault on to defended beaches. Nevertheless it was a challenge that I did not query. I knew the limitations of my craft, their crews and their training, but I also knew their abilities. I was keen to put them to the test.

I went in search of the Commanding Officer of the SBS.

Jonathan Thompson is a quick-witted man (by my standards) whose placid demeanour (by Royal Marines standards) camouflaged an officer of exceptional leadership and human qualities. He had been appointed the first Commanding Officer of the SBS to have come from outside its ranks and it was a measure of his calm professional ability that this was accepted almost more easily by the SBS ranks themselves than by the rest of the Corps. There was little doubt that the SBS was supremely served by Jonathan at a time when, by coincidence, they most needed a man of that calibre.

Later, Jonathan was to command 45 Commando with great distinction in Northern Ireland, a tour which was almost immediately followed by an emergency tour in northern Iraq to help re-settle the hapless Kurds back into their homes and villages, despite the alternative aspirations of Saddam Hussein. He was to be awarded the OBE for the Falklands, was mentioned in despatches in Northern Ireland and awarded the Queen's Gallantry Medal for Iraq.

I went through, again, the good and bad beaches on which his men should concentrate. These were times of deep thought, for I knew that a wrong 'steer' might send men on complicated patrols to look at a location not worth the risk. Not only would the men be in danger but also the ships, boats and aircraft involved in the insertions, recces and extractions. I was confident in those days that I had the facts right, but later on towards D Day I began to wonder if I had remembered everything as it was and worried how much my imagination might have played tricks with my memory.

After lunch we were subject to a bizarre incident which, happily, did not have the dramatic effects that had been first assumed. The date of the landings (which none of the planners knew anyway) had been posted on the ship's notice board as part of the Headquarters and Signals Squadron Daily Orders. From that moment complete censorship of all mail leaving

HMS *Fearless* would be in force. The slightly farcical aspect was that it would not have prevented anyone having a letter posted from another ship; but never mind. All mail would be scrutinized by the two embarked padres. Mail posted that morning (presumably written the night before) would be placed on the tables in the main dining hall and anybody who wanted to remove a letter to re-write it was at liberty to do so. Any remaining, and any sent subsequently, would be censored.

I had nothing to hide and left my mail to be scrutinized. I could have removed some letters to re-write personal aspects rather differently, but I did not want any false feelings being relayed home. However, as an innocent tease of 'the system' I did write a letter to a friend in London, with every word in Arabic script. I doubt if my friend could have read it, but I was just as certain that none of the padres could:

> *"They guessed whose it was and their humour was not found wanting — bought them a whisky or two! We have two excellent Padres with us — both old friends."*

At dawn on 20 April and refreshed by a run around the dew-covered flight deck, followed by a cold shower (my normal morning routine from Arctic to Tropics), I invited John Thurman to the bathroom to see what more we could do in the lecturing line now that we had been tasked with getting the message across to the embarked forces and recently assembled fleet. We both felt that we had to add a greater human factor to our talks so that the audiences could identify with the country as a place where people lived and worked and played. We needed to spice our talks with personal incidents: examples of how and why it takes, for instance, a very long time to walk across country; why the social scene is riven with pitfalls unlikely to be found in the wider social strata of Great Britain; why oranges cost a pound each and why there were no butchers, newspapers, television and few unmarried girls.

We sat and puzzled over our new look lecture. It had to be light and yet fully informative; it had to be militarily relevant and yet give a balanced view of the islands as a whole; it had to be more than an adjunct of the 'ground' paragraph for we needed to appeal to all audiences.

20 April, 1982.

Although *Canberra* had arrived in the anchorage and was a few cables to the north of us I had other tasks to perform before we could start our lecture tour, but what a glorious sight she was as she rode to her anchor facing eastwards and the Island. She was more in her element off a tropical island than we were, but this idyll was spoilt by helicopters swarming around her two flight decks and the scores of marines and paras speed-marching around her promenade decks. A bizarre sight in a bizarre situation.

Closer inshore was another familiar ship, the *AES*. I studied her carefully through my binoculars. She seemed laden and was clearly not going further south for the moment, but her arrival in the Falklands need not have necessarily promoted too much comment. Indeed it might even have been welcomed by the Argentinians. I sought out Jonathan Thompson who agreed that, as nobody seemed to be showing interest, we should. You just never knew.

Without fuss we arranged a Rigid Raiding Craft (RRC) from the 'round the fleet taxi service' which the long-suffering cox'ns had discovered was their less military, but certainly more arduous, duty when at anchor.

Captain Screven, the Norwegian master, and his crew of nine welcomed us aboard. One of the questions I was anxious to establish was whether or not he had any Falkland Islanders among his crew and whether or not he was prepared to continue if given permission, a question that had not been put earlier. I was also keen to look at the cargo manifest, while Jonathan had other plans to put to the Master.

There were no Kelpers in the crew and she was on her way south. Bad and good news respectively. A Kelper coming north might have had valuable information and been able to clear up some of the unanswered questions from the Brize Norton de-briefing; questions that, perhaps, only a nautically minded person might have had a feel for. Going south though could be useful if the Captain was willing to fall in with a couple of outlandish plans that Jonathan and I had hatched on the journey across, but at that moment he was under orders to remain at anchor.

His manifest was more revealing. Not only did it contain the heavy baggage of Mike Norman's detachment but also the 81mm mortars that I had asked for as part of our new-look defence system in 1979. Progress at last I thought. We sat in the Master's cabin with a cool beer and talked of earlier days when Captain Screven had last been in the Islands. The thought of suggesting that he continue in innocence of the seriousness of the situation, but with a couple of 'unknown' stowaways embarked, was put in a roundabout manner. The Master was in favour. We took our leave convinced that here was the germ of an idea that would certainly find favour with the inventive mind of Mike Rose and his team. Jonathan's men would all be committed to beaches and landing sites further afield than Stanley.

The Rigid Raiding Craft re-appeared as ordered, but instead of returning to *Fearless's* air-conditioned interior we decided that we deserved a 'run ashore' even if it was to be exactly that.

We landed at the tiny jetty and made our way to the Royal Marines Church as we called it, although it is more properly known as the Garrison Church. A lovely haven of peace, tranquillity and cool thoughts, despite being continually brought back to the present by the plaques commemorating the deaths of earlier 'Royals' who had served most of their careers in that desolate spot. Many had died with the colours and were buried in the dry grave-yard, some of the thousands across the globe that had caught Major Drury's mind when he wrote his evocative poem *The Dead Marines*.

"...Deep in the tropic jungle where the noonday glare is dim:
On barren hillsides where Korea chants her pagan hymn:
From polar star to southern cross, beneath the sobbing waves:
The dead Marines are sleeping in their widely sundered graves.

"Spent 'empties' flung aside upon the dust heaps of the World,
Who strew the tracks wherever Britain's Flag has been
unfurled,
Lone stragglers from the colours who have long stepped out
of time..."

A poem learnt by heart in my earliest years and now, not for the first time, come to life.

"21 April
"Moved across to Canberra by LCVP. I have packed a toothbrush just in case. Met Col Tom Seccombe and set up shop in the ship's cinema — helped by John Thurman."

It was just as well that I had managed an early night on board *Fearless* for the next days were to become indistinct in a haze of activity. The cultural shock of stepping into a cruise liner in the tropics was quite enough, but on top of that John Thurman and I embarked on the first of our new-style lectures. Each talk, with a question period and short break, would last about two hours and begin again as soon as the audience had changed and we had re-loaded the slide boxes. While I found this fascinating and absorbing (especially the questions), it was with the utmost relief that the last lecture ended each day with the promise of a gin and a cold shower. Almost every evening after dinner there would be more discussions in small groups throughout the ship, as individuals at every level of officer, senior and junior NCO and marine wanted details on various aspects.

"22 April

"Woken by a steward with a cup of tea! Sharing Cabin B56 with Gary Noott. Last night before turning we sat up late discussing the whole problem and especially his part in the defence of the Islands and why he let Mike Norman take command when he, Gary, had been there for a year and knew the form and indeed had been practising the SOPs for long enough. Received the impression that the original SOPs were not in existence any more, which is very odd indeed. He had obviously been keen to let Mike take command.

"23 April

"St George's Day. This is the day I would have liked us to have re-invaded the Islands. Zeebrugge Day. Gave many more lectures. Invited many doctors back to my cabin late at night where they failed to take any professional concern over the amount we all drank!

"24 April

"Met 'H' Jones who burst into my cabin saying he had to find a face he knew so he could catch up with what was happening. Agreed to lecture to his men when they arrive out here."

There had been a knock and in he walked with an enormous smile on his face. We had been contemporaries on the Platoon Commanders' course at Warminster in the early '60s when he would race his Mini Cooper 'S' round the barrack-room huts, but my open Morris '8' had been no match.

"H's arrival is further proof that the MOD really have chosen the best! Heard that part of the Task Force is off SG. I hope they land. Lectured to ship's officers – including many women. Toned it down a little bit."

Much of my talk did include personal views on the Argentinians, Islanders, the Foreign Office and even the Falkland Island Company (who, hardly surprisingly, seldom came out of the talks well). There was a real reason for this: I felt that every man in the task force should be under no illusion about the whys and wherefores, the demerits and the good points of the what, where, when and who of the problem. Some of my views may well have been on the extreme side, but I was determined that men should have the benefit of at least one set of views based on personal experience and not rely on opinions culled from the newspapers; opinions written by journalists whose knowledge was sketchy, if it existed at all from first-hand experience. The marines, soldiers and sailors should make their own judgement. Of course the bulk of each lecture was to do with the military aspects of the subject, but even these had to be balanced by a deeper understanding of the country, its problems and what we were hoping to do about them.

That evening I leant over the Monkey Island coaming..."*watching helicopter operations. It still seems unbelievable with helos operating on the forward and midships flight decks while girls in bikinis sunbathe in the last of the warmth.*"

"*25 April*
"*Took a RRC to LSL* Sir Lancelot *to brief the 1st Raiding Sqn – met by Chris Baxter the OC.*"

The war then burst upon our lives – at last.

"*On the 1500 news it was announced that we had engaged an Argie submarine in Grytviken and at 1700 the MOD announced that an assault had taken place on South Georgia and then, during dinner, that South Georgia was in our hands again. Guy Sheridan, who was commissioned into the Royal Marines the same day as me, commands the landing party which includes M Coy Gp from 42 Cdo with SAS attachments under command.*"

Guy had been chosen as he was, quite clearly, the man for the task, although the fact that he was a 'second-in-command' apparently raised some army eyebrows – I don't know – but once Guy's impeccable credentials had been pointed out his appointment was accepted.

Guy is one of the country's leading biathaletes, with Olympic and international competitions to his credit. He was a member of the Mountain and Arctic Warfare Cadre and had led many cross-mountain ski expeditions in North Norway, the Alps and the Himalayas, notching up a number of notable, and remarkable, 'firsts'. On top of this he had been 'mentioned in despatches' in the Sultan of Muscat's army for operations against guerrillas in the Dhofar mountains of southern Oman. It was therefore with some concern that we heard that his advice not to land on glaciers (backed up by Captain Nick Barker of HMS *Endurance*) had been ignored by the SAS (and 'higher authority') with near-disastrous consequences.

Overall this was excellent news, for not only had we established some military ascendancy over the enemy, but we now had South Georgia if we should need it for cross-decking and training. This was not a popular option but at least it was back on the list.

After dinner I was hijacked, willingly, by an old friend. Corporal Newland crept up behind me in a corridor and with his familiar cry of

"Allo Sir -'ow'y'r doin'" he led me aft towards the Alice Springs Bar. "We heard you were on board and we know how you like a wet after supper." I followed tamely. It was quite excellent for the heart to be accosted by this spokesman for those members of the old NP 8901. I had had no idea that so many of them were on board or even serving in the task force.

Steve Newland was one of my favourite Royal Marines. He had suffered polio badly as a child, with a life expectation drastically reduced, but he overcame that obstacle to gain a black belt at karate and to play a leading and courageous part in 42 Commando's attack on Mount Harriet. It was a memorable evening with nine old 'Falklands' friends.

"*26 April*

"*Apparently the Carrier Battle Group Commander gave an interview on board* Hermes *today that will do little for the morale of those who understand the psychology of leadership. He has committed the cardinal sin of underestimating his opponent in public. We are told that he described the South Georgia success as being an appetiser, with the big match coming up to be a walkover. Some reporters described the interview as inspiring confidence in his men. Most of us see it as providing a 'mood of dangerous and un-warranted optimism'.*"

Subsequently a newspaper cutting dated 29 April arrived which, under the heading, 'Suburban Admiral' read:

"The Admiral said he did not see either the Argentine Air Force or Navy posing a great threat."

"*28 April*

"*Called over to lecture to 45 Cdo on board RFA* Stromness. *Then to* Sir Galahad *where I discovered the lecture had been cancelled. Back to* Fearless *where I fell in off the end of the rope ladder which was an unpleasant experience, and while I may be expendable, my notes, photographs and charts are definitely not. The good news is that there is an invitation to a port and stilton party with the Purser officers (girls) and Nick Vaux, so I have engineered a lecture for tomorrow morning to X Company on board* Canberra...[during the party I was summoned back to brief General Moore in *Fearless*].

For the first time I was to be involved with the decision-making process and, once the choices had been agreed, I was to remain part of that more intimate planning team. It was, by then, too late for my opinions, subjective or objective, to be counted for anything other than what they

18. The Officers' Mess on board SS *Canberra* with the scaffolding supporting the forward flight deck above and the officers below!

19. Brigadier Julian Thompson outside his HQ on 23 May. HMS *Fearless* in the background.

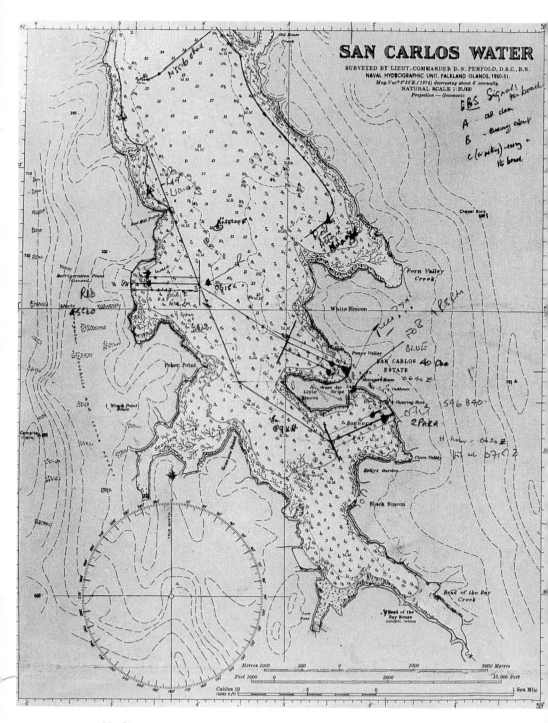

20. Chart used by the author for the first wave on D-Day showing the
landing plan and SBS signals (top right).

had now become: hard advice. An added factor was that, the decision having been made, I would now add to my duties the rather more practical one of commanding the landing craft during what had already become known as 'D' Day. I was no longer a mere Falklands adviser (although I would continue in that capacity until the very end) but I was now part of the command chain − at the very bottom, but part of it.

29 April

By now the staff had whittled a medium list of nineteen meticulously studied areas down to a short list of just three landing options and had decided that, while there might be numerous other beaches worth considering for all manner of subsidiary tasks, we should concentrate on just these. They were all different geographically, militarily and nautically.

The three options (the same three that formed the provisional short list after the 17 May meeting with the Task Force Commander) were presented to General Moore by the Brigadier and the Commodore as those considered most suitable for our revised *modus operandi*. The result of this prodigious work of (military) art by the two staffs would, I presumed, be put before the Commander-in-Chief and, through him, to the War Cabinet. Myself and the key members of the two staffs were on hand to answer questions and help field any 'fast balls'.

San Carlos represented the option with the least number of disadvantages, its greatest drawback being the distance from Stanley overland. Berkeley Sound was a good option, but relied on the enemy not moving his heavy guns into range and would be even better if it could be guaranteed that the Argentinians were on the verge of surrender anyway and needed, quite simply, a face-saving battle. The main naval disadvantage was the distinct possibility of mines off the entrance and, indeed, throughout the length of the sound. The disadvantages of Cow and Volunteer Bays were largely weather-based, the awful going across country, and the inevitable bottleneck at Green Patch. Mines, submarines and Exocet were also very real naval reservations.

While these three were on our short list, we all held a regard for Salvador Waters as a last-minute alternative and I was particularly fond of it. This fascinating area was kept alive as a reserve option by thoughts of its potential for special forces insertions and as a forward supply base if that was the flank to be used for any advance.

"*1 May*
"*A good start to the day. RAF have bombed Stanley Airport and I found my wireless which had gone awol.*"

The news was indeed good, although some of us did feel impotent at the action going on 'down south' with us still off Ascension Island. Personally I wasn't too sure. Sailing south could wait until all was ready; the one thing we did not want to do was sit at sea in the austral autumn in our traditional poising posture. Poising is fine under many circumstances but the South Atlantic in May or June with no lee or friendly territory to hide behind or train across was not so clever. The LSLs had gone on ahead, the men could follow, as surely they must, and go straight in.

Although there were no pauses in our routines of going over the set-piece plans again and again, there was time to indulge in some fantasy. In my case there was a serious side to it. For long I had been aware that everybody was tunnel-visioned. Rightly perhaps, but there were other aspects to our impending journey south and I felt I should highlight them:

> "*Spent afternoon painting recognition silhouettes of the southern ocean dolphins and whales, for the notice boards alongside those of enemy tanks and aircraft. We must remain balanced about these things*"... and while I had the paints to hand I doodled with camouflage schemes for the landing craft, coming up with much the same result as for the Arctic but, this time, with flecks of white, grey and green mixed in. As it happened the craft were painted, as before, with just those dark colours the ships held, which produced two differing and not very artistic solutions, but ones that were workable.

> "*2300. The ship has now run out of port which is very disturbing.*"

Our attentions now turned suddenly to the least favourite of the three short-listed options:

2 May

> "*Cow Bay/Volunteer Bay seems most likely all of a sudden as I have been called back to go over the salient points with the Brigadier, COMAW, OC SBS and CO SAS.*
> *3 May*
> "*Action Stations at 0400. Assault Stations. Heard that the* Belgrano *had been crippled by torpedoes and being escorted home by many ships. Excellent — and how sensible to cripple and not sink. SE of Tierra del Fuego. 0900. News of patrol vessel sunk and*

*another damaged by helos inside TEZ NE of East Falkland. 1024
Just heard that the* Belgrano *has sunk. Despite earlier remark —
better and better when added to yesterday's news of Pucara and
Skyvans destroyed by NGFS, plus three Etendard 'splashed'.
Admiral Woodward in his element and clearly excellent at it.*

"*Session with OC SBS and CO SAS — looking at Salvador
waters — Dan's Shanty — using canoes, RRCs, LCVPs and LCUs
coupled with landings at Cow and Volunteer beaches as a result of
which I have now typed out out full navigational instructions for
Salvador Waters.*

"*Summoned to Bde Commander's cabin to discuss Cow Bay,
Uranie Bay options — vis-a-vis weather. Invited to look at sea area
east of Cape Dolphin but can suggest no landing places until
Salvador Waters.*"

So, I concluded at the time, we had not yet gone firm on anywhere in
particular.

"*5 May
"1415. A very interesting meeting with the Bde Cdr, COMAW,
captain, OC SBS, CO SAS, CO 59, et al, on deception. Helped
produce 19 possible areas for AOA/cross-decking — either for real
or deception. Many ideas put forward by the staff such as dropping
dummy parachutes, leaving a canoe, radar transmissions, false helo
taskings/chatter over the air, loudspeaker noises of ships anchoring.
Also discussed LCVPs for mine sweeping — which fills me with
horror. Looking at Choiseul Sound and Low Bay for deception
areas.*

"*2100. Tim Donkin and Rob Woodard (both great friends)
arrived out here from Northwood. No guarantee of air superiority
can now be given and we will have to learn to live with and plan for
that. Deception plans could take place in Mare Harbour — East
Cove area. We must accept the odd a/c against us — fair enough but
waves of attacks at the most crucial part of an amphib op may mess
us up a bit. We have been assured that Harriers will be based
between the Islands and the mainland until they can be established
ashore. The RAF GR 3s now arriving are designed to live and
operate with ground troops in close support. Bde Cdr and COMAW
very worried about* Elk, Canberra *and the LSLs which must be
close to the beaches — probably now Cow Bay — and their
consequent exposure to air strikes before we can empty them*".

It is interesting that after decisions on the options and priorities had apparently been taken we were still looking very seriously at the beaches closer to Stanley. In subsequent books and articles it has been assumed that the decision to land at San Carlos, once presented to the General, was hard and fast. My log tends to show a different story.

"Rob Woodard and Tim Donkin in the wardroom for drinks before lunch. Highly amusing to hear that last Sunday when Tim met Patricia at a Seaton Barracks cocktail party, just after the sinking of Belgrano, *he had said, sympathetically, that he was afraid that things were becoming rather tense in the South Atlantic. P's reply was, 'On the contrary — things are becoming rather exciting!' It's good to have such positive support back home.*

"1700. Canberra *and the rest sailed leaving* Intrepid *and us to catch up tomorrow. Called to the staff planning room after dinner as I was writing the last letter home. Enemy now reported all round Cow Bay and Volunteer Bay. Back to looking at Campa Menta, Seal Bay and Sand Grass Bay along the coast to the east of Salvador waters. Also looked at Armentine Beach but advised that this was really only of any real value in daylight. SBS recces, who have been ashore for some time, report heavy surf on Campa Menta beach and hard going behind. (The result of the dry summer no doubt.) Also many dead sheep which is interesting. Either the summer was so dry or they have a disease. Either way it is odd, for the islanders are meticulous about burying dead sheep — because of liver fluke and hydatidosis. They also report very different soundings to those taken by me in 1979 — a great build-up of sand apparently. Wrote last letter to P."*

"The Campa Menta, Seal Bay and Sand Beach area had once been a favourite of the Brigadier's, if not the Commodore's, for he has a very real fear of weather and anchorage problems along the north coast. The thought of landing along a three or so mile stretch of coastline and consolidating on a wide front before moving across the good going of 'North Camp' towards Stanley (despite the Green Patch bottle neck) certainly has its military attractions.

"7 May

"Private bad news has crept in on top of all the good military news....Sums indicate that I won't get back in time for the Two-Handed Round Britain and Ireland Race with Roger Dillon which is extremely bad news. I have waited 8 years for this race — much time, money and effort have been wasted by others — I've entered for every one since its inception in 1966. Could not start in '66 because of the Dhofar war, nor in 78 because of the Falklands and now in 82 again

because of the Falklands. At least these are honourable reasons. However, the Falklands come first right now."

Then, at long last, the entry that I, and many others, had been waiting to make in our own personal logs or diaries. The planning would of course continue, but the tension of waiting would be replaced by the altogether more satisfying sensations of suspense and anticipation.

Sailed at 2200. CROSSED THE START LINE!

Silver-grey Fulmar
Fulmarus glacialoides

XII

The Whetted Knife

7 May.

Having once again shaken off all contact with land, we were in for a long day of meetings to confirm our position and assess the plans. Nothing necessarily changes with weighing the anchor but this time the waiting was over and we were very definitely 'off to war'. Of that there was no doubt in many of our minds and so it was a natural time for consolidation, re-affirmation and stock-taking. However, before it all began I made my way up to the starboard bridge wing for a last gasp of fresh air. The south-east trades were more salty and humid now, no longer influenced by the lee of a tropical, volcanic seamount: the sky was overcast and the ocean grey, matching the sombre actions upon which we were embarked. Masefield's words matched the occasion perfectly:

To the gull's way and the whale's way
Where the wind's like a whetted knife;

Green Mountain dipped below the northern horizon. The weather was not very tropical.

This was the first day of 'our' war in many respects. Up to then the 'amphibs' had experienced their own version of a phoney war; it had all been happening to someone else and, whilst we were part of it in the overall sense of things, we had been well out of it.

"Action Stations; Action Stations; assume NBCD State One Condition Zulu." I lay on the chart table in my bathroom as the only sensible place I could think of while the ship conducted its war routines.

Like most Royal Marines of my era I had attended a damage control course at Whale Island, but I had not, unfortunately, been a member of a particular batch of Royal Marines Second Lieutenants who had entered the mock-up of a ship's compartment for their 'end of course' test with anything but the repair of the 'ship' in mind.

Armed with the regulation number of stout wooden shores and a canvas bag full of soft-wood wedges, the officers set about their task, while outside the Petty Officers activated the flood through a 'shell hole' in the 'hull'. Suspicious that after a considerable time the 'ship' was continuing to take in water at an alarming rate and still with no pumps activated from within, the Damage Control Officer opened the 'upper deck' hatch expecting to find a neat shoring up of the damage and some very wet and exhausted officers under training. Not a bit of it; they had built a raft and slowly risen towards the deckhead dry as bones — at least so the story goes!

All ships are so well worked-up in damage control that the best service any 'passengers' can offer is to keep well out of the way. I lay on my chart table. Once 'closed-up' and with everyone in place a ship then becomes almost sepulchral in atmosphere; it is safe then to wander along to another cabin to while away the hours. I once made a backgammon board with the counters sawn from a broom handle, the dice from an offcut of mahogany and the board from two box files. As it was the only set in the wardroom it was a popular use of my Action Stations. On this occasion, though, I made my way to the Amphibious Operations Room from where I was tasked to brief the CO 22 SAS.

This was the first 'operational brief' I gave, by which I mean that it was for a specific direct-action operation. I was not privy to the exact nature of the task and all Mike Rose would say was that his men were to take out an enemy radar installation on Middle Peak of Pebble Island. Navigationally it was not difficult and typical, from the raiding craft point of view, of so much that we practised in the Arctic. The Falklands had their own peculiar sea conditions, weather patterns and topography to be taken into account, as indeed does any other region. But principles remain the same.

The SAS had some ideas of their own which did not entirely match my understanding of the route they should take, nor their method of approach, so I sought out the CO SBS and discussed the procedures they would have adopted.

> *"Alternative, which the SBS prefer, is to launch Gemini rubber assault craft from frigate or submarine NW of Government Island and follow the kelp in. There should be a swell, so it would be unlikely that they would be seen if they use it correctly. Land in Pebble Cove. Good advantage is that the whole journey can be done in one night."*

The fifteen-foot-long rubber Gemini assault craft, powered by a 40 horsepower outboard, is a most useful vessel. In its various versions it can be parachuted and inflated in the water, manhandled across fields to lakes or rivers, easily hidden ashore and launched from a submarine by inflating it once on the casing and floating off as the boat submerges, an evolution I had first met when serving with the French *Commandos Marine* and the submarine *L'Astre* in 1963 off Corsica. During special occasions such as the start of international races from Plymouth Sound they can be seen acting as fast fenders between the competitors and the often badly handled spectator craft. It is then that we paint ROYAL MARINES in large letters down their sides for the television publicity and PARACHUTE REGIMENT on their bottoms in case they turn over while showing off!

I returned to the SAS with two alternatives, and let them decide which one best suited their needs and experience, for I was not privy, understandably, to the detail of their task and therefore was working slightly in the dark.

"Due to be off the Islands on or about the 18th May. Now looking suddenly at the Port San Carlos area again."

During that first day at sea I was called to the Brigadier's cabin and asked to suggest any suitable dispersal airstrips for the enemy to base his Pucara in East Falkland or some of the northern islands. Some areas I knew were suitable, even if they had not been designated as landing strips; others I had heard about in response to questions sent back to the United Kingdom. Sedge Island was a possibility. The airstrip was substantial for that type of aircraft. (I had helped lay it out across the hard and tussac-free ground parallel to the south coast and to the east of the one-house settlement.) It was a clear contender. Beaver Island I wasn't too sure about; Weddell was good; Carcass was good on the flat coastal plain at the west end of the island; Westpoint I didn't know; Darwin and Goose Green were good; Pebble already had a double strip; Stanley had the main airport of course, but possibilities also existed on the old airstrip site and the racecourse (used before by Argentinians) and San Carlos used to have an Auster strip which was still marked on the maps. Although I had never visited them, I assumed that Rob Pitaluga at Gibraltar Settlement and Bill Luxton at Chartres had good strips for their own Cessnas. We did not know much about the operating parameters of the Pucara, but we knew enough to deduce that it was a tough, twin-engined aircraft designed to operate in the counter-insurgency role in rough conditions. It could probably operate from almost any base.

I had seen Nigel Willoughby's excellent document on likely sites across the Colony and had a rudimentary memory of what had been on offer. When I left Stanley in 1979 the procurement of the first Britten Norman Islander was well under way, but I had no idea how far that had advanced and certainly had no idea how far any of the proposed airstrips had progressed.

There were always welcome diversions, but not necessarily the time to enjoy them. At some stage during this period we were required to carry out a jack-stay transfer with our younger sister, HMS *Intrepid*.

I had long fought a battle over the amphibious ships' funnel badges.

Since the earliest days, the ships of the Amphibious Warfare Squadron had had on their funnel that most distinctive badge of Combined Operations, a red anchor with, superimposed across the top, a pair of airforce cap-badge wings and across the middle a rifle. It was convention that the rifle always faced forwards.

During an earlier refit *Intrepid's* starboard funnel badge had been replaced, but not with a mirror image of the one on the port side; hence the rifle pointed towards the stern − a 'crime' as serious, in naval parlance, as wearing badges of rank in the 'going astern' position. It was also an act that would have had many old amphibious hands turning in their watery graves, but, apart from one or two perfectionists in such matters (such as myself), nobody seems to care much these days. I considered it important enough to raise the matter with *Fearless's* Captain, who immediately instructed his yeoman to send a brief semaphore message to the other bridge wing:

"Your rifle is pointing the wrong way!"

The answer from Peter Dingemans was perfect, if 'sartorially' incorrect:

"It is a wise man who keeps his arse covered!"

"9 May. 1100 position is 15°14'; 19°07'W.

"...and more excellent news from the Carrier Task Group. Sea Harriers bombed and SBS boarded a 1400-ton Argie fishing vessel 80' east of Stanley. Let us hope we captured charts showing the mine fields."

Later in the day I was summoned again to the Brigadier's cabin, this time to have my brains picked anew on beaches in the San Carlos and Salvador Waters areas. It was now clear that, despite the red-herring discussion earlier, these were to be the first and second choices. I did not know then that the decisions had actually been made and submitted to England by the Brigadier and Commodore. San Carlos it was to be, but I had a sneaking position, then, that the Brigadier was never happy as he continually kept seeking reassurance in the form of many small, brief and impromptu discussions. Neither he nor the Commodore ever mentioned 'reassurance' but by the continual questioning to which I was subjected that was the only conclusion I could reach. I hope I appreciated that and gave them such confidence, for, once I realized that it really was to be San Carlos, nothing could persuade me to produce any other area with better 'facilities'. That would have led, inevitably, to real and unnecessary doubt.

However, other options for smaller-scale landings were obviously still not ruled out, as I was eventually dismissed with the instructions to write the full sailing directions for Brenton Loch (and particularly La Boca) as "The SAS have 'plans' for it."

No sooner had I finished the guide to Brenton Loch and its approaches and drawn the appropriate chartlets, with every known underwater obstruction marked, than I was called to the Commodore's cabin and ordered to do the same for Salvador Waters.

Verbal briefs with slides and photocopies of my original sketches constituted one thing; producing formal sailing instructions in the exact manner of a 'pilot' was quite another. This was work that, at home, would take weeks of careful study and analysis before descriptions and charts accurate enough for small craft, or in the case of Salvador, large ship navigation, could be produced. On board *Fearless* I reproduced the charts I had drawn on the spot. These were of a larger scale than available from the Admiralty and much more in keeping with the requirement of use at night in very low light. To this end not only did they have to be scrupulously accurate but they also had to have all superfluous information eliminated. Beach exits above the high-water line needed to be tabulated as well as any known hiding places (such as the tussac bogs, Jackass penguin burrows and wrecks), plus tidal streams, kelp patches and sand shoals without kelp. I marked those areas to be avoided. Disturbed animals, for instance, can give away the presence of a human. This was work I relished nearly as much as the collection of the information itself.

There was more good news that day:

"SBS recce of PSC and SC show minimal activity. Perhaps the odd OP."

Whilst the planners welcomed this, I was even more thrilled, for the rest of the signal confirmed that the waters were as described, allowing me to feel at last that I was producing intelligence worthy of the accolade. All could change, certainly, but the lack of enemy interest was encouraging.

"I will lead in the first landing craft waves. As a navigator and as OC LC branch I will like that. After all, 7/8s of the branch is involved and it will be a fitting end to my time as OC. The next piece of good news is that we now have Sidewinder missiles for the Harriers in Atlantic Conveyor *and if the Int-gathering Argie 707 flies over us tomorrow it will be shot down.*

"10 May. 1200Z 21°07'S; 21°17'W

"We have made an Argie flag in case we have to bury any at sea. Antelope *passed us escorting back a ship with the Argie POWs from South Georgia.*

"Outgoing mail transferred.

"Planning, with increased intensity, for what we now know will be certain military involvement. The air and sea blockades are not working. The Commanding Officers of 40, 42, 45 Cdo, 2 and 3 Para, CO SBS, CO SAS, CO 29 etc. flew across for a preliminary brief on their objectives in the Commodore's dining cabin. It was not an easy session for the heat, ship's movement and the vagaries of the electrical supply which kept cutting out during action stations disrupted the lights, air conditioning, fans and my slide projector. Tempers were rather short."

The aim was to give individual Commanding Officers a look at their own areas (now that the decision had been made public at that level) in conjunction with each other, so that all had a view, not only of their own 'patch' but that of their neighbours. The Brigadier had confided to us the individual unit locations, allowing John and me to prepare packages of slides, notes and sketches for every one. Each series was accompanied by a comprehensive verbal brief. The COs eventually departed with their maps and charts suitably marked-up. They would return to their own staffs and produce detailed questions that I would then answer during the next series of flights round the fleet. In the meantime they would have something to work on in preparation for the full, formal Brigade Orders on 13 May.

Plans were now far enough advanced for the Commodore's staff to concentrate on the final approaches to the AOA:

"Advised that eastern entrance to Falkland Sound was navigationally safer but it is the one most likely to be mined.

"Early bed for once — very tired."

The days since sailing had been very full with 11 May no less so. It started with the production of a new navigational plan, followed by a helicopter flight to 2 Para where I remained dogged by lecturing problems:

"Produced charts for the covert landing on Pebble Island — then off to SS Norland by helo at 1000 to lecture to 2 Para. Met by H Jones. Blasted projector wouldn't work and then just as we got it going, half an hour late, we went to Defence Stations for 'Russian sub' and 2 Bear a/c. (Sub was possibly whales.) Sat in Dare Farrar-Hockley's cabin for an hour in a lifejacket.

"Eventually gave 4 lectures, followed by a series of long

171

discussions about the Islands with RAF Chinook pilots and para officers till well after midnight."

'H' and his officers could not have been more delightful and friendly; I felt very much at home during the long evening discussing the Islands and what we expected to find and how we expected the whole thing to turn out for us. The following morning 'H' asked me to join him for breakfast before my next round of lectures. We sat, just the two of us, in the partitioned-off part of the cafeteria reserved for the Battalion's officers. 'H' was in a sombre and reflective mood and a mood I had not seen before. Some conversations imprint themselves on my memory. This was one of the most striking.

"Ewen." 'H' looked at me over a mug held in front of his face with both hands, elbows on the table. "This is my big chance, I'm not going to waste it."

I asked him what he meant. For years he had dreamt of leading his Parachute battalion into battle and it was as simple as that. He asked no more and no less, knowing that this would be the only chance he would get.

"I've also made quite sure that if I don't get back everyone has been well looked after." He mentioned the schooling arrangements he had made for his sons and other detailed provisions.

It was not the sort of conversation that I had had with anyone before, or subsequently, and I tried to change the subject. There was no doubt in my mind then, or since, that 'H' was determined that he would lead his Battalion in action, from the front, somehow, somewhere and without thought for his own safety. There was no premonition of what might or what might not happen, but he knew what he wanted to do with a clarity and determination I found disturbing. While his thoughts were admirable in many ways, I replied as lightheartedly as I could. It was not the occasion to match his prescience.

I was non-committal to his question: "What arrangements have you made for Patricia?"

I had made none, nor had I given the matter any serious thought. 'H' seemed surprised and chided me for a lack of care. I replied to the effect that I had lived life so far as a fatalist and saw no reason to treat my present position any differently. We had met only intermittently over the years, yet despite that, were firm friends. We were, however, a distance apart in our perceptions of how to prepare for life's unpleasantnesses. When it came, I grieved deeply for the loss of a fine man and courageous soldier, but it was no surprise, especially the manner of his going. It made it no easier for that.

"12 May

"On arrival back on board HMS Fearless *learnt that the first Wandering Albatross had been sighted at 30°50'S; 26°00'W and a Wilson's Petrel at 31°56'; 26°00'W. This is very good news and will now give me some much needed relaxation with camera and sketch book. I feel as though I am nearly home."*

The other good news was the arrival of a signal confirming that the landings would take place — and in San Carlos. This ended some anxiety, for not only had we heard nothing on this score from the General since the presentation on 29 April, but, on the assumption that it was to be San Carlos, the final orders had actually been written and distributed that day.

13 May

A milestone in any military operation is the Orders Group (or 'O' group). It is the watershed between planning and execution.

Nothing is more personal than a leader's orders at every level. On them depend the success of an operation; by them men will live or die; because of them battles are won or lost and, on this occasion, the Nation's pride would be increased or dashed. Good orders can, occasionally, lead to defeat, but bad orders seldom lead to victory. Through his subordinates a leader imposes his will; through his personality he inspires confidence in his junior commanders, and, through them, to every individual man. With Julian Thompson there were no histrionics, no false hopes, no misrepresentation of the difficulties we faced, no false bravado.

Amphibious 'O' Groups, even in peacetime, are serious affairs. Men are killed just as easily on the beaches of Browndown or Harstad as they are in San Carlos. The sea and the weather are enemies equally present in peace as in war.

The Wardroom was packed. There is a limit to the number of men that can be jammed into a finite space and it was exceeded. All morning Commanding Officers, their advisers, assistants and staffs converged by helicopter on the Amphibious Flag Ship. Many old faces. Some new faces. All tired faces.

There were the usual last-minute panics; David Baldwin slid up to me with a telescopic pointer (a car's wireless aerial).

"I'll poom for you."

"You'll what?"

"Poom. Point out on map. There's no space for you to move to the screen from the lectern."

It was a new expression to me. I could not have had a better poomer and thanked him.

The senior Commanding Officers sat in comfortable armchairs in the front row, almost upon the lectern and screen. Behind them on soft-bottomed and soft-backed chairs sat their operations and intelligence officers, the officers commanding smaller units, the supporting arms co-ordinators, communicators, aviators, landing craft squadron commanders and Beachmasters, staff officers and liaison officers from ships and other units. Further back the chairs turned to hard-back and soft-bottom until just short of the limit even their bottoms were solid. At the very rear of the briefing men perched or knelt on the wardroom table pushed hard against the starboard bulkhead.

Julian Thompson and Mike Clapp entered the room to a polite silence broken only by the irregular creaking of the ship as she forged her way southwards.

"The tumult and the shouting dies;
The Captains and the Kings depart:"

The strategic planning was, in large part, over. It was now up to the men on the spot to lay the tactical and operational details before their own subordinates. Whatever the Commander-in-Chief in Northwood and the War Cabinet in Downing Street had decided and agreed, it was now up to a Brigadier and a Commodore to 'execute' the country's wishes in their own manner. Seldom, if ever, in recent history has so much responsibility been placed on two such comparatively junior leaders.

This was very much the Brigadier's briefing; the Commodore would hold his own equivalent, the Pre-Landing Conference with his captains, navigators and masters of merchant and Royal Fleet Auxiliary Ships later.

The 'ground' brief opened the proceedings. While everyone present was probably tired of hearing my voice again, that day had a sense of urgency that had not been present before. Objectives described earlier had been just one of the many. Now I concentrated on the detail of the beaches in the San Carlos area, their juxtaposition, their obstacles above and below the inter-tidal zone, the exits, their proximity to, and 'going' under foot towards, the surrounding high ground. I pointed out the areas of population and local high spots that could serve as enemy OPs. Photographs and sketch maps, excellently 'poomed' by David, brought the features to life. Later, and on an 'as required' basis, I would visit all the COs and their officers to highlight individual objectives.

I finished to a complete silence and took my place standing along the forward bulkhead with the other staff officers waiting their turn to brief on their particular subjects.

"My voice has gone after 15 hours of lecturing in 24 aboard Norland. *Wasn't happy with the way I put the ground and weather across but not much I could do about it."*

The intelligence brief was delivered in a soft, slightly Welsh voice by the phlegmatic Brigade Intelligence Officer. Vivian Rowe had an altogether more appreciative audience than during his first attempt to explain the Brigade's concern on the enemy airforce on 16 April and was listened to with an almost nervous concentration. He was followed by the Brigade Major (or Chief of Staff as we now have to call the appointment) John Chester, with the 'friendly forces' paragraph. His was an impressive performance with an impressive list of the ships, battalions and military units ranged against Galtieri's.

Then the Mission, given by the Brigade Commander himself and repeated twice: unambiguous, clear, short, direct and to the point.

The Brigade was to conduct a silent night approach by landing craft in the San Carlos area. The surrounding high ground would be seized on foot, before first light, in order to secure a beachhead into which stores and munitions would be unloaded prior to subsequent operations to re-possess the Falkland Islands. These are my words.

After the subsequent paragraphs on logistics, command and control, the outline naval plot and co-ordinating instructions, the Brigadier stood once more in front of the silent assembly. "Gentlemen," he said, "The operation we are about to embark upon will be no picnic." He had no need to add that it would not be a walkover.

The plan for the initial landings was simple. The amphibious ships would anchor or orbit on a 'race track' to the west of Chancho Point (the southern entrance to Port San Carlos). Landing craft from *Fearless* and *Intrepid* would collect 40 Commando from *Canberra* and 45 Commando from *Stromness*. We would all cross the Line of Departure (LOD — the nautical equivalent of the Start-Line) in line ahead, at six knots, which was about two-thirds maximum revolutions. Off Little Rincon we would split into two groups, form line abreast and at maximum speed land 40 Commando below the settlement of San Carlos. They would take the high ground, dig reverse slope positions, and protect that flank from the north and east. Simultaneously 45's landing craft would turn to starboard to land them in Ajax Bay from where they would take the high ground guarding the west, south-west and sea approaches to the anchorage.

The second wave, for whom the landing craft would return, would bring 2 Para into the beach south of San Carlos from where they would move onto the Sussex Hills to defend the southern approaches, while 3 Para would be landed to the west of Port San Carlos to defend the river and land approaches from the north, east and west. A troop of the Blues and Royals would be landed with 40 Commando and 3 Para. 42 Commando would remain on call in *Canberra* as reserve.

It was simple and neat, provided the weather allowed us to retract the large landing craft and the enemy remained as absent as reported. The anchorage would be defended around its complete perimeter within which we would then conduct an unmolested offload of guns, ammunition, food, vehicles and stores. Ground and sea forces would keep it impregnable from those directions; we were not so sanguine about the air threat.

The orders had been a genuine masterpiece, not only in terms of presentation but in content, confirmed by the absence of questions. John Chester, whose duties included the stage management as well as the co-ordination of the facts, could be well satisfied; it was now up to us to execute those instructions with the same degree of professionalism. There was little doubt that we would repossess the islands.

"Feeling rotten with sore throat and flu (?) so didn't fly across to Intrepid *after O Gp but will go tomorrow to brief Captain and Navigator and speak to 'my' Detachment. Finally finished brief of Brenton Loch for CO 22 SAS − very complicated passages but OK (just) for small light easily manhandled craft in the dark."*

The proposed visit to *Intrepid* puzzled me. The Commodore had grabbed me after the 'O' Group to tell me that HMS *Intrepid* was unhappy about certain aspects of navigating into San Carlos Waters and close in to the Falklands shores in general. He suspected that they had probably read too many signals about kelp and were paying too much attention to the age of some of the surveys as indicated on the Admiralty charts.

It was at about this stage that less bravado and more tension entered my log. Many comments, up to 'D' Day, now take on a more judicious tone. Despite outward appearances, we were all suffering wear and tear to moral and physical well being. The uncertainty, the mismatch of assets (particularly air), the unsuitability of the ships for the job, the worsening weather and the thought of what, at the worst, could lie ahead, took its toll. 'Positive thinking' was the order of the day, but thoughts did stray occasionally! In a ship at sea there is no escape from the job in hand and yet the surprising thing is just how cheerful and supportive everybody was − considering. We all had private concerns, whether or not they centred on home or profession; nobody was immune, but few people indeed showed any adverse sign in public. Each had his own private world into which a dive could be taken if necessary: mine was sketching sea birds and playing 'uckers'; others concerned themselves with the sports results on the World Service or playing chess or Scrabble. Life in anti-flash gear was a constant reminder of the horrors of battle, as were the twenty-four-hours-a-day concern with warfare, the cramped conditions and the canned air. None were conducive to normal emotions and behaviour.

1. Hermione on board the wreck of the *Lady Elizabeth*.

2. Moody Brook Camp in 1978. Condemned for human habitation in 1918 and again in 1945.

3. MV *Forrest* at anchor off Ajax Bay in San Carlos Waters in 1978.

4. "The Beaver float-plane was scrambled from Stanley and flew direct to Goose Green where it moored alongside the yacht *Capricornus*."

5. "The Welsh Guards landed at San Carlos with no firmer orders than to set up defensive positions on the reverse slope of Sussex Mountain."

6. Mortar Troop of 42 Commando setting up their base-plate positions on the slopes of Mount Kent. Lifted in by a Wessex of 845 Naval Air Squadron.

7. "Sniffed at the Z bend but mass of breaking water." Oil painting commissioned by the author from David Cobb showing the lead LCU laden with a company of the Scots Guards turning away from the Z bend on the morning of 6 June, 1982.

8. "Some [of the ruined aircraft] had their noses in the peat…the distinctive Pucara tail cocked in the sky."

My private anxiety was for the accuracy of all that I had told the planners and was to remain with me right up until the day I left the Islands some time after the surrender.

"14 May. Foggy morning. Giving much thought to Exocet and lack of air cover. We enter the TEZ on the 19th and will be completely vulnerable until ashore — 20th? Personally I'm not sure what the fear of the TEZ is. People talk about it as though once in it we are more likely to be attacked by the Argentinians. They have no such exclusion zone and will attack us wherever and whenever they can find us. The TEZ is of our own making. As far as the Argies are concerned we must be just as vulnerable outside it as in, providing they can reach us with their aircraft. So what is the fuss? Canberra will probably be No 1 target and us No 2. Hope the anti a/c screen gets out and is good at its job. The main thing, surely, is to spend as much time as possible in darkness during the final approach to thwart any attempt by their aircraft to disrupt proceedings in the early stages of the landing.

"Quick brief from COMAW and off to Intrepid. *Flew via various ships and some pretty hairy landings.*

"Briefed Malcolm Macleod. Captain and Navigator. Very friendly but with a strange worry over safety.

"Clearly news of the Flag Ship's life-style has reached the ears of those more fortunate. I must say that life in our sister ship seems rather relaxed and certainly uncrowded. There was none of the frantic rushing to and fro that marks life in Fearless. *There is almost a sense of 'it's not really happening' which might well explain the concern over safety. In peacetime this is a valid aspect but in war should have no such high priority. The ship doesn't feel as though it is going into action and while I admire (and even revel in) the atmosphere, I have to say I think it is not quite right under the circumstances. Which I admit is pretty self-opinionated!"*

Waiting for the round-robin Sea King to re-appear I met many old friends at the wardroom bar. I had no need to tell them of the privations we were suffering; many had seen for themselves the extraordinary conditions during their visit for the Brigadier's 'O' Group. To be fair, we were quite well off in *Fearless*: it was just that *Intrepid* was better off! So much better off that I was told to wait for a moment as I began making my way aft to the flight deck and imminent aircraft. I took my time towards Flyco and the Aircrew Briefing Room and at the last moment, with the helicopter on 'finals' a large cardboard box was pushed under my arm. I was already laden with briefcase, projector, slide boxes and roll of charts, but managed to find an extra hand, for it was obviously an important package.

"Don't open this until you reach your bathroom."

I told the smiling Hugh McManners and Dennis Marshall-Hasdell that I would keep that promise.

Hugh was quite one of the most delightful men in the Task Force, a highly educated Gunner and member of that special breed − 148 Commando Forward Observation Battery. He was to be among the first onto the Islands in support of the SBS on D Day and wrote what must be one of the most 'human' books about the conflict, *Falklands Commando* (William Kimber). We served together at Poole and were well aware of each other's taste in food and wine.

Dennis, a tall, laughing RAF Flight Lieutenant and Phantom navigator, was the Brigade Forward Air Controller, and also a friend from Plymouth. Dennis and Hugh had lived in *Fearless* until the port ran out, when they managed to transfer themselves to greater comforts. They couldn't beat me at 'uckers' either but on the other hand I would not have dared play Hugh at chess. There may have been other more military reasons for their move but I was not privy to them.

Back in the peace and quiet of the senior officers' bathroom I opened the box. Inside were two bottles of port, an orange and a quite superb currant cake. It was a Red Cross parcel of the very finest. The orange I ate immediately; the port and cake I saved for a little later when I could share them with the staff.

"Took 2 hours flight back to Fearless *only to find myself back on* Intrepid's *deck! Eventually returned. Admiral Woodward has said that he cannot defend his own task group − let alone us when we arrive − as he simply does not have enough aircraft to defend the carriers, the amphibious ships and carry out ground strikes and special forces missions. This is not his fault but will mean a very careful control of those few Harriers that he does have. We all understand this and his predicament. For the landings, though, we should be given the highest priority to allow us to get ashore safely so that we can begin to win the ground battle from a good start. All else will be vital and probably magnificent, but it is the infantry ashore that attacks and holds ground to secure victory in these circumstances.*

"D Day has been put back, so has H Hour, to allow us more time in darkness on the approach."

This was the first change. The Brigadier had wanted to land after last light so that the troops could approach their objectives under cover of darkness which would have meant approaching the AOA in daylight. It was agreed at one of the many co-ordinating meetings that the priority must now be the approach of the ships in the dark. This was an easily solved problem highlighting the flexibility of planning that comes with years of experience working together.

"*15 May*
"*Flew to Canberra to brief CO and Officers 3 Para on their objective*
− *Port San Carlos.*"

I was frightened on a number of occasions during the campaign and almost all of them involved aircraft. The first occurred that morning:

"*Lifted off by winch from fo'c'sle − lift aborted whilst I was in midair. As I was the only officer waiting to go − huddled with six other staff in the lee of a screen door − I felt it was correct to go first. The fo'c'sle was wild and windy with much spray and a cross wind; the helo was hovering at right angles to the ship which was steaming at 10 knots with about 30 knots of wind on the starboard bow and a heavy sea on top of a heavy swell. I had just slipped the strap beneath my arms at the precise moment the ship's bows plunged fifteen feet. Also at that moment the pilot decided it was too dangerous and pulled his machine upwards, but I don't think he realized I was already hooked on. The look of surprise on my face probably matched those of the officers of the watch as I flashed past the bridge windows about ten feet away and thirty feet below the aircraft to be carried half a mile across a very angry-looking ocean still clutching my briefcase and slides with both hands like a real staff officer going to war! A touch hairy.*
"*Air raid warning yellow whilst on board* Canberra *which we were told was probably the 707.*
"*Back on board* Fearless *and straight into an Int briefing indicating one Coy of enemy N of San Carlos probably on Lookout Rocks. Have asked for a frigate to sail with us when we take 40 Cdo and 45 Cdo up San Carlos Water. Also will need it when we take 3 Para up Port San Carlos. Could be tricky if my memory and notes have been at fault. After all they were written for yachts in peacetime and not for a military amphibious assault − but it is too late to worry about that now. I must retain my faith in my earlier work. I was happy with it then and have to remember that! All in all I think I will prefer to be on board* Black Velvet *on D Day!*
"*Heard the news that the SAS have destroyed 6 Pucara and 3 Aeromaachi on Pebble Island. Excellent news.*

179

"Gale force winds made changing for dinner this evening a little difficult and even hilarious. Congratulated Mike Rose on the performance of the SAS. He was nice enough to suggest that it might not have worked so well without my nav plan, as apparently the recce was done by boat.

"Ship still rolling. Will make some arrangements to keep my camp bed from rolling over the whole time. Suspend it from the deck head — that sort of thing.

"16 May

"Sixth Sunday at sea and the welcome oasis of a church service in the senior rates' dining hall. Air raid warning yellow. Didn't sleep well though, as much going through my mind about the accuracy of everything I have told them.

"This next week will probably be the most dangerous of my life and, in all probability, everybody else's lives — except, possibly, for that week in Dhofar when we came across, for the first time in the war, Chinese Communists operating for PRSY with better and more powerful weapons than those we had. Exciting stuff!

"I shall feel safe when afloat with the landing craft and in charge of my own destiny once again. Like single-handed sailing I prefer it when there is no one to mess things up except me.

"Now advising the Captain to enter between White Rock and the kelp patch half a mile to the east — not between this and Sunk Rock at the entrance to Falkland Sound. Hope I've got that right for this passage is less likely to be mined but is the one NOT recommended by the locals, although I have used it often enough with Jack Sollis.

"The second change to the landing plan was made today. Intelligence reports indicate that a reserve force of enemy have moved to a position north of Darwin and well within reach of Sussex Mountains — 2 Para's objective. Not only that but if they feel inclined they can dominate that approach to the anchorage before we manage to secure it. The Brigadier has now altered the plan so that 2 Para will replace 45 Commando in the first wave. The Marines will land, as planned, across Pony's Valley Bay Beach while the Paras will go ashore in Bonners Bay and make their way straight for the high ground three miles to the south.

"While this will get 2 Para under way as soon as possible it leaves the western flank unsecured until the second wave. Although there are no reports from the SBS in a cave half-way up the hill above Ajax Bay it could be embarrassing if the enemy move into a position to fire up our sterns as we land on the opposite side of the waters. It is an acceptable risk because of the proposed presence of a fire-support frigate.

"There is an enemy position occupying Fannings Head. If they possess a 105 anti-tank gun they can play havoc with the soft-skinned landing craft and their even softer-skinned passengers. This 'Fannings Head Mob' (as Mike Clapp calls them) need to be dealt with by direct action in advance of the landings. A plan to confront this company has come from the CO of the SBS; twenty-five of his men will land by night-goggled pilots flying a Sea King. They will be accompanied by Hugh McManners controlling naval gunfire support from HMS Antrim and Captain Rod Bell.

Rod had been brought up in Costa Rica where his father was a British UN Official. Spanish had been his first language for many years and, of equal importance to the Task Force, he understood the Spanish and Argentinian psychology and social structure probably rather better than he did that of the British. Rod's duty was to test the spirit of the enemy in an attempt to get them to surrender rather than be killed in a fire fight with the SBS.

"Saw a Wandering Albatross and Audubon's Shearwater.

"Thought a great deal about P and the children and generally had a 'low' day — unlike me but am a little concerned about the air threat as we have heard so often that Woodward doesn't think much of it and is not intending to do a great deal about it anyway — but I don't know how much dialogue there is between Brigade and the Battle Group as we do not consider them to be in our own command chain. To be fair there are not that many British aircraft anyway and those that are with us will be pretty busy defending the carriers, but, just for once, the amphibs must be at the very top of any priority list. I suppose it depends if the carriers come close in with us so we are all under the same umbrella.

"17 May

"Gave the 61st lecture on FIs — to ships' officers — not being warned in advance, I was woken in mid-afternoon during a short kip after the 60th to the Bde Air Sqn.

"Rest of the day spent in planning LC assault — Blue Beach One and Blue Beach Two for 40 Cdo and 2 Para in the San Carlos Area and then Green 1 and Red 1 for 3 Para in the PSC area and 45 into Ajax Bay.

"Ship in defence watches the whole time. All of us at action messing, wearing full 'action' kit. Weather is too good for comfort but at least it should get worse just when we want it.

"Another small change — this time with the timings. Brigadier has

decided 2 Para will land first by 10 minutes in Bonners Bay Beach (Blue Beach 2). Will work this out with COMAW's staff tomorrow. Have got over yesterday's 'low' (sorted out by a gin or two) but it annoys me that I have suffered, even briefly from nerves, but I suppose it is only normal when one's fate is in other peoples' hands.

"Saw a Wandering Albatross — we have now lost the Audubon's Shearwater.

"18 May.

"Woken at 1055Z by air raid warning red. Sitting writing this on my camp bed and feeling rather calm and excited about the whole thing. If this is the start, let's get going! Hermes *has sent up two a/c to investigate. She is off our starboard side. Calm, clear day. Good for enemy a/c.*

"Last night Peter Cameron and I stayed up late. We are fully prepared for whatever might be the outcome. It is sad but we have now reached the point where we must put all private thoughts behind us.

"1145. Air raid warning Red again. The ship becomes strangely silent when closed up at Action Stations. Everyone is in his position. Mine is on my camp bed in my cabin to avoid the whiplash effect. I have been told that that is the best thing. I think a hammock would be even better. Strangely exhilarating!

"Wrote a nav plan for HMS Plymouth *who will be our NGFS ship for the run down San Carlos Waters."*

Even at this stage I was still determined that a balanced outlook should be kept, although not everyone shared this rather iconoclastic view:

"Cape Pigeons (Whale Birds) seen. Sent off the bridge by the navigating officer for encouraging the officer of the watch to look for sea birds as well as enemy a/c or submarines. We must remain evenhanded about these things.

"It is a beautiful day — weatherwise — we have met up with the Battle Group — as far as the eye can see there are ships. Merchant tankers, RFAs, LSLs, cruise liners, cross-Channel ferries, merchant heavy-lift ships, LPDs, frigates, destroyers and aircraft carriers. Harriers and helos screaming and buzzing overhead. If Galtieri could only see this lot he would give in. However, our mood is that we must actually win by a feat of arms now! We are prepared mentally and physically. The world will see that Britain really is a powerful nation in intent and determination. On top of that not many countries

could have cobbled together such a task force so quickly and efficiently."

This was the day that plans were changed for the last but most significant time:

"After dinner — summoned to the Joint Planning room to discuss implications of signal from CINC Fleet saying that only one major unit may be in any one ship. Thus 40 Cdo are joining us in HMS Fearless *tomorrow and 3 Para will go to* Intrepid. *The wardroom will be turned into a messdeck.*

"This change has implications beyond that of splitting the major units between ships. 3 Para, about to be embarked in Intrepid, *will have to wait on board whilst her landing craft steam to* Norland *to pick up their fellow paratroopers. It would not have made sense for 2 Para to move to* Intrepid *as they have practised loading through their own ship's side doors one at a time and 3 Para would still have had to be found a home. I can launch with* Fearless's *boats (loaded with 40 Cdo who will now be on board, thus saving them a last-minute cross-decking operation) and transfer into the lead* Intrepid *boat with 'H' Jones before we cross the LOD. He will now land ten minutes ahead of 40 Commando to prevent a fire fight (with possibilities of blue on blue) if the enemy are defending in strength on the headland (Little Rincon) or the settlement separating the two beaches.*

"Issued with a pair of passive night goggles (PNGs). First time I have looked through them. Quite remarkable with bifocal lenses for simultaneous far and short focusing. Everything a bright flickering two-toned green. They do not magnify but a direct light source such as a torch or match can be seen for miles. Otherwise everything else is lit up by whatever ambient light there might be around. Just a few stars are all that is necessary.

"19 May

"Called before dawn to advise the Captain on LCU transfer of 40 Cdo and 3 Para from Canberra. *I reckoned the sea state was OK (some didn't, but I have operated in much worse). The weather seems reasonably settled at the moment and we should go for it immediately. The alternatives are horrendous — individual jackstay transfer of one man at a time might take till after D Day and small sticks of men from flight deck to flight deck will use very precious aircraft maintenance and airframe hours. I warned that there will be some cosmetic damage to the craft but small beer. Captain seemed delighted to have his*

suggestion confirmed.

"The God of battles, in cahoots with the weather deities, has decided it is our turn for good fortune."

In practice they must have been working overtime, for, not only did they give us this most unexpected and quite unusual lull in sea conditions for the middle of the South Atlantic, but during the next day and a half or so, when we needed something altogether different to mask our approach, they again turned up trumps. Thank you, Mars.

"Back to bed via a cup of tea and a grapefruit. Up later – delicious cold shower – last breakfast – probably last cooked meal – before landing. Hamburger, fish cake, bacon, tomatoes, egg. Yuk! – but delicious.

"The collection of 40 Cdo from Canberra *went remarkably well I'm relieved to say. One man fell in between the ship and the LCU but all in all OK. He was rescued, wet, but apparently raring to go."*

The timings for the landings had been backwards and forwards a bit with 'H' Hour now at 0230 GMT to allow us the maximum darkness on the approach and yet give adequate darkness for the troops to reach their objectives. I needed to compress the numerous activities before and during the assault, for we now had more to do in less time.

As the plans and timings were at last firm I was able to concentrate on the fine detail of my pilotage plan down San Carlos Waters.

I had long since chosen the LOD as an imaginary line north-south between Fannings Head and Chancho Point from where I wanted to follow a reasonably circuitous route south, hugging the edge of the kelp along the western shore with a planned passage speed of six knots. I intended to lead the long snake of craft until off Ajax Bay where 40 Commando's craft under command of the redoubtable Bob Edwards would have an agonizing 10-minute wait while I took 2 Para into Bonners Bay at full speed. Without any signal, 40 Commando would then form into line abreast and steam into Pony's Valley Bay. We would meet again off Ajax Bay and return. I would take my craft to *Intrepid* for 3 Para and Bob would take his *Intrepid* craft to *Stromness* for 45 Commando.

There were other restrictions. The whole operation would be conducted in radio silence and without visual signalling. Even in an ideal world where men load in their own ship's landing craft and steam straight ashore an amphibious landing is never easy, for last-minute problems inevitably occur. Timings, dovetailed in with the SBS beach-markers and naval gunfire support (not to mention all the surface, sub-surface and air support and the myriad of fighting, logistic and transport ships) demand that delays and alterations are explained and discussed and this means instant communication. Without it cock-ups can magnify and snowball with terrible consequences. The complication for us on D Day would be that once we rounded Chancho Point we would be out of sight and sound of the Flagship, meaning that even if we were to be so minded there would be no contact at all. We would not be able to seek advice if things went wrong, nor would the command be able to abort or alter. The responsibility for any change would be mine or the cox'ns, some of whom were young Corporals. All the five star and Prime Ministerial planning in the world would count for naught if we were to get it wrong during those vital minutes.

"News at 1200Z (0800 local) was not good. Argie proposals not close enough to Maggie's demands and I am glad to say she does not seem to be swayed by the idea of doing a compromise deal. She must realize that there is only one way to ensure that this sort of thing is stopped and that is to kick the buggers out physically and with as much hurt as possible. Otherwise next time someone else will reckon they can get away with the same sort of thing and end up with a similar compromise.

"Am getting a little tired of waiting. Few of us are sleeping well and this is nothing to do with the impending landings but the living conditions and cramped ship. This is not the way to get the physical and emotional rest people need before carrying out an assault which will be difficult and draining enough anyway without having to start off like this. Oh for the proper ships to do this job and not have to cobble the whole bloody thing together each time! An amphibious landing should be conducted with specialist ships and with specialist officers in command. It's complicated enough as it is and 'at the scholarship level of military operations'. The country deserves better if it wants to hold its head up in these high-profile tasks.

"If this succeeds I suppose the buggers back at home will say: 'There, I told you so. We can do it with what is available.' But would it have been possible to put even this lot together in a few months' time with less ships, coupled with the continuing decline of a once proud (but still vital) merchant fleet.

"We might enter the TEZ tonight, cross it tomorrow and land before dawn on the 21st.

"First action messing with nearly 2,000 men onboard. Queued down the after wardroom ladder past the galley door — a mug of soup and an oggie — back to my cabin to eat it. Colonel Tom Seccombe (and me) not impressed by lack of booze!

"2100Z. By this time tomorrow — providing we have been given the go-ahead — we will be approaching North Falkland Sound.

"The weather forecast is not excellent but it looks as though we shall go anyway.

"Heard earlier this evening that Sea King VT from Hermes to Intrepid has ditched. 21 SAS men are missing. 30 in the a/c. A blow to morale, particularly now, and a loss of irreplaceable assets.

"Action messing dinner was a good stew in a mess tin plus 2 cans of beer and we drank a bottle of port (Thank you, Dennis and Hugh) in Mark Gosling's cabin with David Baldwin, Richard Dixon, and David Dow. Joined by various people who looked in. Brigadier, COMAW, Cdr, Cdr S, and so on. Nothing left to do but wait for the action. Not exactly the guest night before Waterloo but the best we could achieve!

"20 May

"Turned in fully clothed and woken by reveille at 0915Z — 0515 local. Remarkably good night's sleep. Today is the day. If we get through without detection then it will be 'go' for the landings and, barring mayhem on the beaches, once we are established ashore there will be a great chance of overall victory.

"1015. Action Stations. Decided to go to Mark Gosling's cabin again with David Baldwin and David Dow. It's going to be a long day.

"1125. Playing backgammon with David Baldwin and losing! I've only just taught him how to play. 130' from Stanley — heading west. Codeword 'Palpas' (whatever that really means) just received from London to 'GO'. Signal was handed a few moments ago to the Brigadier by John Eddington with a shaking hand for which he was teased. We were joking in Mark's cabin about the FI Governor's flag that I have hung over his scuttle to remind us of what we had to do. 'Put it back where it belongs' — in the words of Rex Hunt when I last saw him. I will." (That same flag was the first to be hoisted at Government House and is now in honourable retirement as an exhibit in the Royal Marines Museum in Portsmouth — still with the mousehole.)

"1530. Air raid warning yellow. News is that 22 Mirages and Etendards (what Brig Thompson calls Super Turds) have taken off from Rio Galagos. Weather is still murky — vis at sea level is about 2 miles. 6 of us sitting in Mark's cabin. John Chester, David Baldwin, Gerry Wells-Cole, David Minords, and David Dow. Full anti-flash gear. Various threats from a/c but at 1650 still only Air raid warning yellow.

"Summoned by Brigadier — intercept of Argie section signal

describing Cameron's House. Eventually decided that they must be at Verde Mountain House. Asking for 6-7 thermos and firewood. Told by their HQ they couldn't have them. Indication of morale?

"Lunch in Mark's cabin of cold chicken and an apple, tomato soup which was very good.

"Summoned again to Brigadier's cabin. For some inexplicable reason we have to rehearse the arguments for and against Low Bay yet again. I do not know the reason why. Nothing has changed to alter my original views that it must be a non-starter and anyway isn't this a little late in the day to start looking at other plans? Brigadier kept his own counsel and was tactful enough not to comment.

"Finally — night has fallen — the weather is still bad — summoned by the Captain to discuss the problems of boat work in N Falkland Sound. COMAW also wanted advice on the best island on which to place an anti-ship OP in the southern entrance. Suggested Great Island — east of Fox Bay. There is no question of us not achieving success; we are talking about the future as though it is Plymouth Sound we are entering. Greatly exhilarated.

"Sea King reported crashed on the Chile coast.

"Now preparing LC Company for its finest hour for some time — pray that we can get this right without breaking radio silence — on time — right beach — no casualties.

"Wind is due to moderate and veer, although I wouldn't be surprised if it backed right round to east and fell altogether and that would be the ideal, I think. An easterly wind to prevent noise reaching the beaches would be best of all.

"2220Z. Packing kit. Loaded pistol. Time for a beer and a quiet think about the job in hand, and home."

There was now no turning back — and not a single member of the Amphibious Task Group would have had it otherwise.

But I longed, momentarily, for the:

"merry yarn from a laughing fellow-rover,
and quiet sleep and a sweet dream when the long trick's
over".

They would come: I knew they would come in due course but sweet dreams have to be earned the hard way.

XIII

On the Beach

No dreams − hardly any sleep.

"21 May, 1982.
"At last − the morning for which we have been planning since the
1st of April: the morning for which we have been waiting with
anticipation, excitement and, at times, trepidation."

With much going through my mind, I had slept intermittently on a camp
bed in the ship's word-processing office, in the end managing a last good
hour. This was reasonably normal for me before any early start − always
fearful that I will not hear the alarm and miss the train, or RV. But, as
always, the deepest sleep comes, courtesy of Murphy's law, just as it is
time to wake.

Having camouflaged my face and hands (and white hair not covered by
my green beret!), checked pistol, charts, note books, landing plans, call
signs and frequencies and hung the necessary bits and pieces (sailing knife,
hand-bearing compass, binoculars, small torch, pocket barometer) around
my neck and waist I was ready for the day. Over one shoulder I slung a
life-jacket and gas mask case (which actually contained a book, chocolate,
anti-flash hood and gloves, an apple, Mars Bar, tin of sardines and one
of bully beef, cigarettes and a flask of whisky) and over the other, the
bulky glass-fibre PNG box. Prepared, at long last, for action, I waddled
and clattered my way up to the Amphibious Operations Room.

Here, in the room where so much of the fervent, often noisy planning
and re-planning had taken place, I found an atmosphere not of future
possibilities but now of cool, quiet execution of well rehearsed drills and
procedures. Suddenly, in contrast to the previous weeks, the AOR was
back to its proper role as the nerve centre of Amphibious Operations.
There was the gentle hum and soft, warm smell of electronic machinery;
everyone seated at his pre-ordained place; order and sense − a clear sign
that the operation had started. Gone were the frantic messengers and
signals, the feverish to-ing and fro-ing of countless staff and advisers. In
their place were the same men now carrying out the clear and unequivocal
orders so well delivered and so clearly understood. Nobody's thoughts

concentrated on whether or not it would be either a 'walkover' or, more likely, 'no picnic'. No one's thoughts were on the consequences of failure or success. The job in hand was the timely landing of four battalions before dawn with their supporting arms. If anyone had thoughts beyond that moment or beyond those immediate shores they were very much in the backs of their minds. As always, for a semi-outsider, entering the AOR was a most impressive military experience. Here was warfare 'at the scholarship level' being carried out by the best in the business.

I squeezed my increased bulk as unobtrusively as possible (conscious of my slightly comical appearance) between the backs of the staff at their desks and consoles and across to the two commanders. Everything was going according to plan − or if it wasn't they certainly gave no hint. A touch behind schedule perhaps? I was told this was due to bad visibility which was a good thing for our terminal approach but tedious as far as accurate and dovetailed timings were concerned.

Concentrated into this small space was information on every man and piece of equipment in the amphibious task force, its landing order, its destination, even plans for its, or his, safe removal if hit or wounded. Into all this were dovetailed further plans for surface, subsurface and air warfare. Intelligence from a variety of obscure and secret sources was fed in almost continuously, assessed, processed, disseminated and reacted upon. Seldom in recent military history had so much information, and so many hopes, been concentrated into such a small space. It would not be over-dramatizing the event to suggest that the aspirations of the whole nation were at that moment focused onto the shoulders of the two commanders (a Royal Marines Brigadier and a Royal Navy Commodore), standing calmly in the middle of that cluttered room. For the next few tense hours the eyes of the nation, and through them, in many respects, those of the whole of the western world (and not a few of the eastern bloc) would be turned towards this operations room, its decisions and reactions.

If we achieved the foothold demanded of us, the British nation could breathe a shallow sigh of relief. If we failed then our country's place as a modern military and influential nation would suffer a blow to pride and morale, and military self-assurance, from which it would take a long time to recover. Like it or not − and it was in the world order of things a minor military operation − the successful landings were of vital importance not only to the Islanders but to the principles of freedom, and they were about to be conducted against odds usually considered unacceptable even with the correct ships.

This moment was also the last chance the Argentinians had to stop us. They had missed the opportunity (or, thankfully, had been denied it by the weather) during our final approach to the Islands, and now they would have to stop us at the most critical stage of any amphibious operation — the approach to the beach and the establishment of a secure foothold. Once that was firm we would take a great deal of shifting, but we all knew that there was unlikely to be a second chance for a successful landing if we failed the first time.

At this point I have to, rather embarrassingly, dispel a serious inaccuracy in Admiral Woodward's book *One Hundred Days*. The amphibious ships did not sail down San Carlos Waters before launching the landing craft as he reports. The ships remained in North Falkland Sound and to the south-west of Chancho Point. This is an important historical fact, which must be corrected, for it meant, among other things, that, once launched, the landings would take place out of sight and therefore beyond the control of, the Task Group Commanders.

Once the small flotilla rounded Chancho Point for the run south down San Carlos Waters no one in the headquarters would know the result of months of planning. Whilst I knew the run to the beaches would be worrying enough for me, I could only guess at the concern that would be felt on the bridge and in the operation rooms of the Flagship the moment my little convoy disappeared from sight. We would be incommunicado until the craft returned — hopefully empty and ready for the next wave. The waiting time would be over two hours and with no radio communications and no way to see over the hill, either with the naked eye or by radar, the staff and their commanders would suffer a severe feeling of impotence. It would not be an easy wait. HMS *Plymouth* could relay messages, but with radio silence and her own line-of-sight restrictions it would be a tenuous and easily compromised link.

With a final look around the specialist desks and their operators speaking without fuss into head-mounted microphones I sidled out again, not so quietly this time as there was much teasing and wishing of luck. I was hoping not to rely on luck, but it would be good to have it! I do, though, remember thinking as I closed the door whether or not I would return and if so would it still be the same quiet centre of calm optimism? Perhaps that was up to me and my cox'ns! The planners had done all in their power. The missile was about to be fired. Its target: the beaches. They could do little but wait until the men were ashore, under direct control, and in their own element once more.

I struggled towards the dock against a tide of camouflaged and fully-kitted Marines. Men for the smaller LCVPs had an uphill climb to the upper decks; men for the LCUs had a descent to the vehicle decks and 'beach'. There was an unreal animation amongst the crews and yet everyone was carrying out pre-sailing checks as though we were off Portland Naval Base. I felt immensely proud of them and, at the same time, a sense of fear for them and their responsibility. It was easier for me as I knew all the options and I was not setting off into the unknown. I had done all I could with talks to the landing craft crews but in the end it was still their 'tiger country'. I had my own fears that no one else could have shared.

For long weeks I had used my memory to assist the planners and although helped, certainly, by confirmation from the SBS ashore, I would remain fearful until the landings were over that my information had been incorrect or, at best, not totally accurate or complete. Now I was to be the executor of those plans. It was a double responsibility. If the landings failed I knew which of the planners to blame! At the worst I felt that my bluff was about to be called and yet...well, I tried not to count too many chickens.

There was another delay as the one-hundred-ton LCUs, sometimes afloat sometimes aground, began crashing together: against the centre partition, against the wooden-battened dock walls and against the dock bottom in the insufficient water depth. The movement was familiar and never easy. Short rolls and yaws with sudden and complete stops made the most experienced of us unable to stand. The violence didn't usually last long as the water depth increased beneath the LCU's flat bottoms, but this day it showed no sign of easing. I was told that there was a problem with the ballast pumps and we would have to be patient, but patience can be a rare commodity on a D Day. I climbed up onto the starboard quarterdeck to focus the passive night goggles and to take a look for the first time for three years at the Islands that were at the centre of my love affair − a passion now heightened by their hour of trial.

It was a typical Falkland morning − calm, cool, clear and starlit. Dangerously typical for our needs.

The stillness was emphasized by the slightest noise from the ships. It seemed impossible that any watcher from the shore could fail to hear, let alone see, the approaching task force; but there was no sign. It crossed my mind that 'they', if 'they' were indeed there, were holding their fire until they could see the whites of our eyes peering over the edges of the landing craft cockpits. Certainly, if 'they' had guessed our destination, they would know that for the rundown towards the assault beaches, the landing craft could only be on their own, out of sight and out of touch with the task group support. What an opportunity to create chaos!

The familiar and unmistakable outline of Fannings Head guarded the northern entrance to the Sound: Chancho Point to the north east, dark against the darker hills above Port San Carlos and only one mile away.

Eight miles to the west the irregular undulations of Mount Rosalie and The Six Hills above Many Branch Harbour, all well-known and well-loved landmarks. Closer still, dark outlines of ships disturbed the long-remembered skyline as they slid, stealthily but visibly, to their allotted positions. Inshore, and recognizable by the whiteness of their wakes rather than by their indistinct shapes, *Intrepid's* landing craft made their way towards *Norland* and 2 Para. They, too, were late, but experience had long since taught me to reserve judgement on nautical events until all the facts were known — and then, usually, to thank the stars that I had not been presented with that particular problem.

I shivered with cold, and probably a little dread for the Islands, and went below to the blue-smoke-filled dock. Some things never change and exhaust fumes from eight three hundred horse-power diesels are among them.

At last (and it was one of the longer waits of my landing craft career) the welcome noise of the stern gate's massive hydraulics drowned out that of air escaping from the ballast tanks. Slowly the dim outline of the far hills to the south and east opened up as the lip of the stern gate swung out and down to sink into Falkland Sound. A cool breeze replaced the heavy blue smoke of the well dock. The sharp motion in the dock eased as the surface water had a wider environment.

"Retract the LCUs." The order from 'Dock Control' to my leading cox'n came over the internal comms. It was the final word of command and came from a Royal Navy lieutenant.

The LCUs backed stern-first into the dark. The sudden near-silence was comforting as the exhaust noise no longer echoed back from the closed steel walls. Men now whispered, if they spoke at all. Most wanted to look over the edge of the tank decks at the first sight of the Islands that were causing all the 'fuss' but the view was, perhaps, rather disappointing. Black hills against a slightly less black sky — although there was another dimension. From across the Sound the 'crump' of naval gunfire was loud and sudden. Four-inch shells landing on Fannings Head, and the long, silent arcs of small-arms tracer, were a telling reminder that this was not Lulworth Cove, Loch Eribol or even Lyngen Fiord. This was real and any sense of 'it's not happening to me' or of exercise artificiality was quickly dispelled. We were now in the war as securely as poor *Sheffield* or the *Belgrano*. The relief that the waiting was over surpassed the pent-up qualms of being involved.

I set up my charts and notes in the radar shack of the leading *Fearless* LCU whose cox'n, like all of them, was an old and trusted Colour Sergeant and friend. C/Sgt Francis was one such man. Quiet and unflappable, I had originally chosen his craft as the lead craft for a rather ordinary reason.

As *Foxtrot One* it seemed to me that it would cause less confusion when things went wrong to have the craft travel down the approach lanes in numerical order. These lanes were simply pencilled on my chart and bore no geographical or military significance, although in another hemisphere and against another enemy they would have been more precisely defined and would have been swept by minesweepers. *Fearless's* boats with 40 Cdo would lead first and *Intrepid's* with 2 Para would follow. At least that had been the original plan when 40 Cdo and 2 Para were to land simultaneously on their respective beaches.

The moving of whole units between the shipping two days earlier and the decision to send 2 Para in to land ten minutes ahead of 42 Commando had caused a few last-minute changes. Although I had left *Fearless* in *Foxtrot One* I would now have to transfer to *Tango One (Intrepid's* lead craft) for the approach to Blue Beach Two, to the south of San Carlos settlement, to reflect 2 Para's need to land first.

Without communications I didn't expect to find *Tango One* easily and as we had already lost much time I was anxious to transfer quickly. *Tango One* was commanded by a cool, direct SNCO whose advice was always positive, unequivocal and, usually, devastatingly accurate. C/Sgt Davies was a friend and colleague of long standing. The only possibility for confusion would be if I failed to meet up with his craft in the dark.

After that, the approach plan was simple enough. We would cross the LOD at 0525Z from where I would lead the snake of craft down my pre-chosen route hugging the west coast of San Carlos Waters. Against earlier suggestions from London that kelp was a problem (written, I had no doubt, by someone who had never seen the stuff) I planned to skirt, and sometimes pass through, the kelp beds that line the shore. I was certain that if the enemy had laid any mines at all they would not be in the kelp. Naturally, there were disadvantages to this plan. We would have to be close to the shore and therefore close to any anti-tank weapons that might be deployed. These would have been deadly against unarmoured landing craft packed very tightly with men: however, if this had indeed been their plan the chances were greater that these weapons would be sited on the east bank.

Without communications, gathering together landing craft from different ships, themselves having loaded men from yet more ships, can be intricate enough, but that morning we had two added complications. I had to swop from one flotilla to another and we had a major delay in the loading of 'H' Jones's men from the MV *Norland*. This was not the fault of the battalion or the ship but simply a function of the convoluted methods forced upon us.

2 Para had not been able to practise this tricky and alien (even to the

Royal Marines) method of going to war by loading one by one through narrow side doors ten or so feet above the waterline into small craft lying, not steadily, alongside. The landing area for any man jumping or climbing down a rope ladder was two feet wide. If he missed by jumping too far out he would fall an extra six feet into the tank deck and if he fell short he would be crushed in the water between five thousand tons and one hundred tons. The operation was being carried out in the dark, with a slight swell running, and with little the LCU cox'ns could do to keep the craft stationary fore-and-aft, and certainly not up and down or laterally. To add to the difficulty there were no mooring strong-points and any line to the deck had to be of great length and to a great height. None of this was ideal. In fact, it was downright farcical.

The delay was becoming intolerable and I was becoming fidgety, despite the welcome presence of Colonel Tom Seccombe who had joined *Foxtrot One* for, I suspected, moral support, although as the Deputy Brigade Commander he had probably felt that the best place for him was not in the overcrowded Amphibious Operations Room but with the first men to land.

Whatever his reason, I was delighted to know that he was embarked with us, not just because of the reassurance his avuncular presence gave but also because he refused to 'take charge'. Others would have fussed over my shoulder. Nevertheless, the increased delay (the third of that morning) was making me edgy. It was making Malcolm Hunt, the normally placid CO of 40 Commando, equally edgy. I was even moved to write in my log that he had lost his sense of humour! It was suggested that we should leave 2 Para to get on as best they could so that '40' could make their own 'H' hour as close to the original as possible. I was minded to agree (it is a matter of pride within the Landing Craft Branch that 'H' hour is met no matter what outside factors combine to dictate otherwise) but sought out Tom Seccombe who was sitting calmly in the unused radar compartment with a cigar.

"No!" was his advice. "The order of landing is more important than a delay to 'H' hour." We would not be able to communicate the alteration of the plan to all the craft and that would inevitably cause more confusion than it solved.

I ordered *Foxtrot One* to close with *Norland*. Up to then I had been anxious to avoid getting mixed up with their loading but we were now late and I needed to find, and transfer to, the leading LCU. The Royal Marine signaller began flashing the previously arranged recognition signal with a pinpoint red light at every craft that came within range. Each one gave the wrong reply, which did not help my humour and rising restlessness. At the same time I instructed the signaller to order each craft to douse his stern light. These lights should have been mere pinpricks, but instead, most craft were complying with the full regulations for the prevention of collision at sea. I had hoped a measure of common sense would have prevailed. Finally, with total frustration, and cursing myself for not specifying in greater detail the dim 'convoy' lights I had wanted, I broke radio silence with three words on the landing craft net.

"Out stern lights!" I hoped that this briefest of transmissions over an unknown frequency (as far as the enemy were concerned) was less compromising than sixteen white lights in line astern!

Throughout this time there had been not one word, by light, from the Flagship. We took this as a sign of confidence. We obviously had a problem, were sorting it out and did not need unnecessary questions or orders from the commanders. They knew we would be doing all that we could to salvage the situation and that back-seat driving would not help. I thanked God for cool sensible leaders, despite the certain knowledge that the frustration they were suffering must have been immense.

I needed to find *Tango One* and, of near equal importance, I needed to find out the cause of the delay to see if I could salvage something. The knock-on effect was eating into the meagre time allowance for 2 Para's land-approach to their objective. Finding *Tango One* was not, in the end, difficult as they were approaching *Fearless's* orbiting craft to look for me. By that time Tom Seccombe and I had transferred to a faster LCVP to hasten the search as answers to my recognition signal were only confusing the scene.

Tom and I jumped across, to find a very anxious 'H' Jones. We were now almost an hour late and I imagined, with embarrassment, the scene on *Fearless's* bridge and in her operations rooms. My ears burned in the darkness.

A paratrooper had fallen between the craft and crushed his pelvis. With hindsight I have always been astonished just how quickly and efficiently they achieved the unloading of *Norland* and great credit must go to the ship's company as well as to 2 Para.

I answered the unspoken question as the fourth and last of 2 Para's LCUs manoeuvred alongside, but some feet below, *Norland's* tiny loading port. "If we leave now with 40 Cdo following, as planned but leaving *Tango Four* to follow when loaded, and if we steam at full speed, we should catch up some time and be about 40 minutes late on the beach."

'H' took no time to consider the hidden question. He knew who would be in the last LCU and had clearly considered the implications of their late arrival at Blue Beach Two. "Let's go."

Tom Seccombe nodded in the darkness.

We closed with Sergeant Garwood's craft and I shouted across: "Follow as best you can. Don't use your radar until the terminal approach and only then if necessary."

We steamed off into the darkness, leaving one LCU to carry out its own version of a second wave. Militarily this was acceptable and outweighed the tiny nautical reservation I held about having one lone craft sailing down the waters by itself. The cox'n would naturally take the shortest route down the middle and if he got into trouble from either mines or enemy fire he would have no mutual support: just as important at sea as it is in infantry manoeuvres.

I told my signaller to flash the formation signal, at the same time ordering the cox'n to make best speed for the southern end of the LOD two cables to the north-east. Exactly sixty-five minutes after we should have begun our passage to the beaches we crossed the start line at full speed. Colour Sergeant Davies was invited to open his throttles to their maximum – and beyond if possible. At long last, and the previous minutes had dragged longer than the previous weeks, we really were heading for the Falkland Islands' beaches.

A strong fire fight was developing across Fannings Head and the continual crack, thump-thump from the supporting naval gunfire was now reassuring. HMS *Plymouth* slid silently (at least we could not hear her above the grumbling of our overloaded Paxmans) southwards half a mile off our port side: a welcome sight and one I did not forget when, years later, she was up for sale by public subscription.

The five-mile passage south was almost anti-climactic and certainly uneventful. Instead of skirting the kelp beds as they followed the coastal contours we took a direct line down the west side of the Waters, the risk of mines taking a lesser priority to 'H' hour.

I recognized Little Rincon (last seen on a typical Falkland Islands day from the deck of the MV *Forrest* in 6/8ths of a gale and bright sunlight) half a mile on the port bow and ordered an alteration of course towards it, signalling to the leading *Fearless* craft as we did so that we had reached their orbiting position.

As we passed through the edge of the kelp off the western point of the tiny peninsula I searched through the PNGs for the outline of the Bonners Bay jetty and remembered clearly the last time I had landed alongside. We were delivering mail and stores from Stanley to find that there was not a soul waiting to meet the ship. This was unusual but explained to me later. There had been some minor feud between MV *Forrest's* skipper and the then settlement manager. On an earlier trip *Forrest* had had onboard the Chief Fisheries Officer from the Overseas Development Ministry who had flown to the Islands to discuss the possibility of inshore, nearshore and offshore fishing. The Manager, a councillor who had apparently asked for

27 April 1978

SECRET

Fannings Head
791

6:0

7:0   Chancho Pt.

Entered San Carlos Waters with Fannings Head an unmistakable land mark. See chart for details of entrance to N. Falkland Sound. Kelp marks all known dangers and does not run-under in the waters.

See chart for full correction and anchorages and landing beaches.

Many Branch Harbour is reported to be a good small boat anchorage but was not visited by us. Well worth a visit.

020° 4'3

2 x Photos 1 of Fannings Head with the lower peak 650 open of the main peak and of Chancho Pt.

Pass close around Chancho Point heading for San Carlos. Straight forward chartwork - keep clear of Fannings Island. From Chancho Point head straight for Hospital Point. If pushed, in a southerly gale, Anchor between Chancho Point and Wreck Point (not named on chart) close in - to Kelp. There is a fresh water pond at back of beach.

SECRET

the visit, turned his guest away with well-remembered and widely reported words that would have been more in place on the trawl deck of a North Sea fishing vessel.

I hoped there would be no such welcome this time. Indeed, I prayed that there would be no welcome at all.

The jetty was the landmark I was most anxious to identify, but before it became clear through the flickering green light of the goggles, I had a moment of fear that perhaps it had been removed in the intervening years. It was important that we landed on the southern side to ensure that the Paras had no buildings to pass. The jetty, flimsy and wooden, would probably not have shown on the radar nor to the naked eye, nor, until close, in the goggles.

The wooden lattice work moving against the low cliffs as we approached at an angle gave me the fleeting identification I needed. It was enough, and some comfort to me that although we may not have met 'H' hour we were at least heading for the right beach.

The next landmark was to have been an SBS signal — a tiny spot of red light low on the water's edge. Using the night goggles one can usually make out the slightest glow of light from great distances but this time there was no sign of anything, which was the worst of the four alternatives that I was expecting.

The signals code I had agreed with the patrol commander and his CO was short, simple and scribbled on the edge of my chart:

"Red light — Beach centre
Alpha - Safe
Bravo - Be careful
Charlie - Enemy on beach
No light — Cock up or enemy on beach"

Translated, this meant that if Alpha was flashed with a pinpoint red light in morse code it would mark the centre of the beach and tell me that the area was clear of enemy: Bravo would indicate that the enemy were about but not on the beach: Charlie meant that the beach was defended and we would have to decide what to do — assault straight into a fire fight as we unloaded or back off, if far enough away, and choose a different place instantly. The first two signals would have ensured that we landed regardless. The third would require a swift change of plan (there was no way I was not going to land the men somewhere); the fourth (no light at all) would require some very quick thinking. I had privately chosen a beach 1.2 miles south-south-west from Bonners Bay on the opposite shore, probably wet and muddy but a beach nevertheless.

The 'No light' signal was the one we were confronted with.

Were there so many enemy that the SBS had not been able to get to the beach — or were there no enemy and our men had simply not been able to make the rendezvous on time? Years of work with the men of the SBS had taught me that their professionalism was absolute, but at that precise moment that did not answer my question. Should we risk the approach or choose another landing beach? If there were enemy on the beach I could see no sign, but then I wouldn't have shown myself either until ready to fire straight down the open ramps of landing craft packed with 600 men.

Our terminal-approach heading, at five cables from the beach and just short of the point where we were to move into line abreast, took us equidistant between Little Rincon and Kelly's Garden, either or both of which could have been defended with anti-tank weapons. With a range of just two cables each, they could hardly have missed us.

During the previous days I had given this moment some thought and had long decided that, SBS lights or no lights, we would land the men. I had not discussed the signals arrangements (or the lack of them) with any of the COs for fear of generating unnecessary and delaying discussions at *le moment critique*. Now that that instant had arrived I was not going to change my mind or plans.

Without considering the problem further I crept forward along the craft's starboard catwalk — the quickest way towards the bows when the tank deck is full of men — to find 'H' who had left the cockpit as we began our final run and as the warning order "Prepare to beach" had been passed to the crew and passengers in a whisper.

"There is no sign of any enemy," I told 'H'. "If you do see any men on the beach and they are taking no action they will be SBS. We should land in two minutes."

The order to beach was relayed through the length of the craft for the benefit of the Paras who had remained crouching in the damp for well over an hour. The men braced themselves with anticipation and shuffled forwards to cram even more closely towards the bows.

I returned to the cockpit to treble-check that we were approaching the right area (the absence of the SBS forming a slight doubt) and that there was still no sign of troops, friendly or enemy. There was nothing, and, in landing-craft parlance we were 'on track, at revolutions'. I turned to Colour Sergeant Davies. "In we go." He needed no encouragement. Power to the winches had been left off until the last moment as that noise carries further than the throb of the diesels. A foot or two of surf would have drowned the hum of our approach and the harsh whine of the ramp hydraulics, but it was all too peaceful.

We checked astern and made the signal for the following craft to fan out either side of us and into the pre-arranged landing plan.

I watched the approaching beach with care and told off the distance-to-run to the cox'n who was all but blind to the dark coastline. There is little room in the cockpit of a LCU and so I had to balance with one foot taking my weight on the cox'n's plinth whilst the other dangled free.

"One hundred yards to run." I was becoming mesmerized by the sight of the two-tone flickering green shadows through the goggles. Still no sign of movement.

"Fifty yards to run."

"Down ramp to horizontal." Colour Sergeant Davies spoke to his engineer on the port side of the cockpit.

"Twenty-five yards to run."

"Ten yards to run."

The LCU decelerated to a halt, silently and without fuss, into heavy, black Falklands mud.

"Down ramp." The briefest of pauses, then Davies gave the final order to 2 Para: "Out troops."

Nobody moved.

I leapt from the cockpit and made my way quickly up the starboard catwalk to 'H'. "We've arrived," I said rather undramatically.

"What are we waiting for?" he asked.

"Nothing. We've given the order but I'm afraid there is about a five yard water gap."

"Right. Let's go."

An officer at the head of the men gave an order more in keeping with the Paras' instructions to jump from an aircraft. "Paras GO!" Somebody further back shouted, "This is supposed to be an invasion," and at that moment (0715Z), exactly 45 minutes late and after 8,000 miles and seven weeks of planning, we landed to repossess that which had been so cruelly and obscenely taken from us.

I broke radio silence with one word: "Putty!" − the traditional codeword to indicate a landing at the correct place. The good news was not received in *Fearless's* Amphibious Operations Room: the waiting staff and their commanders had another three-quarters of an hour before knowing that the first foothold had been achieved.

Either side of us landing craft slid onto the beach, their camouflage colours making them difficult to see with the naked eye. Beyond Little Rincon, behind our port quarter, 40 Cdo started their ten-minute run in to the beaches and there was still no sign of any enemy. We could not believe our luck, for this should have been the Argentinians' last chance to forestall any British re-possession. We knew we would find it difficult to remove 10,000 men from Islands so close to their operational support bases, but we also knew that once we had established a firm beachhead they too would find their task immeasurably more difficult. It was a very satisfying moment.

With a sense of relief probably greater than any I have felt in my career, the cox'n announced to me that he was ready to retract and I was able to tell him to: "Make it so!" He had checked that the other craft had all unloaded their troops without incident. Even the gallant Sergeant Garwood, who must have somehow removed the governors on his 280 horsepower Paxman diesels, had arrived, unloaded and was ready to return with us. It was almost an anti-climax; indeed on the return journey there was a distinct air of humorous relief which we had certainly never felt when transiting the narrow River Foyle on the return journey from landing the AVRE tanks during the barricade-busting operation phase of Operation Motorman in 1972.

As soon as we had closed the western bank − a passage we had proved was safe from mines − the sudden shout, without call signs or preamble, of "Air Raid Warning Red" came over the previously silent radio, from, we presumed, HMS *Plymouth*. It seemed inconceivable that there should be a significant air attack on the craft, but I was not prepared to take chances and invited Colour Sergeant Davies to lead the tiny flotilla into the kelp beds flanking the coast. The western shore is reasonably steep-to with little warning of the approaching rocks once one has entered the kelp. Through the night goggles I could recognize various long-remembered landmarks from a beachcombing walk in 1978 so it was not difficult to judge the correct and safe distance to be off; although I am not sure that Colour Sergeant Davies, nor the implacable Colonel Tom Seccombe had the complete faith in my memory I expected! There were certainly some thinly veiled questions, but, despite their doubts, we hit nothing − and, of more importance, nothing hit us. On return, eventually, to the Flagship I asked about the cause of the Red Warning but there was a rather vague reply. Indeed no one was aware of any such incident at that time.

The complication of the landing phase was now slightly relieved as there was no further cross-decking. However, for planning reasons it was easier that *Fearless's* craft unloaded the men of 3 Para from *Intrepid* whilst those from *Intrepid* (in which I was) unloaded 45 Cdo from the RFA *Stromness*. I had, therefore, to be dropped off at *Intrepid* and await the arrival of the *Fearless* LCUs from their landings on Blue Beach One with 40 Commando. This was to allow me to take the second wave of craft into the one beach yet to be approached. The other cox'ns and officers had all seen the approaches to San Carlos Waters beaches and were then able to judge for themselves where the kelp beds and dangers were.

3 Para were to land on the unexplored Sand Bay Beach to the west of Port San Carlos – Green Beach. This required a night approach across the entrance south of Fannings Head, and the old Fannings Harbour, into the kelp (no mines?) off the south and west coast of Fannings Island. From there I intended to take the craft into the kelp off Rabbit Island and follow it to the final run into Sand Bay Beach. The added complication was that I had never landed on this beach and had only suggested it as a possibility based on deductions from other similar sites in the area, and from various photographs I had taken in more peaceful days. It was the one beach that worried me.

The moment I had been delivered to the red-lit dock of HMS *Intrepid* I made my way to the Amphibious Operations Room to discuss the loading of Hew Pike's men. Hew was understandably anxious. It was long past the time he should have loaded his men: daylight was close. I explained the delay, not that he needed to know the reason, but it was the first he knew that it was due to 'natural causes' rather than high drama on the beaches.

The absolute priority, though, was the speedy embarkation of his battalion into the LCUs. We still had to wait for the arrival of *Fearless's* craft and suggested to the ship that the men of 3 Para should make their way to the tank deck to save time the moment the first craft docked. The atmosphere in the AOR was in marked contrast to that in the Flagship and, while I admired the *sang froid*, it did not help either Hew or myself believe that we would salvage much time. The men would not be called forward until the craft were in and moored. Hew and I bit on our tongues, for we were not amused. We were 45 minutes late at the ship because of the earlier problems before 'H' hour, but this latest delay struck us as inexcusable. There was no more time to lose but at nine and a half knots and with a run of only five miles there was no chance we could make any up. We discussed the matter in a quiet corner, but it is difficult for a visitor to suggest quicker methods of embarkation to another ship.

The AOR staff were quietly at ease, showing an admirable disregard for the imperatives of the moment. In day clothes without anti-flash gear and enveloped in cigar smoke, as an example of coolness it was perfect, but it conveyed the wrong impression to those of us desperate to get to the beaches before dawn. I probably did not endear myself to the ship by making some gratuitous comment about the requirement to have men instantly ready to embark and so, feeling anger welling within me, I went below to meet the arriving craft. I was in a supporting role, the internal business of the ship was no concern of mine.

I was thrilled to be back on board *Foxtrot Four*. Colour Sergeant

Johnston and his crew were the friends with whom, so recently, I had shared many amusing and professional moments north of the Arctic Circle in *The Black Pig*.

A beautiful clear dawn, with us tense and impotent, reminded me of my first daybreak as a Royal Marine in the field. The Colour Sergeant was standing between our first-ever bivouacs with a dustbin full of broken glass and metal bits until frustration finally forced from him words that were never forgotten throughout our training, "Dawn is now breaking for the second time, Gentlemen." Followed by horrific crashing and breaking noises, "Now GET UP and fall in!" I longed to emulate his actions in *Intrepid's* AOR.

I shared a cup of tea — my first of the already long day — with the crew as we waited for the first men of 3 Para to appear.

...and at last they did appear, struggling one at a time between the tightly packed vehicles to concertina their way into the two LCUs on the internal beach. It was a desperately slow affair and it had not been their fault. Once the leading two craft were loaded the next two replaced them. In the lead craft we orbited slowly astern of the ship. Dawn was breaking — pastel blue sky above dark, angular crest-lines. It was a tense time.

Although I chose a straight-line approach to Green Beach I deliberately aimed to cross through some of the kelp beds to the west of Sand Beach and off the southern end of Rabbit Island. The worry of mines still niggled at my brain. A mine of any size would destroy a LCU and, of greater importance, its human cargo.

It required little navigational skill to find the beach for it was exactly as my 1978 photograph showed (also taken in the golden light of a calm Falkland dawn). We were accompanied by four LCVPs containing the balance of the battalion, while two of the LCUs carried the light tanks of the Blues and Royals. These had been placed in the very bows of the craft, in front of the men, and, as a result of practice in Ascension Island, were there to give softening-up fire directly onto the beaches if necessary. Flat-bottomed monitors may have long disappeared from the Royal Naval arsenal but they were being re-invented for a specific purpose. I thought of the Chief Naval Architect's likely views and smiled.

One of my fears was realized about twenty yards short of the narrow beach. I had just gone forward to tell Hew Pike that the men I had spotted at the back of the beach were SBS when we hit the bottom. The craft had grounded forward in about three foot of crystal-clear water. It was not sensible to ask any man to begin a campaign at the onset of the austral winter after he has waded ashore in waist-deep water, so I ordered the other three LCUs to hold off. The enemy were not in evidence, the SBS were on the beach, it was daylight and as the four shallow-draft LCVPs roared past us at ten knots to land their men I shouted to them to back off when empty and moor alongside *Foxtrot Four*.

Heavily laden men then clambered up and over the catwalks, either side of the LCU, to drop into the bellies of the LCVPs to be ferried ashore dryshod. The makeshift operation went smoothly and 3 Para quickly fanned out to begin their advance eastwards and towards the settlement. Behind us, and on the northern shore about a third of a mile to the west, the other three LCUs had each found a rocky, dry landing for the two unwaterproofed Scorpions and the balance of the battalion. The extra delay to the supporting armour and men was annoying but minimal.

All eight craft retracted and formed up in two columns for the return to HMS *Fearless*. We had no more pre-planned assault loads, our orders were now to re-join the Flag Ship when she was anchored.

The SBS men hitched a lift and were clearly relieved to be back in the fold after weeks of living 'behind the lines' although they looked as though they had spent one night on Dartmoor. While the amphibious fleet crept in past Fannings Head I sat in the tank deck sharing a cigarette and cup of well-laced tea with men who until a few minutes earlier had been living on their wits and superb training. They told me of the enemy they had seen and the state of the settlements and the morale of civilians and troops. I listened intently to their experiences (and their opinion of what was still happening on Fannings Head – the fire fight was continuing) and made notes of things that might be useful to the landing craft in future operations.

It seemed wise to wait for the amphibious ships as they made their way in from the Sound to their pre-ordained anchorage positions from where the offload would continue under the protection of a ring of fire (small arms and Blowpipe to begin with) around the surrounding hills. We loitered under Doctor's Head and watched.

"*Returning to* Fearless, *which is steaming up San Carlos Waters – along with* Intrepid, Norland, Canberra, *the LSLs,* Nordic Ferry *and* Plymouth – *the fleet has now come under attack. A Mirage and Pucara have just flown past us being chased by a Sea Cat missile which went straight on into the hill above Ajax bay. Very exhilarating sight but it landed just where 45 Commando are trying to dig in. Once* Fearless *anchored, we asked permission to dock but have just been told to lie off as she is under attack and 'would call us in when more convenient'.*"

It seemed inconceivable that *Canberra* would survive the day (although someone had calculated that if she sank and remained upright her upper decks would still be well above sea level) and that the Flagship, with her huge battle ensign, and her sister would remain unscathed.

With an awful and alien mixture of horror and fascination we gazed at the ships in the anchorage coming under repeated air attack. It is possible that these first waves were short-lived and few in number, but to us watching from the safety of an LCU hiding beneath the cliffs they seemed to be continuous and everlasting. The main thrust appeared to be against the frigates and LPDs and not on the more obvious merchant shipping. We prayed that the pilots did not appreciate the significance of the *Canberra* (full of troops) and the LSLs (full of the supporting arms and stores), but guessed that, perhaps, they wanted to eliminate the defending ships before being able to pick off the transports without hindrance.

At last *Fearless* was able to call us in and we scurried across the sound. I'm not sure whether it was with relief or fear, but either way we were glad to be back 'home' even though 'home' was still under attack. It was, therefore, with a mixture of opposing sensations that we entered the womb-like security of the dock. Here, shielded from the noise and sights of battle outside, all thoughts of that world vanished and we returned to the familiar and everyday routines instantly. I made my way, almost casually, up and along the familiar ladders and passages to the Amphibious Operations Room. The scene was unchanged. As before, nobody noticed my presence as I made my way between anti-flash-clad backs to be de-briefed by my two 'bosses'.

Apparently no man can serve two masters: but he can if he works for the well-established dual-headquarters system which exists in Amphibious Operations. In theory the Commodore Amphibious Warfare controls all the Amphibious Forces during the approach. He retains command of the ships after the Brigadier has been landed with his headquarters, at which stage he relinquishes the ground troops. Up to this 'chop of command' the Commodore will have been responsible for the moving of his ships, the choosing of the landing sites and the deployment of special forces. The choice of landing beaches and landing zones for helicopters (based on the agreed, or ordered, amphibious objectives) will have been a joint decision of course, no one service having the priority. The Commodore will also deploy, with the Brigadier's full agreement, and often at his insistence, any 'advanced force' operations. These forces gather intelligence, thwart counter-attacks after landings or carry out pre-emptive strikes to prevent hindrance of a landing. After this 'chop' the Brigadier relies on the Commodore for support and in many respects their roles are reversed.

In practice, and precisely because it is well practised, the dual command

and control works supremely well and without friction. The Commanders live and work alongside each other in peace as well as in war. Each knows the other's job, his imperatives, his priorities, his restrictions of movement, and on a more personal basis, each knows the other's personal views, foibles, strengths and, importantly, his weaknesses. At this level, this last point is rarely a problem and in the two 'amphibious' Commanders we had on 21 May, 1982, virtually unknown. Indeed, Julian Thompson was to write: "There was plenty of scope for bickering and recrimination, but harmony was the order of the day."

The same applies to the staff officers of both disciplines. From the Royal Marines' point of view most of the staff (officers and SNCOs) know each other anyway, as they will have been through training together, or will have served at some time in a commando together or attended the same staff courses. Despite being a considerably larger service it is also rare for the Royal Naval members to be complete strangers on joining this team. All this makes for the most cohesive and integrated teamwork and it was in full evidence on 21 May, 1982, in San Carlos Waters.

I was met by the Commodore and the Brigadier in front of their huge battle map covering a large section of the after bulkhead. It had always been a habit of mine to make the AOR my first port of call after any landing to debrief the commanders. This was not required by any Standard Operating Procedure but I had always felt that as it was 'their' battle (exercise or real) it was a nice thing to do.

"Heard we had lost 2 Gazelles plus their crews..."

On leaving the AOR I made my way to the bridge to tell the Captain that his craft had returned safely. Strictly speaking I had no reason to do this either, especially as I was not in command of his Royal Marine Detachment nor their craft, but *Fearless* was my home, and the Captain an old friend.

Jeremy Larken was not on his bridge, nor was he in his 'official' place of duty, the ship's operations room. He was, characteristically, on the open gun-direction platform another two decks higher. I felt he wouldn't want to be disturbed as he 'fought' his ship and gave 'Flag Captain' advice to those others within the confines of San Carlos Waters. I went below.

I had nothing to do. For the first time since 2 April there was no immediate future. The troops had been waiting for this moment. Everything they planned began from here. The commanders had been planning for this and would continue to plan for the future, immediate and distant; for my part, everything I had worked for ended with this moment. It was uncanny and abrupt.

I wandered back to my cabin, to the word-processing room where I now kept my camp bed. Coupled with the bathroom, my chart house, this room had been a haven to me and the scene of intense thought. I sat down, but not before I had caught a glimpse of myself in the looking glass by the door. I was appalled. I've never been concerned about how frightful I can look when tired, and my idea of what constitutes a uniform has often failed to impress my leaders. Even so, to my uncritical eye, it was not a pleasant sight − tired, dishevelled, covered in salt-streaked black camouflage cream, and red-eyed. For the previous eighteen hours my diet had been little more than nicotine and adrenalin. For the previous weeks my thoughts had fed only on this moment. Despite previous training and experience in active service areas (with considerably longer periods living without sleep and food), I was tired beyond my expectations. This surprised and annoyed me. Often, and especially when sailing single-handed, I have taken a perverse pleasure in being able to operate for days and weeks tired and hungry.

I suddenly realized, and with some shame, that I was emotionally exhausted rather than physically tired. I am used to lack of sleep and can combat tiredness reasonably well, but this was a new phenomenon to me. I didn't like it and so went in search of companionship.

"Sat on the deck in Richard Dixon's cabin with him, David Minords, David Baldwin and Tony Todd (RCT) through about eleven air raids. Ship hit by machine-gun fire. We fired Sea Cat, 40/60 − Chaff D. Scare charges for underwater attack. We could hear the PWO/AW/Captain's comms all talking to each other of 'incoming aircraft' at such-and-such a range and bearing and mentally we could track them ourselves as they approached San Carlos. Played backgammon with David Baldwin again. Lost twice."

Later in the day the LCUs returned to their duties as ship-to-shore transport and so began the task that they would continue to perform until the Argentinians surrendered.

"It is now confirmed that Ardent *has sunk after a good fight against massive air attacks. 22 dead. Her crew have been transferred to* Canberra *which has now sailed."*

...and so ended my log for 'D' Day, 1982. But there were many unrecorded thoughts at that time and even more in retrospect.

Memories that remain after ten years may well do so because of subsequent events. The unbelievable gallantry of HMS *Ardent*, whose day started when she was the lead ship into the Sound, remains one of the most vivid, and yet I never actually saw her. She bombarded Goose Green airfield, destroying three Pucara aircraft and successfully kept two battalions of enemy infantry pinned down and unable to mount a counter-attack, even if they had been minded to do so. She shelled Camilla Creek and Darwin troop concentrations and she intercepted many aircraft flying up Falkland Sound on their way to attack the amphibious forces. Initially she brought down one Skyhawk and remained untouched. Later she was ordered deeper into the Sound to deflect raids coming up from the south where she became the target for concentrated attacks, eventually sinking off the North West Islands. She had performed way beyond the normal call of duty, with her performance, in the opinion of many of us, matching some of the well-known single-ship actions in history.

The equally noble *Plymouth* riding as our personal 'shotgun' in the dark is a vivid recollection. Although she was not needed, it was comforting to know she was there with her double 4.5 turret. It was with a heavy heart that I was later to watch her twist and turn under air attack, but with jubilation that I saw her escape with minimal damage, belching smoke and steam, bruised but not seriously harmed. Another retrospective memory is that of the Adjutant of the Headquarters and Signal Squadron, Captain Rod Bell, and his attempt to get the Argentinian lookout on Fannings Head to surrender. Armed only with a loudhailer and a twelve-volt battery he had crept to within two hundred yards of the Fannings Head Mob in advance of our passage past the headland. This was not the last time that Rod Bell was called to the front line (and beyond) to use his knowledge of the Spanish patois spoken by the majority of the Argentinian forces. His understanding of the South American temperament was equally as useful in interrogation and tactical questioning. He played an irreplaceable part in the surrender of Goose Green and in the final negotiations before the eventual surrender in Stanley. A great sadness to his many friends was that this brave, calm and dignified officer was to receive no recognition at the end of the conflict.

While on Fannings Head the SBS team discovered a 106mm recoilless rifle sited to cover the approaches to San Carlos Waters — a fact of which I was happily unaware during our runs into the beaches.

The loss of two Gazelle helicopters from Peter Cameron's ubiquitous Brigade Air Squadron so early in the day, and under such tragic circumstances — including the machine-gunning of a wounded crewman in the water — and Peter's phlegmatic leadership (for which he was to be awarded the MC) after such a personal setback is another memory that will remain.

The Paras with their humour and dedication, and tolerance of our strange ways; the Marines with their apt witticisms, enthusiasm and professional pride in spearheading the nation's answer to aggression; the civilians in *Canberra*, and the other similar affable and serene ships, exercising patience and fortitude under the most trying and unfamiliar circumstances; the clarity and peacefulness of the weather; the desolate and majestic beauty of the countryside; all these elements, witness to horrific scenes of destruction and death, make up, for me, a kaleidoscope of reminiscences.

When that day was over no bad memories remained to tarnish the achievements. Delays there might have been, difficulties there certainly were, even the odd over-nonchalant approach to the imperatives of the hour perhaps, but in the end, not one incident had occurred to distract from the ultimate achievement.

Kelp Geese

Chloëphaga hybrida malvinarum

XIV

A Willing Foe and Searoom

"Another day. We were at sea during the night. Woken at 0200 after two hours' sleep as I have been writing my report and planning − on paper − places where LSLs can be beached. A staff officer who was in three watches wanted me to help out. Good grief, I thought − and declined the offer. I had hoped that they would have just given me a moment to catch my breath."

To make amends for my nocturnal mutiny, and there was embarrassment on the staff's part as well, I asked to man the 'offload net' in the AOR for an hour or so, but my real aim was to get around the landing craft fleet and see how the crews were doing and offer encouragement, advice and bring up-to-date news. I was not in the landing craft command chain, but as their own officers were setting up and running Amphibious Beach Units at the two re-supply beaches (Bonner's and Ajax Bays) it seemed that no harm could come of it. Nobody likes to be kept in the dark and it is encouraging to know how things are progressing outside one's own individual area. The landing craft crews were no exception and I particularly wanted to ride with various craft on their different tasks to glean any experience that would be of value in the future.

It had already struck me that the topography (although this particular aspect was no surprise), loads carried and operating parameters were remarkably similar to that of our more regular work in the opposite hemisphere. A useful job could be made out of a 'roving commission' and one which would be of value to us all when we returned to our more normal habitat in the north. There was, though, an ulterior motive − to escape the watch-keeping.

I make no apologies. I am not a staff officer by inclination, although I had attended, and passed, the Royal Naval Staff College, despite an earlier report from the Lieutenants Greenwich Course which had read in part:

"...added to a marked preference for fighting rather than writing...he cannot be recommended for further staff training."

The report was written in 1966 and immediately prior to my joining the Northern Frontier Regiment of the Sultan of Oman's Armed Forces. I had considered the comment to be an accolade and a useful start to the following two and a half years; not so my father who was then the Commandant General of the Royal Marines with rather old-fashioned views on these matters, although reading between the lines of his admonitory letter I had detected a touch of jealousy!

I bore the Staff no ill will. They were all great friends who had every reason to bear me such feelings, for they too were regimental officers doing what they liked least; but it was their job for the moment and I liked to think it wasn't mine!

Uncharitable and ulterior motives had no time to gain the ascendancy as I was suddenly summoned to the ship's bridge for 'an urgent briefing' from the Captain. Without much ado I managed to persuade the duty staff officer, for whom I was standing in, to take back his job and I made off with some relief. Jeremy Larken, a submariner who had embraced the amphibious cause with an enthusiasm rare for an outsider in those days, was a descendant of Sir Ernest Shackleton and had inherited many of the leadership qualities of that great man. He was a firm friend from the Arctic where his ship had accepted my 'cuckoo' into his dock.

He was sitting in the Captain's bridge chair obviously resting from air attacks. Modern naval warfare requires ships to be fought by electronics in an operations room and not from first-hand knowledge from the bridge – or in Jeremy's case, the gun direction platform. But *Fearless* was not a conventional ship with sophisticated defences and the Captain's personal control of her meagre weapons and slow unarmed landing craft was an inspiration.

"*Argonaut* needs a spot of help. Ever towed a Leander with an LCU?"

"No, but each LCU can offer 560 horsepower. It might work."

I knew that *Argonaut* had been severely crippled by bombs and couldn't steam nor hardly fight.

"Right – you've got three LCUs. We need them for the offload, but we must get *Argonaut* in under the protection of the fleet in San Carlos Waters. She is too exposed where she is." He stopped, paused, looked at me and then continued: "I don't know if you know her Captain, Kit Layman, but you may find him a little different. I'm sure you will see what I mean."

Argonaut had two unexploded bombs on board; one in her forward Seacat magazine and one in her engine room. The Seacat magazine bomb, in particular, was in a critical position surrounded by high explosive in a compartment flooded with diesel and sea water. With the bombs likely to explode at any moment, the ship's delicate situation was exacerbated by the rougher water towards the entrance to San Carlos Waters and by the higher chance of further air attacks.

As *Argonaut* could not communicate, at least not on any system that we had, we secured along her port waist so I could discuss with her Captain exactly what it was that he wanted. 'Exact' was probably not the correct word in the circumstances as any towing we would undertake using the LCUs was not likely to be very precise.

I climbed up a short rope ladder and made my way to her bridge, expecting a scene of tense activity, but there was none. There was not a very great deal anybody could do. It would be difficult to imagine a scene that more aptly showed the Royal Navy at its finest under trying circumstances. If I had been a member of the ship's company I would have been in a blind sweat, but I was not allowed that indulgence! Instead, I was offered a cup of tea with apologies for the fact that it would probably not be very hot. Under the conditions it would have been ungrateful not to have accepted.

Smoke drifted up from the forward magazine and I was aware of the second bomb not far aft, lodged in between high-pressure steam pipes: I remembered *Ardent* and did not feel very courageous at that moment, a marked difference to those about me. Nor did I yet understand Jeremy Larken's remarks, unless he had been warning me of Kit Layman's remarkable calmness under horrifying conditions.

I offered one LCU each side, moored with double springs fore and aft so that they could pull or stop nearly three thousand tons of frigate without too much surging. The third craft would be on the end of a long tow forward to give added power, but, of more importance, to aid the steering. Kit Layman would have all his men off the upper deck for the journey while he would pass signals to the three LCUs from his exposed bridge roof: he remained the model of coolness emphasized by a lovely sense of almost Noel Coward-style humour and leadership. Perhaps Jeremy Larken had been trying to tell me I would be involved in a re-run of the film *In Which We Serve*. If that had been his intention it was an accurate summing up. The crew were equally calm, the atmosphere reminding me of an ordinary weekday at Devonport Naval Base spoiled by a rather mundane evolution set by a visiting Admiral. There was drama, certainly, but balanced by a placid, professional approach to mammoth problems, while below decks there were men of extreme valour stabilizing the unwelcome guests and preparing for their removal. In the case of the Seacat magazine bomb this was to take seven days of supreme courage which many of us feel deserved the highest recognition.

Having agreed the plan, I returned to the lead craft to take the strain and as soon as the ship began to make headway the anchor was brought home and we started the turn to port towards a safer haven. From then onwards all was reasonably plain sailing, although after a quarter of an hour at two knots we were worried about being able to stop her. In happier times she could have called upon 30,000 horsepower!

At 1800, whilst keeping a lookout aft through the open door of the cockpit of *Foxtrot One*, I wrote in my log:

> *"Air raid warning Red, which is all we need! Lowish cloud – a little vulnerable in this position."*

But at 1825 I was able to report:

> *"Argonaut safely anchored in San Carlos Waters. Still Red warning. One and a half hours to sunset."*

Before leaving the frigate we moored alongside her bow to say goodbye. It was also an opportunity to ask the First Lieutenant, who was then sorting out the anchoring, for a Lloyds Open Form for our salvage claim. I hoped that the LC Branch Welfare Fund would have been better off by some millions. He promised to speak to his Captain. Six months later I did receive the form, legally and correctly filled in, with a small copper coin sellotaped to the corner 'in full and final settlement'. She was worth every penny! Another supremely brave ship whom the amphibious forces had every cause to thank.

The log continued:

> *"Transferred to F7 (a LCVP) with Corporal White as the cox'n and hoisted to* Fearless *so I could carry out a four-hour stint in the AOR. The officer I relieved returned to his bunk! I only make the point. Ashore early tomorrow to do a job for Brigade. A fascinating day."*

So ended the second day and already, despite my earlier and premature reservations about having nothing to do, a pattern to my life was developing. I was to remain 'on call' for any supernumerary tasks for which others could not be spared. This suited me very well as there would be no routine to my work. There was, though, still much humour around, for before turning in a signal was shown to me by one of the many journalists flitting between *Canberra*, the shore and the Flagship: it was from a colleague in London which read, in part: "Arriving next available schedule flight. Please book into best hotel San Carlos and meet at airport.

Regards." We never knew whether or not it was a spoof but at the time we suspected not!

The following day (23 May) I woke two hours before dawn and caught an LCU into Bonners Bay, an area which was quickly developing into the main landing beach for the Brigade Headquarters and the Forward Operating Base for the Raiding Craft Squadron. There was a great bustle in the headquarters on other matters; so much so that the briefing I was told to expect from the Brigadier was condensed into: "42 Commando need to be moved to Port San Carlos. They are achieving nothing outside the air defence umbrella and are becoming an administrative burden out at Cerro Montevideo. Give it some thought."

I left them to their deliberations, which, I gathered, were the result of some fast orders from London, and wandered back towards the Raiding Squadron FOB.

On the landward side of the isthmus dividing Little Rincon from the mainland, and about one hundred yards up from the beach, was 'the Big House'. As an 'honorary' local I felt it was high time that I apologized to the Settlement Manager for the disturbance. It was as good a time as any. I knocked on the front door and was greeted as a long-lost friend by a man I had never met before. (For some reason Pat Short and I had not come across each other during the year I had commanded NP 8901. He had not then been the manager of San Carlos.)

> *"Pat was delighted to see me with nothing too much trouble and in sharp contrast to the experience of some others in the Task Force who are a little surprised at the lack of emotion from the Islanders. But I suppose as I am not a stranger it is easier for the Islanders to express their emotions to me. As I have explained in my lectures the Islanders have seldom ever met a stranger and have no emotional make-up to deal with one."*

It was as simple as that, but a factor that was never really understood by the British forces and the cause of some uneducated, but, perhaps well meant, comment.

The normality of life was impressive and I thought that if the Islanders could live through this they would survive the aftermath, whatever that might be, for they are a hardy race in both mind and body. All around Brigade HQ children were playing, helping to dig slit trenches, laying out turf blocks to form parapets around the sprouting defensive positions and, by their innocence, helping morale. For the settlement's young there was a carnival atmosphere reminiscent of our Dartmoor village's "Fair in the Square": but amid this outwardly tranquil and rural scene:

"...many air raids. 3 strikes — watched a Mirage hit Antelope's *main mast and crash into the sea.*

"...poor Antelope *hit by two bombs — not yet exploded — but she is steaming around the Sound belching smoke from her funnel. Watching from a RRC on my way back to* Fearless *— stupid really, as we should be under cover but there is a terrible fascination to these raids."*

HMS *Antelope's* bomb exploded later that evening as I was sketching out a chart for 42 Commando's expected move (down the San Carlos River) in my bathroom. I was called immediately to the Captain's cabin (he wasn't there) and hurried on up to the bridge to see at first hand the extent of the problem.

A calm but concerned Jeremy Larken greeted me without taking his eyes off the glare from beyond the bridge windows. The enormous flames flared and died causing alternate light and shadow across the surrounding ships and shore. Through this changing kaleidoscope searchlights from a number of helicopters probed and hunted. It was a majestically aweful sight.

"Can you tow her onto a beach if I give you three LCUs?"

"Yes."

"Right — get on with it. You don't have much time."

We had been down this route before and I rushed to collect gasmask case and charts. On the way I was side-tracked by a staff officer and told I was on watch between 0200 and 0600 in the morning.

There were no LCUs in the dock, so I ran back to the bridge to find that in those few moments events had overtaken me. *Antelope* was burning fiercely, and now continually, with the two LCUs already alongside fighting fires and picking up survivors. I hated the impotence of my position and longed to be able to give some positive form of help; but this personal feeling of helplessness was mollified by the remarkable sight of the boats alongside the inferno, quite clearly acting against the direct orders, being relayed to them from the Flagship, to leave the area. Leading this rescue attempt were *Foxtrot One* commanded by Colour Sergeant Francis and *Foxtrot Four* with Colour Sergeant Johnston. I returned to my cabin with a heavy heart to try and concentrate on my plans for the morrow, but it wasn't easy.

"Survivors coming on board and I was thrilled — but deeply sad — to see Nick Tobin her Captain and great friend. She has lost one dead and a RE Staff Sergeant who was killed trying to defuse the thing. (His Warrant Officer was to lose an arm in the Ajax Bay hospital —

obviously quite remarkable men.) *The LCUs had to be ordered away from the ship before she finally blew up — great work by the lads."*

It was indeed great work by the landing craft crews who man slow and unwieldy craft with no personal protection and I felt immense pride and humility watching their calm bravery. They needed none of my involvement.

A Brigade staff officer gave me a fuller briefing for the move of 42 planned for the next night. Studying the problem in closer detail allowed me to put current events to the back of my mind.

It was not a difficult task; on the face of it a straightforward lift of a Commando from one beach to another; precisely the style of independent support I had always advocated and this time there would be no umpires, or Italians, to complain about fair play!

Before turning in I obtained a brief on the day's activities so that I could pass on the news to the cox'ns first thing in the morning. Some of it, as usual, was exhilarating and encouraging and some of it tragic. During the day we were told that four enemy aircraft out of a wave of four had been shot down and then, later on, nine out of ten had been destroyed. Another wave returned without attacking, but, as someone said, they may well have been in-flight refuelling aircraft who suddenly had no 'trade'. We only existed with the information we received and had no way of verifying anything. It all sounded good news for us, probably too good, but we believed it and that was important for morale. There was also a report that Rapier 'splashed' two aircraft and Seacat one *"....so they are at last proving themselves."* This was just as well for a signal had arrived on the evening of 'D' day telling us to put a bomb under our Rapiers before a bomb fell on them. I noted at the time:

"It was hardly their business and hardly good leadership."

But of course, it was their business as they were Carrier Battle Group ships, which, despite supreme courage, were being hit, although it was felt by our Naval staff that closer air support (by which they meant a longer 'time over target') might also have helped. The 'amphibs' too were taking a hammering.

What we really wanted was the enemy aircraft to be destroyed before they arrived 'on target' and not when on their way home. We knew, too, that the Harrier pilots were equally, if not more, frustrated at their distance from the 'action' — able, so often, only to react to a homeward-bound Skyhawk or Mirage rather than meet them on their way in and before damage was inflicted. Blaming Rapier, in advance, rang a little hollow to the men in 'bomb alley'.

I turned in after finishing my plans for the night transit of the Port San Carlos River, and meeting the LCU crews returning with survivors before they retracted to continue the offload of the other ships in the anchorage. At 0200 I was shaken without prior warning and stood a four-hour watch in the amphibious operations room only to be relieved very late by the next staff officer − a great friend...

...but he brought a bottle of port to the beach later on as an apology.

Two hours' sleep; then at 0800 on the morning of 24 May *Foxtrot Six*, an LCVP, took me to Blue Beach for the beginning of a very full day and night and one that gave me great pleasure and caused me great personal doubt in about equal proportions.

The journey into the beach was disturbed by an air raid across the Sound so we loitered in the vicinity of *Antelope* who was still burning fiercely after blowing up the night before. At 1300 her back broke and she settled with her bows and stern cocked up in the air, resembling an enormous 'V' sign of defiance towards the enemy.

The Brigade Commander's 'O' Group was held in the new headquarters position down the hill from the Big House and dug-in on the seaward side of the isthmus joining Little Rincon to the mainland. The meeting covered, in the main, the plan but not the orders for a raid on the Darwin and Goose Green settlements. At the end I sought out Nick Vaux before he returned to Port San Carlos and tentatively offered him landing craft support, on the assumption that I could prise them away from the offload. His Commando would be saved considerable effort and time, and the certainty of them still being on the move at dawn would be removed, but there was an added complication since my first briefing by the Brigade Commander: the move of 2 Para towards Goose Green would take precedence over 42's local re-shuffling. This advance from the beachhead was on Julian Thompson's own initiative and in response to General Moore's 12th of May directive "to establish moral and physical domination over the enemy." I warned Nick that he might still have to walk.

It was a beautiful day, marked by three air raids during the course of the meeting. When the first 'air raid warning red' was announced we ignored the inviting slit trenches, dug especially for the staff, and stood, or lay, in the diddle-dee watching the action. Two aircraft flew down the anchorage from the direction of Fannings Head, dropped bombs and then altered course towards us, and the hills above the settlement along which they flew, all the time being followed by small arms fire. Suddenly, and noisily, two Rapiers appeared from behind and we watched the gap close.

Over Sussex Mountains and at a very low altitude above the crest two black puffs, almost simultaneous, ended the chase. It was without shame that I recorded that we stood and cheered before re-entering the 'O' Group to join a frustrated Brigadier facing the empty canvas chairs. After that he refused to be interrupted further and we continued unmoved by Skyhawks, except for a Marine guarding the entrance who had a bullet embedded in his puttee. The LSLs *Sir Galahad* and *Sir Lancelot* were both hit by bombs, which, thankfully, on this first occasion, did not explode.

On breaking up from the 'O' group 'H' and I sat in the diddle-dee overlooking the San Carlos anchorage and discussed the various methods by which his Battalion could approach Darwin. That there were simply not enough helicopters had already been accepted, narrowing the remaining options to 'tabbing it' in his words, or travelling by sea.

Ideally, 2 Para would be taken by landing craft in tactical bounds and assault formations (infantry procedures are just as relevant to us as they are to ground troops) up Brenton Loch to be landed in as many mutually supporting waves as was prudent. The best landing beaches were at the head of the stretch of water known as La Boca – the Spanish for 'The Mouth'; close to the settlements and roughly between the two. 'H' gave this considerable 'tactical' thought, although we agreed it would be the beach the Argies would expect us to use for they could deduce just as well the disadvantages of approaching from the east up Choiseul Sound – if they thought we would come by sea at all.

I offered 'H' what I thought would be the number of landing craft that could be spared. We reconciled maps and charts; we discussed timings and alternative landing sites not so close to the final objectives; we studied embarkation points outside San Carlos to avoid subjecting the men to unnecessary and time-consuming sea time. Slowly a plan emerged which involved taking empty landing craft under cover of that night's darkness from San Carlos to one of the five creeks along the north coast of Port Sussex. They would then camouflage out and lie-up during the following day before loading 2 Para, who would have marched down from their eyries along the Sussex Mountains after dusk. We would sail, when dark, for the ten-mile transit of Brenton Loch. Alternative destinations were the many creeks that lead off the eastern and western coasts of the Loch. Unlike the initial landings, we would be on our own with no fire-support frigate; we would be high-value and vulnerable targets in lightly-armed and thin-skinned landing craft. From my point of view, if we succeeded, it would be a magnificent use of landing and raiding craft and an even greater vindication of the previous eight years of trials. If we failed it could mean the near destruction of a complete battalion. The risks had to be weighed very carefully indeed.

'H' was very keen. I was very keen. There were snags. Of all the passages through the Falklands archipelago, that down the length of Brenton Loch is among the more complicated. Peacetime advice was 'never attempt it except in broad daylight and even then as close to slack water, preferably low, as possible'. However, as I had surveyed it in my amateur manner and tabulated all the information that Jack Sollis had given me, I was prepared to 'give it a go'. Nevertheless, both 'H' and I knew that I was proposing a night approach down a waterway with poorly charted, and in some cases untabulated, reefs and shoals. In peacetime I would only attempt the passage with an echo sounder and in broad daylight. If I had had a radar I would have used it unless prepared to sit out a tide while hard aground on a mud or sand bank. In peacetime these were acceptable risks, often taken, often experienced.

But this wasn't peacetime. Not only would we be sailing in the dark, we would not be using radar, we had no echo sounder, we would have nearly six hundred men embarked and we would have no support. A half-troop of maybe four armed AMTRACS were reported to be roaming the area deployed to prevent just such a landing on their own flanks. Both our minds blanked at the thought of the havoc that would be wreaked upon such an armada if caught high and dry in daylight. There were also the Pucara to consider whether we were high and dry or not. While I did not for one moment think that all the craft would be simultaneously stranded if things went wrong (and we could always ferry men ashore in penny packets by RRC) the thought of just one was bad enough.

'H' asked me the obvious question. I gave as a generous sixty-five percent chance of getting all the way with all the craft on time — a greater chance if we accepted a quarter reduction in craft making it all the way. He applied that to his own seventy percent chance of success. The sums did not add up. 'H' stood suddenly and thanked me for the advice. "We'll tab it," he said and walked away back to his own rather more familiar environment. I did not see him again.

I was left to re-think 42's problem, but I was not happy. I had been less than bold in my assessment of the chances of making it down Brenton Loch. With hindsight, I still do not know whether or not the attack straight onto the isthmus would have been any easier or, as some have suggested, even more bloody than the eventual battle. All I do know is that when I heard of 'H's death I felt miserable at not having offered better odds and a quicker approach to the settlements, with, possibly, more supporting arms and ammunition close to the battle. My conscience was slightly relieved on being told later that the beaches and hinterland had been mined and well-covered by defensive fire, but that same conscience was not helped by being told later that the AMTRACS had not existed. In the end I felt that it would have been a more costly battle if it had been conducted from the sea, but that makes me no less mindful of what just might have been.

I wrote: *"Had to make dramatic but, I think, morally correct, decision about the chances of making it up Brenton Loch with the LCUs. Felt wretched at forcing 2 Para and 'H' Jones to walk. I may regret my decision as being rather unadventurous."*

Luckily there was no time to brood, for almost immediately I was approached by a member of COMAW's staff and asked if I could recce San Carlos Waters for suitable areas on which to beach the two stricken LSLs. From the charts and previous visits I was certain I could narrow the choices down without wasting too much time afloat, but I still needed to land in a couple of places for visual confirmation and was allocated a precious Rigid Raiding Craft. These thirty-knot seventeen-foot 'dories' are unique in, and to, the British armed forces. Their main use is offensive insertion of troops, day or night and, with their remarkable (but extremely uncomfortable) sea-keeping qualities and large payload, are used non-stop in most phases of amphibious operations. As they are part of the Landing Craft Branch I knew the Raiding Squadron men as well as any.

A suitable beach about one mile south of Doctor's Point and another almost immediately opposite on the west bank were recce'd, with lines of soundings recorded. Colonel Tom Seccombe had come 'for the ride' which was just as well, for he wisely hauled me back from the west bank beach with the admonition that the area had not been cleared of enemy. We were unarmed apart from one 9mm pistol.

On return to *Fearless* I reported direct to *Tango One* in the dock from where we retracted, in company with *Foxtrot Four*, to head for Port San Carlos and a meeting with the CO of 42 Commando at 1830. At odd moments throughout the day I had been giving the move of the Commando some thought and had considered the possibility of collecting them from as far as four miles up the San Carlos River.

I had sounded up the river four years before in a dinghy, supplementing the rather more formal charted soundings dating from the early 1840s and as a result believed that, although shallow, we might just get away with it. Unlike Brenton Loch, we would only be carrying half the Commando in each wave and the edges of the river were rather more clearly defined. However, some of the dangers were similar. The shores, particularly the southern one, had yet to be cleared and would be close enough for enemy snipers to cause trouble. If Nick decided the soundings were too risky (and

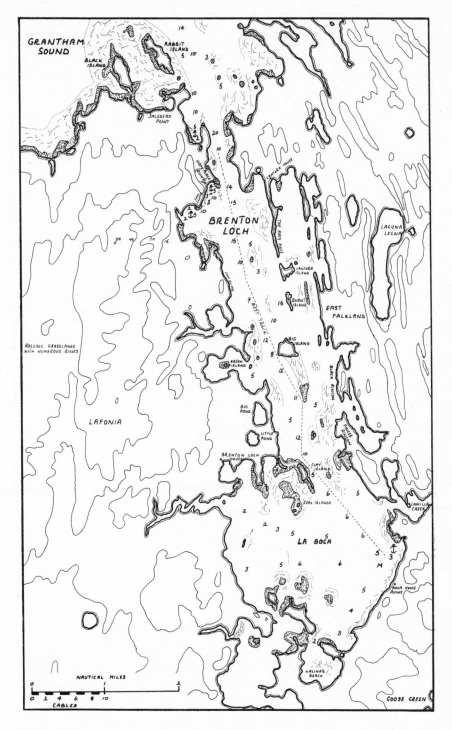

GRANTHAM
SOUND

BLACK
ISLAND

RABBIT
ISLAND

SALEDERO
POINT

BRENTON
LOCH

CANTERA HOUSE

THE ARSE PASS

CANTERA
ISLAND

LAGUNA
LEGNA

BURNT
ISLAND

EAST
FALKLAND

ROLLING GRASSLANDS
WITH NUMEROUS RIVERS

BIG
ISLAND

GREEN
ISLAND

BLACK RINCON

BIG
POND

LITTLE
POND

LAFONIA

BRENTON LOCH
HOUSE

CLAY
ISLAND

PACK
RINCON

CAMILLA
CREEK

SEAL ISLANDS

LA BOCA

M

BOCA HOUSE
RUINS

WALINA'S
BEACH

NAUTICAL MILES

0   1   2

0 2 4 6 8 10

CABLES

GOOSE GREEN

221

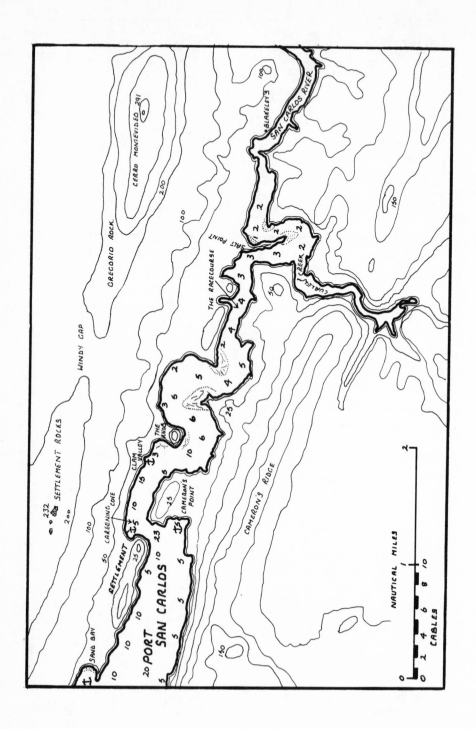

I hoped he would take my advice about that) then I would only be able to pick them up from a position as the Johnny Rook — the nearest Falkland bird to a crow — flies of about one and a half miles from the settlement, but if he accepted the risk I would attempt to reach the far side of Salt Point, a position beyond my earlier recces.

We rounded Hospital Point as the late afternoon sun began turning the white grass and diddle-dee the deep gold so distinctive of the Falklands in fair weather and a low sun. I took the helm while the crew brewed and drank thick, steaming soup.

My thoughts turned back to the night's task.

I was looking forward to the evening with Nick and his men. He was an old family friend and had served under my father at Suez and I had once been the operations officer of his commando. Close navigation, or pilotage, has always held a great fascination for me. Ocean navigation with the associated plotting of sun and star sights is one thing and, of course, a safe landfall after only celestial sightings is always immensely satisfying, but it lacks the adrenalin stimulus compared with the checking, double-checking and hazards of a tricky inshore passage. From the military point of view it had become a particular attraction to me during the earlier days among the Islands, and an art I had continued to practise and teach in the Norwegian Arctic during the intervening three years, which probably explains some of *The Black Pig's* more exotic passages close to the fiord edges at night, without lights or aids to navigation and in temperatures well below zero.

Close in, all the natural elements combine to produce a continuous interplay of nature's hazards and own aids. For instance, among the Falklands the kelp did not hold the fear for me that it did, by proxy, for some of the planners back at home. If one knows the strength of the tide and the type of kelp (tree kelp, frond kelp or drift kelp) the navigator is in a good position to judge, in general terms, the depth of water. Eddies over rocks, the sound of breakers whether from overfalls or shallow water (a different sound) were both useful aids. A sudden zephyr of warmer or colder wind could indicate a valley or higher peak, or even different vegetation, and kelp could break down an onshore swell, as, in a different environment — *The Black Pig* again — could ice floes; or mark as clearly as cats' eyes the twisting passages between shoals. The trick was to know the state of the tide, for kelp 'runs under' in strong currents, its absence not necessarily guaranteeing deep water.

I remembered back to the last visit to Port San Carlos and smiled. In those halcyon days it seemed to me that each Settlement had vied to produce the best welcome and I recalled them by their different qualities: the strongest gins and tonic prize went to Westpoint Island; the most delicious roast beef and diddle-dee pie to Weddell; the finest home-made blackcurrant rum to Beaver Island; the most comfortable bed to Port San Carlos; the most riotous evening Westpoint again; the most relaxed to Carcass Island; the largest whiskies to Pebble Island; the most Drambuie to Saunders; the most unexpected surprises to New Island; the least sleep Weddell again; the most gregarious to Goose Green; the most historic to Saunders; the most like home to Fox Bay East; the best cakes to Keppel; the fullest breakfast 'menu' Carcass again; by far the most chaotic to Sedge...and so it went on. I longed for those days to return, as return they had to.

I wanted to check one or two things with the settlement manager, Alan Miller, a friend and elder son of Sid Miller whose friendship I had been accused of so 'assiduously cultivating' in 1978. Although the Islanders are not by nature a maritime race, I hoped that he might be able to confirm that the soundings as far as Salt Point had remained reasonably stable. I had calculated that as far as the point there should be no problem, although the depths that I had charted ran as a single line roughly down the centre of the passage and would not account for any uncharted rocks either side by less than the width of a LCU.

I put the LCU softly onto the beach west of the Careening Cove jetty, handed her back to her rightful owner and walked ashore across the lowered ramp. In the hills above the settlement most of 3 Para were dug in, while others were using the wool sheds for drying and storing their equipment. I went in search of advice and Nick Vaux.

"Would you be happy," I suggested, "if we risk picking your men up from the far side of Salt Point?" He was delighted. The proposed plan would save his men much unnecessary walking with full kit over foul ground and in the dark. This was more than the simple lift he had hoped for.

At this moment three Kelpers surrounded us, obviously intent on saying hello. I apologized to Nick and turned to the Islanders.

"Welcome back, Ché. We knew you would be involved somehow. Well, it's real great to see you. Alan Miller would like to say hello. Sorry Carol's not here. Well, well, Ewen, you old bugger." Roars of laughter. Carol Miller was giving superb information to the planners back in England and had been since the earliest days, particularly since San Carlos had started appearing on the list of possibilities.

I introduced these hardy men to Nick Vaux and then explained the outline plan for the night. "Sure Ché," they said, "as far as Salt Point will be no problem. Not sure how much further though." Salt Point, 'plus a little bit' was good enough for me.

I looked at Nick, he nodded. We took our leave of the Islanders —

21. "We must get HMS *Argonaut* in under the protection of the fleet in San Carlos Waters. She is too exposed where she is." Three LCUs towing her. Air raid warning red has just been sounded.

22. Uncamouflaged Rigid Raiding Craft in Bonner's Bay with the cox'ns being briefed on the beach for a night operation with the SBS.

23. "The Welsh Guards deployed no less than forty machine-gun teams around the upper decks of *Canberra* during the hours of daylight."

24. "Bluff Cove is difficult to see in the dark..." White Point in the middle distance with East Island and the Z bend in the far distance.

"Cheers for now, Ché" − with the promise that I would call in and see them on my return. Nick and I sat down in the wool shed to plan.

My own charts indicated that as far as Salt Point there probably was enough water, providing we stuck to the line of soundings (which I couldn't guarantee to follow, accurately, in the dark). As luck would have it, it would be a rising tide for both passages, if we left at dusk which was about 1600 local time. Although there would be most water at high water that was precisely the moment when it was least advisable to ground at speed.

Nick seemed rather impressed with the idea of collecting his men from so close to their positions, so while he gave orders over the radio, including the emergency procedures if any craft failed to make the RV, I walked back down to the beach and gave my own sailing instructions.

I only wanted one radar set to be operated and that I would use spasmodically if at all. The best set was *Foxtrot Four's* so it was around that chart table that I gathered the two cox'ns.

Orders were simple enough. Sunset was at 2003Z and high water 0115: we had four hours to cover a total of sixteen miles, each leg being four nautical miles, and we could lift half the commando in each wave of two craft. We would plan to steam at about four knots to give us time in hand for possible obstacles (I used the word on purpose), delays, and loading and unloading times. It was to be a simple matter of 'follow me'. Neither craft would show any lights, but I decided that a method of judging distance-off between the two should be determined. We did not want the rear craft riding over our stern in a rather suggestive manner if the lead LCU were suddenly to halt on a sand bank. I was, though, anxious that the craft steamed as close together as safety would allow in order to give maximum military support, and take men off, in an emergency.

During the run into the beaches on D Day the stern convoy lights had been of limited value − indeed they were downright untactical. They were too bright and, being single lights, gave no indication of the gap between stern and bow. I asked that two dim lights be placed, one on each quarter, of the leading LCU so that the cox'n of the second craft would have a perspective of the vessel ahead, and therefore be able to judge the distance with greater accuracy.

Orders were given for the drills in case of enemy action and in the rather more likely event of a craft becoming stranded. The only communication would be by pin-point red light.

As soon as Nick was ready he embarked and we sailed for Clam Valley, three-quarters of a mile to the east, to wait for darkness. I was anxious not to keep the LCUs on the beach until ready for the journey as Port San Carlos had been bombed and strafed during the previous days: unpleasant enough if ashore, the availability of a handy slit trench taking the sting out

225

of all but the most direct of hits, but potentially disastrous for a static craft. An LCU is a large target and there would be no way it could avoid attention if beached in a military location: neither do the crew have any protection from its rather flimsy construction. The cockpit area is armour-plated but only against small arms and not much use against bombs or rockets.

I also wanted the cox'ns and their crews to get a modicum of rest before the night's work, not least of all because the moment we had safely delivered the second wave of 42 Commando we would return to continue the offload schedules. I also wanted to be free of the shore and the distractions of visitors so I could draw large-scale and accurate charts of the route we would take. To cover all emergencies these needed to be learnt by heart for there would be little chance to study them in detail once we were under way.

At 2100 I gave the order for us to weigh from Clam Valley Creek and proceed up the Port San Carlos River. It was a dark, clear night with a soft westerly breeze; there was no moon but just enough starlight to show the kelp patches. To begin with the tides were not strong enough to run the kelp under, but strong enough to warrant a careful watch on the bends in particular. From the cox'n's position, perched on his 'high chair' it is not easy to read the water nor to see any distance ahead. There were no silhouettes against the river and the dark cliffs behind masked any contrast in tones, but luckily I had kept the passive night goggles and again they were to prove invaluable. Very quickly Colour Sergeant Johnston and I established our well-practised bad-weather routine first tried in the testing conditions of an Arctic winter.

While the cox'n was all but blind I kept up a constant barrage of course and speed corrections based on my radar and passive night goggles observations. As the radar was an unstabilized version – the LCUs had no giro then – all course alterations were relative. To an outsider the continual stream of orders interspersed with relevant anecdotes and reminiscences must have been unintelligible and probably rather puzzling. To someone with a little understanding it would have sounded highly suspect and not very comforting to his confidence, but to Colour Sergeant Johnston and me it was our natural method of working and was developed to mask the drama of our navigational and visibility problems. Paradoxically, we had found that this each-way interplay of orders and double checks and seemingly unconnected banter, kept us both more alert and alive to the task. There was no other way to con the craft.

Behind us, at about two boats' lengths and invisible except when she crossed the reflection of a high star on the water, was Colour Sergeant Davies with *Tango One*. For the first mile or so we kept a fairly constant eight knots, as we had sailed an hour late due to the lingering twilight. As far as could be judged I kept the LCUs in the middle of the river in the hope that we would find sufficient, if not the deepest, water. The first corner had showed me, as we took it a little wide on purpose, that, contrary to the normal rules of hydrodynamics, the deepest part of the river was very clearly not on the outside of the bend! The craft 'smelt' the bottom but did not touch. The shoal was carefully recorded for the return journey.

Although I felt relaxed, if rather busy, running aground was a continuous and underlying fear. The single line of soundings down the river was just that and, although shown as being in the centre, this was a function of the scale of the chart rather than of any degree of accuracy. The only saving thought which does sometimes, perhaps subconsciously, cloud the judgement of a landing craft officer is that his vessels are at least designed to run aground − preferably on flat sand or shingle. If the worst came to the worst the craft astern would tow us off; warps were laid out in her bows for just that immediate task. Despite the clearly rising tide, there remained a small element of self-doubt in my tidal calculations which I had tabulated using the ancient 'full and change' method based on the state of the moon.

Then, suddenly, we hit solid ground. The craft slewed against the tide, which, though rising, was also pushing us harder aground. There had been no warning, no unexplained ripples on the surface of the otherwise flat waters. The undeniable sound and feel of a steel ship grinding harder onto solid rocks and shifting stones quivered through the deck. Colour Sergeant Johnston slammed both engines into reverse − a process, with a 'V' drive, which takes precious seconds to engage. The slope was too gentle, which meant that, although any damage would be minimal, we would have travelled some way across and up the shoal. Astern of us Colour Sergeant Davies had seen the gap between our two stern lights suddenly widen and guessed what had happened. Without altering course he slowed down and brought his bows close to our transom. His crew, waiting for just such an event, and without orders, passed two warps, crossed over, one for each of our quarters. As soon as turns had been taken around the staghorns *Tango One* backed away against the flood stream. Both craft set their engines to full astern and with the same, but psychologically more satisfying noise, we slid off into deeper water. The lines were slipped; I plotted the position of the shoal, judged which side lay the deepest water and the convoy set off again at slightly reduced speed. The teasing between myself and my cox'n took on a different note. Relief on my part and a smile on his. "Like to change places, boss? We need younger eyes for this sort of thing!" I reminded him that the

227

safety of the vessel was his responsibility; I was merely a 'local pilot' in an advisory capacity!

The spit of sand off Salt Point stretched further south than expected and obeyed the rules for deeper water on the outside of bends. We hugged the starboard bank although for a brief moment we did slide silently, and with a few seconds of gentle juddering, over sand. This time I ordered 'full ahead' and took the risk that we would slip into deeper water beyond. We did. If we had not, then the barrier would have prevented any further move up-river. Provided we completed all four passages of the sand spit, two up and two down, before high water we would not hit the bottom in that place again.

As we turned hard 'a port, ahead of us and half a mile away a single steady red light was just visible. We hugged the port-hand bank and ran gently, and this time purposefully, onto the mud. Through the goggles I could see 42 Commando in all-round defence guarding their private beachhead. The second LCU moored alongside to starboard and we lowered our ramps. There was a slight water gap, but as there would be the chance of drying boots back in Port San Carlos – and as they were probably already soaked through – this was not an obstacle. The men filed on board in a quiet orderly fashion while their Sergeants Major called rough roll calls in the darkness in the time-honoured manner of such men, and described so graphically by Nick Vaux in his book *March To The South Atlantic* (Buchan and Enright).

With the known shoals marked on my home-made chart, the return passage was uneventful although I was conscious that, with one hundred and fifty men embarked, each craft drew a few more inches, cancelling out the slight rise in tide. However, we remained fully afloat for the journey and, with boosted confidence, felt able to increase speed. We beached at Port San Carlos just two hours after leaving Clam Valley. As soon as the men had cleared the ramp we retracted for the second run, with Nick remaining to see his whole Commando safely back; although I suspect that the strong cocoa (supplied by *Foxtrot Four's* signaller) and whisky (supplied by me) might have had some small influence on his decision.

Almost exactly at high water we disembarked the second wave at Port San Carlos while Brian Johnston poured us all a well-earned tot.

"....*Damned tricky....Hit the bottom twice....Very close navigation in the pitch dark.... Much of it by instinct.*"

However, the new day was not yet over; the offloading rota was short of two LCUs so we returned to San Carlos Waters at best speed.

I had been concerned for some time that the boats were not being tasked properly and decided to stay for a run or two to see how they were being employed. Neither the crews nor I minded in the slightest working nonstop but as the following diary entry shows some of the loads carried were hardly worth the efforts of tired and overworked men. I was able to see at first hand how the craft were occasionally misemployed and managed to stem the 'disease' before it became endemic. The staff may have been tired (at least they were in watches) but, my God, so were the landing-craft crews.

> "On return we moved in the mist and rain to various tasks, ending up in Fearless − our last load had been Royal Engineer survivors from Sir Lancelot. Then a load of just 10 empty jerrycans. I stormed up to the AOR to find the duty staff officer to whom I could complain about this misuse of desperately tired LCU cox'n's who had just returned from a tricky operation. Good grief, I thought, they have a cushy life. I made the point and took the two LCUs out of play for the rest of the night. We returned with our jerrycans to Red Beach before mooring alongside the Blue Beach Two jetty."

Hallucinations due to tiredness are well-known and much experienced phenomena in the Landing Craft Branch on exercise or operations. They have nothing to do with social habits! In San Carlos some bystanders, when spotting a landing craft at anchor in a sheltered cove, would comment: "If they aren't working they must be idling," although the same accusation was never levied at the helicopter crews! Many of the staff were in a watch system and the helicopters had more pilots than airframes. The landing craft crews had no reliefs.

> "Slept in no 3 hold on a stretcher with 2 blankets. Damned cold but bliss. Letter from Edward Bourne who sent his yacht's Royal Cruising Club burgee which I shall keep and fly and return when it has done its stuff which is to raise my morale."

So ended a long day which by the end had given me great professional pleasure in a job well done with superb friends and compatriots, but that had started with personal doubt over my summing up of 'H' Jones's chances of success. As I turned in in Foxtrot Four's bilges and reflected briefly on the day's events and range of emotions, I had no inkling of what the result of my decision would mean to 2 Para.

XV

The Wheel's Kick

It was indeed a very cold night not helped by sleeping across the bottom plates of the hull surrounded on three sides by the icy waters of a Falkland Islands loch. However, it was peaceful, including a turn in the anchor watch rota, the sort of watchkeeping with which I was more familiar. In the very early morning — after five hours' respite from offloading the shipping, which might have had something to do with my conversation in the Flagship's operations room — the crew tidied up their accommodation and carried out a modicum of 'personal administration', the first since before the landings.

We assumed that 'they' would continue to send strong air raids against us and that if they did our current success rate would ensure that even fewer aircraft would be available for future strikes. No raids, no kills. It might be considered a strange way of looking at air raids, as we, too, were suffering serious losses, but this was how some of us viewed the situation then. It had its parallels in the coat-trailing patrols in the Dhofar mountains in the 1960s: unless we were attacked we could seldom get to grips with the enemy. We were not to know, in those early hours of 25 May, that by nightfall we would have suffered our most significant losses of the war.

Refreshed by a better sleep than usual, following a good night's work, I made my way to the cowshed below the Big House for the morning's briefing. It was good to be part of the whole and my morale reflected this. I passed the Headquarters and Signals Squadron mobile galley. Life was getting even better. The 'Greasy Spoon' sets up its stall from tropics to Arctic with unchanging standards, supplying what British Railways would have called the all-day, 'pusser's issue' general-purpose 'main meal'. A borrowed mess tin allowed me to sit in the diddle-dee devouring, with unlikely relish, a mixture of compo sausages, tinned tomatoes, egg powder, bacon slices and baked beans. Baked beans have never been a favourite of mine, believing, strongly, that they are nursery food but in the cool of a Falklands dawn they were very definitely welcome! The tea could have been brewed by a sergeant major of World War One vintage and was none the worse for that; it was, though, unadulterated.

The Brigadier's briefing followed breakfast.

I was required to take an SBS patrol into White Rock Bay that night

(25 May) by either Rigid Raiding Craft or LCVP – an interesting insertion if they had wanted to be dropped in the upper reaches. The easiest answer was to offer the patrol leader all the alternatives with the varying attributes listed, leaving the SBS to make up their own minds depending on their objectives. I left them with a collection of passage plans. For some days the command had been concerned with the possibility of an enemy observation point high up on Mount Rosalie. It was the obvious place to have had an OP and one that, if it existed, was superbly placed to direct aircraft on to the British ships in the Sound, and, indeed, in the northern approaches. The Mountain and Arctic Warfare Cadre had earlier been tasked with a search-and-destroy style mission but appalling night-time weather had, so far, prevented their insertion.

The good news of the morning was the impending arrival of *Atlantic Conveyor* with tents, general stores and, of the utmost importance, four Chinook and six Wessex helicopters. With this comparatively vast increase in our lift capacity the Brigadier's overall plans for the advance toward Stanley would be able to proceed in militarily sensible bounds, without having to be diverted to 'side shows'. Indeed he did not want to be diverted at all with or without extra helicopters. Stanley was the aim; effort and logistics wasted elsewhere would weaken our chances against the heavily defended hills to the west of the city. Goose Green, though, represented a chance to establish 'moral and physical domination over the enemy' as required by General Moore's directive and, if conducted in the form of a battalion raid, might achieve that objective. But it was not on the Brigadier's route. If it had to be attacked at all, the 24th had been the only night available; but that night the weather had been so bad that no artillery support could be lifted forward and, I suspect without reluctance, the raid was called off. There was probably a great sigh of relief in the Headquarters as all forces and logistics could then be allocated back towards Stanley.

> *"Summoned to the Brigadier to discuss the attack on Stanley. He seems to be under pressure from the UK who don't appreciate the problems of the air threat and the terrain and tend to dismiss them. They also seem to have very large hands spread across very small scale charts."*

During the day there were a number of air raids. I watched one from the bridge of an LCU while it unloaded cargo across the Bonners Bay jetty and recorded seeing a pilot eject over HMS *Fearless*. He landed in the water alongside the ship and was rescued by Colour Sergeant Johnston. He had a badly torn knee but was otherwise in fair shape.

231

Shortly after our brief discussion, the Brigadier asked me to accompany him back to *Fearless* so that he could talk to CINC Fleet.

It was becoming a black time, not helped by political pressure being piled onto military pressure. The Commando Brigade and the Amphibious ships (particularly the ships) had fulfilled their obligations and met, with outstanding success, the aim of 'establishing a beachhead from where operations could develop for the complete possession of the Islands'. The Headquarters was under the impression that any substantial move eastwards would start with the arrival of 5 (Army) Brigade who could then guard our backs, the logistic offload, act as a mobile reserve and, if necessary, open up a second axis of advance.

That was our perception. Indeed no strategy or concept of operations existed for the future after the establishment of the beachhead, although, naturally, Julian Thompson and Michael Clapp discussed ideas continually. The Brigadier's problem was that he, a Brigade Commander, was being ordered by Northwood and not his own Divisional Commander, to draw up a plan which would have an impact on the divisional concept. Because the Divisional Commander (Moore) was incommunicado in the *QE2* Thompson had no idea whether or not his and Clapp's ideas fitted in with the wider picture held only by Moore. Thus Thompson's plans were to be actioned (on Northwood's orders) before Moore's arrival on 30 May by which time the General had no choice but to approve. In essence therefore Thompson and Clapp masterminded the vital first foothold and also sett in motion the chain of events that was to lead to victory. Not only had Thompson wanted to move out as soon as he was ready (but not before) but both commanders had always considered the northern route to be the one most likely to achieve success. With that in mind they had earmarked (before 'D' day) Port Salvador as a stepping stone, which is why from the evening of 21 May onwards the Mountain and Arctic Warfare Cadre had their OPs out covering what would be the helicopter route forward north of the general line of Bull Hill to Evelyn Hill to The Baby. They had considered Fitzroy and the south coast route a good alternative but dismissed it as being too close to the enemy and most likely to be overlooked by Argentinian observation posts.

I do not know what was discussed between the Brigadier and London but it was the only time I saw Julian Thompson depressed. He and the Commodore had more than fulfilled expectations against odds that in the hallowed syndicate rooms of the Army and Naval Staff Colleges would have been unacceptable. Yet he was being pressured, by those with little understanding of the realities on the spot, to conduct further operations (which would have an impact on unknown divisional plans) in accordance with political imperatives and before sufficient forces were available. The fact that we had 'got away with it' during the landings was not a guarantee that this luck (or the enemy's reluctance to counter-attack with anything other than his air force) would last.

25 May was to get worse. HMS *Coventry* was sunk that afternoon, followed a few hours later by an attack on *Atlantic Conveyor*, although we were not to hear of this second loss until the evening.

The sinking of *Atlantic Conveyor* did, though, puzzle the Commodore, for as he had not yet called her into the anchorage (and that was very much his decison and nobody else's) he believed that she was safely to the east waiting to receive his orders. Second guessing amphibious requirements by 'outsiders' isn't, tragically, always helpful.

> *"Managed to grab dinner onboard* Fearless − *the Petty Officer Cook had kept a fillet steak for me which was very kind. In the middle, summoned to the Commodore's cabin to discuss Salvador Waters. Earlier I had briefed the SBS/Raiding Squadron teams for tonight's insertion to Green Island and Teal Inlet. The wardroom is full of survivors from* Galahad *who will return to their ship when the bombs have been defused. I must now think of assault plans onto Stanley but keeping away from those beaches which we know to be mined. Morale is high. The LC branch is performing − as is everybody − extremely well. Turned in fully clothed on my camp bed.* Fearless *went to sea to replenish oil and drop off the SBS team by Rigid Raiders Craft at the entrance to Salvador − going to Green Island to recce the beaches."*

26 May should have been the day when the plans for the advance on Stanley were consolidated but events the day before had forced a change. There were now no extra helicopters. Men would have to walk. Clapp and Thompson, wanting to postpone the advance until the second brigade had appeared, now asked, with even more reason, for a delay until the losses could be made up. They were overruled by Northwood. The only aircraft available would now be used for 42 Commando's move forward to Mount Kent, one company at a time, plus gunner ammunition. At least the attack on Goose Green had been cancelled, releasing the tactical and logistical planners from that diversion, and allowing a Commando to remain as rearguard. Under that circumstance the Brigadier felt that a balanced move forward on foot could begin in advance of the Army reinforcements.

A final complication was that although Mount Kent had been recce'd by D Squadron, SAS, the helicopter landing zone had not been secured due to the appalling weather up in the hills.

The move of 42 Commando was therefore tactically too much of a risk with the remaining battalions and commandos unable to advance in support except by foot over the rough terrain at a very slow pace. The Brigadier decided to revert to his original plan and await the arrival of new helicopters and a second brigade, although he knew this would not meet with approval by those in England. I did suggest that we could take two commandos into the beaches to the east of Green Island in Salvador Waters in one night. If we sailed from San Carlos Waters it would have been, barring breakdowns, an eight- or nine-hour passage which, in open craft in the night-time temperatures, would have been hideous. The alternative was to carry the men to the entrance to Salvador Waters in both LPDs (the only way to get all eight LCUs to the launch position), giving us, perhaps, only a three-hour run through the enclosed waterway. The main snags were that there would be no room for supporting arms (guns and light tanks) and the LPDs would have to return before dawn without being able to wait for the return of the empty LCUs who would have to lie up in open country for a full day before meeting their mother ships undertaking a second night-time run. These were ideas that, although eventually dismissed, were discussed in enough depth for me to write:

> *"Plan is now for me to take two commandos into the beach east of Green Island — which I know well.... There is an element of stalemate about our present position stuck as we are between what is practical and what London want us to do, and what is achievable with the terrain and enemy. If we do move out of PSC we need a garrison to guard our rear and our supply route. We were told to establish a beachhead and that we have done.*
>
> *"However, the Brigadier is not prepared just to sit on the beach despite the loss of mobility and has ordered us to plan logistic support using the few helicopters left to us while the whole Brigade walks to what ever destinations he chooses along the northern flank. We feel we still have the upper hand but do not want to lose that advantage by any hasty plan, ill-conceived by those whose practical experience of the situation is via a satellite link.*
>
> *"Later. The Brigadier was suddenly called to the Satellite Communication Terminal in Ajax Bay for an instant conversation with Northwood. In the Cow Shed we can only guess at the way the discussion is going. We also fear it might be rather one sided."*

The outcome is best described by Julian Thompson in his own book *No Picnic*:

"The radio-telephone was as clear as if the call had been coming from next door. As clear and unequivocal were the orders from Northwood.

The Goose Green operation was to be re-mounted and more action was required all round. Plainly the people at the back-end were getting restless. I returned to my Headquarters and summoned Jones. Chester informed me that the only way that the Brigade could go anywhere, other than 42 Commando's move to Mount Kent, was on foot. It had become quite clear to 3 Commando Brigade that, apart from the whole-hearted support from the Royal Navy, the Brigade was on its own: no assistance or support of any kind would be forthcoming from anyone, either close at hand or back home. It was, as they say in the French Foreign Legion, a case of *'de merde toi legionnaire'*."

The Commodore was to write to me later, explaining that on that day he had "reckoned we could wrap up the AOA and I was thinking of going over to see Julian when I heard that he had had this kick in the arse. 'Move!' They said. 'Get into Darwin and get going'. None of us wanted to go anywhere near Darwin — let it wither on the vine — and so I rushed ashore to find Julian all ashen and I said, 'Look the best thing I can do whether you are ready or not is to free you from the AOA. All the helos are yours as well as my aviation officer. I will leave *Intrepid* in the anchorage with the LCUs to get on with the offload...' and I said, 'Look if you've got to go, the best thing you can do is get on with it'. I sent the signal saying that the AOA was now disestablished and that command had chopped to the Brigadier. I then grabbed Jeremy Larken on 28 May and said, 'Drive like stink for Jeremy Moore, who we then picked up from *Antrim* and took him to meet up with Sandy.

"I briefed Jeremy Moore before we met up with *Hermes* on the 29th. He was asking: 'Why is it that Julian has got himself such a bad name in Northwood?' and I could only answer, 'I didn't know he had. As far as I'm concerned he is doing bloody well,' to which the reply was, 'Christ, Northwood are after him. I'm going to find it very difficult not to relieve him of his command'. And I said, 'What is going on? Who else have you got? There is nobody better. For Heaven's sake, this is a very traumatic event which nobody can judge until they have seen the situation first hand'.

"We met Sandy in his tiny sea cabin which was a bit of a joke because the cabin is half the size of your studio and he and Jeremy sat on the bunk while I stood in the heads with a reporter quizzing them with this huge video camera. Sandy said he was glad to see me alive and I replied that 'I was very glad to be alive, thank you very much — would you like to go in and leave me out here for a change?' But he wouldn't!

"We arrived back in to San Carlos to find that Julian had taken Goose Green and the General was vastly relieved that he had been so successful. He quite rightly saw the political aspects of it, whilst agreeing that it was off the line of march. It is a pity that the politicians didn't always see the military aspects of it all in return. From that time on I don't think Jeremy Moore's great contribution was the running of the battles — the foundations for which had already been laid by Julian — but more important were his nightly reports back to Northwood and the politicians which was the biggest bullshit you ever saw, but Maggie lapped it up. Marvellous glowing reports about Paras standing eight feet tall — they'd been through the valley of death and all that sort of thing and God knows what — it made me cringe but it was what was wanted by the politicians! So, 45 set off for Douglas Station and 3 Para for Teal Inlet on foot — as Julian had planned when we lost *Atlantic Conveyor*."

When reviewing Julian Thompson's second edition of *No Picnic* I was obliged to write: "The war was fought as the result of a breakdown in pragmatic, sensible, forward-looking foreign diplomacy. The battle for Goose Green was the result of backseat driving by those same diplomats and politicians who continued to have no inkling of the problems 'down south' other than in a blinkered political context. As usual, having got us into an awful muddle the politicians, safe from shot, shell and frostbite, forced the pace on the military as though it was suddenly their fault that the whole ghastly affair was not being sorted out quickly enough."

The offload of the shipping was partially halted long before dawn on the morning of 27 May while the men of 45 Commando were lifted from Ajax Bay to Port San Carlos. Ahead of them and 3 Para lay one of the more outstanding achievements of the campaign and one that was to surprise the Argentinians. 3 Para and 45 Commando were to yomp eastwards — an evolution not expected by the enemy. Some in England did not appreciate the problem, for to them it didn't look that far on the map and as one cynic remarked, "So what! The British Army marched all the way from Normandy to Berlin." However, this march of over sixty miles was eventually conducted by men in fearful weather, appalling underfoot conditions, carrying between 80 and 100 pounds and included, before arrival in Stanley, two full-scale Commando assaults and three battalion assaults, in which the Scots Guards were to take their part, against defended positions atop high, rugged features. The advance also embodied numerous fighting patrols and 'minor' incidents, not less in degree of tribulation. It was conducted in just over two weeks.

I had a deep attachment to 45 Commando since commanding a 'half troop' on the Yemen border and a company on board HMS *Bulwark*. My father had led '45' at Suez and during the Eoka campaign in Cyprus. I wished them 'God Speed' as they disembarked across Careening Bay beach.

With the Commando Brigade strung along the northern flank and with the impending arrival of the Army Brigade it was clear that an embryo

Task Force Assault Squadron was required to co-ordinate all the 'boating' assets. Chris Baxter, commanding the Raiding Squadron, and I gave it much thought. His headquarters (on the water's edge in Bonners Bay), although tiny, was the only central point that could be expanded to reflect the new organization. There would be no extra men (except me) nor radios, but it would take under command sixteen landing craft and operate throughout the task force. A small challenge in command, control and logistics.

Chris Baxter had been under my command in various sojourns in North Norway when I had, as now, been 'blistered' onto his unit with my various experimental craft. Despite his fiercely individual ways and idiosyncrasies, he accepted these visitations with understanding. His knowledge of the techniques and craft at his disposal was great, but his penchant was staff work which, in his case, often took precedence over operational concerns. In theory, of course, this is correct, for accurate staff work and adherence to the book should ensure operational success. Sometimes, though, there isn't time.

However, after some initial comments about my coming to 'haunt' him even in the South Atlantic, he accepted my presence and we set-to organizing the future. We agreed a sharing of the communications, elevating the long-suffering Corporal Williams to Task Force Assault Squadron signaller, but, of course, with no extra help in manpower, circuits or sets. Corporal Williams (who, in practical terms, had to accept the greater nuisance) was the epitome of efficiency, good sense and useful ideas. In the subsequent days I was to bless, many times, the drafting system that had given us the good Corporal.

During this reorganizing of the landing craft FOB we were subject to a number of air strikes and for the first time my habit of sitting on the parapet of a slit trench watching the action was shown to be a foolish activity. Up to that moment all strikes seemed to have been aimed at the ships in the anchorage, but tactics suddenly changed:

> "All day (27 May) air strikes including one on to Blue Beach (where 'we are) and Ajax Bay ....'Hostiles SW and closing'... At last light an unannounced Skyhawk attack came over my head. I dived to the ground as the GPMGs and just about everything else opened up. The retard bombs were released about one hundred feet immediately above my head. My first reaction as I saw the tiny white parachutes was that the aircraft had flown through a flock of geese which made me very angry at them for disturbing the wildlife."

The attack on our position had the desired effect on Chris for:

"Very smart new slit trenches are springing up surrounding his Squadron's position." Actually they didn't spring up — although they might have been drier if they had — they were dug down into the peat.

Before dawn the next day, 28 May, Colonel Tom Seccombe took me in a Rigid Raider to look for a second Brigade Maintenance Area to receive the ammunition from *Elk*. She carried the bulk of the Brigade's munitions and as such could not be exposed for more than four hours in the anchorage at night. Her lack of speed forced her to spend much of the useful offloading hours of darkness getting to and from a safe distance from the Argentinian mainland.

We chose the same beach that we had looked at for LSLs on the east bank, and then took the opportunity to nip further on and call in at Port San Carlos. I introduced Tom to Alan Miller and was thrilled to find Terry Peck (the Chief of Police in my days as OC NP 8901). He took me aside in a very conspiratorial manner and told me he had a mass of 'excellent intelligence'.

Terry had 'escaped' from Stanley overland on, I suspect, a motor cycle. Before leaving he had established a comprehensive network of information gatherers and had himself observed and snooped. I sat with him in a corner of the Big House's kitchen and wrote as fast as he was talking until we were disturbed by the threat of an air raid onto the Settlement and took cover in a convenient slit trench outside the back door. Squatting happily in the muddy puddles at the bottom while I continued to write as Terry spoke, we were squashed by three or four others who had, belatedly, heard the news and who jumped in without checking for earlier occupants. I felt safer under that pile of bodies then I did in any other trench, but I wasn't getting my work done, so we excused ourselves to sit in the shadow of a nearby bush where Alan Miller poured very welcome mugs of strong sweet tea.

Terry's information was fascinating but also depressing. The enemy had clearly given the routes we would take towards Stanley some thought and deployed numerous minefields — none of which was marked in accordance with the Geneva Convention.

He believed that mines had been sown across the entrance to Salvador Waters north of Shag Island — not good news. Concordia Beach was also mined — a good waste of mines. Uranie Beach was not mined — a useful beach I was able to continue to keep in mind. Sparrow Cove was mined — I didn't see why. Yorke Bay, Pilot Bay, Gypsy Cove — all mined, which was not surprising and didn't bother us at the time. He gave me the latest information on troop movements and the news that various tracks and mountain passes were believed, and in some cases confirmed, to be free of mines. It was a fascinating view of Argentinian perceptions of how we would plan our next moves. It also confirmed our belief that they still saw us attacking Stanley direct while San Carlos remained a diversion.

There were further interesting snippets: for instance No 10 John Street was heavily guarded (plus an anti-aircraft gun) as was Stanley House, the building offered to us in 1977, with the added attraction that numerous telephone lines had been laid from it to the FIGAS hanger. Government House was surrounded by slit trenches but not thought to contain anyone of any importance. Their Headquarters seemed to be split between the Town Hall and the Secretariat.

On our way back to the beach Tom and I called in at 3 Para's rear echelon to see if they had any news of the Goose Green attack. By an awful coincidence we arrived just as the duty signaller received the message that "Colonel Jones is down." He faced the room. There was no more news.

Tom was anxious to get back to 'base' and see for himself. We hurried down to the water's edge and the waiting raider. The weather had deteriorated badly and the ride back at almost full throttle was as alarming and as exhilarating as any.

"In the middle a Skyhawk flew low overhead and whilst taking avoiding action I cut my face open and hurt my knee. Masses of blood. Rather careless of me."

The news on our return was bad. 'H' had been killed along with, among others, his Adjutant, Captain Chris Wood, and Dick Nunn, a Royal Marines pilot flying in to evacuate the wounded. I wandered back to my new base in deep thought. There was silence as I entered the Raiding Squadron's ops tent and sat at the table to pull out the Brenton Loch charts. I doubted then whether the story would have been much different had we chosen that approach route, and, probably in subconscious reasoning, concluded that it might have been rather worse. This supposition, though, did nothing to allay my guilt at not offering a bolder approach.

Goose Green still had to be taken and the actions of so many men, new-found friends led now by Major Chris Keeble, were humbling. There was nothing any of us could do except wait, and there wasn't anything else to occupy our minds either.

The smart new slit trenches had been dug and were in use but before I had time to inspect the one nearest to the HQ tent I was called back up the hill to discuss the use of landing craft for lifting out enemy prisoners of war. Someone suggested that no such undertaking should be contemplated without an Argentinian guarantee of safe passage and, as this was unlikely at that precise moment, I was told to stand down. I returned to the FOB to continue setting up the enlarged organization. The new Squadron would become the clearing house for all small craft operations throughout the campaign and take the many insignificant and minor problems away from the staff officers' desks. One of the anomalies that would be solved was the command and control of the daily routines of the LCUs and LCVPs. Up to then the Commodore's staff had been in operational control of the craft, although the two LPDs retained command and were at liberty to take craft out of battle if they so wished. Nor were the individual ships beyond hijacking craft for small tasks if they just happened to be alongside at a propitious moment. Unlike the COMAW's staff we would have the time to busy ourselves with the minutiae of the daily tasks and prevent loads of six empty jerrycans.

The Brigade would tell the Commodore of the commodities required ashore, their priority and destination. The COMAW's staff would task the particular ship or ships to enter San Carlos, or, if they could be risked, to stay throughout daylight. We would be told what ships needed unloading to which beach and in which order. The Commodore, too, had his own priorities regarding ships he wished to offload quickly so that they could be ready for other tasks or be sent, empty, to sea in search of comparative safety.

Occasionally a ship needed unloading regardless of whether or not the cargo was required ashore. Priorities changed. Some ships had to sail quickly to meet or avoid a new perceived threat, landing craft became unserviceable, Carrier Battle Group ships could sometimes be spared for escort duties and sometimes not if a 'gunline' task took precedence or if air raids were intensifying. Direct action (minesweeping or towing) and Special Forces tasks (insertions into distant beaches) would intervene at the drop of a hat and the weather (always the weather) had the final say.

It was the start of many many hours of juggling assets, cargoes and part-loads that became known as the Rubik Cube — which by comparison was probably more easy to solve. There would be no logic to the offload requirements and there would be interruptions and restrictions that even the good Hungarian professor himself might have had difficulty in unravelling.

The Brigade (in support of a Division) Assault Squadron's (later to be named 539 Assault Squadron Royal Marines) first full night in existence was a long one, disturbed by yet another high-level bombing raid that this time, we were told, was in the Goose Green area. There were no reports of any casualties.

The news the next morning was that the civilians of Goose Green were still being held (but now as hostages) in the community hall. I offered to take as many LCUs up Brenton Loch as was necessary to collect the prisoners, plus any wounded and civilians, but by 1350 there was no hard news. The surrender arrangements were still being worked out by Chris Keeble and, among others, the ubiquitous Rod Bell, the Spanish-speaking Royal Marine captain.

"In the meantime preparations go ahead for 42 Commando's advance on Mount Kent."

By 1600 things had progressed sufficiently for me to be summoned to discuss yet again the use of the LCUs for the removal of the prisoners of war in daylight and with Argentina's knowledge.

"How many?" I asked.

There was a pause and some laughter. "About eight hundred!" COMAW's staff would need to work out which tasks had the greater call on the landing craft while we turned to the question of mines in the entrance to Salvador Waters.

"Yes, of course we can use the LCVPS as minesweepers!" I wasn't quite sure how and had an instant mental picture of every one of the Corporal cox'ns winning a posthumous medal. But this was serious stuff and I went away to think about it. The Staff Minesweeping Officer had worked out a plan for towing the equipment and it did seem that the prospect was indeed feasible. Although the LCVPs were made of plywood, this was covered down the length of the well deck with armour plating and this, when added to two massive Foden FD6 engines, projected quite a magnetic field for their size.

But there were great advantages. They were light and not likely to set up too much of a pressure zone, their magnetic field would be slight compared with a warship or LSL in the depths of water we were considering, fifteen to thirty metres, and their underwater noise profile would be minimal compared with the ships against which the mines had, presumably, been laid. I felt slightly hesitant at agreeing to their use as sacrificial lambs for the advancing amphibious forces for one powerful reason: I would not be with them. Throughout the campaign I felt strongly that, as we were asking my men to carry out evolutions not within their previous experience, and often way outside the limits for operating what were simple ship-to-shore ferries (an expression I have always avoided but I use it here to emphasize the point), an officer should be the first to lead. I remained reluctant to the end to ask a cox'n to carry out a hazardous operation without my availability to lead them first time. This was not a false sense of bravado. It was wrong for it to have been otherwise, added to which I had a pilotage reason for conducting the first pass. However, I was not to go with them and that was that. We were to continue setting up the Task Force Landing Craft Squadron and the smooth introduction of that organization into the order of battle was my priority as set by the Commodore.

Deep in yet more thought, this time about the effects of a mine against an eight-ton plywood craft, I set off for a walk across Little Rincon, not for the fresh air and exercise, although they were welcome, but for the chance to clear my brain of the conflicting thoughts that had been smothering it. I was also anxious to recce a site close to the shore where we could set up a fuelling site for the Brigade Air Squadron, for Little Rincon was marked on the charts as an Auster Strip. We needed a place where fuel could be either pumped ashore from bowsers in landing craft or close to the beach so that the fuel pods could be lifted across the shingle with a fork-lift truck. There were a number of suitable places with tiny re-entrants leading down to the water's edge from the flat diddle-dee covered grassland a few feet above sea level.

I was also keen to work up an appetite as I had been invited to supper by the Shorts.

Fearless had gone, so I was unable to shave in comfort (which was nothing new) and used cold sea water before presenting a cleanish body in dishevelled clothing at Pat's front door. What a contrast! No sooner had I removed my boots (a standard procedure when entering any Falkland Islands house in camp (similar to that which we observed in North Norway) than I was back into the Falkland family life I had known and loved. The bungalow-style house, the large kitchen and the enveloping smell of peat and natural wool was a familiar and welcoming atmosphere. The smell of cooking was, though, unfamiliar, and it took me a moment or two to recognize roast beef. Where was the familiar 365? Never mind, one could eat mutton any time one liked in the Falklands but to have that delicious tussac-reared beef was the height of luxury. Pat, Isobel and Sis were overwhelming in their hospitality, making me promise to call in at any time and to use their house as my own. Of course I couldn't. My place was with my team down in the mud and puddles of the ops tent a few feet above the high-water mark at the back of the narrow beach; but I did promise to keep them up-to-date with news of how our collective efforts were progressing. I revelled in the warmth of new friendships, although Sis would keep on insisting that we had been drinking partners in the Colony Club in Stanley. I certainly did not remember! Supper took a long time and was a continuous banter between us, reflecting our differing life styles (at that moment) and duties. There were many stories of the past and present. Ears will have burnt that night, but not one with embarrassment other than from praise. It was an occasion of celebration and happiness and for a brief two hours I was able to relax as a civilian for the first time since 2 April. I am grateful for those few moments of peace.

After profuse thanks for one of the more delightful interludes I struggled into my muddy Arctic boots and snow gaiters to return to the ops tent. The Rubik Cube planning conference was due for the night's offload and we needed to address the practical problems of clearing the mines in the entrance to Salvador Waters. The Big House was a long way away.

It was another bitterly cold night on the water's edge and I shivered, between watches, fully clothed in a borrowed, damp sleeping bag. It was no warmer in the ops tent but there was much to take the mind off the cold as the duty signaller and I controlled the offload − an LCU on one engine and finding it difficult to manoeuvre alongside a ship; an emergency load inserted into the plan; a request for a half-hour stand down to replenish lubricating oil; a rope round a screw; a craft stuck on an uncharted shoal while attempting a short cut to a beach; a pallet that had burst its load along the length of a tank deck, that had to be re-packed by hand before the remainder could be lowered in by crane; a fork-lift truck stuck between the ramp wires whilst loading an LCU across the stern gate of an LSL. All minor and normal problems and all met with the customary skill and inventiveness for which the British serviceman is renowned. So the night went on, with little to mark it from any other.

Dawn on 30 May was welcome for the slight rise in temperature it brought, and for the return of the ship carrying General Moore. His presence was particularly welcome for it heralded the arrival of the Army Brigade. The new command would see the problems of terrain, weather and air strikes at first hand. There would be a better chance of those back in England now understanding our problems and accepting how successful the gaining of the initial foothold had been. Our own Brigadier and Commodore could now fight the battle without looking over their shoulder. Somebody else, just that little bit more removed from the practicalities could face up to the politicians and Northwood. However:

"General Moore arrived on the beach by LCVP. He was in a terrible mood as I welcomed him at the water's edge to the Falkland Islands. Stormed past, followed by a rather puzzled-looking staff. He was on his way to Brigade HQ to meet Brigadier Thompson. Smile might have been in order even if he didn't have too much to say. Oh well!"

Otherwise it was a day of air-raid warnings from high-level bombers, the burial of the dead from Goose Green, a photo recce plane overhead which was also not intercepted by us and a final comment in my log: *"Home papers giving all the credit for the landings to Woodward who is being hailed as a hero while Thompson and Clapp receive not a mention in the national press — which is very sad and very wrong."*

Giant Petrel

XVI

Advance!

THE LAST DAY OF MAY and we were entering the austral winter proper. The morrow would bring the month with the second-highest recorded wind speed since records began; the lowest average daily sunshine figures, with less than two hours; the lowest barometric readings; the second-lowest temperatures and the greatest number of days with lying snow. I told the 'ops' tent staff that we had better make the most of it...

...but the day began with bad news:

> *"0830. Canberra strike − low-level bombing run against Brigade Air Squadron. It is unbelievable that a lumbering old Canberra can attack ground troops on a clear night. There was no warning. With all the ships we have surely we can prevent this sort of thing. I slightly hurt. No significant damage to aircraft. So far we have had approximately 140 a/c strikes against us in San Carlos alone. Snow on the hills. Clear."*

Amid all this attempted carnage the unspoilt loneliness and stark, barren beauty of the land, sometimes powdered with the finest of snow coverings, kept my morale high. Many times at dawn or dusk I would sit gazing at the watercolour fragility of the long sloping hills, the golden-hued grass waving along the skylines beneath the untarnished, unpolluted blue of the austral winter sky. To me these seldom-changing scenes had all the power I needed to convince me that the Islands were indeed "worth fighting for." No doubters could persuade me otherwise; indeed on a number of occasions I had to argue fiercely that, apart from the military, political and historical factors behind our need to re-possess the Islands there were, too, strong aesthetic aspects to be considered − but not everyone thought they were beautiful. In my case, and I was not alone, there were also overpowering personal reasons.

I was summoned on board *Fearless* to meet my new military masters, and was delighted to write:

> *"Discussion with Col AQ of Div. Met General in very friendly mood. Slightly surprised him by saying that I had been working on*

Bluff Cove as a hunch for the future. He thought I had actually been there. Not yet, I said, but will go now if required to set up a beach!"

The discussion with the Colonel (Ian Baxter) had ranged over the lift capabilities of my craft, the ability of various beaches to accept loads and storage areas, and my long-term thoughts on the moving forward of troops and equipment. It was no more than we had been planning for, but now that the extent of the extra forces that needed to be accommodated, transported and supported was becoming clear, it was important for us to speak the same language. We still needed to support the Commando Brigade as they made their way along the northern flank of the approach to Stanley; to that support would be added a second 'front' along the southern flank. At least that is what I assumed and why we had begun 'chart recces' of the southern beaches.

The meeting with the General was superbly encouraging, although, as I noted at the time, he and his staff were a little surprised by my thoughts on Bluff Cove as a forward base for the Army Brigade.

It was all hypothetical as there were no plans that I knew of for the advance of the Army Brigade towards either Fitzroy or Bluff Cove. However, everyone listened to this fanatic with polite interest!

I made my way back to what was now the Task Force Landing Craft Squadron Base where an: *"'Air raid warning red' was announced at last light but we took no notice."*

There were difficulties in working out the night's offload of *Canberra, Norland, Atlantic Causeway* and *Baltic Ferry*. Everything had been delayed until 0400Z which we knew was not going to please the ground troops ashore. The cause was unknown at the time and, in some respects, was not our concern. We would unload whatever, whenever it was ready and for twenty-fours hours at a time.

During the 'red' warning, a time when all goes quiet apart from the hooting of the ships' sirens (the quickest and most efficient way of passing the message), I hammered on the tent of 40 Commando's HQ. I felt sorry for them as they continued to guard the anchorage prior to the arrival and establishment of the Army Brigade. They were stoic in their attitude to not advancing on Stanley, yet happy in the thought that once the army were safely ashore they would be lifted forward to join their colleagues. It never happened, although two of their companies were to come under the command of the Welsh Guards later on.

I asked for and, surprisingly, was given, one section from the Commando to help in the defence not only of my Headquarters but of the whole of Little Rincon against parachutists and frogmen, both of which we were expecting − and were to sleep easier for that.

The Rubik Cube for the evening having been solved, delayed and re-solved, I left the ops tent and wandered up to the Big House. There was an ulterior motive. Jeremy Hands, the ITN reporter and very lively company, had breezed in on his way back from dispatching his first-hand report of the battle for Goose Green. Did I want to hear it? I wanted to hear more than the tape, I wanted to hear about the whole battle. Jeremy had a bottle of whisky; there was no better way to thank the Shorts for their earlier kindnesses and so I suggested we took it up to the Big House and I would introduce him to a local family.

The Glorious First of June was anything but, and covered in some detail by my log which ranged over a number of topics. I'm not sure that I would agree with them all with the hindsight of ten years, but they were obviously relevant at the time:

"Air Raid Warning Red at 0800Z (0400 local). Stood down after three quarters of an hour shivering in a slit trench. The smell of oil drifts across the Sound from Antelope. *Clear morning, becoming overcast. Decided to give up slit trenches as a waste of time – literally. Two companies of enemy special forces have landed in Stanley since the 26th. How? Why? Surely we should be able to stop/destroy any C130 which is flying by night? But the Carrier Battle Group is often so far away that their aircraft cannot get to a target in time, or so we are told by the naval staff.*

"A message has been intercepted from Menendez to Galtieri saying the odds he is facing are enormous (particularly after Goose Green) and that they should surrender before too much Argie blood is spilt. I suspect he was given two fingers by Galtieri!

"1400. Air raid red. 1 x C130 splashed to the north – hurrah but in daylight. What about those at night? Gurkhas still streaming ashore across Blue Beach 2 from Nordic Ferry. *Heard 2nd C130 splashed. That's more like it. Lovely story in the HQ about the two things the Argies fear most are the Gurkhas and chemical warfare. There was a plan to send the Gurkhas ashore amidst lots of publicity wearing NBCD suits!*

"42 Cdo in position on Mt Kent – hitting Moody Brook.

"1530. Panic call to drop everything as Commander 3 Cdo Bde believes that Moody Brook is empty and he wishes to get in there now so we should take advantage of this. Two more air raids in pm.

"Certain amount of hilarity in the ops tent this evening. Gave up trying to make up LC tasking for tonight until the loading of Sir Percival *for Teal Inlet is completed as this has priority over everything and is taking up all our assets.*

247

"2 June. Wrote to Hermione for her birthday before going off watch − poor little thing − I love her so much and would give anything to be with her on her birthday − the first one I will have missed − but we must now finish the job we were sent out to do. Turned in at 0200. Up at 0400. Fog − mist − drizzle − bad for enemy parachuting."

The next day, conscious of the men in their appalling conditions down the hill, Pat as always was generous with his offers. He had insisted, some days before, on my Marines using the bathroom and coming in to change and dry their clothes. Now he insisted that we took over the barn vacated by the Greasy Spoon. His family were magnificent; which made it all the more sad when, after lunch, we (including Isobel and Sis) were abruptly disturbed in his sitting room while I spoke, in 'veiled language' on the radio, to another settlement in an attempt to gain local intelligence:

"A RAMC Lt Col strode in wanting to know by what right I was in a civilian house and that he was commandeering it for his doctors as a mess − not even as a dressing station, nor even for his men. I told him; which gave me a little malicious pleasure, particularly as he had no idea anyone in the task force had been to the Islands before. He seemed to disbelieve me when, as part of my explanation, I explained that the Shorts were old friends of mine − which was not quite true but under the circumstances an acceptable white lie. Poor Pat was embarrassed on my behalf and didn't want them there anyway − but as always was the embodiment of good manners and co-operation."

It was a sobering reminder that the military machine that now ruled San Carlos was of a different calibre compared with before and certainly less personally involved. I was saddened by the incident and have always looked upon it as an example of the lack of human interest in the Islands held by some members of the Task Force. To many it was merely a military task to be completed as expeditiously as possible (with which we all agreed) regardless of human considerations (with which we did not all agree).

I walked back to the FOB in deep thought. I was angry with myself for being upset with the boorish doctor's behaviour but there had to be a second dimension to our work − an appreciation that these Islands were homes and livelihoods was a vital factor in the equation. It wasn't a military operation as an end in itself: the overall aim was to return the Islands to their rightful owners. The commandeering of private houses was little better than the Argentinians had achieved in Goose Green. While I would have appreciated the reason if it had been as a dressing station rather than as an officers' mess, I was hurt that my presence should have been the cause of such an outburst. Perhaps 5 Brigade received no briefings about the history and social structure on their way down and, if they had had the benefit of such talks prior to landing, I pondered over who had given them.

I arrived back at the operations tent in a poor mood to be met by Major Roger Dillon, my proposed crew in June's Two-Handed Round Britain and Ireland Race. Of all the officers in the Royal Marines, Roger was almost the last person I expected to meet and the one person I most wanted to see.

The minor and significant incident of an hour back was forgotten. Roger had been sent as a Battle Casualty Replacement (BCR) and somehow, although as a Landing Craft Officer it would not have been difficult, had become attached to the Landing Craft FOB. I dubbed him my own personal BCR, hoping the joke would not backfire, and asked him if he was able to stay. It was easy to hatch a plot, for he, too, was anxious to avoid the Divisional HQ and was seeking an excuse to remain ashore.

Although the tasking duties were not relieved by Roger's presence we were able to share them and take much more of the weight off the gallant Corporal Williams who continued to perform the duties that would, eventually, be carried out by a Warrant Officer, a Signals SNCO and a number of Corporals. It also meant that I would be available for more 'beach work' as plans for the advance on Stanley became firmer. Roger has a clear mind and is able to get to the base of a problem very quickly. His solutions to the offload dilemmas were quick and efficient.

"A complicated juggle for tonight's tasking – all ships are sailing because of some enemy threat. This will not please 5 Bde who are desperate to continue getting their stores ashore. This campaign will show the Army that amphibious ops is a different form of warfare at which the RN/RM are remarkably good.

"At 2300Z took Roger up to the Big House to make the point to the other 'visitors' who kept a low profile in the bedroom Pat had given them. Back to the CP at 0130 for more tasking, then turned in for an hour or so.

"3 June. Up at 0900Z – a 'soft' morning – ships creeping back into the anchorage before dawn. Yesterday was the first day since D day that we had no air raid warnings. It can't last, I feel. The counter-attack by Argie paras is due today. We need low cloud and very strong winds. Rather wish they do come as I believe we will witness – and take part in – their humiliation. In a strange way I look forward to the air raids and am vaguely disappointed if they don't materialize.

*Rather like duck shooting. Killing ducks gives no real pleasure –
only eating them. How odd and detached one's feelings can become.*

*"Offload continues. 3 Cdo Bde now consolidating around Mt
Kent – preparing to move onto Two Sisters. 5 Bde moving to
Fitzroy.*

*"Battle Group has moved even further east. We need air cover by
night as well as by day. All those ships so far away at night when
there are nightly resupply runs into Stanley Airport which must be
stopped. Stanley still being resupplied by C130 for Heaven's sake. I
have not yet seen a friendly aircraft since before D Day.*

*"Bizarre incident with too many air raid warnings. Eventually the
Sgt Major walked across to the village green to see how the army
were getting on and discovered a football match in progress – every
time a foul was given and the whistle blew we dived for cover. They
were 'put in the picture' in an old-fashioned Sgt Majorish manner.*

*"Briefed OC SBS and GI Ops of Div on the beaches at Bluff
Cove and Fitzroy and then walked with Roger over the airstrip. It is
good having him here. Sat in the new ops tent drinking Chris
Baxter's port – out of an empty compo tin that had once had rice
pudding in it.*

*"4 June. Up at 0400 (local) for morning's tasking of the offload
of* Elk *and* Nordic *and the backload of* Percival *for her resupply
run back to Teal Inlet. Tried to get up to Bluff Cove when I heard
that an LPD might be carrying out a landing there with the two
Guards battalions – told I was required at the FOB. But, I argued,
Dillon can do the job better than I, and he has no other tasks at the
moment. Told, rightly, to do as I was told. Oh well – I suppose I
have had my bit of 'front line' fun and can't complain.*

*"Canberra bomber attack on the Bde area in the north but
apparently they were off target and bombed down Berkeley Sound
which is a delightful waste of their ordnance.*

*"Second attack onto the Bde position in the south but as I write
this 30 minutes later at 2250 there is no news of how successful they
were.*

*"Another bottle of port and the papers for 19 May arrived in the
CP tent this evening. Dillon and Cpl Williams set about both
commodities with gusto whilst I was tied up tasking the craft for
tonight's and tomorrow's offload. Not easy as we have all the LCUs
working on loading* Percival *– probably won't end until 0200 when
she sails for Teal Inlet and I must give the crews a break despite Div
HQ's expected complaint; but the weather is atrocious for them and
the handling parties. 40 knots at 0°C – giving a windchill factor well*

into the -20°Cs. *Driving rain from the east. The tent taking a hammering. Sent a bottle and the papers down to the beach for the crews.*

"*Very complicated Rubik's Cube for tomorrow's work off-loading* Elk *and* Nordic *and loading* Sir Tristram. *I think (at 0200) we may have sorted it out. I doubt if I'll get a quiet night tonight as I suspect there will be further air raids and continuing complications over tonight's and tomorrow's tasking.*

"*Heard that last night Hercules were dropping cluster bombs on Mt Kent. Thankfully no casualties but what the hell is happening to allow these a/c to get in? The argument from the Carrier Battle Group is that the war would be over for us if we were to lose one of the carriers. The loss of* Fearless *or* Elk *would be much worse at this stage. But I'm only a bootneck and must get someone to explain it all to me sometime − in the meantime, stop moaning and get on with the job in hand! ...but: the war is here NOW not over 200 miles to the east.*"

XVII

A Settlement Too Far

DEVELOPMENTS DURING THE NEXT few days of Falklands operations are still the subject of earnest discussion, with some aspects still requiring examination. The complete sequence of events will probably never be fully dovetailed into a tidy story, since everybody, from the Prime Minister to the youngest serviceman, saw things from widely differing and individual standpoints. I watched events unfold as an active participant but without the benefit of involvement at staff level. On the other hand the staff received their intelligence and reports in the cool, calm, analytical confines of the Amphibious Operations Room, while those most intimately affected at the 'front' saw them primarily in the context of their own units' requirements. It was natural that, in battle conditions, the parties most closely concerned were unable to appreciate the possible priorities of others.

For the following two chapters I add what I now believe to have been the chronological order of events as they occurred, a good many of which, along with other activities outside San Carlos Waters, I was unaware of at the time. To me this makes an interesting comparison between the inability to provide plausible answers to all questions, while at the same time throwing up new ones. However, my account does, I hope, put various actions (some perceived as correct and some as incorrect at the time) into a more illuminating perspective. The sequence of events highlights a prime example of how personal perceptions coupled with poor or non-existent communications can lead, without any blame at all, to unavoidable confusion and inevitable catastrophe. As an example of that too-often-used excuse for culpable mistakes, 'the fog of war', events leading up to, and at, Fitzroy can have few equals, but in this case, and unlike some, 'the fog' was a genuine pea-souper.

Because much of what was to occur is considered to have roots in the United Kingdom (but mostly in the loss of the *Atlantic Conveyor*) a little background information will be helpful.

5 (Army) Brigade's main role before 2 April had been Home Defence with its Out-of-Area role given a mere 'Priority Two' rating and any duty under this heading expected to be in Africa, Belize, Cyprus or the Middle East. The three infantry regiments at the core of its Order of Battle had

been the 2nd and 3rd Battalions of the Parachute Regiment and 1/7th Gurkha Rifles, but it lacked a full outfit of supporting arms and possessed no integrated artillery or logistic regiment of its own. One of the two Parachute battalions (3 Para) had been on 'Spearhead' making it the natural choice to augment the 3rd Commando Brigade, whilst the other (2 Para) had also been sent south to join the Commandos. In practice, therefore, by the middle of April, 5 Brigade ceased to exist as an operational formation. The 1st Battalion Welsh Guards and 2nd Battalion Scots Guards were 'drafted in' to make up the shortfall, with the specialist equipment for war in an austral autumn being procured and shipped out in an almost, but necessarily, casual manner. Two thousand bergens were bought from just about every civilian outlet that stocked them: the ships were then loaded non-tactically with the comment: "You will be able to re-stow in Ascension Island" but the Brigade never stopped at Ascension Island and there were still not enough bergens – the Welsh Guards being at least one hundred short.

Although there was not the requirement, politically, for the second move from the United Kingdom to be seen to be conducted with the same haste (there was anyway a certain amount of backing and filling) as that of the Royal Marine Brigade, two opposing factors were important. The MOD (Army) were still reluctant to be joining what was considered a naval adventure with a very low chance of success and that any troops they did send would be merely for reserve and garrison duties when things either went wrong or were satisfactorily resolved. This, though, was certainly not how Julian Thompson and Mike Clapp viewed the impending arrival of 5 Brigade which they needed urgently to help balance the advance on Stanley and to guard against any counter-attack from West Falkland as the Commando Brigade began its move out of San Carlos. Neither were the three army battalions themselves under any illusion of their eventual duties – they were coming south to fight.

No matter how much the Brigade would have liked to have re-stowed on the way south nothing would have altered the unsuitable vehicles with which it was issued, nor the lack of its own heavy-lift helicopters, although just before sailing His Royal Highness The Prince of Wales gave the Welsh Guards a three-wheeled, rough-terrain 'buggy' as a personal gift which proved invaluable for internal communications and was much envied by the others. However, it is right to have sympathy for the position 5 Brigade faced on arrival in the Falklands and the situation they inherited at Goose Green, and to remember that luck refused to help even then, but, in truth, nor did they make their own luck.

Whilst understandably not specifically trained for the same military tasks as the Commandos and Paratroopers (their roles are, after all, rather different in peace and war) the Welsh Guards were not unfit for battle, as some commentators have suggested. Indeed they were a more natural choice for sudden inclusion in the depleted 5 Brigade's Order of Battle than, say, the Scots Guards, and they were certainly expecting to be chosen first. The Welsh had returned from a concentrated military training period in Kenya just before Christmas and were appointed the Spearhead Battalion from February to March, 1982, before being relieved by 3 Para. Among other aspects, this tour of duty ensured that of all the battalions available to replace 2 and 3 Para in 5 Brigade the Welsh Guards were one of the very few that were fully up-to-strength in men and with a complete 'battle scale' of equipment. Indeed so complete were they that they were able to 'lend' the Scots Guards one mortar section for the duration of the conflict. Apart from some practice, and minor, parades no full-scale public duties had been undertaken since before Kenya, contrary to perceptions at the time. Of their physical fitness (at least of fifteen of their company) it is indicative that the Battalion won the Army Rugby Cup for the eleventh time just before sailing.

The whole of this newly constituted 5 Brigade carried out exercise Welsh Falcon, in the Brecon area of Wales designed to test, in similar conditions underfoot, every battle procedure from section to brigade. It has been described privately at senior level as a vexing period with too many staff from outside the Brigade Headquarters interfering and dictating, with little experience, how the 'newly formed' Brigade was to approach its immediate future.

On the way south on board the *Queen Elizabeth 2* life was more cramped for the 3,000 men than it had been in the smaller *Canberra*. With no space capable of holding more than thirty men for training, even the synagogue had to be commandeered as an intelligence office. Larger briefing spaces such as the cinema did exist, but many of the practical lessons were conducted at right-hand bends in passageways, so that double the amount of men could see the lecturer standing in the apex. Physical training did take place relentlessly. It was only when the men cross-decked to *Canberra* that this aspect took second place and for sound reasons. What should have been a two-day journey (during which it had been planned to rest, attend final briefings and carry out incessant live firing) turned without notice into four and a half days of appalling weather which, for most of the time, put the upper deck out of bounds. In addition to any other duties or tasks (and regardless of the weather and sea-sickness) the Welsh Guards deployed no less than forty machine-gun teams around the upper decks during daylight, including the six .5-inch Brownings of the Machine Gun Platoon.

"30 May. Decision made that 5 Brigade should move towards Stanley along the southern axis. COMAW prepares to send a team of mine clearance divers and an SBS section forward to find and check beaches and hinterland in the Fitzroy and Bluff Cove areas and to establish if reinforcement by sea is possible. I confirm likely areas as well as beaches in Swan Inlet and Mare Harbour.

"1 June. Four-man Mountain and Arctic Warfare Cadre patrol established in Winter Quarrie on the southern slopes of Mount Smoko, four and a half miles north west of Bluff Cove. Supported by another in the vicinity.

"2 June. Gurkhas arrive onboard MV Norland. *SS* Canberra *anchors San Carlos Waters before dawn with the Scots and Welsh Guards embarked. Offload of troops takes twenty four hours."*

The Welsh Guards landed at San Carlos on 2 June with no firmer orders than to set up defensive positions in grid square 6080 on the northern reverse slope of Sussex Mountain.

"2 Para return under command of 5 Bde, seize Fitzroy and Bluff Cove but with no established lines of communications or supply. Div HQ and COMAW now occupied with the unwelcome problem of reinforcing forward troops before movement assets are available from the northern flank and before secure and reliable lines of communication are open. At 2110 the Winter Quarrie M and AW Cadre patrol report one Chinook and one Scout flying west to east dropping troops at Fitzroy before returning along same route. Before this visual sighting "many helicopters heard." Reported by voice. "Artillery fire mission called." Described as a "heavy build-up of enemy troops." Fleeting glimpse through the mist reveals these to be friendly aircraft. Fire mission cancelled. (This was the first indication that Divisional Headquarters had of Brigadier Wilson's 'great leap forward'.)

"Target date for 5 Bde's completion of build-up along the south coast now end of first week in June. Most, if not all, medium support helicopters allocated to 3 Cdo Bde to complete their investing of the northern flank. 5 Bde left with legacy of 1200 prisoners of war and a great deal of unstable ammunition including weeping napalm.

"By 2 June 3 Commando Brigade open up northern route without resistance or any attack against shipping anchored off Teal Inlet (despite BBC World Service announcing on 4 June that Teal Inlet was the Headquarters of the force preparing to attack Stanley). Units of the Brigade move up to Mt Kent – Mt Challenger and close on the enemy

on Mt Longdon, Two Sisters and Mt Harriet. By 4 June Commando Brigade deployed between Mt Estancia, Mt Vernet, Mt Kent and Mt Challenger. Probing attacks take place against Mt Longdon.

"3 June. M and AW report to Div HQ: '03 1530. Eight BV 202s moving east to Estancia House. 1630-1700. Continual helicopter activity in areas of Bluff Cove and Estancia House. Underslung loads and troops. 1700. Green, Yellow and Red smoke seen at various intervals during past hour.' 2 Para and a battery of 105mm guns. Ammunition follows the next day."

The Commanding Officer of the Welsh Guards gave his first full 'O' group during the afternoon of 3 June, having come from a similar meeting with his Brigade Commander earlier in the day. The main points to emerge were that the Brigade was to consolidate at Fitzroy and Bluff Cove and that the bridge linking the two settlements had been blown by the enemy. As a start to this phase the Welsh Guards' initial mission was to reach High Hill (five miles north-east of Darwin and overlooking the Darwin – Bluff Cove track) by first light on 4 June. This was not an unusually tall order as their objective lay fourteen Johnny Rook miles by land, but, as they were offered no 'ground' transport whatsoever it was not going to be easy.

Johnny Rickett, the Welsh Guards' Commanding Officer, had learnt from the misfortunes of others and was determined that his Battalion would take forward as much heavy kit as possible. 5 Brigade's Commander had been particularly scathing about 2 Para's lack of equipment on Sussex Mountain until two days after the landings (a fault he laid at HQ 3 Commando Brigade's door); an attitude that no doubt heavily influenced Rickett's decision. Of course the Brigadier had not been there and so was unable to judge at first hand the causes and effects of those dramatic first days. It was, though, to be an important point, for the Guards would have been well able to yomp to their objective with light scales and no transport. However, with uncertainty (due to the lack of helicopters) over when they would be married up with their large packs and ammunition the Commanding Officer's decision was correct; both commodities were vital, the one for sustaining the men in fighting trim, the second for beating the enemy. Nothing else counted at that stage.

The Battalion was therefore allocated whatever vehicles could be found and to this end three tractors were commissioned into service, two large and one small. The advance was due to start at 2100 (after sunset) by which time only the small tractor and trailer had appeared and was allocated immediately to Prince of Wales Company. This leading, and only, vehicle made it as far as the northern slope of Sussex Mountain

25. Burnt-out RRCs on the beach beneath 26 Ross Road West after the abortive special forces attack on Wireless Ridge.

26. "Two minutes later, after Griff Evans' indescribable smile had reappeared...he staggered on to the green with a huge Union Flag."

27. "Our first stop was San Carlos Settlement to pick up Max Hastings and Michael Nicholson…" Max and various SBS ranks embarking in Peter Manley's Wessex to take the surrender of Pebble Island.

before it became immovably bogged in the sodden peat. Without any prospect of reaching their destination with anything with which to fight or survive, the Commanding Officer ordered the march to be abandoned shortly before 2200, fifty minutes after setting out. It took another hour for the Battalion to retrace their steps to their earlier defensive positions.

Throughout 4 June the Welsh Guards sat at the bottom of water-filled holes in frustrating inactivity with two vital days lost. There were two reasons why time was short: firstly the men in the mountains could not wait indefinitely for those on the right flank to catch up before they themselves became increasingly unfit for any future attacks, and secondly parties of men varying in size from section to battalion were now spread along a thirty-five-mile axis bordering the south coast and vulnerable to disruption by the enemy along its entire length. Those most at risk were at the eastern end and, although well dug in, they had no mutual support, defensive weapons of any great consequence nor had they established lines of supply, support or communication. If the enemy had any inclination to launch a counter-attack, or even the occasional small-scale raid, any hope of a right-flank advance on Stanley might have been destroyed.

Brigadier Wilson was, it is reported, 'a man with a mission' and one not averse to playing cap-badge politics to ensure that his Brigade was first into Stanley. While his Brigade's 'great leap forward' was certainly full of bold initiatives, it was, equally certainly, full of unrestrained impulses which were to require a series of urgently and hastily planned moves to restore the military equilibrium.

"3,500 men of 5 Bde (plus 12 guns, light helicopters, signals vehicles, combat supplies of every commodity) have no option but either to walk or go by sea. It is suggested that it might be sensible to wait to complete their move once helicopters are available, the troops along the southern flank are so far forward and cut off while atrocious weather is affecting the men in the mountains − neither bodies of men can wait indefinitely. Helicopters can not cross the Wickham Heights from Teal Inlet to assist those on the southern flank as low cloud is covering the East Falkland from at least Bluff Cove to San Carlos − making all helicopter operations difficult if not impossible.

"4th June. Scots and Welsh Guards ordered to assemble at San Carlos in preparation for a sea move.

"In view of low cloud COMAW agrees to send an LPD to deliver four LCUs plus one Guards Battalion to Bluff Cove to provide greater defence in depth and relieve the parachute battalion. COMAW also agrees to send in one LSL to Fitzroy and no further in a one-off trip not to be repeated once surprise has been lost or visibility improves.

Orders LSL to be loaded with four Rapier and the Field Ambulance Regiment and just the stores that can be unloaded in one day as has been happening successfully at Teal Inlet. (LSL (Sir Tristram) eventually sails — on the night of 6/7 June — without the Rapier or Field Ambulance as the low cloud prevented the Rapier being lifted down from the heights but when she does sail she is overloaded because someone thought that, as there would now be four LCUs at Fitzroy, they could cope with a more laden ship in the same time-scale)."

On 4 June, though, I had asked if there was anything I could do, to be warned by a member of COMAW's staff that two LSLs might be tasked to take the Guards battalions direct to Bluff Cove. This worried me for I knew there were no suitable LSL beaches in the area and so we would have to use LCUs, but with their maximum speed, even when empty, of under ten knots I was not sure how we would get them forward. If the LCUs went in their mother ships then so could the men, but an LPD could not get close enough to either anchorage due to the shallow water. We could load LCVPs as deck cargo on the LSLs and un-ship them at the destination, but whatever we did the whole enterprise would need sea and air protection.

This was all considered and after a late afternoon discussion I was told to return to my HQ. Some alternative method was to be actioned for the troops (to which I was not privy — but see above) and as I assumed that this would probably be LCUs sailing up Brenton Loch from Port Sussex I prepared my charts and notes accordingly.

Twenty-four hours later during the early evening of 5 June a Rigid Raiding Craft swept in to Bonners Bay. Marine Davenport cut the 135 HP engine and tilted the propeller clear of the water as he approached the thin kelp covering shallow rocks. He squelched his way to the HQ tent. Almost immediately Chris Baxter emerged out of the gloom, a signal fluttering in his hand.

"You're wanted by COMAW — the cox'n will take you back — lucky bugger!"

We bounced and surfed towards the Flagship at thirty five knots.

I was anxious to be involved in any operation that took me away from San Carlos, which was fast becoming a mere maintenance and stores area. I was not the only one who wanted to put San Carlos behind them. 5 Brigade, for rather more relevant reasons, was anxious to get on the move, and any distance eastwards that I could take them by landing craft would be a bonus.

I braced myself for the inevitable teasing as I entered the Staff Planning

Office (the Chapel), after which the officers warned me that they were now looking again at the Cantera Beach option.

"COMAW is very keen to give it some more thought as the risk of sending LSLs round the south coast may be too great."

How many men? How much kit? Vehicles? Wheeled or tracked? Loose stores? Timings? From where? When? Questions answered by the staff.

Can you do it? Yes. I was ready to brief the Commodore and made my way forward.

I spread my charts over the desk.

"Last night we discussed the possibility of a move from San Carlos to Cantera Beach. I can take men further forward if you wish, Commodore, but if it is to be in daylight I will need combat air patrol over the craft. I can make the entrance to Brenton Loch and back in one night but not much further in the same time."

Commodore Clapp stopped me: "Of course the men will still have to move forward from Goose Green. The Divisional Commander wants both the Guards battalions as far forward as Bluff Cove to relieve 2 Para and from where they can deploy into the pre-attack positions."

"I can't take them that far in one night unless we move them closer in an LPD and I lift them ashore by LCU. We can at least hide in the creeks after we have dropped our passengers. Alternatively we could sail by night in LCUs from here and stop for the day in a creek or two that I know."

"We are looking at that but may decide to use an LPD − probably *Intrepid* as *Fearless* has to refuel. In the meantime thank you for your advice to the staff on the possibilities in Brenton Loch. We'll let you know."

Again, it was a question of don't call us, we'll call you. The options of Brenton Loch had been spelt out to the staff; the possibility of lifting men ashore from an LPD had been discussed. The LSL option for men, cursorily mentioned previously, had not been raised again. The choices had been laid before the Amphibious and Divisional staffs. Now it was up to them to juggle the nautical and military preferences and produce the best solution. This was not work for me: I only offered facts not opinions. Anxious to be involved in whatever method was chosen and yet with no desire for self-gratification, I suggested that if there was to be any move by sea I was the landing craft officer who could be spared most easily, I also knew the way, but I was dismissed in a friendly manner and so went in search of the wardroom chef before returning to the beach...

...where I found that the evening's tasking had been further complicated by the sudden departure from the anchorage of all the 'transports' for, as I understood it, "some enemy threat." I noted something to the effect that this would not, again, please 5 Brigade who:

"are desperate to continue getting their stores off and consolidate forwards."

It is easy to criticize the impetuous rush forward of the army Brigade (as I have done), but every moment they delayed jeopardized the ability of the Commandos and Paras to mount an effective assault on the hills surrounding Stanley. It was, though, a question of 'the how, the where and the when' of 5 Brigade Commander's 'rush' that was less welcome than the rush itself. Bluff Cove, in practice if not on the map, was just that little bit too cut off by land (the bridge was blown) and by sea (the passage by day or night passed perilously close to likely enemy positions and observation points) to make sense until Fitzroy had been fully built up and lines of communication forward and back well established with helicopters that could be spared and that could make it over the hills. Later on Brigadier Wilson was to complain that he had been ordered to take Bluff Cove and Fitzroy by the Divisional Commander and yet when he had done so he was not thanked. Wilson thought that cap-badge politics were rife within and between the Divisional and Commando Brigade Headquarters (which they very definitely were not), believing that if he had been a Royal Marine displaying such boldness and initiative he would have been well supplied with helicopters from the beginning and well praised at the end. The truth is that anyone else would have achieved the aim slightly more judiciously while acknowledging the real reasons for the sparse helicopter support. I feel able to comment, for not only was I in a position to view the feelings at 'command-interface' level but I was also one of those charged with closing-up the southern flank gaps over the next few tense days.

There was, though, much sympathy for the newly arrived Brigade because they had little understanding of the imperatives of Amphibious warfare and the nature of the art exposed to the whims of the enemy and, more particularly, the weather. It was always difficult explaining to visiting 5 Bde Staff that ships with precious commodities embarked had just sailed ten minutes before, due to some threat. We are used to it — we like it no more than they — but we do understand and accept the reasons.

There had been some good news from the Commodore: the Harriers now had a forward airstrip from which they would be able to give closer air support without hundreds of miles in round-trips from the aircraft carriers.

The 'commissioning' of HMS *Sheathbill* was of great importance to the amphibious forces. This temporary Sea Harrier strip was operational at Port San Carlos and, although fit to supply only fuel and not munitions, it was a tremendous boost to the morale of those of us who worried about close air support. The Fleet Air Arm name their air stations after birds and had chosen a particularly appropriate one this time. The Snowy Sheathbill is one of the less attractive Falklands inhabitants. All white, with a short, stout, green, yellow and brown bill and a permanent bleary look due to a patch of bare skin below the eyes, it scavenges for food and is especially attracted to the regurgitations of penguins and cormorants. With a fondness for eating seals' faeces and stealing eggs, it does not endear itself to many. Although its toes are un-webbed, it can swim well if pushed! The Fleet Air Arm chose well!

"During the day (5 June) Sir Tristram *loads Rapier and gunner ammunition (but no firing points) by LCU and mexeflote. Both Guards Battalions begin loading in HMS* Intrepid *during the afternoon until COMAW reiterates his orders that no LPD is to be at sea during daylight so Welsh Guards ordered back to their slit trenches: time available at the launching point for the LCUs would be too tight to allow two waves inshore in darkness. This first restriction on the use of the LPDs operating forward is on the Commodore's initiative at this stage and not, as widely reported, from CINC Fleet. CINC Fleet's restriction on all 'large ship' movement comes later. (When it did come the Commodore "spent all day trying to establish from CINC Fleet's staff whether a 'large ship' included the LSLs" but received no reply and so reverted to an interpretion that suited the military imperatives of the moment.)*

"Told I could go back to the FOB yet again. I did. Ten minutes after landing back at Bonners Bay I was ordered to return to Fearless *under the impression I would be taking the Welsh Guards straight from San Carlos to Cantera Beach but told I was to lead a four-LCU approach to Bluff Cove from* Intrepid *(who will return empty of craft) with the Scots Guards and be prepared to come out to meet the Welsh tomorrow night. This makes sense for the troops will be spared a long yomp — and a warship makes sense too, even if the move has to be spread over two nights."*

This (the Scots Guards' move) was the only move to Bluff Cove sanctioned by Commodore Clapp. From then onwards he expected everything that moved forward to go only as far as Fitzroy with the Welsh Guards moving, on foot, through the Scots Guards to take up a position as the most easterly battalion.

Carrier Battle Group staff speak to COMAW's staff on 5 June and discuss details of the proposed move by Intrepid. *PM — COMAW briefs Admiral Woodward by secure voice on proposed operation. Admiral agrees and informs Commodore that 'as far as he knows' there are no ships allocated to the south-east gunline tonight and therefore no deconfliction between his and the Commodore's forces should arise... (Clapp's parish only extends from Salvador Waters westabout to east coast of Falklands Sound)... and yet... mid-afternoon* Cardiff *and* Yarmouth *detached from the Carrier Battle Group for operations in the Port Fitzroy area without a warning to the Commodore and without themselves being warned of LCU movements through the area."*

There was no time to nip back to the beach to collect my charts, for *Intrepid* was already laden and anxious to be off, but, I was assured, her navigating officer would supply me with the necessary information. I was not entirely happy with my memory alone as an aid to navigation nor with the information taken from an uncorrected chart but as we would be taken as close as possible (so I was told on board *Fearless*) and as little should have changed, hydrographically, over the years I was able to confirm to the Commodore that I could find my way and he wished me luck. The Commodore: "We had discussed two routes. West of Lively Island into Choiseul Sound or eastabout. I expected *Intrepid* to get you to Middle Island or possibly Elephant Island but not much closer, leaving you with a four-hour journey at 6 knots or even a two and a half hour journey if you could manage your full speed."

Intrepid's Captain, Peter Dingemans, met me in good humour, although what he was about to say did nothing for mine. As soon as we were clear of Fannings Head he told me the bad news, which I recorded immediately afterwards in my log:

"Intrepid *is not, politically," (her Captain's words) "allowed further east than Lively Island. The risk to an LPD is too great." In* Fearless *I had been shown the likely arcs of a shore-based Exocet (from information sent back from Stanley) and they extend in a semi-circle south of Stanley with the western arc ending at an angle of about 215° from the most likely Exocet position. This leaves a clear passage up to three miles offshore from the eastern reefs off Lively Island at the approximate maximum range of Exocet. Pointed out that this was going to be tricky enough for us in the LCUs without a 15,000-ton ship failing to reduce our navigational problems by taking us closer or up the inshore route.*

"My pleas have fallen on decidedly stony ground which is a pity.

"I suggested to the Captain that the loss of 600 men of the Scots Guards was, perhaps, the greater risk at this stage of the war and the loss of an LPD would be of small beer compared with them. Not only that, but the ship would return after dropping us and would take her frigates with her. Good grief, I thought! That's rather selfish. I therefore demanded that I had a frigate escort to East Island (where I was told on board Fearless *I might be dropped), and Combat Air Patrol at dawn if I am still at sea, which Heaven forbid. But I will have no navigational aids at all, and not even my own notes since I thought I was taking the Guards to Brenton Loch.*

"I have asked for a 'flash' signal to be sent and one has been drafted. I also want something said to the effect that to do this from such a distance from the objective (probably a five- or six-hour run) will be hairy enough but to do it a second time unless I can be dropped closer, and I can get my charts from the FOB, will be pushing our luck. The enemy will be alerted to the route and will see a 'push' building up and try to stop it. I am due to take in the Welsh Guards tomorrow night. I realize the importance of getting these two battalions in, but there will be great risk to these men unless I can be dropped closer — and where would we be if we lost a battalion? Worse off, I would suggest, than if we lost a frigate, or an LPD or even perhaps Invincible."

The two of us discussed this side by side, leaning over the chart table. Although it was an amicable conversation, it was not an easy one and I was forced to put my case vigorously. The forthcoming operation, to my mind, was as important as anything conducted since Plymouth.

We were about to launch six hundred men in four small, very lightly armed, unarmoured and unprotected craft designed to operate in ship-to-shore movements of a few miles under continual visual guidance of a mother ship or, in the 'old' days, an LCR (radar). We were going to transit hostile waters, with a thirty-five-mile open-sea approach towards, and then along, enemy-held shores, in the dark. We did not have up-to-date or large scale charts, we had no log for speed and distance through the water, we had no echo sounder, we carried no hand-bearing compass and the only steering compass had at least a 30° error, we would pass through a known area of magnetic anomalies, we would not be able to use the radar except in limited and very short bursts and we would be launched from an uncertain position: but we did have my memory (!) and the priceless gift of night vision goggles. We also had masses of determination.

That was, of course, my perception at the time: as it turned out it was not very accurate. Firstly, the Commodore had personally assured the

Captain of *Intrepid* that there were to be no ships on the gunline; secondly it had been the Commodore's decision (not Peter Dingeman's) that no frigate would accompany us inshore as it would lessen the chance of surprise. The air threat at night was minimal, particularly in view of the low cloud base, and the two enemy ships known to be in the area were accounted for: one was lying stranded on the north shore of Choiseul Sound and the other was known to be securely moored alongside in Stanley. Also unknown to me was the fact that the shores were not enemy-held, at least not unless we approached Bluff Cove from the east, and nobody in the Flagship expected us to do that − did they? Despite all this, the navigational problem remained a very real worry if we were not going to be dropped where I had hoped, which was either east of Lively Island or at the entrance to Choiseul Sound.

The British press were to report this operation and they, too, regarded it as something special: "Acts of Great Daring" and "Dangerous Landings Under Their Noses" were two headlines in the *Daily Telegraph*. "The British push is really on" and "There are under way at this moment operations which I can only describe as extraordinarily daring, which cannot be revealed until they are completed," and "In a daring operation under the noses of the enemy the 2nd Bn Scots Guards have moved 50 miles forward."

No credit for these dramatic accounts should be laid at my door. The 'great daring' if it existed, was in the planning and risk-taking by the Commodore, to whom all praise should be given for the imaginative way in which the land forces' problems and aspirations were being met and solved. We, the landing craft and infantry, were merely carrying out orders (sometimes with the odd query!) and proving the value of good training. We had no time to consider the boldness of the 'push' in terms other than of our own environment and military situation.

Later, the Commodore was to tell me:

"The plans had of course been gestating many days between the General, Colonel AQ and myself, and the decision was made over lunch in my cabin with the General and both Brigade Commanders. All the problems which occurred and several which did not were thrashed out and the risks considered reasonable. 5 Bde opted for Fitzroy as a Bde HQ but made it clear that they would like the Scots Guards taken forward to Bluff Cove. Brigadier Wilson assured me that there was a ridge of high ground between Fitzroy anchorage and the Argentinian position which would hide any LSLs or LCUs at Fitzroy, should the cloud base lift sufficiently for the OPs to be able to look that way. There, together with 5 Bde's inadequate briefing of the WG (who should have gone to Fitzroy) hangs another tale − for much of which I seem to have taken the opprobrium despite the fact

I still believe it was a gallant, courageous and essential attempt to pull 5 Brigade out of a deep mire (into which I still sometimes think they and the Division blindly walked!) and upon which the success or failure of the whole expedition now depended, by courtesy of the Royal Navy.... It was about to be a very uncomfortable and probably very bloody situation, the outcome of which, if we had not taken those decisions, would have been far less certain, but would certainly have been even more bloody and have meant greater RM casualties. I feared deeply for the LSLs but believed the risk was essential and, in the prevailing weather conditions, worthwhile. It was the weather, I stress that because it was always, always the weather that gave me the courage to go ahead with the operations. If it hadn't been made clear to me that the weather was nasty and likely to stay I would never have sent any of those ships in."

I make much of this preamble now (I certainly did then) to the night's move as I believe that the makings of a disaster existed in large proportions. The fact that it did not happen was through the Grace of God – although He led us a pretty trot before deciding that, for that night at least, we were to be spared. This operation therefore has more to offer in the way of lessons to be learnt than the rather more preventable tragedy that was to occur a few days later. It deserves a close study: briefings, de-confliction, orders, command and control and protection for amphibious or joint operations (no matter how small and insignificant the craft, or number of men conducting them) are all matters that need careful dovetailing. Often the smallest vessels carry the greatest value and need precise orders for safe conduct – orders which themselves must fit in with other simultaneous operations. There was plenty of time for this all to have happened. Churchill once said that amphibious operations are "A very specialized form of warfare. They have to fit together like a jewelled bracelet."

"Told the Captain, 'I think the whole fucking thing stinks,' and asked him to remember my words and my requests if the thing turns sour and I fail.

"Navigationally it will be awkward as my memory is about all I have but On! On! I suppose. Once we get going it will at least be fascinating and, possibly, great fun!

"Militarily it could be awkward as there will be no friendly ships on the gunline and, of course, no escorts in case we get into trouble. The Captain confirmed that any ships we see will be enemy. I asked this two or three times and was assured that we will be on our own. Not good but at least I know where I stand. I asked for the ship recognition signal 'just in case' but he does not know the one for the

Battle Group ships so could not give it to me — but then, as he pointed out, there will be none!

"Thank goodness I can rely on the cox'ns to act correctly if there is either a navigational cock-up by me or an enemy-induced drama. I remember the day I took the LCUs with the AVREs embarked up the Foyle into Londonderry during Operation Motorman and how we planned that with such meticulous care. Writing lying on the deck of the AOO's cabin whilst trying to get some rest."

There was work to be done, and no matter how much it was to be spoiled, for what I considered to be a ha'p'orth of tar, it was imperative we got started. It was also vital that none of what had been discussed in the chart house should be revealed to my cox'ns, although I felt that the senior Scots Guards officers should know.

"6th June. (5th June local time). Hermione's birthday.

"0230Z Embarked in T1 (C/Sgt Davies) — loaded up 600 men of the Scots Guards in the four LCUs.

"0430 Retracted from Intrepid *into a moonlit calm sea with haze."*

It has often been reported that the weather was bad at this stage of the journey. It was not. It was deceptively good, apart from that most important ingredient — visibility. As long as there was poor visibility the Commodore was prepared to send his ships forwards, but even visibility can be a two-edged weapon in wartime. I needed to see; we did not want to be seen.

"No land on radar. Intrepid *has dropped us (I think) two miles or so to the west-south-west of Lively Island, leaving me with a hideous passage. Apparently the Scots Guards were told at San Carlos that the journey will take a couple of hours. I reckon it will be more like six at the least — the rhumb line course is about 38 miles assuming I don't find the Z bend. Watched* Intrepid *sail away to the west with her escorts. Feeling rather lonely."*

We were on our own. I asked Major Ian Mackay-Dick (Second-in-Command of the Scots Guards) and John Kiszely (commanding Left Flank Company and a yachtsman) to join me in the navigation compartment. It was tiny but at least we could discuss our problems in private and I was close to the cox'n to give orders. My first concern was to tell Ian and John exactly how I viewed the situation.

"We will make it to Bluff Cove. It will be a long passage. We are not escorted navigationally or militarily. If we see another ship it will be Argentinian. If the weather holds, we will be ashore by dawn. There is no food. Smoking can take place below the level of the catwalks."

The Scots Guards were on their way and that was all that mattered at that moment. I was on my way too and, at last, as master of my and the Guards' destiny, I could relax into my own familiar world.

"At about 0400 HMS Cardiff *detects a fast radar contact moving west to east beneath the Wickham Heights. Engages with Sea Dart.*

"Heading NE to hit Lively Island to obtain a position as nothing showing on radar. Sighted Lively through PNG binos. Visibility clearing quickly. Many flares to the north of Lively – possibly enemy signals. Nothing like the chart on the radar echo so am a little puzzled but assume the echo is bouncing off higher ground or being affected by the kelp.

"Now I know where we are I have reversed our course and we are taking a mighty dog leg – an Admiralty Sweep – to round Prong Point. I must get three miles south and west of the land to clear the kelp reef. We were dropped, it appears, in the bight of clear water north-west of the kelp reef – but I can't be quite certain."

Through the mottled two-toned green of the night-vision goggles – the distinctive smell of rubber and plastic triggering my anxious senses as a reminder of D Day – I was able to make out the kelp banks ruffling the surface of the water. Without prior experience it was easy to mistake them in the dark as mud flats or shingle banks. The goggles did not magnify and so we were, once again, out of sight of land and relying on a certain amount of guesswork. I knew from a passage along this coast in April, 1978, that the kelp extended at least half a mile further offshore than charted. That much I had remembered, but I worried about what I might have forgotten.

"Rounded SE corner of Lively Island – experiencing quite a westerly tidal set – shortly after Dangerous Point. The radar has now packed up. I have been flashing it on and off as necessary, which is probably why. Position fixing is primarily from rare glimpses of the headlands as caught, momentarily, in the night vision goggles. It is not particularly precise, and not to be recommended when the stakes are so high, but there is no alternative."

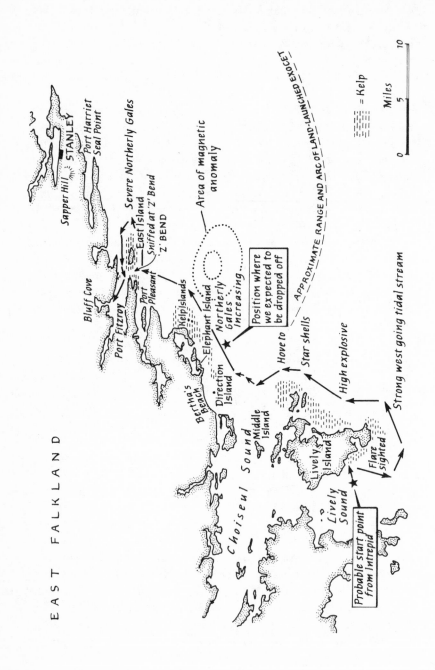

EAST FALKLAND

Sapper Hill
STANLEY
Port Harriet
Seal Point
Severe Northerly Gales
East Island
Sniffed at 'Z' Bend
'Z' BEND
Bluff Cove
Port Fitzroy
Port Pleasant
Area of magnetic anomaly
Kelp Islands
Elephant Island
Northerly Gales Increasing
Position where we expected to be dropped off
Bertha's Beach
Direction Island
Hove to
Star shells
APPROXIMATE RANGE AND ARC OF LAND-LAUNCHED EXOCET
High explosive
Choiseul Sound
Middle Island
Strong west going tidal stream
Lively Island
Flare sighted
Lively Sound
Probable start point from Intrepid

= Kelp

Miles
0   5   10

268

Although the stakes were indeed high, we had safely rounded three major headlands and my confidence grew. We had one last alteration of course to make, but, quite without warning, and as I was expressing my relief to Ian and John, further outside influences burst, literally, into our lives:

"We have just come under artillery or mortar fire but for some reason impossible to tell from which direction but it can only be Lively Island (mortars?) or the mainland to the NE (artillery?)."

One theory suggested long afterwards was that the high explosive bursts in the sea around us could have been bombs from an Argentinian Air Force Canberra. Others have often suggested that we were shelled by a British Battle Group frigate unaware that amphibious forces were on the move that night. I don't know. 'They' missed us anyway.

This inaccurate shelling was subconsciously expected and certainly did not affect my plans. There were other concerns. I wanted a fix for two reasons: we needed to make an intelligent guess of the source of the bombardment as an area of coastline to avoid, while an accurate departure point was essential prior to crossing the entrance to the Sound. I switched on *Tango One's* radar. There was no sign of life, just a blank grey-green screen. Using a pin-point red Aldis lamp the signaller flashed the craft with the next-best radar and ordered it alongside:

"Rafted alongside T3 to try Colour Sergeant Garwood's radar. While working this I saw what appeared to be an aircraft passing down our starboard side at 350 knots."

Enemy aircraft was the one thing I had not bargained for when spelling out my fears on board HMS *Intrepid*. It was sensible to return to the lead craft and the Guards officers. *Tango One* was still alongside allowing me to hop across the wet, black chasm and be grabbed, roughly but securely, by one of her crew.

"We have split up and all craft following us at maximum revs. All guns mounted."

As there were no signs that we had actually been spotted, I had time to think and plot. Even the apparently defunct radar stopped sulking and grudgingly flickered into life. What had been an aircraft metamorphosed into two ships and I realized what had happened. The landing craft had been swinging violently as we stopped, loosely moored together with the blip on the radar in *Tango Three's* un-gyro-stabilized radar showing as a very fast-moving contact. They (for the blip had split into two as it closed our position) appeared to 'slow down' as the LCU's heading steadied.

> *"Radar suddenly working again — 2 ships 4 miles astern — closing at about 20 knots, although I think I would prefer aircraft right now. Star shells now being fired over us. Much flashing from the direction of Stanley just before this and loud bangs overhead. Seems just like more artillery or mortar fire at us — but we also connect the star shells with the ships; clearly we are under fire from the frigates."*

It was then that my first real doubts since sailing began to take shape and at this precise moment I remembered, vividly, the conversation I had had a few hours previously in HMS *Intrepid* and the statement from the Commodore that the Admiral would not be sending any ships to 'our' area during the night. The relaxation into my familiar world had been a touch premature.

There was no doubt that the ships were enemy and yet intuition (and Ian and John who had not been privy to my earlier 'briefings') told me that this was impossible. As a direct result of the sinking of the *Belgrano* no Argentinian naval ship had, as far as I knew, been involved in the war. They wouldn't dare now to be this close in; yet why not? Maybe they too knew that there would be no British ships on the gunline that night. What an opportunity to make a quick, bold dash, to return some of the bombardment medicine! Either way, I was not prepared to risk a battalion of men in an award-winning show of defiance. I called Ian Mackay-Dick and John Kiszely to the navigation compartment.

"God knows who they are," I said, pointing to the intermittent echoes on the radar, "but I think we should see if we can hide among the islands behind Dangerous Point. If nothing else, if we are hit out here, about five miles from the nearest point of Lively Island, there is no chance. If we are close in men may be able to swim ashore before they die of cold."

John (the more nautical of the two) asked about our relative speeds. Earlier we had begun to slow a little because of the rising wind and sea, but an alteration in course would make it easier to increase speed again with safety. I didn't emphasize that the relative difference of an increase from six to nine knots against a possible thirty knots only a few miles away was unlikely to alter our circumstances very much.

We looked at each other in the glow of the radar; all knowing that, whatever I or they suggested, there was little choice and even less chance of escape.

I gave a further alteration in course (while we discussed the very few options open) to take us not to the nearest point of land, but to somewhere along the northern entrance of Choiseul Sound. We would not make it before the ships caught us, but it might, if they were enemy, give a different clue to our destination, and a shorter swim!

"I feel that if we can make shoal water before the ships get to us I know the Islands better than the Argies. But we are already well within range of any gun they might have. It seems inconceivable that they are Argie ships but I had been told quite clearly that there will be no British ships on the gunline tonight — and anyway I do not have the recognition signal even if they are ours and they have been firing at us."

It was a pointless gesture. The ships by then were visible through the binoculars. The sea, now at an obtuse angle to the bow, was soaking the troops even more than before: the increase in speed only marginal. Every five seconds or so the craft rolled, dipped and slammed their flat bottoms and equally flat sides into the short, icy seas, hurling solid water across the starboard bow. The freeing ports, just a few inches above the waterline, designed to let surface water out, were actually flooding the tank deck. One hundred and fifty men in each craft were being assaulted from above and below. Navigation, station keeping, even life itself, were fast becoming a hit-or-miss affair. It was not unlike the struggle in a small yacht in a gale of wind. Although I felt at home it was not the occasion to reminisce or delight in a personal tussle with the elements. I ordered the cox'n to return to the original course for Bluff Cove. The slamming was worse but it was marginally drier with the seas flung back clear either side and away from the open tank deck.

"After quick consultation with Ian Mackay-Dick, during which I put the options open to us in rather stark language, we had a whisky. He is happy for us to continue to head towards East Island and Bluff Cove as planned as there is simply nothing we can do about it. If they are Argies they could even mistake us for their own but this is really a forlorn hope, and they haven't yet fired HE at us — or have they? Someone has been. With 600 men on board and no protection or serious weapons, we realize that there is not a lot we can do. It seems ironical to me that for the initial landings into waters that might have been mined and might have been covered by enemy heavy weapons we had a frigate in support, and yet here where we are much more vulnerable and where the danger to the frigate must be considerably less, we are on our own. Navigationally. Militarily.

271

"A tiny red light from the leading warship has just indicated that we should heave-to. We did. She then flashed 'Friend' in morse code. I invited my signaller to reply 'To which side?' Without further conversation they have turned away to the SE at fast speed leaving us even more vulnerable than before, for not only have we been lit up but if the Argie's land-based radar had not spotted us before (and someone clearly had) they will now know for certain that we are British and can probably guess at our destination. I feel anger and dismay at this disregard for our problem and can only speculate at the background to such perfidy and ignorance."

In his book *The Royal Navy and the Falklands War*, David Brown identifies the ship and states that *"Cardiff's* alarms were not yet over." He does not mention ours! He goes on to say that she (the frigate) *"encouraged"* us on our way, but, as I wrote in the margin of my copy of the book *"This was not how I saw it!"* It was not my idea of encouragement to be lit up by six starshells; badly frightened by being closed at speed; being ordered to heave-to without recognition and then to be left alone with intemperate haste just when we needed a little love and attention. Nor were the Scots Guards impressed. From their positions in the bottom of a near-freezing and awash tank deck, the whole episode of high explosive, illumination, followed by two unidentified frigates at close quarters in three parts of a gale of wind off an enemy-held coastline was regarded rather dimly.

A year later and late at night I was told by a Royal Naval officer that the captain of HMS *Cardiff* had tossed a coin with his gunnery officer to decide whether or not to fire high explosive or star shells first. I have always felt this rather personally as I was at the Nautical College Pangbourne with Mike Harris — the Captain. Thank God it was 'starshells first' but who had targetted us earlier is still a mystery. Nine years later, when confronted by me for the first time with this story, Mike vehemently denied it. I was not to know then that earlier in the night *Cardiff* had hit a British helicopter with a missile as it, too, moved forward along the southern flank. Like me Mike Harris had been told that there would be no friendly movement along the southern flank. This is strange as his Admiral had been informed by my Commodore about the move forward of the Scots Guards and in the same conversation the Admiral had confirmed that he would not be sending any Battle Group frigates to the gunline, thus leaving the way clear for us. Having been ordered to the gunline, Mike was waiting for opportunity targets such as the Argentinian C 130 Hercules flying regular resupply flights at night and understandably had had every

272

reason to think that the helicopter was it. Presumably he assumed, until very close, that we were enemy coastal or amphibious craft who deserved the same treatment.

In his book *One Hundred Days*, and to Michael Clapp, Admiral Woodward admits that he knew of our move, although he says he, personally, should have prevented it for he believed that the Guards could have covered the distance in just two days (which, in itself, is indicative of an ignorance that could have had further delaying consequences if he had had his way), but, with respect, it was not his job to prevent, alter or encourage amphibious plans, only to react favourably in their support. When questioned in 1992 by a *Western Morning News* book reviewer why the LCUs had been 'shot up' his all-too instant reply was:

"The landing craft were late and in the wrong place."

It is difficult to know where else we should have been and at what other time, and, besides, that was hardly a reason for dismissing the near loss of six hundred Scots Guardsmen so perfunctorily. As it happened we were almost exactly where HMS *Intrepid* could have dropped us and at about the same time.

> *"It's just as well that someone on board the frigate knows what a British LCU looks like — and that is not as stupid as it might sound."*

With my earlier fears well-founded, we returned to the pressing problem of crossing the entrance to Choiseul Sound. I had established that my LCU had a compass error of at least 30°. So far it had been rough and ready pilotage, but I now needed an accurate position for the penultimate stage of the journey.

We were off Dangerous Point and intending to head, on the chart, for the seaward end of East Island. An error of only ten degrees (and with no log to warn us when we had 'run our distance') would take us to a similar headland (as viewed in the dark) within a mile of the coast below Sapper Hill which, if rounded, would lead us to Port Harriet and, to mis-coin a Crimean phrase, "Into the jaws of death sailed the six hundred." I was keen to avoid that.

Although it was important that I obtained a correct assessment of the compass's true error before taking our departure from Lively Island, an added concern was the area of magnetic anomaly somewhere along our projected course, a fact not recorded on Admiralty charts but only on mine. I knew this anomaly to be roughly between Lively Island and East Island but with my own corrected charts lying in my slit trench at San Carlos I could not remember exactly where.

"Luckily I have just sighted Direction Island as the only recognizable echo on radar − most fortuitous as I can now take the convoy across the Choiseul Sound entrance and find the kelp reef off the Kelp Islands. Direction Island and the sweep of Bertha's Beach behind are about the only unmistakable radar echoes in the area for they and their juxtaposition are clear and never altered by kelp or high ground. How lucky I am to get just a fleeting glimpse from two revolutions of the radar aerial before they disappeared in the clutter which is now getting worse.

"Weather now deteriorating very quickly. North wind producing even shorter, steeper seas. The troops are becoming very weak. Slowing down makes no difference so we have decided to push on at max revs and get there quickly. Even so we are not making much progress over the ground."

We had reached the point where I knew I was going to have to make a decision that would affect the outcome of the journey as surely as any 'enemy' frigate or shore battery: the 'Z' bend. Navigationally, a simple short cut in calm weather, but if the land to the north was held by the enemy the 'Z' bend was an operational imperative.

As soon as I recognized the passage through the binoculars I realized that the 'Z' bend was out. We had to risk the long option and it would be a worrying, and thrilling, time. My assessment of the compass error had been about right though, so at least we were going to round the correct headland.

"Sniffed at the Z bend but mass of breaking water − turned for east end of East Island and so within just a few miles of Sapper Hill and Stanley and below land probably held by the enemy. Rounded kelp reef off the eastern end of East Island as close as I dared in this murk and dark then hit the kelp patch to the ESE of White Point − not marked fully on the 'modern' charts."

It was with profound relief that then, after seven or so hours of intense concentration, I spotted White Point showing, quite dramatically, as light and dark green in the goggles. I called Ian and John: "You owe me a whisky. I think we've made it." There was nothing medicinal about the tot: we deserved the 'celebration'.

Ignoring the possibility that either side of the narrow entrance could have been held by the enemy we squinted through the gloom for signs of friendly life − the Parachute Regiment. Huddled beneath the wool shed two men were waving us in onto the makeshift slip, and with no regrets at all the Scots Guards prepared for a shallow wade ashore: they could not get any wetter.

"Bluff Cove is difficult to see in the dark. Full revs to get through against 40-70 knots of wind in the entrance. Violently gusty but no rain. Hit the beach by the sheep hut at 0930Z (0530 local on 6 June). Landed a very stoic battalion of Scots Guards and wished them luck. I hope they are satisfied but they probably do not know how close they came to disaster from natural and manmade obstructions to our safe passage. Three cases of exposure and one damaged knee. I hope the Guards are grateful and that they do not know of all the dramas that nearly prevented us from making it.

"Ian, John and I shook hands, wished each other luck and turned to our different tasks. For their part they are glad to be back in the element they understand while I am glad to be returning to sea for I know what it will be like in the hills in June, even without a determined enemy. It has begun to rain. Driving, penetrating stuff. Poor show from the Almighty – but then He must remain impartial!"

Two years later when I was asked to support John Kiszely's membership of the Royal Yacht Squadron I remembered with great enthusiasm his help that night and willingly wrote to the Membership Committee. It might not have been the confirmation of 'yachting' experience the Squadron were looking for but I'm glad to say that it did his membership proposal no harm!

Despite my fears, we had made it. For much of the journey I had been fearful of my memory, fearful of the enemy and, for a significant period, fearful of our own ships. However, we had made a safe landfall, although much of the navigation had once again been by instinct. I was exhausted but content as a result and ordered the LCUs to raft up to the east of the wool shed in the only patch of suitable deep water to lick our wounds and rest.

Before leaving San Carlos I had been informed that the second night of this reinforcement plan would involve sailing *Intrepid's* LCUs from Bluff Cove to a rendezvous with *Fearless* south of Elephant Island. She would have her landing craft pre-loaded with men to save time and I would simply transfer to her lead-craft while the empty *Intrepid* boats swopped places and returned to San Carlos. I had learnt this before joining *Intrepid*, which made that ship's reluctance to continue further to the north or east of Lively Island even more puzzling.

We had made it safely to Bluff Cove and as I stared, red-eyed, past the rain-smeared navigation compartment windows then being washed of salt

I said a heartfelt prayer to the God of Amphibiosity. It was becoming a wild day, ominously clear at sea-level but still overcast. Skuas screeched and fought around the kelp-lined beaches inshore and under the cliffs to the east. Upland Geese, in their hundreds, walked, heads down, through the waving grass beyond the water's edge, pecking at anything they could find. If it was too windy for them, then it was too windy for us.

If we were to do the same thing again that night with the Welsh Guards I wanted one or two things clarified and made up my mind to fly back to San Carlos — or at the very least find a secure radio net.

Tango One slipped from the trot and took me back to the landing point beneath the wool shed where I hesitated before going ashore. We had received a message from a Para officer (whom I knew well) requesting a lift for his men across Bluff Cove creek once the Scots Guards had taken over his defensive positions. Was this acceptable? Of course it was.

Telling *Tango One* to remain on the beach for the moment I hitched a lift in a Land Rover along the boggy, deeply-rutted, water-filled single track that led to the settlement, the Scots Guards communications centre and, hopefully, a link with COMAW.

"Mike McKie and Tim Dobbyns (co-owners) hijacked me down to the big house."

We had last met on Carcass Island in 1979 during one of the many memorable evenings given to us by Rob and Lorraine McGill. As I sat briefly with old friends I longed passionately for those days of laughter and sunlight to return, but we all knew that they wouldn't if we sat drinking tea all morning. I made my way through the mud and wind to the Scots Guards' Headquarters.

The Guards had set themselves up in sheds, using various scraps of canvas and polythene sheeting to increase protection from rain and wind, although they deserved better after their hideous ordeal. Any thought of talking to their own Brigade HQ, let alone to HMS *Fearless*, was out of the question. There was nothing for it but to get back as quickly as possible, in person. With amazing luck, a Sea King landed unannounced that moment on the village green *en route* for Port San Carlos and with no help from the crewmen, who thought I was a bum looking for an easy way back to comfort and safety, I was on my way after sending a note for Colour Sergeant Davies instructing him to remain at Bluff Cove no matter what (or who), until I returned with the night's orders. I warned him that it would probably involve sailing shortly after dark for a rendezvous with *Fearless*.

Give White Point a clear berth. Distinctive white sands with a behind which in on the west side of the entrance. A good sheltered anchorage can be found between Tussac Island and the mainland to East / of Fitzroy in 1½ fathoms over thick mud.

— Bluff Cove entrance is very difficult to see —

Port Fitzroy is a beautiful, sheltered expanse of water where dinghy sailing is great fun — plenty of dolphins and where landings can be made to see Jackass penguins — a few on East Island and gentoo around the corner in London Cove. Great 'explor' for children up to Rock Point, Fitz Cove and North Basin. Anchored off the entrance bearing 010°T in 4 fathoms. Mud. Just short of Kelp.

Ashore try opening through Gorge. Strange strata. I opposite hut :)

<u>— BLUFF COVE —</u>

George and Rose Stewart
    (Owner)
Gus and Son (Here)
 + George's Daughter
    3,400 Sheep
Could carry 6,000 Sheep

NOI NAVIGABLE

FARM

HUT

WHITE POINT

on east side in 1½ fathoms.

Suggest a moor as not much room to swing if ship is longer than 50 feet.

<u>19ᵗ April</u> 78 ditto weather

Bluff Cove to Stanley, via south of East Island

To leave Bluff Cove steer 117° from White Rock this is direct to the N of East Island and will keep you clear of Kelp NE of East Point. Beware of Tussac Island, this appears further off than it really is. This is because Tussac from a distance resembles large bushy trees but it grows to about 8-11 feet — an illusion that could be dangerous.

NISSEN HUT
Kelp   EASI ISLAND
Kelp TUSSAC
ISLET Kelp
COVE

Z BED

"Flew back to Fearless *v.v low and v.v fast. v.v. exhilarating. At the last moment a para Major RE jumped aboard and asked me if I was responsible for landing the Scots Guards in the wrong place and five hours late − he went on and on about it − I nearly pushed him out of the bloody door. Considering they were lucky to get there at all (and in the right place and within my own timing estimate) his remarks were rather unnecessary."*

It was a great relief to see, quite suddenly as we crested Sussex Mountain, HMS *Fearless* − home − where she should be and offering a touch of peace, sanity and warmth, a hot shower and a plate of food. As it turned out, and apart from the warmth of friendships, there was no time for such luxuries!

I was well received by the staff who seemed happy that this sudden and rather unexpected move of ground troops had, so far, gone well. I explained without anger and, I hoped, with some relevant humour, how well it nearly did not go! There were lessons for the future and, as I was likely to be involved, I wanted them to be well learned. There was no doubt that COMAW and Div HQ wanted these moves to be completed as soon as possible.

The Commodore again:

"I had always tried to keep the Admiral informed of my intentions, and although not my duty, of what I believed were the General's needs and arguments. This was not an easy task as the Admiral often preferred to transmit rather than receive and although I was co-located with most of the General's staff I never felt wholly in the military picture. The situation wasn't helped because the Admiral never really seemed to know if he was in overall command which I felt he wanted and tried to achieve, or what his role as *primus inter pares* was. Both General Moore and I were pretty clear how we saw each of the Task Group Commanders' roles and how they interlocked but we were, of course, spending a lot of time together, eating meals in my cabin, briefing and sometimes going ashore together, whereas the Admiral was a long way away and getting a very different feel for the campaign and, it seems, speaking to a very different crowd in Northwood. The Admiral seemed quite embarrassed and contrite the next morning, after I pointed out we had lost all hope of surprise as a result of his ships' actions, and that the subsequent reinforcement of Fitzroy − albeit further south − would also be jeopardized."

The move of the Welsh Guards would, subject to weather, continue as planned. The even better news, from my point of view, came in confirmation that Jeremy Larken was to bring HMS *Fearless* to within two miles of the southern end of Elephant Island and we would have two frigates on the gunline to help if necessary. If the weather continued to moderate (but with the visibility remaining poor in our favour) the plan was without unforeseen hitches. I was given the recognition signals and an up-date of friendly sea and land forces in the area of Choiseul Sound and Lively Island. I was happy. I was, actually, more than happy. We had tested ourselves to near the limit and had achieved the aim without loss of life. We had all now learnt the lessons and were about to conduct a no less dramatic repeat performance. This was what I was employed to do and what I enjoyed doing.

> *"Arrived on board and briefed by Captain for tonight's task....* *Looked longingly at my cabin and bunk − no time even for a shave* *or shower. Writing this at dusk whilst waiting in the half-light on a* *bitingly cold, wind- and rain-swept flight deck for the helicopter to* *take me back to Bluff Cove. I don't like flying.*
> *"During the day (6 June) the weather prevents* Sir Tristram *completing her loading for Fitzroy with the Rapier firing points. She* *continues to load ammunition and stores. The Field Ambulance arrive* *too late and miss the ship. Welsh Guards embark in HMS* Fearless *at noon, bound, according to the Commodore's orders for Fitzroy.* *These orders are not translated correctly by Divisional Headquarters* *(for only COMAW could order ships' destinations). The Welsh* *Guards are instructed by them 'to sail to Bluff Cove'."*

The Welsh Guards embarked in HMS *Fearless* during the afternoon, leaving behind only their 'B' Echelon. Early that evening the Commanding Officer gave his 'O' Group. Following instructions he had been given by the Divisional Staff, the Battalion was ordered to land at Yellow Beach (Bluff Cove, western bank) and then to move on foot through the Scots Guards' position to the area of Grid Square 2167 astride the track to Stanley where the Battalion was to dig in pending further orders. *Fearless* was to sail with just two of her LCUs, leaving the other two to continue with the San Carlos offload. The 'naval' plan was for her to rendezvous with 'my' four *Intrepid* LCUs, retract her own two pre-loaded craft, bring in two of *Intrepid* boats, load these quickly with men and retract them. She would then bring in the two empty *Intrepid* boats, shut the stern gate and sail for the comparative safety of San Carlos. To save time it made sense for the two pre-loaded craft to be laden with the stores and equipment that would otherwise take time to embark. Men loading into the 'second wave' would take just a few minutes. Therefore in the 'co-ordinating instructions' paragraph to his 'O' Group the Commanding Officer ordered that the two *Fearless* craft would be pre-loaded as follows:

Foxtrot One
Four Land Rovers (fitted for radio) and trailers.
Recce Platoon.
Battalion Headquarters.
Foxtrot Four
Stores, compo rations.
Machine Gun Platoon.
Anti-tank Platoon.
No 2 Company.
Balance of Battalion Headquarters.
Section of Royal Engineers.

The remainder of the Battalion, consisting mostly of the other two rifle companies and the mortar platoon, would load into the *Intrepid* boats and the flotilla would sail in company. No mention was made to the Welsh Guards of the possibility of landing at Fitzroy, nor was there anything to suggest that the bridge linking Fitzroy and Bluff Cove was other than impassable due to earlier enemy action. I have to say, too, that I had no illusions about my destination once I had changed craft at *Fearless*. Without any notice to the contrary it was 'back to Bluff Cove' as far as I was concerned.

Fearless sails at dusk in company with *Avenger* and *Penelope*.

"Arrived back at Bluff Cove in appalling weather at sunset after an 'interesting' flight. Storm force winds and low cloud − mist. Craft have all dispersed during the storm − unable to contact them immediately."

In fact we found one craft in the vicinity; just outside the entrance to the Cove, under the inadequate lee of White Point. It was a dramatic and forbidding sight worthy of the best Hammond Innes novel. The crewman and I sat in the open door of the aircraft while the pilot struggled to maintain a hover fifty or so feet above the craft to allow me to be winched down.

'Christmas!' I remember thinking to myself as I sat in the door watching the LCU between, and below, my muddy ski-march boots. 'Do I really have to!'

'Yes, you bloody well do!' A familiar voice from the past − my Godfather − broke in. It was rather uncanny! I had once refused to climb the sixty-foot mast of his Bristol Channel Pilot Cutter at the age of seven and was sent home on a fourteen-hour lone train journey with a grubby note for my mother: 'You sent your son to me to learn seamanship – he has failed!' My mother, totally unabashed, sent me back by return, with an equally terse note on the reverse of the original: 'I sent my son to you to be taught seamanship – you appear to be failing!'

Any decision I was making to myself was superseded by the crewman shouting in my ear.

"No go, Sir!"

I wasn't sorry – and yet would things have been different if I had joined up with at least one LCU? I would have become even more out of touch with the command but I might have been in a better position to learn, in time, what had happened and then round up the landing craft, although at sunset no craft were able to move anywhere with safety.

It was all but dark and the pilot was as anxious to return to San Carlos as I was to get off anywhere from where I could talk to COMAW. He landed me on the settlement green and we parted company, both glad to be free of one another's differing requirements. I left a message for Headquarters to the effect that, at that moment, the weather was bad but expected to moderate. I did not mention the lack of craft as I was confident they would return with the decreasing wind. I went in search of a radio link with COMAW to explain the predicament more fully.

Back onboard *Fearless* the arrangements continued as planned.

I was concerned at the lack of craft, but hoped, as I sat later with Mike McKie and a dram in the kitchen of Bluff Cove's Big House, that they would reappear as the weather started to moderate. The weather did moderate: the craft did not appear. I puzzled for most of the night why the cox'ns had decided to seek shelter elsewhere, for that is what I assumed they had done. Bluff Cove was the best 'bolt hole' in the area.

A radio link was opened between the beach and the Scots Guards to inform me if any craft materialized in the steadily decreasing winds, but by midnight, with the weather considerably quieter and even within the Chief Naval Architect's safety limits, there were still no craft. I shivered myself to sleep in my sodden clothes.

Fearless arrived at the rendezvous on time, docking down at 0200. There was then an anxious pause while the two laden craft snatched at their lines and crashed against the dock's batter boards. Without my arrival only half the Guards would be on their way, and not a very balanced half at that. The loading tables had been drawn up so that all the heavy equipment would be pre-loaded, but with only these two craft available to make the journey it was not the equipment that the Colonel would, by choice, have sent in first, if there had been a choice. Now, not only was he having to send it in first but it was to be the only part of his Battalion to go ashore at all. The departure time, 0300, came and went. Johnny Rickett was so anxious not to split his Battalion that he sought out the Land Force Commander and told him he was not sure that it was wise to continue with the plan; he wanted all ashore or nobody, and particularly he wanted his rifle companies ashore first. Jeremy Moore was reassuring: "Don't worry − I'll get the other half to Bluff Cove tomorrow night;" and with that, and with the ship unable to wait any longer than the critical 0400 (by which time the LCUs had to sail to make Bluff Cove before dawn at 1000 local), the Commanding Officer embarked in *Foxtrot One*, leaving *Fearless* with over three hundred of his men still on board to sail at best speed back to San Carlos.

In his book *Operation Corporate* Martin Middlebrook implies that there were 'misunderstandings' over the arrangements for the transfer of the Welsh Guards at the half-way hand over. There was no confusion at all. The Welsh Guards' Commanding Officer knew exactly what he wanted to do (be landed at Bluff Cove). *Fearless's* Captain knew exactly where he wanted to launch the LCUs (south of Elephant Island at the entrance to Choiseul Sound), and I knew exactly where that rendezvous was to be and when.

What did happen was that I had sent the signal from the Scots Guards' HQ suggesting that, as the weather was so bad, we might have to delay the operation. That message was, surprisingly, received, but not until *Fearless* had closed the RV (which might explain why this one did get through when it did). Nor, as Middlebrook goes on to explain, did I fail to sail to make the rendezvous; "because of the battering [my] craft and [my] crews had suffered the previous night while carrying the Scots Guards." We had received no such battering and were able to continue operating the moment we had landed the troops at Bluff Cove.

Apart from the navigational and operational difficulties I describe above, we were working just within the limits of our experience; although I accept that the Chief Naval Architect may have taken a different view of the wind and sea conditions, but then I have never seen eye to eye with the boffins of Bath and their unreal computer predictions of landing craft stability. The conditions were extraordinarily difficult and violently unpleasant but apart from the enemy (and HMS *Cardiff*) they were not, in my opinion at the time, dangerous. There is a great difference between the two, as I have always taught my cox'ns. We certainly had not been battered into unseaworthiness, or unwillingness.

"7 June. Woken by Tim Dobbyns before dawn. Quick cup of tea in the big house. Disturbed by 2 Welsh Guards provost on motorbikes who said the Welsh Guards had just landed in LCUs! I dashed down

to the Cove in Mike McKie's Land Rover. F4 *was on the beach. Good effort by Tony Todd who had been shaken by the Captain when* Fearless *reached the RV to find us not there and told to guide the craft to Bluff Cove."*

Commodore Clapp: "I assume someone must have said we had better send them in to Bluff Cove and not Fitzroy to see what has happened to Ewen. I don't know; but my instructions had been for them to go to Fitzroy. I was learning fast that 'orders and intentions' mean different things to the different services!"

Reflections from my log written a little later: "*It was excellent weather with them, yet with us just 12 miles north-east it had been frustratingly bad to begin with – an academic problem, as I had no craft anyway. The embarrassment of not having all the craft will not be known as the weather has intervened, but at the time we could have sailed and didn't. Remembering back to midnight I know I would have given it a go if the craft had been available as instructed. Where the bloody hell are they? Tony admitted that it wasn't easy, even though he possessed a 'satnav' system and only had a twenty-mile passage and one headland to negotiate. Nevertheless it was a really impressive performance* (for which he was Mentioned in Despatches) *as he does not know the area and so missed the Z bend – which would have been passable. So, we have half the Welsh Guards (and the wrong half by all accounts) ashore at Bluff Cove. What next?*"

XVIII

A Bloody War
And A Sickly Season

I WAS FURIOUS. I was also relieved that Tony Todd had had a safe passage, but we still had to conduct, somehow, yet another night approach with half a battalion. We had got away with it two nights running, but I knew that the reason why we still had men 'on the move' was the fault of myself and the landing craft crews.

I knew the Commodore would ask me if I had at least tried and whether or not I had 'Gone out to have a look' but I had been denied the chance to do just that and knew that we had failed the Commodore and the Welsh Guards, some of whom were returning for the umpteenth time to San Carlos. At that time I was not prepared to explain the real reason for my inactivity and just let everyone think it was purely the weather. I also knew, as I sat on the beach pondering the situation, that the cox'ns must have had a very good reason for not being available when I returned from San Carlos and an even better one for not being on the beach ready to sail at midnight. I needed to know what it was.

Tony briefed me on the situation he expected to find at Fitzroy and suggested that we sail immediately, but I wasn't too sure. It was an outstandingly beautiful and clear day and, although the flat calm meant that we could transit the 'Z' bend in safety (as far as navigation was concerned), it would have been a most listless enemy that would have let us complete this daylight passage of ten miles 'under his nose' and the one thing the Argentinian Air Force was not was listless. Yet there was obviously urgent work to be done at Fitzroy and not many craft with which to complete it. An LSL was waiting to be unloaded. I agreed to sail for Port Pleasant, Fitzroy Settlement's anchorage − not to be confused with Port Fitzroy off which leads Bluff Cove, a fact that may have caused some of the misunderstandings between the Commodore's staff and the various military staffs.

The Commodore picks up the story: "The Colonel AQ on the General's staff begged me to have one more and last go. We had been prevented by the weather in getting the Rapier on to *Sir Tristram* and the Field Ambulance had also missed her. We now had half the Welsh Guards to get forward as well. My only reasonable and reluctant solution was to use *Sir Galahad*, which, of all the LSLs, had had the worst time with unexploded bombs and I wanted her to get to sea and safety but she had arrived in San Carlos and was the only one empty and available."

Back in San Carlos the Captain of *Sir Galahad* (Phil Roberts), having just returned that morning from Teal Inlet, was ordered by the General's staff (wrongly by-passing the correct chain of command for the tasking of shipping) to load the Welsh Guards direct from *Fearless*. This the Captain did under the impression that he would be taking them (and his recently loaded four Rapier firing points) to Fitzroy as ordered by 'his boss' – the Commodore. The Welsh Guards embarked content in the belief that they would be dropped off first, and straight into Bluff Cove as suggested by a junior member of the Commodore's staff, which, paradoxically, confirmed the orders given by their own Commanding Officer as he left *Fearless* earlier that day with the General's promise still fresh in his mind.

> "The plans for the landing at Bluff Cove changes a number of times during 7 June. While still on board Fearless the Welsh Guards are told that Sir Galahad would go direct to Bluff Cove, disembark them (the method was not specified but was assumed by them to be by beaching) and then the ship would move to Fitzroy to unload the Rapier urgently need to protect what was becoming the main logistic base for both Brigades' assault on Stanley. Other variants include the Sir Galahad rendezvousing with 2 LCUs south of Elephant Island, from where the guardsmen would be taken to Bluff Cove before dawn. A later plan suggests that 2 LCUs would meet them at Fitzroy, though there were no definitive instructions covering this idea, to ferry them to Bluff Cove. All in all an understandably confusing time.
>
> "On 7 June CINC Fleet orders that no 'large ship' is to operate forward at all, ending his signal with the words that 'the man on the spot, however, must decide. This came before the decision on the use of Sir Galahad, forcing COMAW to argue with Northwood over the use of LSLs. Were they or were they not 'large ships' for this purpose? He received no confirmation either way. The LPDs had been put at some risk two nights running and it appeared that the possibility of disaster was now too much for Northwood and the Cabinet. It is possible that in the United Kingdom it was assumed that a major amphibious operation was planned rather than a secretive small-scale affair. All movement was to be by some other method than an LPD from now onwards."

To add to this confusion none of the military participants in the mounting saga appreciated (and nor should they necessarily have done so) that without a suitable beach or jetty in the area the only way that any vessel was going to be unloaded was by landing craft and helicopter; this added to the muddle over place names. At that moment there were no helicopters and six out of a Task Force total of eight LCUs were at Fitzroy not Bluff Cove. The remaining two were now at Teal Inlet. Four, though, were about to be returned from Fitzroy to San Carlos which had been denuded of assets, so anxious was the Commodore to 'rescue' the situation.

An added complication then appeared on the scene, although as events were to turn out their presence in the Fitzroy area was to be fortuitous. 16 Field Ambulance (5 Brigade's medical unit) still needed to be brought forward to cover the impending attacks on to the hills surrounding the western approaches to Stanley. This organization was in some disarray on the beach, having failed for various reasons, one of which was the lack of landing craft, to sail to Fitzroy in *Sir Tristram* the night before and now it took a further seven hours after the Guards were embarked in *Sir Galahad* for them to follow suit. Their destination was very definitely Fitzroy: plus Rapier firing points, plus ammunition, plus one Sea King to speed the offload.

Captain Roberts was now concerned not only over the delay in loading by the Field Ambulance but also with the differing destinations expected by his passengers. He asked COMAW's staff for a delay of twenty-four hours in order to sort this out and to ensure that he had the most hours of darkness in which to sail to both anchorages. COMAW's staff refused this request and ordered him to sail immediately for the very good reason that nine hours of darkness were left to cover the 130 miles to Fitzroy, his only destination. The staff now explained, quite correctly, that offloading craft were available at Fitzroy and not Bluff Cove and that no suitable beach for an LSL existed in either area. *Sir Galahad* sailed at 2200 with 470 Embarked Military Force. The Welsh Guards were very much party to the general reluctance to be at sea in daylight but were given assurances on board that adequate protection would cover any offload. Apart from anything else the order to sail at the eleventh hour was seen by them as confirmation that COMAW's staff were aware of the risks and by implication had provided for them.

> *"During the day the Argentinian observation post on the Wickham Heights requests an air strike against Fitzroy."*

It has always been accepted that the Argentinian OP had been in visual contact with the shipping in Port Pleasant but, at the war's end, the

Commodore stopped his helicopter returning him from Stanley so that he could stand on the very peak above the enemy OP. From this even higher position he could only see the top three feet of an LSL's mast through very powerful binoculars. He was then in no doubt that the air strikes called for were the result of a considerable increase in signal traffic in the Fitzroy area.

"HMS Intrepid *sails forward night of 7/8 June to collect the four LCUs so frantically needed back at San Carlos."*

The Commodore was to comment later: "We were always worried about West Falkland and the need to continue offloading stores at San Carlos which is why I was determined to get the LCUs back — and the only way was by LPD. Thinking the way that we were, I still believe that even then I did not give West Falkland as much thought as I should, although others back in England seemed to think we were giving it too much attention. Jeremy Moore certainly thought he was very extended when he considered what could happen quite suddenly behind our backs."

So, back to the morning of 7 June at Bluff Cove where there was not a cloud in sight and not a breath of wind....

We had to sail, collect the dispersed landing craft and organize a swift offload of *Sir Tristram* at Fitzroy, mobilizing all the vessels we could muster for as long as we could. There was no alternative. With strongly-crossed fingers we sailed into that astonishingly calm, beautiful, sunlit, dangerous morning.

The 'Z' bend, precisely marked by the kelp, showed as a well-defined track curving between the shallows. The South Atlantic was as flat as any millpond with the dazzling blue reflections broken only by the smudges of kelp and the occasional eddy as the gentle tide meandered through the pass.

All eyes were astern and to the north east. Every man was alert with his weapon; the GPMGs swivelled aft to face the expected Pucara attack. There was none, and we sailed at full speed into the *"comparative protection"* (an ill-considered opinion in my log as it was to turn out) of the Fitzroy anchorage on the north shore of Port Pleasant, accompanied by two Puffing Pigs and numerous Black-browed Albatrosses. Once again I was diverted by the wildlife, and while this distraction could have been dangerous, it was a most heartening sight and one that often kept me sane and determined throughout the campaign.

As soon as we had berthed on the settlement jetty, I called for a report from the *Intrepid* LCU cox'ns over the problems of the previous night. Their story did nothing for my humour. Shortly after I had left for the

Flagship a Parachute Regiment major gave instructions for a move he wanted to make between Fitzroy and Bluff Cove and not just across the local inlet as I had agreed. Corporal Angel had answered his original request over the radio with a perfectly correct "Wait out" while he fetched his cox'n, to receive the reply: "I want a fucking answer, not a 'wait out'!" There was talk of a pistol being produced and all manner of unpleasantness. The cox'ns had no charts, the weather was marginal, they had no aids to navigation and they had never seen the area before. They were also acting under my orders to remain where they were for future operations.

In his book *2 Para at War* General Frost describes his version of this unfortunate incident and implies — to my reading of it — that the production of a pistol had been a necessary act due to the incompetence and reluctance of my landing craft crews, but I will staunchly defend my cox'ns against any argument from someone who was not there, was not a seaman, did not know the Falkland Islands and was not trained in amphibious warfare.

Three LCUs then set out on this unplanned voyage just before the weather again turned foul, by which time they were storm-bound at Fitzroy and unable to return to Bluff Cove to collect me and make the rendezvous with *Fearless*. If there had been communications between the army at Fitzroy and the embarked Divisional staff co-located with COMAW's staff it is just possible, with hindsight, that I might have been diverted to the settlement on my way back from the *Fearless* briefing on the evening of 6 June, but Fitzroy had remained incommunicado with the outside world and I had remained in ignorance of my crafts' movements.

This continual lack of communication was the cause of so much that occurred during those few days. I was told later that neither CLFFI nor COMAW were aware that 5 Brigade could not talk to their forward troops. The loss of the relay station (and particularly the loss of Major Mike Forge, the Brigade Signals Officer, flying forward to repair it) was a prime contributory factor, but the lack of understanding of the third dimension, the sea flank (with its command and control peculiarities), added to this non-amphibious Brigade Headquarters' loss of tight control.

Whether or not the weather would have actually prevented me from sailing from Bluff Cove in time to meet *Fearless* I do not know, but I do know that I had been given no choice but to miss the rendezvous. That is why no craft attempted to RV with HMS *Fearless* and that is why half the battalion of Welsh Guards were eventually (and I believe therefore, unnecessarily) forced to embark in the RFA *Sir Galahad*.

288

28. "Below us and half a mile away lay the settlement. It was a tranquil and idyllic scene…sweet peat smoke drifted over the hill on the early morning breeze…." Pebble Island settlement on the morning after 'their' garrison had surrendered.

29. "As we crested the slight bank at the back of Elephant Beach the skyline was broken by ruined aircraft in a variety of positions."

30. The *Rio Iguazu* "...half out of the water and listing to starboard - an eighty-ton lightly armed vessel and one of those I so feared earlier."

31. Moody Brook was "burned out beyond recognition to all but the most sentimental."

After four breakfasts (there is usually an unwritten competition between LCU crews to see who can produce the best breakfast for 'the boss') I cooled my temper with a walk up to the local Royal Artillery Blowpipe section on the hill above the jetty.

"Tried out the aimer. This team have two enemy aircraft to their credit. Sadly none came whilst I was with them as, so far, I have only once fired my pistol at a Skyhawk – and that was solely for morale purposes! For the record – I missed!"

I was keen to shave, change my clothes, wash and replace my congealed camouflage cream. The offload was going as quickly as I dared hope and for a brief moment all seemed to be right with the world again. We had had problems – we still had problems: half a battalion had somehow to be brought forward but that was someone else's concern. Mine were, momentarily, more personal.

Morale was raised a further notch:

"Heard that 2 a/c shot down over San Carlos today."

The day continued. Once orders had been issued I was superfluous to the offload and so felt clear to renew old Falkland Island acquaintances. There were altruistic reasons and not just a desire to go 'coffee-housing' for Fitzroy contained many citizens from Stanley who had left the capital when the occasion had presented itself. There was much useful information to be gained by talking to friends who had witnessed at first hand the awful early days of Argentinian occupation of their homes.

"Went ashore to see, among many others, Janet Blakely – our elderly baby sitter – many tears and much love to Patricia and the children. How muddling for the emotions to be back in time one moment as though on an old fashioned patrol around the settlements in the MV Forrest, *and the next deep into the vagaries and harsh realities of war."*

As sunset grew nearer I made my way back to 'clock in' with the Army headquarters to discover that at dusk we were due to lose the four *Intrepid* LCUs, leaving us to re-juggle the offload priorities, procedures and timings. Some signals were obviously getting through. I think that this one was via *Sir Tristram* but I could not then trace it.

5 Brigade's embryo Headquarters had been set up in the wool shed with lamps blazing beneath huge skylights pointing to the stars. It was warm and comfortable with partitions and rooms dividing the various functions. As a set piece it was superb, but I could not help casting my mind back to the Commando Brigade who had eschewed outside lights and anything

near civilian-occupied buildings to avoid helping an air strike which could have homed in on their radio transmissions. Although the skylights would have been in among the settlement and therefore, to a Canberra on a night bombing run, part of the normal collection of lights, I thought the concept rather dangerous, but it was not my place to say so.

In the wool shed I was introduced to a Parachute Regiment Major, Barnie Rolfe-Smith. We met as old friends and I immediately recruited him as an ally in order to brief him on the problems in the anchorage as I saw them. I was particularly keen that nothing prevented the speedy offload of *Sir Tristram* and to that end we had to devote every craft we then possessed, which were now two LCUs and one mexeflote. We knew we could not complete the task that night, but if we worked fast, I suggested, she might, just might, be ready to sail the following night.

During this conversation it was suggested that we send one of the two LCUs to Darwin to collect the Brigade radio vehicles so urgently needed. While the collection of the radios was vital for 5 Brigade, there were distinct disadvantages in transporting them by LCU. On the other hand there were two other ways of getting the vehicles to Fitzroy − overland or slung beneath a Sea King. These, though, were also fraught with difficulties, not least of which was the average speed over the peat at that time of year and the lack of helicopters. 5 Brigade tasked a number of Sea King sorties but no such request reached Divisional HQ due to the continuing lack of communications. On General Moore's arrival all helicopters had been 'chopped' to Divisional HQ, plus naval aviators as the liaison/tasking officers. The Colonel AQ then decided the allocation of aircraft, back to COMAW for the offload for instance, or between the two Brigades.

Now that we had lost *Intrepid's* four we needed both the remaining LCUs, working flat out, to ensure that *Sir Tristram* was unloaded in time for her return journey to San Carlos after dark. Secondly, as we could not tell the garrison at Darwin that the LCU would be on its way, I was hesitant to risk it when I knew that the Gurkhas had orders to destroy anything that moved up Choiseul Sound. I have great respect for the Gurkhas and knew full well that they would do exactly that. Thirdly, if I did send a LCU it would not be available until the next night as, Gurkhas or no Gurkhas, it was clearly a target for Pucara over the Sound by day. The radios would not be at Fitzroy for at least twenty four more hours if they did come by sea and it could take as long across country. I was being cautious, but also trying to ensure that the LSL was given the first priority. My arguments were accepted with good grace although, once again, I felt that I was not perhaps being bold enough. The unloading of the LSL and the safety of the LCU were, rightly or wrongly, uppermost in my mind at that stage. 'Once bitten twice shy' was seldom more apt although Nelson would not have approved of those sentiments for they were hardly conducive to 'engaging the enemy more closely'.

During a brief discussion with Colour Sergeant Johnston he helped me with my decision by stating: "LCUs have been shot up by the Royal Navy on both flanks [he had been challenged twice when on a run back from Teal Inlet] and I would rather not face the Gurkhas. My luck may not last." These were to be tragically prophetic words.

The beach we were using forced upon us another small but significant factor which affected the availability of craft and timings. It was in a cove facing south west towards the prevailing winds, about half a mile from the settlement. The landing point was awkward as there was one exit through the low cliffs offset by some yards from the only clear patch of water for an LCU's approach. Outside two or so hours either side of high water the beach was operational, as equipment could be landed at the waterline and then run along the shingle to the exit, but at high water this lateral track to the cut in the cliffs was submerged and then landings, of very light kit and men only, had to take place directly on to the southern end of Fitzroy Jetty.

I insisted that the crews stopped as much as possible during this natural 'break' around high water and got rest, showers and hot meals as best they could from the ship.

"*Went onboard* Sir Tristram *to find that before sailing* Intrepid's *LCUs had been instructed to rendezvous in Low Bay which is even further west than Lively Sound and difficult to believe when one considers that* Fearless *came up to Direction Island only last night. I hope they make it. Offered a shower, dinner and a cabin. Accepted.*"

I entered the officers' saloon with some care. Although clean in body my clothes were still filthy and as standards were being maintained throughout the ship because of the situation (rather than in spite of it), I was keen not to abuse the hospitality. Everybody wore spotless Action Working Dress and carried equally spotless anti-flash gear. I didn't look the part and was privately ashamed that it was in deep contrast to my days in the Hadramaut when, with no facilities whatsoever apart from a cold-water bath I had made out of an oil drum and that I kept in the rushes on the edge of the wadi not two hundred yards from the enemy fort we were watching, I had changed for 'dinner' (sand grouse baked in an ammunition tin) every evening. My Baluchi 'bearer' would produce clean clothes in time for the dusk 'stand-to' and nightly skirmish with a sniper who had taken it upon himself to prevent this very English habit.

I need not have worried too much for the RFA's good manners and understanding of displaced persons are well known. The Captain, Robin Green, asked me to join him at his table. Dinner, served by impeccable Chinese stewards, was conducted as though there was no outside world.

Having been rebuked by Robin for knocking the 'weevils' out of my biscuits during the cheese course – an old and harmless affectation which did not reflect on the ship's purser – I felt I should repay the officers with a bottle of port. The conversation touched only fleetingly on the business in hand; for the most part the meal was a lovely oasis of civilized behaviour and amusing stories with old friends and colleagues set in an angry and arid desert. I revelled in it more perhaps than I should have done.

After dinner we repaired to the Captain's quarters for a brandy where the two of us were happy to end the evening with a quiet talk about the more pressing subjects so carefully avoided earlier.

I had met Captain Robin Green a few times and knew him as an officer immensely proud of his ship and his crew. His loyalty to *Sir Tristram* and his Service was absolute and added emphasis to his worry. He did not want to be seen to be complaining yet he was intensely concerned for his ship's safety. I did not help him in this concern by agreeing, fully, with his views of the position in which he found himself. It was a risk, we all knew that, but it would have been less of a risk if he had had a modicum of protection. There was none, and we knew that with only two LCUs and one small mexeflote, he would still be unloading cargo the whole of the following day. We did not then, appreciate the problem a frigate would have faced in such confined waters and saw the risk only in terms of our own predicament.

"Robin is very distressed. I don't give much for his chances in daylight tomorrow – but he will probably have to wait until the next night before sailing."

I turned in.

"8 June.0200. Woken by Barnie Rolfe-Smith to tell me that MV Monsunen *has returned from GG and has comms with the RN and is prepared to escort F4 up Choiseul Sound so I have now ordered Colour Sergeant Johnston to sail but to make absolutely certain that he remains in comms with* Monsunen *in whatever way he and they deem fit to ensure that the Gurkhas know they are transiting the Sound. Told him that under no circumstances is he to sail back until dark tonight regardless of who orders him to do so."*

I debated whether or not I should go too but decided against it. *Monsunen* had a local skipper and (at COMAW's insistance to prevent hijacking) a naval officer in command. She had full communications with her destination, the sea-level visibility was fine and I was bound to be needed to advise 5 Brigade if there were to be any other offload or amphibious tasks during the coming day. We would need to re-plan yet again now that we were down to one LCU and the small mexeflote. It was another decision I was to regret and possibly the one I regret most. Whether or not the subsequent loss of *Foxtrot Four* would have occurred if I had been embarked, I cannot, of course, tell: I may too have felt the same sense of frustration and determination to help as expeditiously as possible, as did Brian Johnston that following afternoon.

I was later taken to task, quite rightly, for myself sending an LCU on an 'unauthorized' journey as it was in the area specifically to unload *Sir Tristram*, but I had, by then, changed my mind and now believed that the 5 Brigade communications vehicles had the utmost priority and readily agreed, once it was safe to do so, to help them out. It was, after all, the lack of communications that was the root cause of so much that happened in the area.

> I turned-in fully clothed in case of problems and then: "*Up at dawn; woken by Captain Green who took me immediately to his bridge to show me* Sir Galahad *at anchor about a cable to the east. Robin simply can't believe that another ship has appeared. With Tony Todd we looked through the binos to see that she is full of men who are cluttering up the stern gate whilst there is a mexe (half full of ammo) moored alongside the stern ramp (it appears to be ours) on its way to the beach. Not sure what we are going to unload* Sir G *with, but whatever we do, I think these ships are in grave danger. Writing this on board* F1 *as we cross to* Sir G. *Have just ordered the LCU to moor alongside the port side of the ramp − not quite sure what I am going to find − nor what we can do about it.*"

The Commodore's staff had assumed, quite understandably, that *Sir Tristram* would be empty and that the one Sea King brought by *Sir Galahad*, two LCUs and one mexeflote would be sufficient to unload the second LSL within the day but they were not to know that *Sir Tristram* had been overloaded and that I had despatched one LCU to Goose Green and therefore lengthened the unloading time even further.

The next few minutes are very clearly etched in my memory.

Foxtrot One moored down the port side of the stern ramp. On the ramp and filling the tunnel leading to the tank deck were men in camouflaged combat clothing and helmets. To begin with neither Tony nor I had any idea who the men were or what the rest of the ship's cargo was, although we guessed that the bulk of her payload must have been ammunition and food. The men were a mystery to us.

Watching our arrival from the lowered ramp were a number of officers representing various organizations and, apart from a couple of Royal Marines in green berets, all wore combat helmets masking their corporate identities; among them were two Army majors. To this day I cannot identify them as individuals (personally, I have never attempted to do so) and could not swear to their regiment which was never mentioned at the time, although, by inference, it became clear. One of the two, seeing yet more officers about to join the throng, asked us who was responsible for unloading the ships in the anchorage. Although not specifically charged with that duty, Tony Todd, as the COMAW's representative would assume that mantle. I had no such duty other than that of adviser on the practicalities and the area; as I did direct to COMAW himself.

We explained this to the assembled company adding that if they told Tony where it was they wanted to go I was prepared to discuss the feasibility of the move. The men wanted to get to Bluff Cove, as ordered by their Commanding Officer. The Rapier firing points, gunner ammunition, Royal Engineer Troop and Field Ambulance needed to be offloaded at Fitzroy and were destined to form the nucleus of 5 Brigade's forward support area. On the face of it a simple and easily solved question of priorities and planning.

"Nobody is going to Bluff Cove today – unless they walk." I felt that that option had to be scotched early on. "Stores can be unloaded just as soon as we finish with *Sir Tristram*."

Everyone and everything that was on board, I explained, would be unloaded into Fitzroy and anybody that needed a further move to Bluff Cove could travel that night in a landing craft (providing we had finished the offload of both LSLs, which was going to be unlikely) or during the day on foot. I suggested that the men had to be removed from the ship first due to the possibility of air strikes and that they could all be put ashore using the LCU and mexeflote then alongside. The craft would then concentrate solely on *Sir Tristram*, which was nearly empty, after which they would return to *Sir Galahad*. I emphasized an important factor: large bodies of men in an LSL clutter up the confined spaces making the movement of vehicles and stores even more protracted and awkward.

This did not find favour with some of the officers on the stern of *Sir Galahad* who wanted to get to Bluff Cove immediately, "as ordered." It was a perfectly understandable request and one with which I fully sympathized, not least of all because it had been my Squadron that, no matter for what reason, had failed to unload them earlier. However, it simply was not practical. We had nothing with which to take them to Bluff Cove unless we stopped unloading *Sir Tristram*, and that was out of the question because of the priority to get the Rapier operating as quickly as possible. It would take two, possibly three, loads in the one LCU and each round trip would take about two and a half hours, assuming the 'Z' bend was passable. It could not be done in daylight and there was a perfectly feasible alternative: they could walk the seven miles to their defensive positions via the bridge (which I knew, but they did not, had been repaired sufficiently well to take men on foot) while some of their kit was transported by tractor. I could, if essential, take the balance of their heavy kit round by night, assuming that *Foxtrot Four* returned about five hours after sunset.

"So, I'm afraid you will not be able to get to Bluff Cove by sea today."

They seemed not to understand the problem.

"Why not?"

"Because the LSL cannot land men there without either landing craft or helicopters and there is nowhere to beach her. We can not sail there in daylight in anything anyway as we will be right under Argentinian OPs."

"We were told to land at Bluff Cove."

"So you can — if you wait on the beach till sunset."

"In which case we will stay on board until dark."

"Sorry. The men must wait ashore, they are in danger and they are in the way." I recounted the reasons.

"So what do you suggest?"

"That your men are put ashore and you decide which way you go to Bluff Cove. The bridge across the upper end of Port Fitzroy has been repaired, at least well enough for men walking."

I was not to know that the Royal Engineer Troop embarked in *Sir Galahad* was specifically tasked to repair the bridge. Their presence on board indicated to the Guards officers that the bridge (despite what I was saying) was still impassable to everything. I would probably have come to the same conclusion!

"How do we get ashore?"

I pointed to the half-laden LCU and the half-laden mexeflote further forward: "In those — now. We are wasting valuable time. I can have all your men safely ashore in under twenty minutes if we cram them in for such a short journey. The other troops can follow on but I suggest you move first so that you can start walking."

"That is simply not acceptable! They are full of ammunition."

"So is this ship!"

"No. We stay on board and you can take us tonight. We have been messed around too much already since we arrived in the Islands."

"If I take you tonight I shall pick your men up from the beach. You are not staying on board. I will have to make three runs – two if we are lucky and you don't have too much kit. If you walk you will all be there before dark tonight."

For the reasons given above the Guards officers did not believe my sums as their calculations naturally took no account of the short cut across Port Fitzroy. To my mind it was seven miles of poor 'going' to the Battalion position, compared with 14 terrible miles round the head of the waterway and across River Camp. Of course I did not know we were both working on different distances.

I had hoped that the message was getting through for precious time was being wasted: we were well into daylight and each minute, as far as I was concerned, brought the chance of an air attack closer. This is not hindsight. With hindsight, I can feel much sympathy for the officers concerned. They had been messed about a fair amount in San Carlos and then, again, in HMS *Fearless*.

My own feelings, at the time though, were not very charitable but now I can view the conversation and the reasons behind some of the decisions from a wider perspective. The Battalion had indeed been treated like the Duke of York's ten thousand men and now, to the officers on the stern ramp of *Sir Galahad* that day, the overriding imperative was to join the other half of their Battalion as soon as possible, a Battalion which they rightly assumed was vulnerable and exposed without two thirds of its 'bayonets'. As they saw it, they were to be landed in the wrong place and in circumstances that would take them further from, rather than nearer to, their objective. Believing the Fitzroy bridge to be down (and they certainly were not going to believe someone who, from their viewpoint, was telling them otherwise to add weight to his own argument) they thought it would entail a full day's march – or more – to join up with their colleagues, and even then without the ammunition and heavy kit they were anxious to carry with them.

They had seen no enemy air activity since they first landed at San Carlos, which doubtless contributed to their different perception of those risks. They had been given assurances that there would be local air protection for any offload, an assurance that had been repeated onboard *Sir Galahad* with the added confirmation that CAP was being provided. (It was, but when they were needed most the one pair of Harriers earmarked for Fitzroy was diverted to chase enemy aircraft elsewhere.) Too much faith was unfortunately also being placed in the speed with which the Rapier on board *Sir Galahad* could be landed and deployed, and, possibly, in the protection it would offer. One way and another they did not share my view of the imminent risks and dangers of air attack.

It was clear that I was achieving nothing and so, in desperation, I gave a direct order for the infantry to get ashore with or without their kit in order that we could get on with unloading *Sir Tristram*.

The officers ignored my order. In doing so they explained to me quite clearly that no orders would be accepted from an officer of equivalent rank. I was amazed. Rank did not come into my equation: common sense and experience were behind my instructions, not rank.

I was not prepared to enter into the farcical discussion of the relative ranks of Royal Marines and Army officers which is a minefield of confusion at the best of times. When under the Naval Discipline Act, Royal Marines officers equate to one rank above their army counterparts. In practice they do the whole time, as pay and other privileges testify. That was not the point at issue: professional advice should have been accepted irrespective of rank. Not to do so was an irresponsible act for which I did not feel inclined to be accountable. I said so, and then:

"Are you getting off this ship?"

"No."

"Very well then, but I want you to know that you stay onboard against my advice."

It was vital that I sorted out the impasse by finding someone ashore who could act on my behalf but not compromise my plans. *Foxtrot One* cast off and we headed for the beach and while the LCU returned to continue unloading *Sir Tristram's* ammunition I made my way to the wool shed and Barnie Rolfe-Smith.

"Barnie. I have just come from the latest LSL. She has three hundred and fifty men of the Welsh Guards on board."

He stopped me: "I think you are mistaken. They were all landed the night before last at Bluff Cove by *Fearless'* landing craft." We had not discussed the earlier problems during our previous meetings as they were, to me, old news and my mind had been on the timely offload of *Sir Tristram* and the despatch of *Foxtrot Four*.

"They didn't all get off, some of them returned to San Carlos. They must now get off that ship and on to Bluff Cove as quickly as possible."

It was Barnie's job to insist they got to Bluff Cove by the most effective means available and it was my job, as I saw it, to advise him on the nautical options available. I explained the two main reasons why I wanted the men off the ship, regardless of where they eventually ended up and ran through what had occurred on *Sir Galahad's* stern ramp.

Not keen to undergo a repeat performance I persuaded Barnie to agree that, as he was 'their' staff officer, he should take over negotiations with the Guards. Before he left I gave him a potted version of amphibious operations, Fitzroy-style, with the priorities as I saw them: get all the men off *Sir Galahad* regardless of regiment; point the infantry towards the Fitzroy Bridge or tell them to wait on the beach; unload and sail *Sir Tristram* at dusk; unload *Sir Galahad* of ammunition and hospital stores; take infantry heavy kit to Bluff by landing craft.

All this Barnie understood perfectly.

I was very unhappy indeed with the situation I had been obliged to leave and the failure of my powers of persuasion, but I believed that I had done my best. With as clear a conscience as I could muster under the circumstances, and still angry that my initial advice had not been taken, I said farewell to 5 Brigade's Headquarters and went in search of 'Smoko' with a local family. There was no more that I could do.

During the interval between my briefing Barnie and 5 Brigade's orders to the embarked troops the one LCU and the one mexeflote were kept busy unloading *Sir Tristram*, while the Sea King ferried ashore the Rapier from *Sir Galahad*.

When it was apparent that they would not be getting off straight away, the Welsh Guards offered to put men on *Sir Galahad's* deck with their personal weapons for local air defence. The ship declined this offer, the collective view being that it was not necessary with CAP cover and the Rapier being set up ashore. After the discussion on the stern ramp (of which he was unaware) *Sir Galahad's* Captain asked if they were going ashore. The Welsh Guards senior officers said, 'No — but they would get off immediately they received orders from 5 Brigade or their Battalion'. In his book *Operation Corporate* Martin Middlebrook partially correctly states that 'the next plan suggested was for the one landing craft present to be unloaded of its cargo (on the beach) ...and run (the Guards) around to Bluff Cove'. Middlebrook does not say who suggested this plan — but the second part would certainly not have had my approval until after dark.

During the afternoon a verbal message was received via the ship's staff saying that the guardsmen were to disembark and that the LCU was being despatched to relay them ashore. Although the message was ambiguous the Guards understood the orders were from 5 Brigade and that their destination was to be Bluff Cove, although it is possible that this was either not stated by the originator or was added on by a communicator exercising initiative. From their point of view they had received the instructions for which they were waiting anxiously and so set about organizing their disembarkation without further ado. As they prepared their heavy bergans and mortar ammunition in bundles at the after end of the tank deck ready for shifting across the ship's stern ramp and directly into the LCU, the landing craft was quite suddenly and unexpectedly commandeered by the unfortunate Commanding Officer of the Field Ambulance (whom I had first met when he was being so boorish in Pat Short's house) .

Prior to this the mexeflote had also been 'hijacked' from its urgent ammunition offloading duties to take ashore Field Ambulance vehicles. As an army Lieutenant Colonel, John Roberts felt he was the senior embarked officer and thus able to countermand any order received in the ship; he also appreciated that delays to his own offload would occur if the one LCU was to be away for so long on at least two round trips, each of about two hours, to Bluff Cove. (He would not have known that once I became aware of the destination I would have vetoed the move except to the immediate shore.) There was, or there should have been, no urgency for the Field Ambulance to take priority with the use of the landing craft, for the attacks against the perimeter defences of Stanley had been delayed until, among others, the Welsh Guards' fighting companies were ready, although, in Roberts' defence, he was not to know that. In the end, it was fortuitous that there was immediate medical care available ashore later in the day but if I was a Welsh Guardsman I would not be inclined to see it that way and would feel that here was another cause for their too-long stay on board.

Once most of the Field Ambulance had been put ashore the landing craft returned to *Sir Galahad* to carry out the cox'n's original orders from 5 Brigade to go to Bluff Cove (?) but it was now over one hour after the Guards had agreed to leave the ship.

By the time the LCU had returned from its Field Ambulance trip it had developed an hydraulic failure in its ramp winches. If the LCU's ramp had been working it would have been a simple job to dock on the ship's stern ramp allowing men to manhandle their stores into the landing craft at the same level. However with the bergans and mortar ammunition lashed onto ten pallets beneath the after hatch it was decided that the only quick solution now was to move the LCU alongside the port waist of the ship and crane the netted bundles straight into the LCU, and when that evolution was complete the ship's ramp would be lowered and the LCU moved aft to allow the men to scramble swiftly over the low side from the horizontal ramp. While the LCU moved up the port side to receive the pallets the ramp was closed. (This will be seen shortly as an important decision but for unplanned reasons.) As it was not in use it was raised in accordance with the ship's standing orders to safeguard watertight integrity from action damage and to 'maintain habitability' as the guardsmen were using the tank deck for accommodation. The port side mess decks had been put out of action by the unexploded bomb of 24 May and rather than having some men in the luxury of the starboard side accommodation it had been agreed that all should be billetted in the tank deck.

Incidentally when the ship was hit on 24 May in San Carlos Waters by a 1000 lb bomb she had three hundred men of the Commando Logistic Regiment embarked at a time when air attacks were regular and sustained and yet, despite the Captain's signalled concern to COMAW and Brigade HQ, it was deemed an acceptable risk — or so Phil Roberts assumed from the lack of response to his message. Because of this he, too, felt that under the circumstances on 8 June he had no reason to put the men ashore until they were guaranteed safe passage direct to Bluff Cove and so did not insist.

Ashore, the Rapier teams lifted by the Sea King had been set up to cover the Fitzroy area with one firing post aimed across the eastern sea approaches. By yet another terrible coincidence it was this one team that had sustained the only damage in the transit — spare parts were just ten minutes from being fitted but until that moment there was no anti-air cover facing seawards.

As though there were not enough factors ranged against the LSLs and the Welsh Guards that day, HMS *Sheathbill* was rendered unserviceable at 1030Z by a GR3 Harrier crashing on take off. The knock-on effect was substantial, for 800 Squadron Harriers based in *Hermes* now had nowhere local to refuel. Normally this would not have altered the 'on station' timings significantly but the day before (7 June) the Commander, Carrier Battle Group had ordered his flagship to steam another one hundred miles further east to clean her boilers — an extraordinary decision made against the advice of his Flag Captain who felt that such a vital and delicate moment in the war was no time for routine maintenance. This extra distance, coupled with the sudden lack of facilities at San Carlos meant that, just when they were to be needed most, each CAP patrol had less than fifteen minutes on station. To put this into perspective, an LCU steams two miles in this time and an LSL just four. Of course, nobody could have foreseen the accident, but it was another tiny piece in this terrible jigsaw.

Keeping the aircraft and their carriers safe was an admirable policy but allowing the Harriers sufficient time to do their job would have been an even more admirable concept.

Yet more misfortune attended those in Fitzroy. Just before 1700Z 800 Squadron's CAP was diverted from its patrol area to chase enemy Dagger aircraft, while five Skyhawks from a different formation approached Port Fitzroy overland from the west. Turning south over the sea an Argentinian wingman spotted the masts of the two LSLs in Port Pleasant. The flight hardened its turn and ran in with well-fused bombs.

When the bombs hit, much of the blast through the internal vehicle decks had no escape through the closed 'stern gate' compounding the degree and severity of the burn and flash injuries, and while that was the informed opinion of some who were there, another eye witness states: "This is a reasonable view but not one I agree with. I was in the tank deck about half way down the narrower section towards the rear ramp when the bomb went off. The fire-ball filled the tank deck but due to the lack of oxygen was snuffed out after a few seconds. There was then a period of some thirty seconds before fires started. In that time many had the opportunity to escape. If the rear ramp had been down there is no doubt in my mind that the flue action would have intensified the fire and that the pallets of ammunition down the length of the tank deck would have caught fire immediately. Almost everyone on that deck, totalling about two hundred would have died...the bravery of the LCU crew undoubtedly saved many lives, including my own."

Captain Roberts, awarded the DSO for his handling of *Sir Galahad* throughout the campaign, and particularly on this day, told me much later that his ship was hit by three 500 lb bombs. One passed through the starboard side and, without exploding, pierced the diesel ready-use tank, setting it on fire. Two other bombs passed through the starboard side into the stern trunk leading to the ramp where they deflagrated as opposed to exploded: the explosive burning off very quickly creating a massive fireball effect.

Despite the earlier unfortunate decision not to disembark there must remain a great measure of sympathy for the Guards for so many outside factors were contributing to this impending disaster not least of all the countermanding of 5 Brigade's orders.

Amphibious warfare, despite some contrary views, is not the sole prerogative of the Royal Marines, but it does require specialists who learn, early in their careers, that this form of warfare is complicated enough without subordinate commanders altering plans or applying their own appreciation of the situation. These amphibious specialists are not stifled of initiative but they do understand that continuity of planning must proceed in an ordained order. Of greater importance, they know that plans are dovetailed, in the most complex manner, into the many activities which run concurrently and which may well be unknown, for good reasons, by all participants.

After leaving Barnie to his deliberations I had made my way via many old friends, cups of tea and delicious home-made cakes to end up walking alone across the slight rise beyond the buildings. My thoughts, spurred on by the many greetings and inquiries of Patricia, Hamish and Hermione, were of home and children, dogs and yachts, quiet glasses of port by the large log fire in my cottage on the edge of Dartmoor after a day's shooting; of lazy evenings at anchor, single-handed in my little gaff-cutter, landlocked by beech woods and sloping river banks in the upper reaches of the Tamar River; of the companionship of my marines in the old Naval Party 8901; of the previous occasions I had been 'in action': the Yemen border in 1961 (and again with my detachment from HMS *Anzio* during the Radfan campaign) and those halcyon days as a second lieutenant in command of a 'half troop' of 45 Commando patrolling for days through the 'jebels' above Dhala's tented camp: my magnificent soldiers in the Oman's Northern Frontier Regiment during the Dhofar war and their quite unbelievable valour against communist insurrection; the landing craft crews up the River Foyle during Operation Motorman; my crews, at that moment working their backs off under trying circumstances; the armed and very fast 'snake boat' chases through the darkened waters of Hong Kong's cluttered harbours, without charts and lights, where the stakes were probably higher than in anything else I had done and where these same landing craft crews demonstrated every quality required of a Royal Marine.

I leant against a wooden paling and gazed across the tranquil waters of the aptly named Shallow Cove towards Port Fitzroy and Bluff Cove a bare three Johnny Rook miles away. I thought of the Scots Guards now digging in and preparing for the final (I remember thinking with absolute clarity that I hoped it would be the final) offensive. If it wasn't, and we had to fight for Stanley itself.... I turned, all thoughts of dogs and yachts gone, and headed back to the present. I had had no sense of foreboding but something had drawn me away for that brief hour to be alone with my memories and hopes.

I made my way to a house I knew well. There was laughter from the kitchen and the voices of young women as I struggled to take off my muddy boots outside the back door. I knocked and was welcomed back into a family I had not seen for three years. We sat at a table beneath the window facing south across the anchorage, with tea, cakes and Tennants lager.

Abruptly, the revelry and pent-up excitement ended; it had been very short-lived.

"*1710Z. Air strike on* Galahad *and* Tristram. Galahad *already burning badly as I write this at the rush with a hand shaking with anger. Must dash down to the beach to see if I can help.* Tristram *seems to be OK at the moment.*"

The windows shook, everyone turned; those of us sitting half stood as the sound of fast jets died and explosions rattled the loose fittings. We watched, silently, as the first wisps of smoke and flames burst into something altogether more menacing and sinister. We knew instantly what we had just witnessed. These were not the 'misfires' I had seen in San Carlos, these were deathly accurate bombs, and they had been fused to perfection. Slowly, that awful silence was replaced by a quiet, intense sobbing from the three or four girls in the kitchen. The men swore harshly but softly.

I had never been in the company of civilians during combat; it was not a pleasant experience. All the compassion I could muster welled up. I was to blame, not for the bombing but for them witnessing it. Suddenly, it was not something that happened to the 'military', it was happening to them and I was the spokesman for all those who had brought war and death and destruction to those tranquil islands.

Later I wrote: "*I was sitting with the Stewarts in Gus's mother's house with George Stewart and Gus and Coleen Read and some others. All the girls were immediately in tears as this was the first that they had seen of the war at first hand and so, suddenly, it was real — I suppose that up to now it was rather distant to those who were in 'Camp' and who hadn't actually seen anything happen.*"

"How could they? It isn't happening. Tell us, Ewen, tell us. It isn't happening."

I couldn't, and with an anger as intense as any I had felt in life I left the room and the devastated family with whom I had been laughing — and then consoling. I did not know what I was going to do but one thing was obvious, there were going to be casualties on a scale as yet unknown. My friends in the house at the top of the hill knew the ships had been hit; that was bad enough: only I knew that many men would have died.

I sat against the peat stack and lit a cigarette before pulling on freezing, sodden boots. I was in a hurry and yet I could not bring myself to rush.

Down to the settlement jetty: men coming ashore in lifeboats, in the LCU, by helicopter. A shortage of stretcher bearers; grabbed the 'empty' end of one and stumbled up the hill to a shed. A casualty clearing station — makeshift — set up by members of the Field Ambulance brought ashore earlier. Stripped to shirt-sleeves; formed teams of bearers — from the beach to the clearing station — from the clearing station to the helicopter landing site. A Royal Marines corporal marshalling aircraft — impeccably.

The events of those few hours remain jumbled in time and space. In what order did events take place? I do not know. At some moment the Chief Officer of *Sir Galahad* asked me for a biro and a piece of paper. I gave him my gold propelling pencil quite happy never to see it again if it was to be of any use. Chinese crewmen wandered across the green in trances, wrapped in blankets; scenes from newsreel footage shot at any one of a thousand disaster areas.

Horribly mutilated bodies — all alive that I saw — and I carried many of them — lifted with infinite care across the settlement: too much care perhaps — speed was of more importance.

One landing craft alongside the burning *Sir Galahad* remains the most vivid memory, the courage of the cox'n (Colour Sergeant 'Connie' Francis) directly exposed — unlike any other — to the heat and noise and smell of the burning hull glowing and towering above him whilst men struggled slowly, painfully, on board. No swift escape for him or his craft or his passengers if there were to be further explosions. Then, equally as suddenly as the original detonations, silence. There was no one else to be lifted ashore. Helicopters running the airlift back to San Carlos were all that broke the quiet. The noise was better. It diverted thoughts and made conversation, already stilted, awkward and self-conscious, not worth the effort. One lone and long scream still remembered: a severely burned man lying on his stomach; four men holding him down, a surgeon smoothing Flazamine cream across the whole of his back, his legs, his arms, his now-hairless head.

> "F1 *was alongside* Galahad — *sterling work bringing off the wounded. A ghastly sight. Spent an hour as a stretcher bearer and helping the Chief Officer of* Galahad *to account for his men. Not fun. Two more Skyhawk raids.*"

During the later air raids I walked with Tony Todd (who had been enjoying a mug of tea on *Sir Galahad's* bridge when the Skyhawks screamed in) across the settlement green. As the subsequent raids developed we knelt, rather nonchalantly, but awkwardly, with cold-stiff knees, under a convenient and rusting old wagon. Each time the tracer and Blowpipe missiles died down, and the aircraft had roared and jinked beyond the hills to the south west, we stood, lit a cigarette and continued our conversation. During a longer than usual pause Tony casually lifted the lid of the 'water bowser'. It was full of the settlement's emergency fuel. We chose another refuge, while trying to analyse the events of that morning and where we had gone wrong.

I blamed myself for not insisting with even greater vigour that the men be removed from the ship. While Tony was kind enough to tell me that I could have done no more, I was not so sure. I am still not sure.

Someone rushed up to me with a message, sent from the radio in the back of a 5 Brigade Land Rover embarked in *Foxtrot Four*; there was more awful news:

"2000. F4 reported sinking — 6 wounded 11 dead or missing."

A cool army signaller had managed to get a message through while his Land Rover remained chained to the sinking LCU. I ran back to the beach to find *Foxtrot One* and her exhausted and gallant crew resting from their horrifying but remarkable rescue attempts. Colour Sergeant Francis was to be awarded the Distinguished Service Medal for his rescue of men from the burning HMS *Antelope* earlier and for his equally brave work alongside *Sir Galahad*. I had another rescue task for them:

"Sent F1 to search for lifebelts/liferafts/people. Called in at 5 Bde but unable to contact COMAW."

There was other news, only partially good as the damage had been done: *"CAP has destroyed the aircraft that attacked the LSLs."* Subsequent and conflicting information made even this one piece of good news doubtful but what was never in doubt was that of the four Argentinian aircraft that attacked *Foxtrot Four* three were shot down with their pilots killed.

"Walked down to the jetty — still no sign of F1 *or* Monsunen. *Wandered back from the ABU with the burning ships behind — tragic sight — expecting* Tristram *to explode at any moment. Survivors and the injured being lifted out by Sea King back to San Carlos/Ajax Bay for the night."*

My thoughts, though, were for Colour Sergeant Johnston and his men.

"Who the hell ordered F4 *to sail back in daylight down Choiseul Sound I would like to know."*

I do know now. Colour Sergeant Johnston, having loaded his craft, turned to the senior passenger and said: "Bugger the orders. The Brigade needs these vehicles forward now. We'll sail." He was a brave man who was to be awarded, posthumously, the Queen's Gallantry Medal for refusing, despite being ordered, to leave the side of HMS *Antelope* as she burned in San Carlos Waters.

305

"0245. Arrived on board Intrepid. *Debriefed by Captain and AOO. Heard that Colour Sergeant Johnston, Sergeant Rotherham, Marines Rundle and Griffin and Mechanician James are now officially missing presumed killed."*

The Commodore was to write later: "The appalling thing is that a frigate under those conditions only has two 40mm Bofors — the same as an LSL and some have only two 20mm oerlikons as close-range weapons. The 4.5 inch gun is no good as it largely depends on radar and neither the gun nor Seacat could react in time in that area with land all round. By sending in a frigate I would have provided another target without any increase in air defence. In other ways I do now regret not putting in a frigate because it might have interpreted the air raid warning signals correctly and could have suggested to the Captains that they place as many small arms around the upper decks as possible. My view is that the LSLs did receive the air raid warnings but for some reason thought they were only for San Carlos. I don't think they knew we were getting our warnings from a submarine off the Argentinian coast and that they covered the whole area and could not be specific. I was placing too much reliance in the RFA captains' understanding of maritime warfare Falklands-style and I should not have. If I had known the weather was so clear I would have ordered the ships back under cover of darkness but that would probably have been too late under the circumstances."

"9 June. Slept on the deck in the Commodore's dining cabin on board Intrepid *— left at dawn by LCVP for Blue Beach 2 — found the FOB in good health but sad for the news."*

It was pleasant to get back to my own headquarters after the dramas further east and to be able to scotch rumours and report events at first hand. Immediately I was immersed again in the everyday problems that were so much part of life. We would have missed them greatly if they had not cropped up to keep us on our toes. Life was, apart from the obvious tragedies, still stimulating, varied and never, never dull.

"Returned to Fearless *— after 2 air raid red alerts. Surprised (and heartened!) to find people were glad to see me back safely.*
"Much sadness over the loss of F4 — it seems so unnecessary — they were my Black Pig *crew in Norway and among the very best.*
"10 June. Warned that the Argies are now planning a gas attack (signal intercepted stating that they were planning to 'drop some

306

*parcels in a lake' and this is assumed to mean San Carlos Waters).
My gas mask is on the beach as I use the container as a carrying bag
for more important items. Have been warned off to go to* Intrepid *to
navigate four LCUs each with 66 tons of ammo up to Fitzroy tonight
to replace that which has been lost in the two LSLs.*

"On board Fearless — *briefed for tonight's run — moved back to*
Intrepid *by LCVP at 2000."*

The ammunition was vital. The 'bayonets' of 3 Commando Brigade
were in position among the hills to the west and north of Stanley whilst
those of 5 Army Brigade were moving forward to the start lines in the
foothills to the south and west. No attack could take place without the
southern flank's munitions and so failure with this next move would be
catastrophic as far as any assault on Stanley was concerned. It was as
important a task as any we had undertaken for men could, in extremis,
yomp eastwards but ammunition, in the bulk required and in the time
available, could only move by sea.

*"Ground attacks could start tonight. Enemy have been heard
discussing '15 small ships at sea tonight' so it sounds as though we,
too, should expect a landing...? Gunline frigates tonight onto
Stanley."*

The briefing for the night's operation was held in the Commodore's Staff
Office where I joked with the staff that even less did I want to be
starshelled that night with that load; they understood, and assured me that
all ships knew of our presence. I was even given the night's recognition
signal. I was happy.

Intrepid's wardroom was its usual friendly self and I spent a pleasant
hour or so chatting to friends who commented on my unkempt appearance
which contrasted so vividly with theirs. I was hardly surprised for I had
long lost any sense of military sartorial perfection and was clothed in what
I considered the most suitable rig for the nomadic, cold and damp life I
was leading. Starting from the bottom I wore Arctic ski-march boots and
snow gaiters over two pairs of loop-stitched socks; going up, long-johns
under denim trousers which had yet to dry from the salt water dousing of
five nights earlier; hairy khaki shirt and 45 Commando silk scarf beneath
a white submariners woollen jersey topped by a special-forces, oiled-cotton
hooded jacket. On my head I wore a beret during daylight but at night I
wound my green Northern Frontier Regiment *shamagh* around my neck
and head. Although often cold and nearly always wet with salt water I was
very rarely uncomfortable. I was permanently tired.

"Quite a swell running as we wait for the ship to dock down — each LCU has about 60 tons of ammo onboard — could be a problem retracting — 0350 as I write this — Tango One beginning to crash all over the place. Will write more when retracted from the dock.

"Star shells to the NW — over Lafonia this time. Uncertain of where Intrepid *has dropped us as nothing on radar. Was sent an initial vector over the air which is not good security but they couldn't give me one when I called in on the bridge before saying goodbye.*

"At least I have my own charts but the compasses have an estimated error of about 50° with all this ammunition on board. At least I think it is 50° — certainly more than 30°.

"11 June. Arrived at the beach at 0706. Usual diet of nicotine and adrenalin."

Sometime during the day General Moore arrived on the beach and although he clearly had other more pressing tasks he took me aside for a private briefing of the situation in the mountains. At that moment the Commanding Officers of 3 Para, 42 and 45 Commandos were giving their orders for the attacks onto, respectively, Mount Longdon, Mount Harriet and Two Sisters; a convex crescent of defence surrounding the western approaches to the final objective. If all went well they would be in British hands by dawn on the 12th. From there we would exploit forwards via Wireless Ridge to the north and Tumbledown and Sapper Hill to the south. After that... "If the Argentinians surrender then that will be the end. If not, we fight through Stanley."

Before he left, the General instructed me to look hard at the amphibious options involved in a landing against West Falkland. It was great to be back, in a positive way, in the business I understood. Having first-hand knowledge of the situation was also good for the heart and spirit.

"Either way any success in the east will not necessarily affect what happens behind our backs. General reckons West Falkland will still have to be captured. About 800 men at Fox Bay and Port Howard. I'll call in at Int. HQ back in Fearless *to suggest beaches and approaches. Hope to lead the next lot of landings. This is all very good news indeed."*

I passed on all the snippets of news gleaned from the General to the crews and the Amphibious Beach Unit before beginning plans for yet more landing craft operations.

"Called back to RV with Intrepid *in Lively Sound (why will she never come further east?) at 0330 to bring 4 craft back here laden with more ammo as none of the other cox'n's have led this transit before – so, another long night of adrenalin especially as the RV is so far away. Grabbed an hour's precautionary sleep in the Amphibious Beach Unit's tent and a borrowed a still-warm sleeping bag.*

"2130. Retracted – half an hour late due to unloading Tristram's *undamaged stores.*

"0130. Hove to waiting for Intrepid.

"0230. Star shells over Lively island – again.

"Altered course to 3° south of Lively Island towards an intermittent radar contact. At last we have met up with Intrepid *who is not where she said she would be. Thank God we have found her or we would be at sea in daylight trying to hide amongst some islands with no time to get back to the comparative safety of Fitzroy.*

"Not required to return as she is unexpectedly empty so spent the night onboard. Heard that Cdo attack going well and that Glamorgan *hit by missile – which we think we watched as we steamed down the east coast of Lively Island.*

"12 June

"Bed, on board Fearless *eventually – but immediately summoned by Captain (in my silk dressing gown) to be told he didn't want me to discuss the events of Fitzroy as the Commodore was likely to be pilloried and the press had already got hold of it. Jeremy Larken gave me quite a hard time although I was so tired I didn't realize he was doing so to begin with. He had offered me a coffee and I rather rudely said: 'Could I have a whisky, please?' He gave me a very large one and then a further rocket about not everyone sharing my love of the Islands – or of going to war – and that some people would prefer it if I quietened my enthusiasm for both!*

'It was a difficult and courageous decision,' he said and I agreed. The same risk has been taken at Teal without loss. I suppose we were just unlucky. The bad visibility that was so crucial to the decision making had cleared unexpectedly and, an interesting point: if no one had been killed in the attacks, despite losing two ships, would there be any comment?"

Later that morning I bumped into a Royal Marines SBS Corporal who, unsolicited, told me of a recent encounter which, although he could laugh about it later, at the time made him so angry that he was only prevented from striking out by his 'oppo'. Having returned two hours earlier from fourteen days 'behind enemy lines' the corporal was walking, shaved and smartly dressed, through *Fearless's* tank deck where he passed a group of men from an unidentified regiment who jostled him angrily. They had just returned from twenty four hours ashore. "It's all right for you living in luxury in this ship, mate! You should try some soldiering! It's bloody tough in the front line." I report the words verbatim to show how easily perceptions can become distorted and how feelings can be soured, and remain so for many years, by unconnected and trifling events — just as mine were to be a few months later by RAF Support Command's misuse of a Hercules aircraft when it imported from Gibraltar a private motor car instead of my raiding craft.

> *"The next day — lost count of the date — choosing and brainstorming beaches on West Falklands. The excellent news is that the Paras, the Scots Guards — on to Wireless Ridge and Tumbledown. The Commandos secure on their original objectives."*

As a summing up of the whole Fitzroy/Bluff Cove series of operations Commodore Clapp wrote: "When I briefed Peter Dingemans he was clearly concerned at the use of an LPD. He seemed to think that damage or loss of an LPD was too great a price for the success of the land campaign. I suggested that the Navy could never raise its head if it let the soldiers down now just when they needed us most. He was thinking like a pure naval officer and not really understanding the military needs. Anyhow he obviously chose to drop you with the Scots Guards somewhere in Lively Sound for reasons of his own.

"On my side there was clearly a cock-up as I never realized the fact that Tony Todd had been ordered to Bluff Cove with the Welsh Guards. He was supposed to have gone to Fitzroy because all I agreed with Ian Baxter (the Colonel AQ of the CLFFI staff) was that I would take a risk one off in using Bluff Cove and it would be in my view one hell of a risk which was totally dependent on the weather remaining much as it was. I reckoned then it was just reasonable to put the Scots Guards in in four LCUs in a rush. Anything moving forward after that I would not dare to send that close because we may have lost surprise and beyond Fitzroy you are getting into enemy gunfire range: the Welsh Guards had to go into Fitzroy. Brigadier Wilson gave me the impression that he was perfectly happy with that as his Bde HQ was to be at Fitzroy and we had discussed the likelihood of the LSLs being hidden by the high ground.

"It comes back to the lack of an agreed strategy. Julian's and my theory had been that in the absence of any directive we could only afford to open up a southern flank once the extra helicopters arrived. When Jeremy Moore arrived with his additional troops it was decided that they weren't to be left behind as a garrison for San Carlos and Darwin (we never thought they would be) but they were to be used in the front for political reasons as much as anything else. Poor old Hunt in 40 Commando was left behind, partly, I suspect, because I had said I wanted Royal Marines to remain as the garrison on the premise that they understood naval and amphibious operations best if they were to be needed in a rush. I was dead worried about Port Howard and Fox Bay. I worried that the latter in particular could be easily reinforced by a determined Argentinian air or sea attempt.

"Losing the *Atlantic Conveyor* forced us to change our plans about the move forward, not so much along the north where we always planned to use landing craft but particularly over the support of the southern flank where 5 Brigade had not helped the overall situation by becoming so vulnerable and wrong footed. They did not seem to understand amphibious problems or the problems of an open sea flank and the vulnerability of logistic support. Mind you, Divisional HQ could have advised them better, but that, again, is hindsight – or perhaps we should have attached a naval officer to 5 Brigade's staff."

Discussing the LSL losses the Commodore continued: "I felt dreadful as far as the LSLs were concerned as they were being asked to take the worst risks and had already had a decidedly unpleasant war with unexploded bombs. Both Captain Green and Captain Roberts asked to see me after they had been brought back to San Carlos. We sat in my cabin somewhat at a loss for words, staring at each other. There was very little any of us could say. They were both shaken up and Green said to me as they went out of the door: 'Thank you for seeing us. I don't envy you the decisions you have to make.' I was immensely relieved and took that to mean that 'OK, we're with you.' Both of them have certainly been extremely loyal ever since. I just said: 'I'm terribly sorry, it didn't go as well as I had hoped. I had hoped the weather would have been alright for you and you would have been OK. There is no way I could have protected you properly'."

For the moment the events at Fitzroy and Bluff Cove were behind me and I was able to concentrate on assault beaches for an attack on West Falklands. It was not, though, the end of my involvement with the 8th June.

XIX

Victory

I WOKE ON 14 JUNE to mixed feelings. On the wider scale of things the news was quite excellent: Julian Thompson had ordered his Brigade into 'hot pursuit'; we were drawing up outline plans for a Commando raid onto Port Howard and I had seen my first friendly aircraft when a Sea Harrier landed on *Fearless* the night before for emergency fuel. Closer to home I wasn't so sure. I was very worried about *Tango One* from whom I had not heard since she was despatched to make a lone journey to Fitzroy the night before. I had been asked to navigate her but had declined for the reason that the cox'n knew the way and my continual involvement would undermine my crews' confidence. It has sometimes been difficult persuading a few of the LPD captains that a landing craft Colour Sergeant is trained and capable of such journeys unsupervised. They certainly needed no wet-nursing from me on this occasion.

Other snippets of news filtered in. Some of it very bad indeed. Sue Whitley, Doreen Burns and Mary Goodwin had been killed by a naval shell, with Steve Whitley and Mrs Fowler badly wounded. For me, this was the worst news of the war. I had known Sue before she married the Falkland's vet Steve Whitley, and Mrs Goodwin was a much respected member of the Falkland Islands, and the eldest inhabitant of Stanley.

I needed some action to take my mind off this tragedy and it came soon enough from David Minords, COMAW's Royal Marines staff officer and lynchpin.

"The submarine *Onyx* is off on a patrol around the western islands to look for enemy observation posts – it will be useful if go with her."

However the *Onyx* plan was superseded almost immediately by a request from Jonathan Thompson to accompany him in the requisitioned trawler *Pict*. This was rather more to my liking, and more in line with the dwindling services I had left to offer as the land and coastal battles drew to a close...but even this was superceded by the superb news that broke into *Fearless's* Amphibious Operations Room:

"1555 – 'White flag reported over Stanley. Cease fire except in self-defence.' We must watch the AAF very carefully."

I poured a:

"Very Large Port to celebrate the beginning of the real end."

We had been in at the start and, unlike a number of campaigns in which some of us had taken part, we were about to be in at the end as well. Many had joined conflicts in the middle and left them in the middle — Cyprus, Borneo, Malaya, Aden, Dhofar, Northern Ireland — Suez was an exception, so was the Radfan but ...

...more work beckoned and whatever was happening in Stanley did not, yet, reflect what was happening elsewhere.

HMS *Pict* lay alongside *Fearless's* port quarter. Red and rusty, workmanlike and efficient; bustling with activity in a slightly incongruous manner with her large stern-trawling gear oddly out of place in a war zone.

On the double-ended bridge (an aft-facing control station commanded the trawl deck) I met David Garwood the captain, a young Lieutenant Commander with a fascinating, and dangerous, mission. His ship was employed as a makeshift, but most effective, minesweeper — one of five such ships which, apart from their minesweeping duties, were used as work horses from South Georgia to West Falklands. An amusing story is told of a sister ship in Grytviken. HMS *Cordella* had manoeuvred alongside the passenger liner *Queen Elizabeth 2* to transfer troops between her and *Canberra* as the Cunarder was not allowed further into the war zone. The great liner's Captain leant over his bridge wing to shout down at the salt-stained and rusty trawler: "Which one are you?" The Royal Naval officer, without hesitation, shouted back: *"Cordella.* Which one are you?"

Lieutenant Roger Armstrong of the SBS, and Jonathan Thompson, accompanied by some of his men also embarked in time for us to sail at 2000. We were to collect the team that had spent much of the war watching and reporting on Carcass Island and then drop off stores, covertly, for the Pebble Island section, allowing them to continue their surveillance in case of counter-attack or similar trouble from the garrison. Argentinians had never landed on Carcass and so the British team's presence there was no longer necessary.

Once we had sailed our briefing, and journey, were interrupted by a signal indicating that the SBS on Pebble Island were 'in trouble'. We knew no more but prudence dictated a stronger force; we returned to collect another section.

In the dark, at slow speed, without lights and little noise we approached the island beach from where the close observation team was due to be lifted. There was no sign of opposition, although we believed there to be thirty or so enemy garrisoning the whole island. The Gemini was lowered and, without hint of the difficulties we had been led to expect, the team was lifted back to the trawler incident-free. Not now having to support them in a fight and break out they were safe on board without the Argentinians knowing they had been ashore.

Another team on Saunders Island — the site of the original Royal Marines settlement — were lifted, but this time we did not leave behind an inscribed lead plaque. Despite the conflict drawing to a satisfactory close it remained vital that the SBS left their hides undetected so that in the event of any cease fire affecting only Stanley (or just East Falkland), or failing altogether, they could return, uncompromised, for further tasks.

The final undertaking of the night was to close with the southern coast of Carcass Island and lift its surveillance team. As we approached with great caution yet another garbled message was received, again indicating the possibility of trouble. David took his ship to the south of Sedge Island, the scene of two hilarious lunchtimes in more peaceful days, and towards the aptly named Needle Rocks before turning sharply north-westwards into Port Pattison.

At about 0515, in a rising southerly gale, and with ambient temperatures producing a wind-chill factor of -10°C *Pict* inched, as stealthily as a trawler can, towards the pre-arranged pick-up point off Ram Paddock (the bluff that forms the western entrance to the anchorage) until 0530, when, with a lurch and grinding familiar to a landing craft officer but not the *Pict's crew*, the ship hit something very solid.

I looked, white-faced (I assumed), at Jonathan Thompson but before he had time to comment the Captain's voice shouted down from the bridge:

"Where's that bloody Marine who thinks he knows all the rocks?"

Presuming that he meant me, although I had never made that claim, I rushed up the bridge ladder. The ship was lolling from side to side in that uncomfortable way ships do when they are perched, with only ninety-eight percent of their available buoyancy taking effect, on an underwater obstruction.

I made my way to the chart table. We appeared to have anchored to the west of the position agreed, certainly in an area I had not visited before. To confuse us further, the echo sounder was steadily recording 12 metres of water as David and I studied the Admiralty chart. Trawlers, for all their lack of creature comforts, are built to withstand great pummelling in heavy seas and *Pict* was no exception. We wriggled free, breathed again, and weighed the anchor. The Gemini was recovered with its relieved crew and passengers and we were able to make our way to the east for the run back, north of the outlying islands.

Apart from my own hand-drawn charts the area was covered by two Admiralty charts. Before the Argentinian invasion the only chart covering Carcass Island was number 1354A to a scale of 1:224,000; too small for accurate inshore navigation in any size of vessel. On 23 April the Hydrographic Department had issued a 1:50,000 chart (no: 2514) which covered the north-western islands from New Island to Pebble Island, but it, too, was a little small for the type of work in which we were engaged. Quite clearly, at the bottom of this latest and monochrome chart, was the instruction "Provisional Chart only. To be used with published charts."

Our alarms were not yet over:

"0605. Had just started a large whisky when: two very loud bangs. Thought it was a salvo of shells hitting the ship. The Captain thought watertight bulkheads were bursting as a result of us sitting on the rock. Emergency stations. Dressed quickly in appropriate clothing. Ship has list to port. Going flat out for San Carlos. Wind strong from the south which may explain the list. Bloody cold. Not a night for a swim. Even persuaded Jonathan to have a very large tot! — probably his first ever. Explanation is the anchor coming home or banging loose against the ship's side as it was not tight into the hawse pipe. However — this is the first time that I have ever put on a lifejacket for real. It was a civilian model (Board of Trade) and I couldn't work out how to use it!"

We arrived back in San Carlos Waters after dawn. Standing on the starboard bridge wing I stared south down a grey and overcast Sound. The strong south-westerly wind, enhanced by the occasional 'woollie' off the Coastal Ridge, scratched and tore the seas into white horses, short and viscous, the only splash of colour of the morning. We still had had no confirmation of the jumbled signals of the night with their hints that the enemy on the outer islands were still active, but we did know that fifty miles to the east talks were taking place that, with any luck, would end the battles around Stanley for good.

But what of the west? A second front? More special forces insertions? More landings? More land battles? More air battles? More ships sacrificing themselves to ensure a modicum of occasional air parity?

There would be no rest until the whole of the Falkland Islands were free, and seen to be free. Stanley had been the primary objective, but the perverse nature of the Argentinian military mentality might continue to make our life awkward until they were physically beaten in every corner of the archipelago. If that was their desire, so be it. We were tired but ready, and certainly willing.

"1130 — terrible weather — 40 knots — hail and snow from the south-west. Entered San Carlos Waters."

It was 15 June.

I climbed up the swaying rope ladder dangling from *Fearless's* port waist and shouted down a final farewell to David Garwood. It had been at times an amusing, frightening and heartstopping few hours which encapsulated in many ways what I enjoyed doing most. (David was to be 'mentioned in despatches' for particularly hazardous minesweeping duties in Berkeley Sound a few days later.)

Following my usual custom I called in at the Amphibious Operations Room for a short debrief on my way to my cabin. Someone handed me a signal. I sat and read:

"From CLFFI to COMAW. Copy of signal to CINC Fleet.

"In Port Stanley at 9 pm tonight 14th June 1982, Major General Menendez surrendered to me all Argentinian Forces in East and West Falkland together with their impedimenta.

"Arrangements are in hand to assemble the men for their return to Argentina; to gather their arms and equipment and to mark and make safe their munitions.

"The Falkland Islands are once more under the Government desired by their inhabitants.

"God save the Queen.

JJ Moore."

It was all over bar the shouting, and there was much of that to come.

The signal, a marvellous piece of 'victory' prose, was copied into my log. It had been written with an economy of words that perfectly suited the occasion; the penultimate sentence encapsulating, exactly, the reason why we had been fighting

War was one thing, peace was quite another matter. Safety and regulations would take an increasing share of our thoughts; that and fair play to a now-beaten foe who must be treated with magnanimity (which is less easy than with guile and cunning).

I returned to my bathroom to contemplate the port bottle and my mail. I achieved opening neither. David Minords, always the bearer of either excellent or frightful news, knocked and came in.

"Who do you think your boss is?"

I shrugged my shoulders.

"The General, the Commodore and the Brigadier all have different tasks for you. If I tell you what they are you can choose the one you want

316

to do and I'll then tell you under whose command you are!"

That seemed fair to me.

David outlined the three tasks. I do not remember what two of them were but the one that appealed most was the one required by the Commodore.

There was no time for mail or port; there was no time for sleep or washing; a helicopter waited on the flight deck. It was to be another five days before I saw my cabin again.

Waiting to load was Jonathan Thompson (who had asked the Commodore if I could accompany him), his Sergeant Major, and the SBS Operations Officer, Captain Colin Howard. My orders had been as straightforward as I could have wished and exceeded even my autonomous desires by leaving me unbridled scope for initiative. I was to accompany the OC of the SBS in the surrender of Pebble Island and after that to gather any *ad hoc* team I could and with the same Wessex helicopter go on to secure the surrender of Weddell Island, if necessary, before ending up at Fox Bay. There I was to meet HMS *Intrepid* and the CO of 40 Commando, who would have taken the surrender of the enemy at both Fox Bay settlements and that of Port Howard and wait for new orders.

Our first stop was the San Carlos settlement green to pick up Max Hastings of the *Evening Standard* and Michael Nicholson of *ITN*; new friends with whom I had spent many interesting hours listening to their intelligent and individual views on the conflict in particular, on personalities in detail and world events in general.

We took off at 1430 for the twenty-mile hop across to Port Howard where 40 Commando, under the ever-patient Malcolm Hunt, had been given the task of accepting the surrender of that Argentinian garrison.

Lines of dejected enemy turned their backs from the increased wind chill of the helicopter's down draft as the pilot flared out and landed on the grass. The CO SBS jumped out to collect the intelligence about Pebble Island from 40 Commando that they themselves had gleaned from a prisoner of war. Nobody was sure that, outside Port Howard, the enemy understood or even knew about the unconditional surrender terms signed by their general in Stanley.

Jonathan returned to the helicopter. We had to stop at Port Purvis house to collect a 'deserter' from Pebble Island known to be hiding there. He would brief us on the situation across the intervening twelve miles of water. It didn't ring true but I kept silent. The whys and wherefores were not my concern and I was anxious not to interfere unnecessarily.

The house was empty and rather eerie and we thought it all strangely suspicious, with the term 'a come-on' from Northern Ireland in our thoughts. We were, though, committed, and after a thorough check, carried out tactically in case of ambush or booby traps, we climbed back into our machine.

This time we streamed a white sheet from the door with the pilot turning the aircraft starboard-side-to as we approached the eastern end of the three-humped, long, thin island, so that it 'fully deployed' underneath the fuselage rather than flowed in a long, narrow streamer aft. It was slightly bizarre and could have meant that it was us that were surrendering to the garrison.

> *"Passed a land rover with four men taking cover in fire-positions..."*

The pilot saw the men before we did and landed quickly. We jumped out and surrounded them to find they were planting mines on the hill to the south of Ship Harbour which we believed was a clear indication that not only were they unaware that the 'war' was over but they were clearly expecting it to spread westwards now that Stanley had fallen. They spoke, or at least pretended to speak, no English, and were clearly surprised at this sudden encounter with their enemy. However, as they had not fired at us and had no radio that we could see, there was nothing to do but continue the five miles along the southern coast until the settlement opened up. It was difficult to know whether we were being foolish or bold, but we decided through intermediate shouting into cupped ears that we were being audacious and that we should 'get on with it'.

The helicopter swooped in at sea level, climbed the few feet to the level of the green behind the jetty and wool sheds and landed on the gently sloping grass. We leapt out, again not knowing whether to look sheepish or belligerent but, either way, anxious not to force a fight with those who might have thought that perhaps we had come prepared for one. They were not to know either that between us the only arms we could muster were my pistol, Colin's sub-machine gun and the Sergeant Major's rifle; the pilot may, too, have had a pistol.

There was no firing, so in a tight group we walked towards the only men we could see, off the port side of the aircraft and below the 'big house'. Quite suddenly, puzzled Argentinian faces appeared around the green. We were surrounded. Max Hastings and Jonathan Thompson strode towards the apparent leader.

The Lieutenant, who seemed to be the most senior officer present, was a dapper little man with black hair and a trimmed moustache. His appearance was greatly at odds with ours of tired, drawn, barely shaven faces, caked and streaked in old camouflage-cream. Our 'uniforms' were a mixture and far from clean. The Argentinian was even shorter than me: Max, Jonathan and Michael towered over him. I think it was Max who spoke the order:

"You have surrendered!"

There was a short pause while the enemy officer looked up into his enemy's face, unsmiling and unarmed. He looked past him to his many men surrounding the green and the now-silent helicopter. Slowly a smile spread across his neat features. He spoke in English.

"Oh good, the men will be pleased. I'll go and tell them."

We all smiled.

While this short exchange had been going on, and before we knew the result, it had become obvious that we were surrounded not by thirty-five men ready to be disarmed but a vastly larger number.

"How many men have you here?"

"Over one hundred!"

Their 'exercise' was over and they were going back to Buenos Aires. They would be home before us. I left the group, already discussing arrangements, and strode off to the 'big house'. The front door was opened timidly by an Argentinian soldier – an interpreter. Behind him was the worried face (he was never normally worried by anything) of Griff Evans, the settlement manager. He recognized me instantly and pushed past.

"It's all over Griff, Where's your Union Jack?"

Two minutes later, after Griff's indescribable smile had reappeared for a photograph, he staggered on to the green with a huge Union Flag. It was taken from him and nailed to the highest part of the roof by one of the more agile kelpers.

"Griff Evans gave us all a whisky and I read the General's signal to as many of the settlement that could fit into the Big House's sitting room. Many tears and hugs."

Before the evening got into full swing, though, I walked around the settlement with Griff. It was my first glimpse at what lay behind the rumours and stories surrounding the facts of occupation and it was clear that the rumours were correct: officers had lived very well indeed. One house, that had been used as their mess, was stocked to overflowing with cheese and luxury foods that would have graced any Fortnum's hamper.

In another of the commandeered houses, which no Islander had been allowed to enter since the invasion, Griff and I found a Racal radio, still switched on and tuned in. Before altering the set Argentinian frequency I gave a number of blind calls, in English, stating that the war was over. There were no replies so I re-tuned to the Falkland Islands' own frequency and within moments was talking to Goulding, Kepple and Carcass Islands. None of them knew that peace talks had taken place, indeed that the battles around Stanley had been successful in our favour. It was one of the more satisfying moments of the campaign and watching Griff speak to his friends for the first time since 2 April, and with such good news, was indeed a moving experience.

While the men were all herded into the wool shed for the night (the officers trying unsuccessfully to be segregated) the helicopter took off with some of our original party and a promise to return at dawn.

The following morning, Jeorge the interpreter had been allowed by his Commanding Officer to return from the sheep shed to say farewell. He made his way rather self-consciously up to the Big House and, amid very genuine tears on both sides, promised to return, but as a tourist when the peace had had time to be properly established, in contrast to a few of the others whose final words were as defiant as Galtieri's had been at the very beginning. This time (I had refused to do so the day before) I shook Jeorge's hand in genuine gratitude for his support to the Pebble Island people. He had apparently been one of the few 'good' men; an unwilling conscript who had used his privileged position living with the Evans' family to everyone's advantage.

JACKASS
PENGUIN

32. "We stopped, once, for me to take a photograph of an Exocet missile...lying in a ditch."

33. Peter Manley's Wessex with the author embarked "hit the ground very hard after one of the blades broke ten feet up...it then chopped off the tail behind where we were sitting."

34. The author and Patricia, Hamish and Hermione with the *Yachtsman of the Year* trophy awarded at the 1983 London Boat Show.

XX

When the Long Trick's Over

*"Listened to the 0000Z news which gave Michael Nicholson's account
of how Pebble Island had surrendered to the three of us. Made it sound
a little more dramatic than it was."*

But it was good to hear for all that and allowed us to drink a further
toast or two.

*"Eventually turned in on the floor of a bedroom. Very
comfortable."*

I woke at six o'clock (local time). There was no time for breakfast before
hauling the protesting Argentinian Lieutenant out of the wool shed; he
did not approve of sharing his 'accommodation' with his men: a complaint
that provoked me into reminding him that if he and his colleagues had
done so more often and shown even a modicum of understanding for those
under their command the outcome of the war might have been very
different. I'm not sure that he got the point.

We then took him, his engineer (and an interpreter to make quite sure
that there would be no misunderstanding about instructions and orders)
on a tour of the settlement and its immediate surroundings. We were
anxious to have any booby traps or mines pointed out to us and to get a
full understanding of the defences that had been prepared and which were
still in place.

Whilst 'they' were dealing with one such horror I found time to write
navigational notes for Elephant Bay, although the Argentinians were a
little puzzled by this diligent note-taking particularly as I faced away from
them and their work and stared out to sea taking bearings.

Carrying on with our circumnavigation of the settlement we ended at the
airstrip, scene of the dramatic, and classic, SAS operation and were the
first British to witness in daylight the havoc that had been wreaked by the
night attack on the parked Argentinian aircraft. It was quite a sight.

As we crested the slight bank at the back of Elephant Beach the skyline
was broken by ruined aircraft in a variety of positions. Some with their
noses in the peat, the distinctive Pucara tail cocked in the sky, others down

321

by one wing, some just burnt out with a few recognizable bits jutting from an otherwise amorphous jumble of blackened metal and pipes. Almost all, at least those that had not been burnt out completely, had been damaged in the same place to ensure there would be no cannibalization, making it possible to refit one or two damaged aircraft from the remains of the others.

Below us and half a mile or so away lay the settlement. It was a tranquil and idyllic scene and, if one put one's back, and mind, to the wrecked aircraft, un-altered in decades. Sweet peat smoke drifted over the hill on the early morning breeze to disappear across the wide expanse of Elephant Bay. There was the noise of a settlement coming to life, touching reminders to those who had not heard its familiar babble or smelt its familiar scent for over ten weeks. If there is a smell and sound of freedom then we were experiencing them.

On the way back to the big house and my meagre selection of kit I was able to 'liberate' a piece of equipment that I was lacking.

Binoculars; a small pile of them and other such 'attractive items' lay on the grass. It was obvious, even from a casual glance, that most had been smashed as they had been discarded, along with other pieces of military impedimenta. I rummaged. There was one pair of small field glasses, unbroken and with a thin leather strap smelling powerfully of cheap scent − a male officer's! Trying not to breathe I hung them round my neck and walked on hoping that no friend would come too close and suspect things!

"All POWs seem absolutely delighted to be going home and keep asking me when the aircraft or ship will arrive to take them away. It cannot happen soon enough for us either but at the moment I am unable to answer their questions, and merely echo their views that as soon as they are out of the place the more delighted I will also be."

Eventually our own faithful Wessex arrived, piloted by the calm and humorous Peter Manley, allowing Colin Howard and I to continue our peripatetic journey around the western islands and settlements. Although I sent a signal saying that Elephant Bay was suitable for a landing (I was taking a bit of a risk there) I never did discover how the Pebble Island Argentinians were repatriated.

We flew low over Goulding, to whom I had spoken the night before, and waved. We knew they were safe and so needed no immediate visit. As a tangible sign that we, the British, were back in business, I would have liked to have flown over the other two settlements I had contacted, but we needed fuel and Peter had fixed to land on HMS *Intrepid*, at that moment steaming slowly south down Falkland Sound.

We took off again for Weddell Island where, although not certain of any welcome we might receive from stray Argentinians, we were certain of a tremendous reception from Bob and Thelma. We flew in with all eyes straining at every window and door searching for signs of enemy hand-launched anti-aircraft missiles, but there were none and with some ill-disguised relief (at least on my part) we landed safely.

"Many hugs and tears from Bob and Thelma."

As soon as we landed, the SBS team came down the hill from where they had kept the settlement under surveillance since the very beginning, appearing much to Bob's astonishment, for he had no idea they had been there at all. By sheer chance, for she could not possibly have guessed there would be so many friends to lunch, Thelma, in her expansive style had roasted ribs of beef and baked a mammoth Tea Berry pie. Bob, in his equally distinctive style, produced the largest and strongest gins and tonics I had tasted since leaving England.

The SBS team, though, were not to accompany us back, being re-tasked to meet the submarine HMS *Onyx* for further duties.

We returned to *Intrepid* for orders where I reported to the Captain who had assumed command, on behalf of the Commodore, of all that was happening in the amphibious world outside Stanley.

I was now to advise on West Falklands and Lafonia with a view to searching those areas for any likely observation posts or places where crashed pilots might be hiding out and who may not have heard the news. After agreeing an overall scheme I was ordered back into the Wessex to fly to Fox Bay East. This was unexpected as I had no reason, other than social, to visit Richard and Grizelda Cockwell.

We landed, and I hurried to the big house. I remember the next few moments with immense pleasure and not a little retrospective sadness, if one can mix such emotions.

I had no time to bang on the door before it was opened. Even less time to say "Hello Grizelda" and she was crying on my shoulder, which was not difficult for she is taller than me. How nice to be welcomed in such a way; unwarranted, for I had done so little to help in their freedom compared with those further east, who were still suffering fearful privations and awful weather conditions. As on one or two occasions before, I supposed that I represented those that were taking a more active part in all that had occurred recently.

It was bliss to sit in comfort in the civilized surroundings of a house that would have been perfectly in place on the edge of Dartmoor. There were differences! I was shown a massive hole in the scullery roof through which the spent casing of a Royal Navy star shell had punched its way. I knew how they felt about this one and wrote:

> *"Their tales of the Harrier strikes and naval bombardments were quite horrific. They had 21 living in the house — including the 'strange' doctor from Stanley — and had built a superb cellar-style funk-hole beneath the drawing room floor which was only about three feet high. They all lived in it each night."*

We settled down to an evening *en famille* to have our celebrations rudely interrupted by the news that:

> *"Galtieri has admitted the fall of Stanley 'against superior odds and equipment with the help of other nations' but he does not agree that hostilities have ceased. We have 10,000 Argie prisoners with 600 of them between the two Fox Bays which we could keep as hostages. The plan is that HMS* Intrepid *will lift them out tomorrow."*

Richard, realizing that on the morrow I would have to continue my travels, asked if that evening I would walk with him around the settlement for the first time since the enemy had arrived. He was anxious to see for himself his men, their families and problems, material and emotional, without the duress of war. He was keen, too, to inspect the material damage suffered by his settlement as soon as he could. I had the impression that he needed an 'outside' friend to walk the route with him.

The sight was depressing and mirrored that which I had found elsewhere. The community hall was a shambles and vandalized in the most repulsive manner. Human excreta in piles against the walls, dried puddles of urine, lewd drawings, smashed and broken furniture and fittings. Richard was very visibly shaken. There was little structural damage, other than to plaster, windows and doors, but it was a disturbing sensation to witness such obscene abuse of a place in which a whole village lived, danced, drank and sang; in which couples married and children were christened; from where the elderly were buried; a place in which the Christian festivals were celebrated and which formed the focus for all that kept such tight communities together and vibrant.

I took notes for Richard as he tabulated the damage and initial assessment of the work that needed to be done to bring his much loved settlement back to its peacetime standards.

Although forewarned, mentally and physically, by seeing the effect that the Argentinian occupation had had on Pebble Island, it was no easier to accept at Fox Bay East. Hatred — an unpleasant and unnecessary emotion at the best or worst of times — had no place but pity, in huge measure, did.

Back in the Big House I listened intently as Richard and Grizelda, their hands spread across maps and charts, worked out a sensible itinerary fo patrolling and searching the western islands.

At 0400, happy that I could brief the Captain of *Intrepid* with a time-effective scheme, I turned in.

"17 June. Up before dawn. Formulating final plans for advising Intrepid. *Must check out Coastal Ridge. The enemy are reported to have laid 4,000 mines and although they say that they have lifted them all they only took a day to do so! I'm not sure that I can trust them to have lifted very many. Dunnose Head needs sorting out. Jasons. Speedwell Island. George Island. Lafonia. Lively Island and so on. A busy time ahead."*

HMS *Intrepid* was not off the settlement at dawn and so, with time to fill in, I wandered off, particularly fascinated by the black ship leaning inwards over the end of the settlement jetty. She was a familiar shape, but cold and silent, and I could not place when, or even why, I had seen her before. Listing about eight degrees to port she was clearly settled on the bottom, but, as the water was shallow, she had settled very close to her marks. She was a tempting sight, and one I didn't resist.

There was something uncannily familiar about the troop transport and as a rope hung tantalizingly over the end of the jetty, I climbed up. It was all too inviting. She was clearly built to civilian standards and I was familiar with her layout. The memories were happy but I couldn't place them at all which was most most puzzling, for there was something more positive than just *déjà vu* at work,

I stopped in the bar, which I found without losing my way! It was a shambles, although bottles still stood, just, in various racks. I was tired, it was peaceful, and for the first time since leaving England, and even some considerable time before that, I was alone. There was silence and it was eerie. The squeak of a rat broke the spell before I heard many more scuttling about unseen. I sat back in a chair that had slid against the inboard bulkhead. The silence and the *Mary Celeste* atmosphere slowly replaced the earlier complacency of happiness. There was something very odd and it wasn't quite right.

I walked forward into the officers' saloon and it was then that I realized; the curtains were still there, the furniture and layout, although disturbed by the list to port, were familiar, but what drove it home effectively was the pattern of polished tiles covering the deck. The last time I had stood in that position I had been dancing with Patricia at one of the more amusing and relaxed evenings of our Stanley sojourn in the late '70s. The ship, the *Bahia Buen Suceso*, had called to remove the remains of the old airstrip at Hookers Point after it had been blown upside down during a dramatic gale on the night of 1 November, 1978.

The Argentinian officers had held a 'black-tie' dance on board which had been notable for the sophistication of the ambiance and the courtesy of our hosts. It had been an evening memorable for conviviality and style, but now I was back as an enemy and trying hard not to savour the fate of such a friendly vessel.

I was not enjoying the experience now and made my way quickly to the bridge. Call it looting if you must but my father had given me a beautiful light alloy German sextant 'salvaged' in Wilhelmshaven when he had commanded the first Royal Marines battalion to enter the town to take the surrender of the German ships there. I thought I should continue this tradition and so made my way to the navigator's caboosh abaft the bridge where I found a number of battered wooden boxes of which three held sextants and one an anemometer. There were other instruments and navigator's impedimenta which I lined up on the deck and knelt among while choosing what I considered to be the best of a reasonable bunch.

Following a loud clattering of heavy naval boots on the steel ladder leading from the accommodation I looked up without a hint of embarrassment to see a great friend of mine whom I had not met for years. Nick Harry, a Lieutenant Commander and Engineer Officer of HMS *Avenger*, stood staring in disbelief.

"I might have guessed I would be beaten to it by a bloody Bootie!"

I stood and we shook hands, roaring with laughter. It was good to see Nick again, his arrival dispelling any earlier morbid feelings for the ship and her crew. They and their troubles were forgotten and I was back in the present and the reason why we had been fighting these particular people.

We bundled the boxes into a sack and prepared to leave. Nick had more military and official reasons to be on board and returned to continue his inspection of the state of the ship. I had one last port of call – the ship's safe. My 9mm pistol, not surprisingly, failed to reveal its contents which was a pity, for I was to discover later (when it was blown open by *Avenger's* clearance diving team) that it yielded thirty thousand used American dollars. I was told that they found their way into the Royal Navy's coffers via a legal route but I would have had other plans for them!

As a postscript, the *Bahia Buen Suceso* was eventually towed to Stanley, de-stored of her ammunition, taken to sea again, this time to a position south of Falkland Island Sound where she was sunk by every conceivable RN gun and a torpedo from the submarine *Onyx*. She was even depth-charged as she went down. It was Trafalgar Day 1982.

The thought that HMS *Avenger* was in the area gave me the germ of a plan so it was with great delight that I caught up with the familiar figure of Captain Hugo White striding across the green towards the Big House. Hugo had been my 'dormitory prefect' at the Nautical College, Pangbourne, in the late '50s, and, having heard of my presence and the reason for it, had also been hatching a plot.

"We have devised a scheme for clearing West Falklands using Avenger *and her helicopter, reckoning this to be far more cost-effective — and more fun — than with* Intrepid. *It will suit me better as I can get on with the job more efficiently and quickly and it certainly suits* Avenger. *Approved by* Intrepid *— for two days at least."*

Having received the permission from our '*in loco parentis*', Hugo invited me back on board, and so, when his Lynx helicopter landed later that afternoon, I was away on another fascinating task.

On board *Avenger* I sat down with the Captain to work out a progressive search of the western isles and mainland. It was a large task which would involve many helicopter hours, especially as *Avenger* herself was partially crippled due to a blade missing from her port propeller.

There were a few 'personal admin' jobs to be taken care of first as I possessed only what I stood up in, and I was not very proud of it. I needed a bath, but, of more importance, I needed some clean clothes and a pair of shoes suitable for the wardroom and the ship's immaculate decks. I also needed somewhere to lay my head.

"The ship's supply officer is another old friend. Martin Cooper is more than kind and has lent me all sorts of things I had long regarded as luxuries. Slippers! Clean handkerchiefs! Socks! Even a dressing gown, dry towel and a bunk in the sick bay."

We took off at 0915 (local) the next morning into low cloud with me sitting in the Lynx's port doorway studying the ground below. Although I knew where we should go and for what we should be looking, we were also required to keep a watch for crashed aircraft or downed pilots — alive or dead.

For long it had been expected that Port Edgar House might have been used as a base for special forces. Highly regarded down the centuries by the British Royal Navy, Port Edgar was once considered the finest anchorage for a Fleet in the southern hemisphere and, because of this, was chosen as the place where the Royal Family should spend the First World War, on board a capital ship. At least, that is the story the Islanders tell. It never happened for much the same reasons, I would have thought, that the Family refused to leave London during the Second World War blitz.

We shot in though the entrance, to give anyone watching no advance warning of our arrival, and flew at almost sea-level straight onto the small flat patch to the east of the tiny two-storeyed shanty. This was to become a well-practised routine over the next days, but at that stage we had no idea of how to operate. I had to assume each time that there might be someone holed-up in these isolated buildings, either surviving or observing − either way, prepared to defend himself.

I drew my pistol and ran into the house, stopped and listened. I felt rather foolish, but speed and surprise were the order of the day each time and I did not want to be caught through an over-casual approach.

There was another eerie silence, emphasized, strangely, by the wind through the eaves. It was damp and cool. Hitchcock could probably have made something rather sinister of the whole thing, but there was no sign of recent human occupation, at least not on the ground floor; nor should there have been if a professional had been in residence and determined to stay there.

I climbed the stairs. Nothing. I relaxed, replaced my pistol and took a moment or two to gaze out of the window up the length of that beautifully sheltered anchorage with its numerous inviting creeks and valleys. A couple could spend an idyllic honeymoon at such a spot: a dinghy with a simple sail or small outboard, food and wine, a wind-up gramophone, plenty of candles and a fresh stock of dried peat and one would never be bored.

"...tell the Beaver float-plane to come back in six weeks...!"

I returned to the present and made my way back to the aircraft. Total time − less than three minutes: away to the next on our list.

Black Shanty, six miles to the south-west and below the imposing Little Molyhawk Hill, was destroyed, but there was no sign who had done it. There were many other shanties but nowhere was there a sign of occupation and I began to feel rather absurd carrying out my one-man assaults with drawn pistol. However, neither I nor the helicopter pilot were prepared to take risks so close to going home.

The morning's aim was to end at the Robertson's settlement of Port Stephens to hear their news and see if they had any ideas or information on the possible whereabouts of hiding Argentinians.

"Rum and coffee with Peter and Anne Robertson — she is an Argentinian. They were delighted to see us. They had only seen Mirage and Skyhawks flying down the waters at 100' — in and out. The only thing they wanted to see now were Sea Harriers — which I shall fix on return to the ship — not quite the shopping list I was told to get from the settlements. Immediate needs that had been denied them during the war — like flour and sugar and butter for instance!"

The afternoon was very much the same as the morning although I was puzzled by the state of one house and the sudden announcement from *Intrepid* that we were not to touch Lafonia: an instruction that Hugo decided to ignore on the basis of his own greater intelligence (military, I assumed, rather than personal).

"Returned to the ship... then up the Coastal Ridge... Port Howard.... Swan Island....all the small tussac islands.... Port King...found two life boats but no sign of humans...Wreck Shanty. Also Mary Celeste like. Fire still in the grate. Bedrooms awful mess as though someone had left in too much of a hurry and unexpectedly — rather suspicious and almost sinister. Flew back to Avenger *at dusk."*

The next day we landed on the high bluff that forms the western entrance to Fox Bay allowing me to inspect the gun positions guarding the approaches. The pilot then flew off to a safe distance as I suspected there may have been booby traps; he was not keen to be damaged if I was to set one off! In the end I deduced that all was as it seemed, although not before carrying out a number of unusual methods for testing for ordnance. I managed to climb above the emplacements and with a one- or two-second dropping-time rolled boulders onto likely booby-traps while using those few seconds to duck behind the crest. Nothing was detonated and I felt safe enough to investigate closer. There were certainly masses of spent shell and small-arms cases indicating a busy time for the gun crews during the preceding weeks.

The Argentinians had definitely visited George Island and, judging by the mess, stayed for some time, but the circumstances were, again, a trifle odd. If 'they' had been 'observing' in an official capacity they should have been fed better, so I suspected the occupants had been surviving. The Upland Goose carcasses would not have been unusual, but the remains of a number of Turkey Buzzards meant that they must have been very hungry indeed and, possibly, in extremis. The Buzzard may well have been palatable but it had never featured in my essays on survival.

For as many years as I had been involved with the Falklands I had held a desire to visit the furthest island from the mainland – Jason West Cay. With Jack Sollis, and against various wishes, I had landed on Steeple Jason in 1979 but the weather had not then been kind and any thought of heading further west had been out of the question, even with such determined people as myself and Ian Strange wishing it otherwise. It was unlikely that on that particular islet there would be anyone unless he were a survivor for not even the most imaginative mind would have suggested it as an observation post, but it was just possible that a pilot could have struggled ashore there.

There were, too, other reasons for wanting to have a look at Jason West Cay – the 'Elizabethan' wreck and the possibility of finding traces of *En Avant* – both of which had occupied my mind in 1978. As Jason West Cay was on our route, if we took the longest and safest course, it was easy to persuade Hugo White that we should, at the very least, overfly it. Having established the outline plan I recounted my interest in wrecks and the Jason West Cay wreck in particular.

Hugo decided to come with us for the first aerial sortie of the day, but not before church at 0630:

> *"I always like the Royal Naval prayer and no more than now does it mean something. '...a security for such as pass on the seas upon their lawful occasions'."*

It was a cold, windy, overcast day. Thousands of birds, mostly wandering albatross, dazzled brilliantly white against a dark, blue-grey dawn. The decks streamed with tiny rivulets of blown spray and rain as we huddled in the lee of the hanger while the pilot went through his checks. When given the 'thumbs-up' we crouched forward against the wind and below the blades to embark. Notebooks, charts, camera and my gasmask bag full of the usual impedimenta in case we came down and had to survive, cluttered the seat between us in the back. A new film had been loaded into my 1934 Leica camera and the equally ancient light meter was firmly attached.

From somewhere west of New Island we left the ship steaming northwards at eight knots under the command of her First Lieutenant, Tony Bollingbroke. The next rendezvous would be north and east of the Jasons after we had inspected the two main Islands of Steeple and Grand.

On the 'land maps' Jason West Cay is marked as being just under two-thirds of a mile long and on the charts about six cables. In actual fact I believe the island to be considerably less but am not likely to argue. It rose above sea level, at that state of the tide, (and I made no record of what the state of the tide was) to only a few feet and looked tiny from the air with nothing to add perspective except a few very scrawny tussac plants. It seemed an unlikely place for a wreck to have survived longer than a tide or two. As our visit to this Cay was a sideshow we were not due to do anything other than make a close pass. At one hundred feet above sea level and from about a cable off it resembled hundreds of other tiny white-fringed islets, or even half-tide rocky outcrops, that would be swamped in a full gale at high water. Anything that might have been stranded would almost certainly have been washed over and off the leeward side. It was rather an anticlimax and through the headphones Hugo shouted that "yes, it was a lovely sight but we should get on to Steeple Jason." I agreed.

"But wait!" We shouted together. The briefest shaft of pale, filtered sunlight had caught a straight line against the ragged silhouette of low rocks and sea-torn tussac. "There's something down there." We banked back to port and came in low from the east, at an acute angle to the lie of the islet that runs north-west to south-east.

Unmistakable: the frame and timbers of a ship. No orders were given. The pilot, who had been briefed on the old story, swung the Lynx in over the coastline. The wind was from the south-west and accelerating slightly over the low and rough ground. Skilfully, and with the 'observer' leaning far out of his open door to look underneath, the pilot found four reasonably flat rocks that exactly fitted the 'footprints' of the helicopter's wheels. There was little doubt that we were the first men to land on the island and, although not by sea, (my preferred method, for romantic reasons), it was a supremely exciting moment.

Well weathered and torn apart, it seemed to me that the remains twenty-five or so feet above us, and about sixty feet long, were probably the middle third of a vessel. I doubted that she was old enough to be Elizabethan and there were certainly no skeletons, neither of which diminished my thrill at the discovery. No inspection of mine could determine the age or origin of the ship and so I removed a thin sliver of wood and a couple of fastenings for analysis by experts. Much later I sent these samples off to the National Maritime Museum at Greenwich and the South Street Seaport Museum at Mystic, Massachusetts, but even now I still await answers! There are only two ships 'known' to have been wrecked on this particular island. The *Alto*, a 200-ton American whaling barque under the command of Captain E.W. White (no known relation to Hugo), 37 months out of Bedford, New Jersey, with a crew of 26 was:

"...wrecked this day – 12th July 1870 – on Jason West Cay during terrific storm on the night of the eclipse of the moon...;"

The *Lady Dufferin*, a 1,300-ton British ship went ashore at three o'clock in the morning of 17 February, 1882, under the command of Captain J. Fea. Her crew rowed to Westpoint Island — itself quite a journey.

I am certain that the remains that now lie high and dry in the middle of Jason West Cay are not the *Lady Dufferin*, but, neither am I sure that they are the *Alto*. In the absence of any other clues I harbour a lingering hope that, if not Elizabethan, she is at least earlier than nineteenth century. Maybe one day we will know.

> *"A tremendously exciting find and the satisfaction of a long-standing ambition."*

Seven miles to the east lie the first of the main Jason Islands, if approaching from Argentina. It had long been suggested that at least one of them harboured an Argentinian observation post or radio beacon for guiding aircraft from the mainland towards targets among the islands. They were, too, likely places for a damaged aircraft to have made for before the pilot ejected on the way home.

We could not search the whole of the islands in great detail but we did cover the obvious places. There was no sign of any occupation, apart from the hut on Grand Jason which had been used by Cindy Buxton and Annie Price when making their film about Falkland Islands wildlife in 1979 and 1980.

Carcass was the next 'inhabited' port of call and we touched down to a fantastic welcome from Rob McGill. Lorraine was still in Stanley, which was sad for us, but to see Rob fit and well was good news, as it was also to hear that his beloved island had remained unmolested. I told him how close he had become to being the landlord of a forward air base with all the attendant horrors of noise and pollution and possible enemy air attack that it would have brought. He was as relieved as any of us that this decision had not been taken and I recounted to him how I had explained (unashamedly, subjectively) to the planners what a poor choice Carcass would have been for such an undertaking! He owes me a drink.

We had not planned to stop at Pebble Island settlement, but were due to search the northern coast from the air before heading back to the ship for fuel. During the air battles occasional reports filtered through suggesting that one or two pilots had baled out over that last piece of ground before heading north-westwards across three hundred or so miles of inhospitable water.

The first aircraft was unmistakable, the crumpled silver wings contrasting starkly with the surrounding blackness of disturbed peat on the flat plain between Pebble Island's North and Middle Peaks. We turned back and landed a few yards away. The aircraft, one of a pair of Lear jets flying unarmed, at about 39,000 feet, had been shot by HMS *Exeter* at the maximum range of her Sea Dart anti-aircraft missile. The second aircraft was allowed to return, which it did with alacrity, to tell others that San Carlos was not a wise place to be in unprotected civilian aircraft.

What we found was unpleasant. The main body of the aircraft and its engines had buried themselves deep into the peat with the wings folded over the top, like a bird settled awkwardly on the water, the whole wreckage covering a remarkably small area. We were anxious, in accordance with our instructions for such occasions, to see if we could identify at least one of the crew so that the Argentinians could be informed as soon as possible. Digging was out of the question and we were also not able to move too much structure as the shallow crater surrounding the surface remains was full of aviation fuel. Lifting up one piece of wing, as gingerly as we could, we saw the tops of three heads in the peat and wreckage: hands flopped from the wrists above the surface: a coat lay across the grass a few yards away which contained enough material to identify at least one crew member. We noted carefully the position and with a few backward glances at the impromptu burial of men and machine we took off, steeled for further such sights.

> *"Next aircraft was a Mirage (Dagger). Bits of the pilot scattered around — teeth — piece of skull — backbone — elbow. Underpants. All flesh has been eaten by birds.*
>
> *"Next aircraft — another Dagger. No sign of the pilot or his seat so let's hope he escaped safely. Both a/c behind Pebble hills on the northern slopes."*

All pilots and crew were later recovered and buried with military honours.

We needed to refuel from the ship which was then approaching the anchorage in Port Egmont opposite the original Royal Marines settlement. This allowed us to fly back via Hill Cove and the shores of Byron Sound. There were no further signs of aircraft.

Refuelling took a few minutes during which time I persuaded the Captain to accompany me in a further bout of nostalgia. Figures had been seen approaching Settlement Cove and I believed that, with the few minutes of daylight left, we should have a look at where it all started. I also believed that the men ashore would have come from the family at Saunders Settlement and it was right that we should 'make our number' as soon as possible for there would be no time the next day. We flew ashore and landed above the broken stone remains of the old accommodation huts. Tony and Bill Pole-Evans were there to greet us and grateful for our arrival. It was another lovely meeting.

It was the end of a long day of mixed fortunes and emotions and, officially, the end of my task, but by the end of the next day, through a little subterfuge, I had managed to re-join HMS *Fearless* and have a signal sent, as though from the Commodore, to HMS *Intrepid*, re-tasking *Avenger's* helicopter to search for signs of *Foxtrot Four*.

The night before I had stared long and hard at charts of the entrance to the Sound imagining the scene on the evening of 8 June, and deduced that the landing craft had probably been no less than one mile south of the Island when she was hit, or when she was finally abandoned by the remaining crewman and the passengers from 5 Army Brigade. Taking into account the weather and tidal conditions and the likely windage on a sinking and heavy hull, I was able to produce an area of greatest probability. There was much guesswork, but also some practical experience, in my calculations.

I wasn't sure what I wanted to find for *Foxtrot Four* had last been seen:

"...drifting 190 in a slowly sinking condition."

I was certain her crew were dead. Certainly no sign of those that were missing was found after she was hit, but I was anxious to see if by some extraordinary piece of good fortune at least someone had managed to scramble ashore. As survival is possible in the islands under the most remarkable conditions, it was just conceivable, but the most forlorn of expectations, that the craft herself had not sunk before beaching on the southern shore of Choiseul Sound. She had been carrying a full load of Land Rovers and communications trailers and so at the least we should find some sign or clue to her final resting place, if only a thin leak of oil rising slowly to the surface.

We searched for three hours, flying low and slow along every possible stretch of coastline. There was nothing, absolutely nothing. We followed a supposed route from the attack position looking for oil. Nothing. There was brief excitement when we spotted a bright flash of colour (there is little jetsam in Falkland Island waters and anything man-made stands out as being unnatural) to discover on landing that it was a lifebelt from *Sir Galahad*. I picked some tussac grass roots for 'elevenses' and climbed back in the helicopter, but the crew stuck to their bars of 'nutty'.

What we did find, though, were the remains of one Puma and one Skyhawk. Both were tabulated and reported to the Flagship. Thankfully there was no sign of the aircrew, and again we hoped that they were safe and sound elsewhere. There was enough fuel to allow us to take in a last sweep along the northern shores of the Sound. There was no sign of my landing craft but we did come across a damage-control team from HMS *Penelope* working on a beached Argentinian patrol boat, believed at the time to be the *Rio Iguazu*. She was half out of the water and listing to starboard — an eighty-ton lightly armed vessel and one of those I so feared earlier.

"Penelope's *engineers asked me to go into the flooded engine room aft to check if the mass of something nasty in the far corner was a dead body. I went below and reckoned it was but as it would have meant swimming round the engines in the dark to get to it I declined the offer to look closer! I thought it was their problem. Later heard that my diagnosis was correct and it was indeed a body.*"

We returned to HMS *Fearless*. There were no more tasks, and although satisfied that I had achieved all that was asked of me and *Avenger*, I was sad that I had not been able to establish the final fate of *Foxtrot Four*.

"*The Commodore has moved ashore. The Brigadier is taking his Brigade on board* Canberra *and I am on my own again. Militarily, for me, it is at last all over.*"

Wilson's
Petrel.

XXI

Ask Me One On Beaches

HAVING VISITED ALMOST EVERYONE I knew while 'on duty' around the western isles, it was time for celebrations in Stanley.

As HMS *Fearless* had been ordered to sail on the morrow (23 June) for England I had only a few hours in which to find my friends. It was necessary to act as quickly as the peacetime boat routine (how quickly we reverted to routines) would allow. A hasty shower, then down to the starboard waist and a cold, wet, two-mile bash to windward in a LCVP. I travelled with, amongst others, David Minords, for so long my link with the Commodore and the General and the orchestrator and organizer of much that I had been asked to do.

"Whose command are you under now?"

"Why? Does it matter?"

"Yes it does. You have to belong to someone so that you can find a bunk for the journey home. In the bugger's rush you will be forgotten. You are not officially on anyone's books — and who is going to write your confidential report?"

I had never considered any of that and as far as any report was concerned I really was not too worried whether I had one or not. Overall I had enjoyed myself (in the professional sense) and felt strongly that to be reported on for helping in what was for me an emotional experience would have cheapened my meagre contribution. I suppose, subconsciously, I felt I had done my bit to the best of my ability and that was good enough. I had known the country and had had a very personal reason for being physically involved in its rehabilitation.

On reaching the public jetty, and having put all thoughts of reports and bunks well behind me, I headed briskly along Ross Road towards an un-arranged programme of visits.

I had tried to prepare a list of those whom I wanted to see most but this had proved impossible as there were too many clamouring for a high priority; and so I let events take a natural course in the manner of some out-of-season first-footer who according to legend, should be tall, dark and handsome and bearing coal, bread and salt. I am short, ugly and white-haired and bore two bottles of whisky. At some stage throughout the night I met, by design or coincidence, over forty Islanders.

336

Monsignor Spraggon and his priest, Father Monaghan, were first, and I was greeted with the opening of a magnum of whisky and tales of bullets through their house and a bible. I would not see the Monsignor again for he was to die as the result of his gallant rescue attempts during the subsequent hospital fire: I should have stayed longer with that remarkable man. Nor would I have left Jack Sollis's house so soon after a delicious dinner if I had known that I would not see him again either. He died in England from an illness from which he suffered for so long without complaint. In both houses we talked and teased, laughed and mourned. Jack had always been a controversial figure, never frightened to air his views about 'The Company' for whom he had a certain disregard, or the Argentinians for whom he had an even greater distrust, or the FCO against whom, like so many, he felt an unhealthy but utterly understandable suspicion. For the present British Government and the Prime Minister he had nothing but praise.

I listened to the authentic voice of the islanders, sometimes equivocal, sometimes less so; always ready to argue with each other but always ranged together against outsiders who dared to impose their own self-appointed standards on a community which had long learned to live with its own apparent drawbacks and which, despite outward signs, had more to offer the outside world than it needed in return.

I was back among the community with whom I had spent such a fascinating year, although even with the passage of time it would be foolish to pretend that it had been a period of total tranquillity and happiness. I was, and will always remain, like every expatriate, or casual visitor, an outsider.

Officially out of bounds to troops (which I did not consider too much of an obstacle as it was a restriction placed by Des King, the owner, and not the military) I was keen to end my meanderings through Stanley at the Upland Goose Hotel. Understandably, although not appreciated by the military, Des did not want hundreds of men drinking his establishment dry. Although considered by some to have been hardly tactful under the circumstances, it is difficult to see what sensible alternative Des had to protect his hotel, but his decision helped to fuel a common feeling among some of the British troops that they were not always welcome.

Des King met me with subdued enthusiasm, which, considering that I was, as it were, a local and one who had helped in liberating him, was not frightfully boosting to the morale. It amused me, though, to delight just slightly in his embarrassment at feeling he ought to let me in, and in this he was not helped by a noisy crowd drinking at a table behind the door; Max Hastings, Robert Fox and others greeted my arrival with considerably more glee than the landlord: a drink was ordered and Des, seeing that he was beaten, even bought it and smiled!

There was much drinking, laughing and story-telling, during which the tale of the search for, and finding of, the wreck on Jason West Cay was recounted. No sooner had I finished the saga than Max disappeared to return after a very few minutes to announce that the story would appear in the next evening's London *Standard*!

All good parties run their course, eventually, and I realized very late indeed that I had to find a bed for the night. I asked Des King if he had a spare room. He did not.

But Des does have a silver lining; as I was leaving he stopped me and offered me the room Rob Pitaluga (from Gibraltar Station) had used during his internment by the Argentinians. The room had not been cleared since Rob's departure, but it was bliss, even though I was certain I would be charged the full amount. I slept the sleep of the less than righteous.

After an excellent sleep I used the remains of Rob's shaving gear and presented myself for breakfast for which I was more than prepared to pay. No such luck! Ning King (Rob's sister and Des's wife) was adamant that everything was on the house and I was to relax with bacon and eggs eaten without pressure of time or operations.

"Des King even refused to charge me which must be a record and/or a great honour."

Paul Howe, a young man working in the hotel, offered to give me a lift out to Moody Brook on his tiny moped (for which he was granted permission) and we spluttered off along Ross Road West; two rather large and cumbersome riders on a very small two-stroke. We 'tacked' in between the potholes and numerous groups of men, mostly Paras and Marines, chatting and laughing, many in various states of near nakedness as they washed and aired their clothing and bodies. The route, lined by Union and Regimental Flags, as far as the old sea-plane hangar, had the air of a country fête about it. It was overcast, but clear and dry, and the atmosphere was reminiscent of a crowd at a point-to-point or the party after a rugby match. (Probably the Army/Navy match at Twickenham.)

At one stage we were stopped while negotiating with circumspection a large group of red-bereted Parachute Regiment soldiers. They looked at my green beret.

"Aren't you the Marine Major who told us how to catch Upland Geese?"

Indeed I had, as part of the survival lectures. For the Paras benefit only, I had explained that the best way was to lie on their backs with legs and arms in the air until the goose, inquisitive to the last, came within striking distance. Then they had to roll over very quickly, catch the animal by its neck, take its clothes off and cook it. Simple.

Now my little tease was about to rebound. I tried to tell my driver to make off quickly. Too late. The Red Berets closed in.

"Well, sir," they shouted, "it works − it works!" I'm not sure who, in the end, was teasing whom!

We passed 26 Ross Road West with its own huge Union Flag and then out into more open country past the shattered hangar and the remains of at least one of the Beaver float-planes. It was a sad sight indeed; those marvellous little bright-red aircraft with the black stripe, that had served me so well (but in various livery and with differing landing gear − wheels or floats) from the Oman to the Falklands.

If I was sad at the sight of the sea-plane hangar and its battered and broken customers I was not prepared for Moody Brook. I knew it had been bombed and I knew, too, that I had long fought for its replacement, but in the end a strong paternal feeling towards that haphazard complex of old stone-built buildings and pre-fabricated single-storey huts and chacons swept over me as we rounded the slight bend past the western corner of the Belsen Block. Condemned in 1918 and again in 1945, it had finally paid the price without the PSA having to lift a finger.

The place was burnt-out beyond recognition to all but the most sentimental. Black smudges stained the once-white walls above each window. The green corrugated iron roof above the central block, the galley, was still intact, but above my old office, the officers' and SNCOs' mess, our cabins and operations room, just one pair of charred and pitted rafters angled skywards. The rest had fallen in. There was no point in seeing if my pictures or Patricia's curtains and cushions had survived. Of the men's accommodation nothing remained at all above a blackened jumble at ground level. Without any particular twinge of despair, but with a feeling of sadness I climbed off the pillion and tugged the Leica from inside my jacket front. Just two photographs were all I needed for the record since I certainly did not feel like prolonging or intensifying the agony by rummaging through the wreckage. I had seen enough and my emotions were already stirring for I had not thought that I could harbour such strong and protective thoughts for an unlovely structure I had tried so desperately to have pulled down. We turned and motored slowly down the Stanley road without a backward glance, except at the Belsen Block: I would have rejoiced willingly if it had been reduced to a similar state as the camp itself.

I called in briefly at Government House, but it was too reminiscent of military headquarters anywhere in the world for my liking, with worried staff rushing hither and anxious clerks running thither, all scurrying to and fro at beck and call. It was no place for an itinerant officer dressed for sea in a white submariners' jersey. 'My' flag flew defiantly from the flag pole − still with the mousehole in the upper section of the central crest − and after taking a photograph to show the children where it had ended up, where it really belonged, I left that beehive of military industry.

The back streets of Stanley held more tragic sights, the burnt-out shell of the once magnificent Globe Stores being the most striking. Magnificent? Yes, for it had been the only real old-fashioned emporium in Stanley, housing, before total destruction, an amazing collection of items in the manner of a Victorian ironmonger or village shop. Upstairs in the attic had been stored in haphazard profusion many of the salvaged remains from the cargo of the *John R. Kelly* now lying submerged and broken up in Pilot Bay after hitting the rock to which she gave her name in May, 1899. Before I left in 1979 I had been presented with three full bottles of ink from this cargo, en route for the west coast of America. The ink, made by the Hudson Writing Ink Manufacturing Company of New York in 1898, is still used sparingly with quill pens I keep on top of the word processor to remind me of a more reliable method of keeping records when falling trees cut the South Devon power lines.

The smell and squalor of the capital, although infinitely improved (so I had been told) since the day of surrender, was still noisome and depressing.

Strong black coffee and kisses greeted me at Ian's house (the kisses from Maria I hasten to add) preceding tales of life under the Argentinians from one of the more resourceful members of the community who had refused to move out − although Ian with his own Island out to the west could easily have done so. The Strange's house was closest to the Stanley Airport and from it he had watched the attacks by Harriers and Naval gunfire.

He was keen, as a simple matter of curiosity, to see the result of the bombing that he had witnessed for so long and so close at hand, and so was I. Promising him the authority I had no right to grant, we climbed into his now working Land Rover (he had rendered it unserviceable as far as the occupying forces had been concerned to prevent it being taken away and used) to drive along the airport road with his normal scant regard for speed limits or safety rules; we stopped, once, for me to take a photograph of an Exocet missile half out of its corrugated square box and lying in a ditch.

It had been a puzzle to many of us that despite the reported hole in the surface of the runway (which I had seen on the aerial photographs) the Hercules of the AAF had continued to use the airport with impunity up to the night before the surrender.

We found no sign of any crater on the runway which made me even more certain that the Argentinians had shown remarkable guile in camouflage and deception. It is possible that the concrete had been damaged by the Vulcan bombers and that the damage had been repaired after the end of the war and before our arrival, but, if so, the repairs had been remarkable.

Some thought they had wheeled a makeshift 'bomb crater' across on wheels to make it look as though it was unusable to our photo-recce a/c — which is what had been suggested at one stage.

"*I gather from Ian Strange that often the Hercules were on the ground for over an hour and yet we were unable to do anything about them. I am sure there must be a good reason and I hope when all this is over someone will explain how the AAF was able to operate with such disregard for us — including a reported fourteen flights the night before the surrender!! I'm sure the Fleet Air Arm are just as anxious to know the reason why.*

"*Everywhere piles of ammunition and kit. They were a remarkably badly led and dispirited army with tales of the dead being collected from the mountains and dropped out to sea from helicopters. Also tales of young men being told they were in Patagonia facing the Chileans and having their boot laces removed so that they could not run away from their positions — of how few officers were ever found and captured when defences were overrun by our own forces — and men being shot in the feet to prevent them leaving their positions. How, despite awful stories of begging soldiers knocking, nightly and covertly, on civilian doors in search of food, there were massive stocks of rations untouched, most of which had been available only to the officers. It is a disgusting and disturbing litany of appalling leadership and class distinction. What I found on the outer islands was not an isolated example.*"

I left the Stranges' house slowly and with much reflection. I had enjoyed the war professionally, which is not to deny that I had been frightened, cold and uncomfortable on many occasions, but it had been a most stimulating experience. I was not enjoying much of the 'peace' that I found during my brief wander through Stanley, for it only reminded me of the real tragedy behind this latest episode in Falklands history. I wanted to leave before my almost uncontainable emotions concerning the despicable but temporary regime that had wrought such human and political turmoil got the better of me. It was time to go — to return in more settled years.

A *Fearless* boat was, by chance, waiting at the public jetty. Unlike the previous occasion on the deck of *Endurance* I did not look back, preferring instead to remember the Islands as they had been while looking forward to my next visit — a visit that I hoped would be made once the memory of any military occupation (British or Argentinian) had long faded. A forlorn hope indeed! One factor did allow me the luxury of looking to that happy day: the Falklands were now in the forefront of Foreign Office minds back at home and that, if nothing else, should ensure that they would never be eased to the sidelines again by a British government. But was a huge British garrison, already being talked off, the method by which Utopia could be achieved? I wasn't sure.

As I stood waiting to embark in the LCVP a 'senior visiting officer' had come up to me.

"You the fellow that knows all about the Islands?" I had never made that claim and so nodded ambiguously.

"Then tell me," he said pointing to the western skyline, "which is Mount Longdon and which is Tumbledown?"

I couldn't answer his question. I didn't know. I suddenly realized that I could not distinguish the hills overlooking Stanley. All I could do was mutter something to the effect that if he was to ask me a question about the beaches there was a good chance that I might get them right — and I think we did.

It began to rain — fine, wind-blown mist from the west. I jumped down into the well-deck of the landing craft, just forward of the closed Arctic cover.

"Let go forward! Let go aft!" The cox'n manoeuvred his craft away from the Public Jetty. I pulled the hood of my jacket over my head and stared seawards.

Dolphin Gull

XXII

Wives and Sweethearts

"EXCUSE ME SIR, the Captain would like to see you in the Commodore's day cabin."

"The Brigadier has asked that you join his team, in *Canberra*. You are most welcome to come home with us — the choice is yours. We sail shortly and I believe *Canberra* leaves tomorrow but right now she is back in San Carlos." There was no choice: if I joined *Canberra* I would almost certainly make the deadline for the Two-Handed Round Britain and Ireland race without having to resort to 'crab air' for the last leg via Ascension Island and *Fearless*, but my loyalty to Jeremy Larken and his ship was an overriding factor:

"If I may, I would like to come home with you, sir."

Below, later, I dressed leisurely for dinner, for there was now no rush, I was not dashing off somewhere after a quick change of working clothes. In practice the ship was still at absolute readiness for action, but certain routines had been relaxed and the wardroom and main galleys were back into peacetime menus and timings. I had no duties to attend to, no men to worry about (my 'Squadron' had been dissolved as unceremoniously as it had been formed), no lingering doubts over the next set of orders for another dramatic dash along the coast.

"Good night onboard Fearless *as the captain has persuaded me to stay for the journey home. Celebrated with a port or two."*

I had turned-in expecting a full night's sleep, a 'first' since well before the landings but at some stage I became conscious that the ship had altered course significantly, the different motion and rate of pitch and yaw alerting me to some new plan. I thought little of it and rolled back to sleep, thinking, only lightly, that perhaps we had simply moved out of the lee of the northern coast. The morning brought a rude shock.

"24 June. Woke to find that we are back in Stanley so the port we drank last night in celebration was a little premature! Apparently Woodward has ordered Fearless *back with a Flash signal at 0300Z asking for 7 questions to be answered."*

At anchor again in Port William I sought out the long-suffering navigation officer, John Prime, tearing up his previous passage plan. He had no idea when he should start a new plan to 'weigh and proceed for England'. I sympathized with him, but also studied my own selfish position for it was now less than likely that I could even get to Ascension Island in time to make the start of the Round Britain Race by air. From the beginning it had been a forlorn hope.

Suddenly and unexpectedly the ship went to Flying Stations and a hunch took me up to 'Flyco'. A Wessex was due in five minutes for papers that had to be delivered direct to *Canberra*. "Was it full?" "No." "Could they take one more passenger?" The Aviation Officer called the aircraft. "Yes". There was no spare time: on deck for seconds only, they would not be shutting down their engines.

How I managed to pack I do not know, but on my dash back to my cabin I collected a number of paper sacks; everything I possessed was thrown in while other bags were stuffed with the necessities for travel home in a luxury liner. My precious charts and newly gained sextant were cast aside in the hope that we would eventually meet up somewhere, somehow, in England. I apologized to the Captain, who quite understood, and ran back to the flight deck.

If I had had a warning of the terror we were to be subjected to ten minutes later I might have found the need to catch the helicopter less compelling. Nor did I know that even *Canberra's* arrival in home waters would be delayed until after the race start date.

"Took off thinking this is my last helo flight of the war and I have got away with it so far. What ill-timed thoughts! We called in on another ship at anchor outside Stanley harbour and two minutes later whilst coming in to land at Stanley Race Course picked up a large reinforced-polythene sack in one of the blades. The helo was the one I had travelled round the west in and was still being piloted by Peter Manley. No seats. Not strapped in. Five of us, my large paper sacks and two brief cases.

"We hit the ground very hard after one of the blades broke when about ten feet above the ground. The blade, which had bent downwards, continued to cut a circle around the aircraft. It chopped off the tail just behind where we were squatting on the deck. Helo continued to leap around committing suicide. I thought of jumping out as I was thrown near the door but the crewman who saw what I was thinking stopped me which was just as well as the blade was cutting the turf for 360°. Exceptionally violent motion − like dice in a cup. Horrendous noise as the aircraft was cut in two and the out-of-focus

blur of the outside world, and safety, beyond the open door − but no way past the deadly revolving curtain. Forty-five seconds was an eternity before the thing stopped and the pilot (who had wrecked his shoulder) shouted down between his legs for us to get out before it caught fire. We needed no encouragement.

"We were being watched by Monsignor Spraggon about to embark in another helo for his very first trip in one. He looked a little ashen, so I rushed across to reassure him, although I felt in need of reassurance myself! He was off in a Chinook for a memorial service at Goose Green.

"Grabbed another Wessex and flew safely to Canberra *in San Carlos Waters. Had a certain amount of difficulty getting on board as 'The Beagle' [Captain Christopher Burne − the Senior Naval Officer] spotted me getting off the helo and wanted to know why I was there. I explained that the Brigadier has asked me to travel back with his Brigade and that was as good an excuse as I could think of. Nick Vaux told him I needed a sporting chance to get back for the race. He relented and I was, grudgingly I thought but remembering earlier parties, with good reason probably, given a cabin to myself. I suspect that Julian Thompson and Nick Vaux had some hand in the final decision which, I gather, was touch and go.*

"My cabin is A75. Inside, so I can't see the sea, which is a pity, but at least I am on board and very grateful − although I shall miss Jeremy Larken's superb company and my many friends in Fearless.*"*

The ship slipped quietly out past Fannings Head: in the Crow's Nest Bar we felt the gentle heave and roll but took no notice. We called at Port William to collect the remnants of Brigade Headquarters and then, at 1722 on 25 June, weighed anchor for the last time in Falklands waters and headed north.

During the next days I prepared a report for John Chester, the Brigade Major, on the use of Landing Craft in support of two Brigades. The report was also the ideal vehicle by which I could expound my theory on the formation of an independent landing craft squadron as a separate unit within the 3rd Commando Brigade.

The Commando Brigade, an amphibious organization, was lacking a vital degree of flexibility by not possessing its own 'navy'. It retained its own 'air force' (the Brigade Air Squadron and attached Naval Squadrons); its own Gunners (29 Commando Regiment Royal Artillery); its own Sappers, special forces, Mountain and Arctic Warfare Cadre and so on, but nothing afloat which it could call its own. It was true that the 3rd Raiding Squadron was part of HQ and Signals Squadron, but they were very light indeed and really only of value to the SBS and very small groups of marines from the Commandos working with submarines or helicopters.

If landing craft support was needed, and the fiords of north Norway and the lochs of the Falkland Islands had proved this to be a vital requirement, the Brigade had to rely on the LCUs and LCVPs of the amphibious ships. Whilst the Commodore and the Brigadier were complementary to each other, there were numerous occasions when the 'mother' ships simply were not available or had left the AOA for some other task. It was a rare occasion indeed that they sailed without their own dedicated landing craft; thereby leaving the Brigade 'boatless'.

My actual report on operations was short and to the point. We had not learnt any new lessons except, perhaps, the importance of 'de-confliction' to prevent the 'blue on blue' contacts from which I and a number of my crews had suffered. What we had done, though, was to prove that all our years in the Norwegian Arctic in winter had been worthwhile. The deeply indented coastline of the Falklands archipelago had produced very similar operating conditions to those in the north. Loads carried had been similar, operating conditions on muddy and shingly beaches mirrored the earlier problems for which we had long since adapted our operating procedures. Sea conditions, temperatures and wind strengths had also been similar, for which, although unpleasant, we had been thankful. In simple terms, therefore, we had operated within well practised and familiar limits. In the north we never expected to have full air superiority, but, at the best, air parity in the fiord bottoms. In the Falklands, as far as the landing craft were concerned, we never even achieved air parity, for not once did we see a friendly aircraft on the wing. We saw, at close quarters, too many of 'theirs'.

Preparing the report took a couple of days, at the end of which I really could concentrate on preparing myself mentally for the homecoming. On the face of it the ship and its 'embarked force' had two differing requirements. The Brigade's 'home port' was Plymouth, the ship's was Southampton. We would pass Plymouth on our way up channel, so what could be easier and less trouble for the men and their families than to be offloaded straight into Stonehouse Barracks?

But feelings were divided. Back at home 'they' wanted us to offload in the West Country but took little notice of the relationship between ship and Brigade — nor the practicalities. Those of us embarked were keen to return home as one company for we owed at least that much to the Great White Whale. It was settled by three factors in our favour. The embarked force were happy to accept the problem of travel by road back along the south coast and to east Scotland; the ship could not enter Plymouth Sound as it was too shallow, which would make the offload a convoluted and lengthy affair and, finally, the Brigadier sent a signal explaining that, despite any other argument, we all wanted to arrive home together. That settled it. London capitulated, setting in motion one of the greatest 'welcome-homes' in recent British military history. Not one of us would have missed it and, for my part, I willingly gave up any chance to make the Round Britain Race to be part of it.

There were also the men of 'my' NP 8901 who were travelling back with the Brigade. On the way down I had enjoyed the company of nearly three-quarters of my detachment but on this return journey we were short of one or two − most notably Corporal Steve Newland who had been wounded in both legs as he led his section up and through the crags of Mount Harriet in a selfless action that most believed deserved the highest award for gallantry that can be bestowed. It certainly matched, and probably outshone, any others of the time. Even after being hit at very close range this most gallant Corporal continued to encourage his men and to direct fire on to the enemy positions right alongside his own. By coincidence his place had been taken amongst those heavily defended enemy positions by the equally remarkable Lance-Corporal Sheppard (also ex-NP 8901 of our year) who had then been the Company Clerk. It was immensely humbling to hear their tales and to know that for some brief period in their various careers I had been their 'boss'. It had been entirely my privilege.

A moving Thanksgiving Service was held in the ship's cinema on 27 June, led by Captain Dennis Scott-Masson, followed by a 'splicing of the main brace' by the officers and men of the Brigade Headquarters in the Alice Springs Bar. Splicing the Mainbrace with 'under-proof' bottled rum out of cardboard cups may not meet with the approval of the souls of departed chief stokers (who, rumour has it, reincarnate into seagulls) but it certainly met with the approval of the 3rd Commando Brigade and was the start to a lengthy lunch which for the officers continued in the Crow's Nest and, I've no doubt, continued in the Alice Springs Bar...and why not, for few Splicings had been more justly earned. That evening my presence on board was finally endorsed by being invited to drinks in the Captain's cabin followed by dinner at his table in the main dining saloon. In preparation for the morrow when the end of hostilities, as far as the ship was concerned, would be announced, Peter Cameron and I changed into Red Sea rig − the only proper rig to be worn in the evenings at sea, war or not − and which was, for us, the final metamorphosis back to peacetime.

John Ware (Commando Forces Director of Music) and his musicians organized what could only be described as a 'mini prom' in the ship's concert hall. It was magnificent and as many of the embarked passengers as possible crowded into the theatre where the band beat retreat, the corps of drums counter-marched and the audience took part. There were the usual songs straight from the Royal Albert Hall and the evening ended with the traditional naval 'Sunset' and evening hymn. This was only a tiny part of the band's routines; for they were in demand non-stop with discos, pop groups, jazz groups, classical ensembles and even impromptu operatic arias. Let no one take them away from us for their presence in action is an integral part of the morale (including their medical support duties) of the Royal Marines, and morale has an irreplaceable role in achieving, and celebrating, victory.

During these days there was much informed and some less intelligent talk on the wireless about the conduct of the war and the immediate aftermath. Among the suggestions was one that the Islands should increase their population by two to three thousand people, a view that introduced me to the the phenomena I was eventually to call 'second-hand hindsight' by those who only knew the islands from 2 April, 1982, onwards.

Capital investment – yes. But not, surely, a doubling of the population by outsiders. For a start the Islanders fiercely and rightly guard their own heritage. The kelpers have maintained this staunchly British outpost as British and on behalf of Britain, and they would not be likely to take too kindly to such a large injection of outsiders. All they wanted was a guarantee of their security plus financial support in return for those benefits so readily taken up by absentee landlords and the British Government. Capital investment was certainly needed for such as the new 'land' aircraft, the Darwin Road, the senior school and so on. It was hoped that even the swimming pool fund (open since the 1930s) might bear fruit at last.

At that particular moment, though, I wrote, once again, that all the financial help they really wanted could be obtained through proper control of their own gross national product, without it being controlled, as seemed to be the case, by the shareholders of the Falkland Islands Company. I was moved to write at the time:

"...ie nationalization of the FIC, a sensible control of the farms with perhaps diversification amongst landowners to allow more kelpers to take a personal interest in landownership and therefore a more direct say in the GNP; a realistic tariff for the shipping and fishing rights.

"The defence of the colony, naturally, comes in for some pretty hefty discussion during the late night sessions held over the bar in the Crow's Nest.

"Of course the defence problems are great and will now be greater. Whatever happens, it is bound to include a longer airfield and probably a military port and base for ground troops. This could make the Islands an even more attractive target — to a wider sphere of interested parties — than they were before. It could be that although the sword they worried about has indeed broken it may be replaced by a heavier one. One thing is certain. Although the way of life in Camp and in Stanley may not in the end change very much, the Falklands will never again be the out-of-the-way backwater that made them so attractive — the raison d'être *for the inhabitants' acceptance of such formidable hardships.*

"I hear that there will be 1,500 RAF people stationed there. They have already called the airport 'RAF Stanley' which has upset the locals as it is still their airport, with the RAF as squatters. A small point but one which highlights the need for a greater sensitivity from the services. I am sure that life in the settlements will return to normality once the mess has been cleared up. Indeed some settlements were never physically touched by the war at all.

"Personally, I think the best possible thing to happen would be to send back the original-sized NP 8901 with the threat of a nuclear submarine and, perhaps, a half-squadron of Fleet Air Arm Harriers. We could then raise two fingers to the Argentinians and dare them to do it again!"

I still hold to that opinion and regard with horror the vast military base now in existence.

At some stage we passed MV *Elk* who fired a salute from her forward 40/60s Bofors Guns bolted on for the journey south. Her delightfully eccentric Captain, John Morton, and Senior Naval Officer, Andrew Ritchie, (plus a very-much-alive parrot, contrary to press speculation) were great favourites in the Task Force for a remarkable acceptance of their peculiar dangers and the many methods they employed to overcome them. At one stage we had feared for the whole of the San Carlos anchorage if she was to be hit by a properly fused bomb, for she carried the largest proportion of the Task Forces' ammunition. It was for this and many associated reasons that she was knighted in acknowledgement of the part she played alongside those other knights of the round table — the LSLs. "Arise *Sir Elk*" was the final accolade in a signal wishing her *bon voyage* for the remainder of the passage home. It was a fitting gesture to a most brave ship.

We closed Ascension Island and were warned that we would be embarking many extra people. We had also put in a stores demand for

2,000 cases of beer, and some salad. The beer arrived, the salad did not. The newcomers were met with mixed feelings, for by then we were a well-established community and looked with concern upon the decision to be joined by, amongst others, service psychiatrists.

The psychiatrists might have found something to make of the differences in behaviour from the wildly jingoistic journey south to the reflective return, but we put that down to a perfectly understandable reaction amongst fighting men and was nothing untoward or unusual in people who have experienced, for the first time in action, the ultimate in the responsibility of leadership. Of course everyone is in a position of responsibility if only to his fellow and equally ranked friends within the confines of each small organization or team.

Before Ascension I had realized that to make the Round Britain Race would be touch and go, and, perhaps, irresponsible of me under the circumstances, and so, reluctantly, I sent a telegram to Mike Cobbold, the yacht's long-suffering, patient and generous owner, explaining my position. Naturally it came as no surprise to him, and probably as a great relief. I immediately began drawing up plans for the next in 1986. These fascinating and navigationally demanding races are held every four years and alternate with the Single-Handed Trans-Atlantic Race.

Once we were well out of the war zone, telephone links with the United Kingdom were opened, allowing me to make a signal to Patricia saying simply that I was well and looking forward to getting home. Just to establish communications was enough.

I received a reply that read: "We will be there with flags and tomahawks." This surprised me a touch for I could think of no particular reason why I should be scalped on return from a voyage that had not included runs ashore in the West Indies or the Far East. I sent back: "Query Tomahawks." The message, by return, was more comforting: "Yacht Squadron Signal book. For tomahawks read champagne." I needn't have worried.

In the old signals book of the Royal Yacht Squadron one of those messages sent in a four-figure code was "Send more Tomahawks" (Others were such as "May I borrow your washerwoman"). For years my father had sent simply the signal letters for a resupply of tomahawks whenever he wished to celebrate or congratulate. I didn't know that Patricia had remembered this delightful idiosyncrasy. It was a nice touch, for it is exactly what father would have said, my only regret being that neither he nor my mother would be there at our arrival. My parents had long regarded me as (in the words of a report from my prep school — Stubbington House, which Admiral Woodward had also attended): "Something of a dilettante and a rather lazy one at that" but even father might have finally acknowledged that there was some good in the boy at last.

Other links were established when I was called to the bridge during the penultimate day as we sailed along the south coast of England and crossed tacks with the yachts in the Round Britain Race. Once one yacht had called on the maritime VHF frequency to welcome me back others took up the cue and some hilarious exchanges and moving tributes to the Task Force were relayed from that fleet of two-handed sailing eccentrics. It was a very nice gesture indeed and will always be appreciated, for these were my friends from another, altogether more carefree 'nautical' world to which I hoped to return in due course.

It became clearer as we headed east (and there had been more than a hint during the radio conversations) that the greeting in Southampton was to be something special, although quite how special was a surprise right up until the event itself. Captain Dennis Scott-Masson took his 'Great White Whale' slowly along the south coast of England, curving in and out of the familiar bays during that last afternoon and evening at sea. The weather was perfect with, eventually, a hazy pink sunset sending the last of the small flotillas back to their home port.

During the last night at sea champagne was laid aside for the morrow's breakfast and at dinner the toast was, as always on Saturday nights at sea in HM Ships (and no more appropriate night than this): "Wives and Sweethearts" – to which the youngest member of the wardroom is required to rejoin in a quiet voice: "May they never meet" – but which my Squadron officers were later to bastardize further by adding "May they never know they've met!"

XXIII

Sir, I Have The Honour

THE WEATHER, THE DAY OF THE WEEK, the time of day and of course the reason, formed an unbeatable combination for such a homecoming. A stately, but slightly battered liner home from war, laden with success − a scene as old as the British Empire and still as evocative to the patriotic.

Prince Charles, accompanied by the Commandant General, Royal Marines, and the Commander-in-Chief, Fleet, landed on by Wessex. The officers and SNCOs gathered in the Sergeants' Mess as a brief part of the reception. I stood with others as the Royal Party made its way round the packed room through much laughter and happiness.

As warned (and Prince Charles himself had hinted at it), there was quite a reception waiting in the Solent, although all along the south coast since the Lizard small vessels and light aircraft had flitted about us offering a taste of what was to come.

The excitement of the day was highlighted rather than dampened by the early morning mist. *Canberra's* huge, white and rusty hull appearing slowly, almost wraithlike, out of the heat haze, will remain one of the most arousing sights of the whole campaign for those watching on television as much as for those actually there. I stood on the monkey island well away from the press interviews with senior officers taking place on the starboard bridge wing. As we approached 105/106 berth, Southampton Docks, I tried to make out Patricia, Hamish and Hermione, but with over 35,000 people (the police lost count at that figure) filling the docks alone it was not going to be easy, and I still was not quite sure if they would be there. Then, amid the mass of flags and messages painted on sheets, a lone Royal Cruising Club burgee on a very long stick: unmistakably the Tailyour family!

There was no point in prolonging the 'get away' to a quiet picnic in the New Forest with the dogs and children, after which Patricia drove us to the Officers' Mess at Poole, where she had stayed the previous night. Lunch was in full swing and we joined in before heading west. At every cross roads, every bridge, every lay-by, every building there was a reception party. The eccentric joined with the more conventional, the very young with the pensioner, the old soldier with the hippy. Landlords gave

352

free beer and it took an hour to pass through Dorchester alone as pints were passed out to the men.

We arrived, elated and exhausted, at the cottage with me expressing mock surprise that Cornwood was not 'en fête' although I would have been acutely embarrassed if it had been. It was also just as well for at crack of dawn the next morning I received two messages. Firstly, I was required back at Poole that day to call on my CO and, secondly, I was required in Stonehouse on the morrow to take part in the Commando Forces/3rd Commando Brigade debrief of the Captain General of the Royal Marines – HRH the Duke of Edinburgh. It was unexpectedly reminiscent of the hectic days before leaving. The special leave (and Easter leave) which we had been granted would have to wait. It waited for a very long time!

HRH's lunch and visit was a success, although I think we would have had to work hard to have prevented it being so. The Duke was, as it were, in his element. We had a story to tell, he had family involvement, and as our Captain General he was in the company of a familiar organization without press or people likely to quote or draw mischievous conclusions.

It was a perfect seal to the campaign, and as he left the barracks we felt that now that we had 'reported back to our leader' we were free to go our own ways.

For my part I had work to do at Poole. There was an outstanding report waiting to be completed on the winter's Arctic deployment which, for some reason, the CO had assumed I would have completed during our sojourn in the south. He was already a touch irascible about its half-finished state. I also had to prepare the handover of the Landing Craft company to Roger Dillon. Moreover HRH was due to pay Royal Marines Poole a visit for which OC SBS (accompanied by a senior LCU cox'n and an SBS patrol leader) and I were invited to give a private two-hour presentation on our respective organizations' role in the war. The Illustrator's Branch built a huge relief model of the Falklands and erected this impressive structure in one of the anterooms. This working visit was the most fascinating brief/debrief with which I have ever been involved. Animated, relaxed, informative, with hard questions and much laughter, particularly when my cox'n (Colour Sergeant Barry Davies) described being strafed by an aircraft so low and close that both machine guns' beaten zone passed down each side of his LCU without a hit being registered. Later we repeated the performance for HRH Prince Harald of Norway (later, the King), the Royal Marines' Honorary Colonel.

After all that it really was the end as far as I was concerned. On 29 July I brought *Black Velvet* alongside the seaward pontoon at the LC base, laden with the appropriate ingredients and entertained every marine and sailor under my command to considerable quantities of Guinness and champagne.

The Sergeant Major presented me with a magnificent brass engraving of an LCU in its Arctic guise mounted on a highly polished piece of mahogany as a reminder of all we had tried to achieve during the previous eleven years, and with much embarrassment from the cheering, we (Roger had joined me as crew) sailed away from the Branch I had joined in 1963 – at least that is what I thought at the time. A section of Rigid Raiding Craft shot out from behind the pontoon and proceeded to 'white-wall' us as we made our otherwise stately way down Poole harbour.

About this time Sir Peter Johnson of 'Nautical Books' (which were then an imprint of Macmillans) had been badgering me fairly consistently with offers for the original pilotage notes I was determined to call *Falkland Islands Passages*. We quickly reached an agreement although I had to give in over the title and call the work *Falkland Islands Shores*.

Granada Television were anxious to make a documentary of the war and, despite my misgivings about taking part, the Corps insisted that I and a number of others did so. This was a role which, despite outward appearances, I was loath to undertake.

I was even more loath to take part in an appalling TV panel game called *Tell the Truth*. The Corps insisted. I found the whole episode acutely embarrassing and decided that I would never do that sort of thing again, no matter who ordered me.

Probably to prevent any internecine arguing between the Commandos I was asked to lead the Commando Forces contingent through London, a march-past which the City had offered the Services. It was a most generous gesture in thanks for a job well done, and why on earth not? Military celebrations are a proper part of military events, and with as much panache as possible in my view. I was told that, as I had led the Commandos and Paras, into San Carlos I had better not get them lost meandering through the streets of London.

As the Officer Commanding Plymouth Garrison, it was my duty to receive the envelopes containing a letter from the CGRM for distribution to those members of the smaller units of the Commando Brigade about to receive honours and awards. It was not a day to which I had been particularly looking forward, and when it did come I was more saddened by the omissions than I was elated by the inclusions. Decorations are a very personal and sensitive subject, but when I and others saw the full list we were astounded by several whose participation had certainly been less worthy than others who received no mention at all. Where, for instance, was Captain Rod Bell, the quite remarkable Spanish interpreter and interrogator who had accompanied the SBS on Fannings Head, 2 Para at Goose Green, who was the first to contact General Menendez and who was largely responsible for negotiating the final surrender? Throughout the campaign he had been not only where the action was but sometimes even in front of it to secure success. The Task Force and the country still owe him an immense gratitude. There were many others.

What saddened a large number of the 'naval service' was certainly not the award of Victoria Crosses to the Parachute Regiment alone, rather that, back in London, the MOD (Army) submitted two names for this honour without the Royal Navy being aware of this decision. 'Down south' it had been decided that there were no Victoria Crosses to be awarded and none were forwarded, initially, to the United Kingdom by the senior commanders on the spot responsible for such matters. The unilateral decision in London was an unthinking gesture that failed to appreciate the superbly calm valour of the Royal Navy's ships' companies supporting the Royal Marines, themselves fighting some of the hardest and most successful battles of the campaign.

On the morning of the march the press were allowed in to the Honourable Artillery Company's field where the parade was forming up. An abiding memory for me is of Corporal Steve Newland, with his brand-new MM ribbon on his chest, dropping his trousers to reveal for the TV cameras the leg wounds sustained under quite unbeatable circumstances among the crags of Mount Harriet. He was still in considerable pain but insisted on taking part.

The march ended at the Guildhall and a magnificent banquet, the largest ever given at one sitting by the City. Quite how the caterers provided hot plates, hot food and perfect service through the many rooms remains a source of admiration. Towards the end a shy sailor (is there one?) rose from his table and amid inevitable thoughts of over-indulgence from the more stuffy (for the wine was flowing abundantly) approached the top table. From behind his back and much to the immediate concern of the surreptitious 'minders' he asked, very quietly and politely if the Prime Minister would sign his copy of the menu. There was no hesitation and Mrs Thatcher did so with a flourish and to great cheers. It was a clear signal for everyone else to do the same and so to a continuous roar of approval a long line of servicemen queued with their menus. It was a lovely sight and quite in keeping with the day.

Towards the end of the year I received a most unexpected surprise in a letter from the Chairman of the Association of Yachting Journalists. My name was on the short list to be elected *Yachtsman of the Year* for 1982 and while the opposition was strong (Naomi and Rob James for their Round Britain success and David Cowper for his Round the World single-handed achievements) it was likely, I was told, that in the final ballot I would emerge as the winner. "Could I be at the January 1993 Boat Show on the first Thursday?" Genuine modesty made me decline the award for I had ploughed back my amateur 'chart-work' for the benefit of the amphibious forces and through them for the Islanders and that was satisfying enough. It was better, I argued, that it went to someone more deserving, but the AYJ were adamant.

The Boat Show means only one thing to me since the introduction of glass fibre into the industry and that is the Guinness Stand and friends. This day was different of course and I was required to spend much time away from my usual haunt being interviewed in front of various craft and mounds of equipment. It was all rather fun and included a reception after the presentation and much celebrating. The only event to mar the occasion was the association of my award with the obscene spectacle of a Sea Harrier suspended above the Earls Court pool chasing a Pucara which, in real life, had been shot up while on the ground. I thought this crowing over an enemy distasteful in the extreme and particularly as it had been the AAF that had performed with such admired distinction in battle.

Very early that morning I had been interviewed on the BBC Radio Four programme 'Today' by Brian Redhead which was another amusing, stimulating and enlightening experience and just before leaving Earls Court in the evening I received a telephone call from John Dunn, the BBC2 interviewer. 'Would I care to be a guest on his show that evening?' These were two of only three interviews that I willingly underwent.

Unfortunately the John Dunn show, at least my part in it, was not enjoyed by the Chief Hydrographer of the Royal Navy, for a few weeks later I received an anxious letter from the Royal Marines Chief of Staff. Even at that stage I could not, it seemed, avoid controversy, although I was more saddened by the tone of the Admiral's enclosed letter than its content. He stated that neither he nor his Department knew of the involvement of my charts in the planning and conduct of the war (we found that difficult to believe) and if they had they would have preferred a qualified surveyor to have supplied specialist advice to the Amphibious Task Group. He should have known that the Commodore had been approached by his Department with offers of help before we sailed, but these had been turned down for the reason that COMAW needed an overall view of the shallows and not intimate knowledge of just the passages that had been surveyed by individuals. On top of that I was 'at fault' for not offering the information 'obtained in service time and with service materials' to the Admiralty in 1979; the threat being that I would now have to reimburse the service and that permission concerning Crown Copyright for certain aspects of my book would not be forthcoming. It was, by any standards, an unnecessary example of pique.

The Royal Marines asked me to draft a balanced reply. This was not difficult for I was able to refute all the points raised in the Chief Hydrographer's letter. All the work had been conducted in my own time, if travelling as a passenger on patrol in *Forrest* could be described as such, and certainly no service materials had been used specifically for my work. I had offered all my notes to the hydrographers on board HMS *Endurance* during the return journey and again to the Royal Institute of Navigation on reaching England. The first of these august bodies told me that as the work represented the 'amateur jottings of a yachtsman' it was of no interest to their Department (the Chief Hydrographer was the professional head of that Department) and the second (on whose committee the Chief Hydrographer himself sat) dismissed the work as being of no interest to them either! It was a sad little saga that contrasted poorly with the Directorate of Naval Plans' request to me in May to help choose Mare Harbour as the 'naval' port for the construction of the Mount Pleasant airfield. My contribution for them contained exactly the same hydrographic detail as those earlier brainstorming sessions.

Back to more pressing matters. I had accepted the post of Officer Commanding Plymouth Garrison under the impression that it was a stepping-stone to forming the Brigade Assault Squadron. On enquiring of Headquarters Commando Forces about the unborn Squadron's progress, I was told that it was nothing to do with me, which, to a large extent, was of course true. But I did feel that it was perhaps some of my business as I had set the scene and trialled the embryo organization in peace and war over eleven years, although, unknown to me at the time, there were a number of senior officers angling for the credit of bringing the Squadron to fruition and my presence was certainly not going to help their own aspirations in this respect. Long after it was formed, one could hardly meet a senior officer who, on hearing of its eventual birth, would not mention loudly that "Yes, wasn't it excellent news as it had been all my own idea!" 539 Assault Squadron would claim a vast parentage!

The truth of the matter was simple. Lieutenant-Colonel Sir Steuart Pringle (as he then was) had given life to the idea in north Norway in 1971, Commodore Michael Clapp and Brigadier Julian Thompson had 'baptised it with fire' in the Falklands, Colonel Richard Preston had taken up the cause as Chief of Staff to the MGRM Plymouth after he had pushed hard for a similar 'pool' of craft, while CO at RM Poole, and I claim a little of the credit for worrying at the heels of these, and other senior officers, over the years.

357

Actually, I was nearly a victim of my own success. At a meeting held in Hamoaze House sometime in 1983 (my diary for that year was last seen on the Dover to London express) a huge blackboard was set up in a staff officer's office. Representatives from throughout the Corps were called to the meeting. As a humble garrison commander far removed from the operational scene, I was not invited. It was decided there and then where all the facilities – men and equipment – would come from and where they would be based if the Admiralty approved the formation. By some subterfuge now forgotten, I had managed to attend and was horrified to see on the blackboard among all the other corrections, alterations and insertions in chalk on the 'wiring diagram' for the proposed organization, that the Officer Commanding would be a captain. This boded ill for my own aspirations.

As I had already been dubbed, quite needlessly (but, privately, rather pleasingly!), a pirate and buccaneer by the senior officers of the Corps, I felt that I had every excuse (and the opportunity) to get some pleasure for my punishment. A convenient stand-easy gave me that ideal moment. While everyone was out of the room collecting coffee I slipped back in and quickly replaced 'Captain' with 'Major' in as similar a chalky-hand as I could muster in the time.

On taking up the meeting nobody noticed the change and so with well disguised relief I was able to watch the board being taken down at the end to be transcribed by the clerks into a formal submission for the Department of the Commandant General.

Some weeks later I received a call from 'head office' saying that the proposal had been accepted and that they were looking for a suitably qualified Landing Craft Major and as there was only one would I mind being considered? I feigned surprise.

"Delighted," I said. The penultimate and second most satisfying tour of my career was on the starting blocks. Many skirmishes lay ahead, but the main obstacles seemed to have been solved. Our winter base was to be close to Harstad in the Norwegian Lofoten Islands from where (among other duties) I set about a four-year study of the beaches and sea approaches for landing craft operations. Thankfully these have never been needed. As in an earlier incarnation the wildlife took my mind off the more sinister aspects of the job.

At about this time I published *Falkland Islands Shores* to remarkably good reviews, which gave it an importance far beyond its real value. There had nearly been a hiccup when it was suggested by the MOD that it should not be issued for fear it would aid a future aggressor, but thankfully common sense won and it was given an official blessing; after years of work it had been an anxious moment.

The book was finished, we bought an abandoned South Devon farmhouse with enough acres to keep us occupied and I commissioned the Commando Brigade Assault Squadron. All was well until early 1986 when the idyll was disturbed by an incident that led, ultimately to much unhappiness. Patricia received a telephone call from a Mr Ratcliff-Genge of the *Daily Mail*. Could he come and talk to me about the forthcoming Two-Handed Round-Britain and Ireland Race? It seemed a fair request and one which would not give any trouble to the Royal Marines public relations watchdogs.

When the *Daily Mail* man appeared at the back door on a Sunday I was astonished to be told, before he even came into the house, that it was actually about the Welsh Guards that he wanted to interview me. I tried to push the door shut but he was quicker than me and obviously had much practice. He put his face close to the crack.

"I think you will be interested to hear what I have to say."

"I doubt it."

"I've been asked by my editor, who has been approached by the army, to run an article putting the blame for the loss of the Welsh Guards on the Royal Marines in general and you in particular. I need your version before I go any further."

This was a very different slant on the subject. The last I had had to do with the affair was a Granada television programme which was factual, and, in its way, innocuous enough. It had offered a fair description of the outline facts of the incident and little more.

"You had better come in, but I may not be able to help you."

I could help him by explaining the facts as I saw them and as I remembered them. They had not altered from all the interviews and, indeed, from the evidence I had given to the Board of Inquiry.

At the end of the discussion I warned Ratcliff-Genge that I would be telephoning the Royal Marines PR office that evening and that they would probably wish to get in touch with him. He accepted this and drove back to London leaving me with the feeling that he had had rather a wasted voyage. For my part I was deeply disturbed by his news and lost no time in leaving a long message on the PR Officer's MOD answering machine.

The Royal Marines' PR Officer telephoned back the next day to say that they had known nothing of the army's request to the *Daily Mail* but that he would be speaking to the appropriate public relations officer. Like me, he doubted that this proposed story had emanated from the army *per se*, rather from an individual. A later call confirmed this to be the army PR officer's view as well and that they would be conducting their own investigation.

Later in the week Ratcliff-Genge telephoned me to say that he had recounted my version of events to his editor and that as they were sound and had been verified, the newspaper would not be running the story and would dis-associate itself from any further such requests.

It was this piece of averted skulduggery that was in my mind when Yorkshire Television approached me to ask if I would appear in a programme titled 'Falklands War — the Untold Story'. I didn't think there was an 'untold story' to be told and was more than hesitant at the thought of taking part until I was told that if I did not appear it was likely that 'an army chap' would be interviewed instead with his version of the *Galahad* incident. I reluctantly agreed to the request. Filming of my part took place in a London hotel and, in accordance with requests passed through the RM PRO, I was dressed in the clothes I wore 'down south'. This was, from the waist up, a white polo neck submariner's jersey and my green beret. Unfortunately the large, plain screen that started off behind me when we practised the shots was moved and the programme went out with me in my version of 'combat' clothing framed by potted plants and gilt-edged pictures. It looked rather incongruous. During the interview I recounted my anger at failing to persuade the troops to get ashore from *Sir Galahad* and, in doing so, re-affirmed my view that I could have had them all off and in comparative safety within twenty minutes. I did not mentioned any regiment and certainly no names.

In April, 1987, a week before the programme was due to be screened, the *Daily Mirror* ran an 'Exclusive' under two-inch-high front page letters "50 HEROES LEFT TO DIE. Falklands Major accuses fellow officers." One paper had me being court-martialled for 'letting the side down' (the charge might have been difficult to frame), another had me being 'tipped for promotion'. I'm glad to say neither 'impostors' won the day. The simple truth was that nothing was 'exclusive' and nothing was said that had not been analysed in numerous books. It was an old story. However, the matter did not end there and I was ordered to call, formally, on Nick Vaux, now my General.

I don't suppose Nick enjoyed the interview any more than I did, especially as he was acting under orders from 'head office'. Apparently 'the army' had complained formally to the Department of the Commandant General Royal Marines accusing me of blaming a regiment by name and, worst of all, blaming individuals by name. I knew the identity of the Regiment of course, but had never known, nor bothered to find out, who the officers were. Others knew and indeed identified them in public, including eventually Simon Weston in his book *Walking Tall*. I did not, and, in truth, to this day still cannot tell to whom it was that I spoke on the stern of *Galahad* that awful morning.

Instead of receiving support there seemed to be anger at my defence, as

I saw it, of the truth, no matter how unpalatable that might have been in some quarters. I also remembered well the visit of Ratcliff-Genge to the farm and the reason behind it. Throughout the interview with Nick I kept silent: the 'system' was upset and I did not know why. It would not help my side of the case, even if I had been asked to put it (which I was not) by defending myself at such a 'meeting'.

As I was leaving Nick stopped me: "and never wear that bloody white jersey in uniform again. Many senior officers have spoken to me about it."

I then realized that perhaps that was behind the apparent opprobrium I was receiving. The Royal Marines might have been more inclined to stand up for me if I had been 'correctly' dressed. If that was what all the fuss was really about it was best it was soon forgotten — but I continued to wear the jersey in my landing craft. My squadron expected nothing else!

I wanted, though, to make it quite clear that as I had appeared with the sanction of the Corps I felt that it should have been able to support my appearance afterwards even if, in retrospect, it did not approve. Instead, the Royal Marines were now supporting the army's view that I should be reprimanded for 'talking out of turn' about 'brother' officers. "It was not a very gentlemanly or officer-like thing to have done," was a view relayed to me by a third party.

I went home thoroughly depressed and unhappy. I didn't know whether or not I had done the right thing and clearly in the eyes of my own service I had not; but neither could I reconcile that with doing what I thought was correct. The story was old hat and well tabulated in other television and wireless programmes and most 'definitive' books on the subject. I had tried my best to get the men off the ship; I had been privy to a 'private' attempt to divert blame; I had not identified either regiment or individual, I had not 'blamed' anybody, but simply recounted the facts and I appeared in the clothes I was told to appear in. I could have refused to appear on the programme; I could have told a different story; I could have been conventionally dressed; I could have lied to make every one feel better.

As an added precaution I had a transcript from the programme read and checked by the Royal Marines PR Officer whose job it would have been to have been present if he had considered that I was likely to talk out of turn. He could find nothing that he would have deleted if he had been present. I was beginning to wonder what all the fuss was really about (and who had actually started it), especially when I read a news report quoting a spokesman for the Brigade of Guards saying that there was no blame to be attached to anyone for the loss of the men in *Sir Galahad* and that as far as they were concerned the matter was closed.

There was one action I could take, and without being asked, I sat down and 'rendered my reasons in writing' for saying what I did and appearing as I did. I did not expect it to be read by anyone but I would feel that I had at least said my bit.

"Sir,

"I have the honour to render my reasons for appearing on Yorkshire Television recently…"

I sent my 'reasons in writing' to my Brigade Commander (now Robin Ross) on whose desk it arrived unannounced and probably unwelcome. On the telephone I expanded the reason why I felt it necessary to put my case. To have been involved in an 'incident' in which so many men had died needlessly, did two things to me. It made me very sensitive indeed to the subject and it made me determined that the truth, however unpleasant, be known in full.

In thirty-two supremely happy years in the Royal Marines this is the only occasion that I pondered on the lack of support for its members the Corps could sometimes display. I have not led a blameless career, but on this occasion I had genuine cause to think I was right for once. I still find the reasons behind the reprimands difficult to fathom and I remain equally sensitive, not to the *Sir Galahad* incident itself so much, but to the aftermath.

There was yet a further twist to this saga which hurt every bit as much as the 'interview' with Nick Vaux. Shortly afterwards and by some terrible coincidence I sat next but one to an army officer's wife at a play performed on the lawns of a country house in Dorset.

Before the start this woman leant across the empty chair between us and said:

"Are you Ewen Southby-Tailyour?" She was polite enough. I smiled back and said that I was indeed.

"Do you know who is about to sit in this chair between us?" She wasn't quite so nice now. I shook my head.

"The officer whom you accuse of refusing to take his men off *Sir Galahad.*" I was appalled, not by the seating arrangements rather by her assumption. I did not know who the officers were on the stern of *Sir Galahad*, had never bothered to find out and did not know at that moment who I was about to sit next to. Frankly, I wasn't interested.

Unfortunately the matter was not dropped. I was asked what rank I now held. I told her.

"Still a Major? Well that probably shows you whose word everybody is taking. My husband is now a Lieutenant Colonel, and by the way never ever put your face into my husband's officers' mess. You are most definitely not welcome." I did not bother to tell her that I too was about to be promoted to Lieutenant Colonel nor did I point out that that rank was the equivalent to an army Colonel. It all seemed so pointless.

362

I said I was sorry to hear that, as I had tried to save them from a fate I knew to be inevitable. My attempts to stop this woman from further invective were as unsuccessfully conducted as had been my attempts to get her husband's men ashore. Her continued comments about me and my career are still too unpleasant to report even now. It was another deeply saddening moment and not without much hurt. When the husband did appear to take his place, his wife whispered the name of the person sitting on his right. He turned to me and said, "Hello, I don't think we've ever met before." To which I could truthfully reply that I certainly did not recognize him!

There were, though, more bright spots than black holes. I was elected to the Executive Council of the Falkland Islands Foundation under the then Chairmanship of Sir Peter Scott. The FIF later changed its name to Falklands Conservation and I was appointed Chairman of the Sub-Committee on Wrecks. This fascinating challenge came at the same time as an even greater honour in this field when I was elected Chairman of the World Ship Trust whose aims are to 'rescue' world-wide, historic ships that have no known owner or benefactor. All this is the direct result of my 'Falklands involvement' and I am most grateful.

Some good news took a very practical form. At the beginning of the 1983 sailing season I received a letter from the Chairman of The East Coast Mutual Yacht Insurance Association Ltd (the oldest yacht insurance company in the World and with whom I insured *Black Velvet*) that in recognition of my part in the Falklands conflict they wanted to offer me free cover for one year. I accepted with great pleasure, although I had to tell them that by doing so they would successfully prevent me from daring to raise a claim! Thankfully I did not have to.

The chance to return to the Islands came, inevitably, through my interest in wrecks. A San Francisco entrepreneur, Edward Zilinsky, (who was heading a team named the *Bring the Vicar Home Committee*) asked me to accompany him to Goose Green and the wreck of *The Vicar of Bray*. The great interest in her revolves around the fact that she is the only remaining 'gold-rush' ship from 1849 and so naturally, she has a place in the affections of that city. I do not believe the wrecks should be removed, willy-nilly, from the Falklands waters but *The Vicar* is different.

It was the start of a glorious fortnight. By strange good fortune, for us, our visit coincided with the departure of Rex and Mavis Hunt, the 'out-going' governor. As soon as they heard I was coming down we were all included in their private end-of-tour celebrations. Not only was this a great honour but it gave much credibility to the team from the west coast of America. We wined and dined superbly, drank much too much in the Colony Club, who, very kindly, renewed my membership from years back for the duration of our stay, and sampled old-fashioned, unchanged-by-the-war hospitality in Camp; we also gave a massive cocktail party in the Upland Goose where we stayed in some comfort (thanks to Des and Ning King). We spent much time with *The Vicar* and a perfect day on Carcass Island. I was able to 'walk the course' of the Goose Green battle by myself and we were all able to revel in the newly won freedom. In many respects I felt I was back home and so many people made me welcome that any unpleasantness I had suffered in England was not only put into a real perspective but was forgotten during our stay.

The one telling 'post-war' point was made by our reporter from the *San Francisco Examiner*. On first seeing Mount Pleasant airfield he stopped, clearly surprised by the sheer size and complexity of such an establishment.

He looked at me as we stood braced against the westerly gale: "This isn't built just to defend the Falklands. This was built to launch an attack against Northern Ireland!" The point might have been trite; it was also perceptive. It is indeed a huge military base.

I found the Islands remarkably unchanged outside the Mount Pleasant area. Camp life still continued as before; Stanley still existed as before; I read the lesson on Sunday in the cathedral to the same congregation; the potholes in the roads still remained un-filled and, now that most servicemen are out-of-town, the military presence seemed as light as when I had commanded the garrison. The wind still blows, but there are still beautiful calms at dawn and dusk. The peat smoke pervades everywhere and everything, the tea berries still bloom, the albatrosses still glide on the up draughts and the Arctic skuas still fight and scream, while the penguins and dolphins continue to delight. There are differences. Of course there are differences, but they are well contained.

As we waited to board the Boeing 747 (British Airways ran the flights for a very short time) for our flight home I wandered absentmindedly away from my fellow passengers to take a last look at the Wickham Heights and Mount Kent. A worried RAF Flight Sergeant ran across the tarmac towards me.

"Are you lost, Sir?"

"No, thank you. It's alright, I know where I am."

Next time I really will return by yacht!

XXIV

Reflections

IN REFLECTING ON MY PART in this lengthy saga, a part that was closely involved in peace and war as no one else was privileged to be, I am bound to regret some things, while others I will continue to champion with vigour.

I regret my relationship with Governor Parker in 1978 and 1979, but still believe it was over worthwhile principles, although in the end I had achieved nothing concrete for NP 8901 other than plans and proposals: not one practical aspect for which we had fought in 1979 was in place by 2 April, 1982.

I am sad that I failed to convince anybody at the Royal Naval Staff College in 1979 that the Falkland Islands were worth bothering about, but my fellow students, the Directing Staff and a number of visiting lecturers only had eyes for the North Atlantic and the Central Front and yet, as Julian Thompson was to write in the magazine *Command* "Anyone who preaches on the theme that 'it will never happen' thus undermining the flexibility of our armed forces, deserves to be censured in the strongest terms."

I was ashamed at my failure to stand up to Admiral Woodward at that first meeting north of Ascension Island, for had I been able to put across the authentic voice of the Falklands and my views on the coastline, the people, the topography and the weather, he might have had a better understanding of the place the amphibious forces would be assaulting and he would be supporting. He says now that at the time he was not interested in the detail, only the overall plan. But plans can only be drawn up, given a priority and then chosen and implemented from the most up-to-date intelligence.

I regret having to offer 'H' Jones such poor odds for the sea approach to Goose Green. The risks may well have been worth it, although, as I have mentioned, hindsight still shows that the decision we took was probably the correct one, but I don't really know.

I wish most of all that I had accompanied Colour Sergeant Johnston in *Foxtrot Four* to Goose Green from Fitzroy.

I regret, fervently, not having applied even more pressure to get the Welsh Guards off *Sir Galahad*, but the Battalion has never looked for scapegoats and took their severe knock firmly on the chin — like any first class boxer, of which they had many. I hope, therefore, that I have explained their reasons (most of them totally understandable) for not getting the men off *Sir Galahad* immediately, but more than that I hope that I have catalogued correctly and fairly the extraordinary chain of unfortunate incidents (many seemingly unconnected) that caused them to be afloat at Fitzroy in the first place, and also why the enemy aircraft were able to attack with such apparent impunity.

I am glad that my private work was of such value, but I would not rate it more highly (as others have kindly done) than simply a means by which we saved time in planning and reconnaissance. I am certainly proud to have been part of Mike Clapp's and Julian Thompson's teams and of the part I played in helping them to choose San Carlos — an inspired choice if I may say so!

My conscience did not allow me to review Admiral Woodward's book *One Hundred Days* for the *Western Morning News* (for whom I am their naval book reviewer). Reluctantly I returned the copy with the opinion that a fairer review would be written by someone who had either not been there or who had a background in military psychiatry. The sadness is that, despite the uneasy self-portrait, the book contained some excellent material worthy of positive comment — such as the decision to sink the *Belgrano* and the preservation of our meagre air assets, but as an historical document those who were 'down south' (especially those inshore and ashore, where the Admiral was not but about which he wrote) found a great deal with which to disagree.

What is particularly unfortunate, though, is that no one has ever acknowledged the quite indispensable part played by Commodore Michael Clapp and his 'amphibious' ships from the initial assault of San Carlos to the final surrender. To dismiss the most crucial operation of any undertaken throughout the war — bar none — in one short, inaccurate section Admiral Woodward (who could, and should, so easily have reversed this omission) compounds the error. Without the successful amphibious landing (composed and orchestrated by Clapp) the Islands would still be under Argentinian occupation and of that there is no doubt, but Michael Clapp was retired at the war's end with the rank of Captain. Of even more significance, he was not de-briefed on his return, thus leaving his crucial experience untapped for the benefit of future exponents of the art and untabulated for use by future Amphibious Task Group Commanders.

The war, once inevitable, was not, in my view, an 'unnecessary war' as has so often been portrayed. It was a vital war that not only cleared the air of much muddled FCO thinking (in the manner of a thoroughly good thunderstorm) but it showed to the world Britain's practical commitment to peace and freedom among so many timid governments.

The greatest joy of all, though, was that we won; despite everything, international law was upheld and a dictator was put back in his box. Of course, success *per se* should not preclude criticism, for, as I said at the beginning, although the means may well have justified the end this does not guarantee that the same amount of luck will be available next time. We should therefore analyse very carefully the triumphs as well as the disasters and, next time, make sure that we have the right ships and equipment, we use the well-proven command structure that exists and we begin with a firm, positive aim. The enemy next time will be better trained, better motivated and better led.

Finally, we were to build one of the largest tri-service bases in the southern hemisphere, thereby making the Islands for many years to come a formidable military obstacle (and target?) to those with sinister aspirations.

In that context, I can foresee the possibility of Mount Pleasant one day becoming an American base very much in the mould of Diego Garcia, for despite glasnost I cannot accept that the United States will ever allow a vacuum in the area. I still remember the 1979 assessment that Russia would have moved in within three weeks if Britain had done nothing in the event of an Argentinian invasion then.

If I may paraphrase Rex Hunt's final comments in his book *My Falkland Days* (David and Charles):

"Sea communications are still of vital importance to the West. The futures of Central America and South Africa are uncertain. South America is volatile. The traditional trade routes through the Panama Canal and round the Cape of Good Hope could be put at risk; but the Cape Horn route is safe as long as the Falklands remain in British hands."

The Islands still guard the southern entrance to the Pacific with their massive military base; they are still the closest ice-free port to that part of Antarctica most likely to contain recoverable minerals, or be in need of ecological protection, and they still hold the key to the continued expansion of sustainable white fish and krill catches, let alone undiscovered, but highly probable, reserves of oil.

And what of future British parliaments and the possibility that we may one day elect a government willing to accede to continuing Argentinian posturings on sovereignty or, who, quite simply, may wish to withdraw militarily from 'Fortress Falklands'?

I suggest that a sword still hangs over the Falklands, and next time the thread will be cut by politicians and diplomats, not the military.

367

BIBLIOGRAPHY

Books:

ADKIN, Mark. *Goose Green*. Leo Cooper, 1985.

AKEHURST, John. *We Won a War, The Campaign in Oman 1965-1975*. Michael Russel 1982.

BILTON, Michael; KOSMINSKY, Peter. *Speaking Out*. Andre Deutsch 1989.

BROWN, David. *The Royal Navy and the Falklands War*. Leo Cooper 1987.

CABLE, Sir James. *Diplomacy at Sea.*Macmillan 1985.

CAWKELL, Mary. *The Falklands Story 1592-1982*. Anthony Nelson 1983.

ENGLISH, Adrian; WATTS, Anthony. *Battle For the Falklands*. Osprey 1982.

ENOKSEN, Arne. *Med Capricornus Over Alle Hav*. Anse Grafiske 1982.

EVANS, Michael. *Amphibious Operations. The Projection of Sea Power Ashore.*Brassey's 1990.

FOX, Robert. *Antarctica and the South Atlantic*. BBC 1985.

FROST, John. *2 Para Falklands*. Buchan and Enright 1983.

HADFIELD, William. *Brazil, The River Plate and the Falkland Islands*. Longman, Brown, Green and Longman 1854.

HASTINGS, Max; JENKINS, Simon. *The Battle for the Falklands*. Michael Joseph 1983.

HUNT, Sir Rex. *My Falkland Days*. David and Charles 1992.

HYDROGRAPHIC DEPARTMENT: *South America Pilot. Volume II. Fifteenth Edition*. 1971.

JOLLY, Rick. *The Red and Green Life Machine*. Century 1983.

McMANNERS, Hugh. *Falklands Commando*. William Kimber 1984

MIDDLEBROOK, Martin. *Operation Corporate*. Viking 1985.

MUXWORTHY, JL. *The Great White Whale Goes to War*. P & O SNC 1982.

OAKLEY, Derek. *The Falklands Military Machine*. Ravelin 1989.

SEYMOUR, William. *British Special Forces*. Sidgwick & Jackson 1985.

STRANGE, Ian. *The Falkland Islands*. David and Charles 1983.

SOUTHBY-TAILYOUR, Ewen. *Falkland Islands Shores*. Conway Maritime 1985.

THE SUNDAY TIMES. *The Falklands War*. Andre Deutsch 1982.

THOMPSON, Julian. *No Picnic*. Leo Cooper 1985.

WARD, Sharkey. *Sea Harrier. A maverick over the Falklands*. Leo Cooper 1992.

WESTON, Simon. *Walking Tall*. Bloomsbury 1989.

WOODS, Robin. *Birds of the Falkland Islands*. Anthony Nelson 1975.

WOODWARD, Sandy. *One Hundred Days*. HarperCollins 1992.

VAUX, Nick. *March to the South Atlantic*. Buchan and Enright 1986.

Publications and articles:

COMMAND. Editor: Hugh McManners. Summer 1992.
FRANKS, Lord. *Falkland Islands Review*. 1983.
MARSHALL CAVENDISH PUBLICATIONS. *The Falklands War*. 1983.
ROYAL FLEET AUXILIARY.
RFA Newsletter. April 1983. The Falklands.
SECRETARY OF STATE for DEFENCE.
The Falklands Campaign — the Lessons. 1982.
SHACKLETON, Rt Hon. the Lord.
Economic Survey of the Falkland Islands. 1976.
SHACKLETON, Rt Hon. the Lord.
Falkland Islands Economic Study. 1982.
SOUTHBY-TAILYOUR, Ewen. *Give a dog a bad name*. Royal Cruising Club Journal 1978.
SOUTHBY-TAILYOUR, Ewen.
A Winter's Cruise Amongst the Falkland Islands.
Royal Naval Sailing Association Journal Spring 1979.
SOUTHBY-TAILYOUR, Ewen.
Ask me one on beaches.
Royal Cruising Club Journal 1982.
SOUTHBY-TAILYOUR, Ewen.
The Reluctant Pilot. Yachting Monthly, December 1983.
SOUTHBY-TAILYOUR, Ewen.
Two and a half landings. Falkland Islands Foundation Journal 1983.
SOUTHBY-TAILYOUR, Ewen.
Corporate Decision. Elite Magazine 1987.
SOUTHBY-TAILYOUR, Ewen.
Beachhead: Falklands. Soldier of Fortune. September 1988.
SOUTHBY-TAILYOUR, Ewen.
Arctic Notebook. Royal Cruising Club Journal 1988.
SOUTHBY-TAILYOUR, Ewen.
Her first — my last.
Yachting Monthly November 1989.
SOUTHBY-TAILYOUR, Ewen.
Arctic Notebook. Ocean Navigator July 1990.

INDEX

Ranks and titles used are those at the time or on first appearance.

Middleton, Capt RN, L, 152
Military Medal, 355
Miller, Alan and Carol, 38, 67, 224, 238
Miller, LMEM, D., 99
Miller, Sid, 65, 67, 69, 224
Miller, Tim, 67
Mills, A/Lt RM, Keith, 118, 119
Milne, Harry, 60, 66
Ministry of Defence, 4, 8, 11, 17, 21, 23, 24, 31, 32, 47, 52, 55, 61, 63, 64, 66, 68, 69, 85, 97, 102, 158, 159, 253, 358, MOD (Army), 355
Minords, Maj RM, David, 186, 207, 312, 316, 336
Monaghan, Father, 337
Montevideo, 19, 92, 93, 117
Montrose, Duke of, 98
Moody Brook, 10, 20, 23-28, 30, 32, 35, 38, 40, 44, 46-49, 53-55, 57, 61, 68, 72, 77, 83, 86, 87, 89, 247, 338, 339, attacked, 119, state of bridge, 116
Moore, Maj Gen, Jeremy, 114, 118, 143, 160, 161, 164, 217, 231, 232, 235, 236, 243, 245, 246, 259, 260, 264, 278, 282, 285, 287, 288, 290, 308, 310, 319, victory signal, 316
Mount Challenger, 255, 256
Mount Estancia, 256
Mount Harriet, 39, 160, 256, 308, 347, 355
Mount Kent, 108, 233, 247, 250, 251, 255, 256, 364
Mount Longdon, 39, 255, 256, 308, 342
Mount Pleasant, 357, 364, 367
Mount Rosalie, 192, 231
Mount Smoko, 255
Mount Vernet, 256
Mount William, 39
Mountbatten, Lord Louis, 98
Mullet Creek, 39, 119
Murrel River, 39

NAAFI, 10
Napier, Roddy, 80
Napoleon, Emperor, 142, 143
Narrows, the, 20, 23, 35, 90
National Maritime Historical Society of America, 85
National Maritime Museum, Greenwich, 331
NATO, 94, 101, 108, 153
Naval Party 8901, 1, 2, 7, 9, 12, 16, 17, 19, 22, 23, 25, 26, 29-34, 36, 40, 41, 42, 46, 47, 48, 50, 53, 54, 60, 61-63, 66-72, 83,

85-90, 92, 93, 116, 117, 131, 133, 214, 238, 302, 347, 349, 364, 365, arival in Falklands Islands, 20, 'buffer' detachment, 12, defence of Government House by (1982), 118, 119, pre-embarkation training, 17, suggested replacement by Royal Engineers, 27, 86, awarded Wilkinson Sword of Peace, 41-43
Naval Discipline Act, 297
Naval Security, 97
Needles, The, 314
Nelson, Admiral Lord, 139, 290
New Forest, The, 352
New Island, 81, 315, 330, 340
New York, 340
New Zealand, 38
Newland, Cpl RM, Steve, 159, 160, 347, 355
Nicholson, Michael, 317, 318, 321
Noott, Maj RM, Gary, 117, 118, 129, 158
Norman, Maj RM, Norman, 117, 118, 156, 158
Normandy, 236
North Camp, 146, 164
North Sea, 94, 198
North Peak, 332
North West Islands, The, 208
North West Passage, The, 3
Northern Ireland, 154, 313, 317, 364
Norway, 98, 107, 154, 159, 223, 242, 306, 358, 1940 campaign, 100, coastal forces, 101, northern flank of NATO, 97, 152, 237, 346
Nott, Rt. Hon., John, MP, 96, 103
Nunn, Capt RM, Richard, 239

Odling-Smee, Lt Cdr RN, Peter, 3
Oman, 339, Chinese involvement in war, 180, Dhofar War, 1, 46, 49, 112, 159, 164, 180, 230, 302, 313, Hadramaut, 291, Northern Frontier Regiment, 112, 211, 302, 307
Operation *Motorman*, 201, 266, 302
Ordnance point, 47
Organisation of American States, 73
Overseas Development Ministry, 7, 44, 63, 196

Pacific, 96
Panama Canal, 94, 95, 367
Pangbourne, The Nautical College, 131, 272, 327
Paris, 7, 19, 92
Parker, Diedre, 20

378

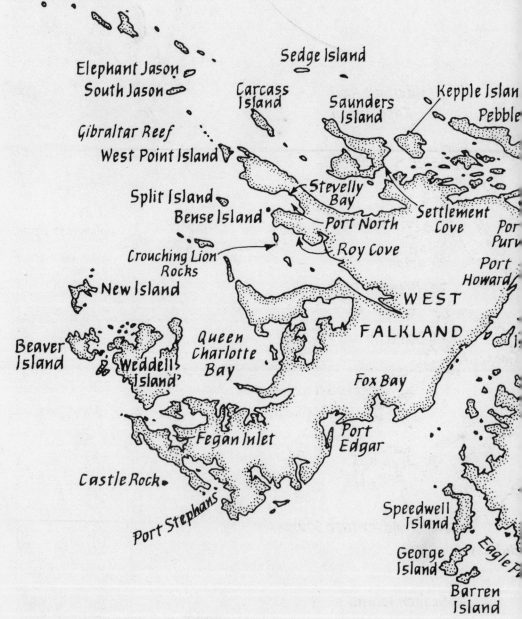

Jason West Cay

Sedge Island

Elephant Jason
South Jason

Carcass
Island

Saunders
Island

Kepple Islan

Pebble

Gibraltar Reef
West Point Island

Stevelly
Bay

Settlement
Cove

Por
Purv

Split Island
Bense Island

Port North

Roy Cove

Port
Howard

Crouching Lion
Rocks

New Island

WEST

FALKLAND

Beaver
Island

Weddell
Island

Queen
Charlotte
Bay

Fox Bay

Fegan Inlet

Port
Edgar

Castle Rock

Speedwell
Island

Eagle P

Port Stephans

George
Island

Barren
Island